We Sh
Not Be Moved

The story of British wrestling

Vol. 2 1975-1979

By
Tony Earnshaw

Introduction

This is the follow-up to my first book, The Saturday Afternoon War, which looked at the history of British wrestling between 1980 and 1988. This book concerns the period between 1975 and 1979.

We Shall Not Be Moved is intended to be a factual record of the period rather than wrestlers' reminisces of their time in the ring. That subject has already been covered in two excellent books in the past and whilst I have contacted or spoken to certain wrestlers to clarify points this book's purpose is that of something to document the history of the sport in the designated period.

The mid-seventies was a low period for wrestling: there was a dearth of new faces on the bills and most if not all of the headline attractions were the big names of the previous decade. At that time, Mick McManus was jealously guarding his position as the top star for Dale Martin Promotions. As he was the company's booker/matchmaker, it was a pretty easy job for him to do. Meanwhile, Eric 'Tug' Wilson's matchmaking for Best Wryton Promotions had failed to fill venues such as Belle Vue, Hanley, and Liverpool Stadium, and he was relieved of his position in May 1975.

The man brought in to replace Wilson and arrest the decline was Max Crabtree. Crabtree had been promoting his own shows for a few years and they had been very successful, although his bills at the Eldorado Stadium in Edinburgh were well known for getting out of hand. News of his appointment made the sports pages, with the Liverpool Echo commenting: 'This summer's professional wrestling Friday night presentations at the Liverpool Stadium are to get a facelift. Top grappling promoter Max Crabtree takes charge of events on behalf of Joint Promotions—the Saturday afternoon TV wrestling contractors'.

Veteran promoters such as Ted Beresford and Norman Morrell were near retirement and their venues were eventually amalgamated into a beefed-up Best Wryton Promotions, run by Crabtree.

Dale Martin, on the other hand, didn't see the need to change things and Mick McManus continued to run the wrestling side of the organisation. While the wrestling side of the business was stuck in the sixties, the financial side of the business remained in rude health. The vast majority of shows put on by Dale Martin were paid for out of local corporation entertainment budgets. Dale Martin would be paid a set fee to put on an evening show at a given venue, providing the wrestlers, the officials, the ring, the advertising posters, programmes, and whatever else was required. Any box-office profit was split between the promoters and the hall owners. The arrangement died a death once Margaret Thatcher became Prime Minister, because local authority funding was slashed and it became unprofitable to run wrestling in many places. The ITV contract for wrestling on World of Sport was another gold mine and, together with the paid shows, it made the mid-seventies a very profitable time for the Joint Promotions cartel.

The independent circuit was very much a fragmented affair in 1975. The departure of Jackie Pallo and his son JJ from Joint Promotions in 1974 had given the independents a boost, especially when Pallo set up his own promotional company, The Star Who Presents the Stars. Brian Dixon's Wrestling Enterprises promotions formed the main competition for Joint Promotions, and Dixon's wife Mitzi Mueller was his star attraction. Other independent promoters were of the more dubious type, advertising wrestlers who didn't appear and then referring to the small-print explaining their right to change the proposed bill.

We begin with the 1975 to 1976 winter season, when wrestling was about to witness monumental change, thanks to Max Crabtree.

1975

September

The first wrestling of the month on ITV's World of Sport (6th September) featured three matches from Wolverhampton. The main match saw Bobby Ryan become the new European Lightweight Champion when he beat Jim Breaks by two falls to one. Breaks had taken the lead by submission in the third round before Ryan equalised in round four. Ryan then stunned Breaks with the winning move in the fifth round.

Kendo Nagasaki, who was back wrestling for Joint Promotions after a stint on the independent circuit, beat the Jamaica Kid. The Kid had been the recipient of the Kamikaze Crash in the second round, which left him with no hope of beating the count. The preliminary match that week between Paddy John Faye and Roger Green had ended in a No Contest when Green was unable to continue in the fourth round.

The following week saw Nagasaki back on TV, when he was part of a four-man knockout tournament broadcast from Blackburn. The other three participants were Big Daddy, Jim Moran, and the much lighter Mike Marino.

The first semi-final saw Marino take on Moran over six rounds, with victory going to the first score. Moran threw Marino towards the ropes in the opening seconds and as Marino hit them, they broke. The match was stopped while the ropes were repaired and referee Ernest Baldwin restarted the match from the beginning of the first round. Moran, who suffered from acromegaly (a rare condition where the body produces too much growth hormone), immediately used his size and weight advantages to overpower Marino and to weaken the lighter man. Referee Baldwin issued his first public warning to Moran in the third round following his illegal use of a closed fist. It was Marino who got the winner in the fourth round, with a neat reversal for a folding press.

The second semi-final saw Kendo Nagasaki, preceded by Gorgeous George, make his way to the ring first. George

1

immediately grabbed MC Stan Ryland's microphone to make his usual speech introducing his man. Opponent Big Daddy entered the ring to a mixed reaction. Once more, the match was fought over six rounds, with the first score winning. Commentator Kent Walton wasn't sure if Daddy had weighed himself recently, but estimated that Daddy was around the 25-stone mark.

Nagasaki's pre-fight rituals were cut short, much to George's anger, but once the salt had been thrown the action commenced. Immediately, Daddy went on the attack and used his superior strength to throw Nagasaki around the ring. A belly butt knocked Nagasaki out of the ring and when he returned to it Daddy tried to unmask him. When that failed, Daddy tried a neck-lift suspension. The ending came suddenly when a double back-handed chop floored Daddy and Nagasaki pinned him for the only fall needed to win in the first round. An angry Daddy chased Nagasaki back to the dressing room, and so began a feud that would do the rounds for the next couple of years and which produced some incredibly heated encounters.

The other match saw Vic Faulkner take on Alan Woods over six rounds, with two falls etc. needed to win. Both were excellent wrestlers and after a nip-and-tuck affair it was Faulkner who got the winner in round six with a double-leg nelson.

The final of the knockout tournament between Kendo Nagasaki and Mike Marino was the centrepiece of the World of Sport broadcast on the 20th, which again came from Blackburn. Surprisingly, it was Marino who got the first score with a leg-stretch hold that saw Nagasaki submit in the third round. Nagasaki equalised with a submission in the fourth round, employing a grapevine hold that forced Marino to submit. With things getting out of hand and Nagasaki getting a final public warning, the masked man won the match in the fifth round. An attempted flying tackle from Marino saw both wrestlers go over the top rope and when he attempted it again, Nagasaki threw Marino over the top rope, meaning that Marino had no chance of beating the count.

Alan Dennison's match with John Naylor ended in a No Contest when Naylor was unable to continue in the fourth round. An interesting appointment saw former heavyweight star Jack Pye referee the match between Count Bartelli and Mark Rocco. Bartelli won the contest, pinning Rocco for the one fall needed for victory in round three, with Pye ensuring that Rocco adhered to the rules.

Woking was the venue for the wrestling shown on World of Sport on 27th September, with Les Kellett taking on Bobby Barnes as the highlight. Kellett took the honours by two falls to Barnes' submission. Kellett took the first fall in the third round before Barnes equalised with a submission in the fourth. Shortly after Barnes received his final public warning in round five, he was pinned by Kellett for the winner.

A heavyweight match saw crowd favourite Steve Veidor beat muscular Welshman Johnny Yearsley by the only fall needed in the fifth round. In that week's other bout, John Elijah defeated Billy Torontos again, by the one fall required that time, in round four.

Around the halls

Kendo Nagasaki was the main attraction as Belle Vue in Manchester commenced its new season on 13th September. The Max Crabtree effect was already being felt due to the bigger number of matches on the bill, along with more stipulation matches. Nagasaki took on fellow masked wrestler The White Angel. There were no rounds, no falls or submissions, and victory had to be achieved by a knockout. Nagasaki won after nine minutes, when the Angel failed to beat the count and was then unmasked as 'Gipsy' Joe Romero.

The Royals were also in action, taking on The Dennisons (Alan Dennison and Sid Cooper), with Bert and Vic winning in eighteen minutes. The Farmer's Boy beat Tally Ho Kaye by disqualification in round five in the opener. Tony St. Clair had an upset victory over British Middleweight Champion Brian Maxine by pinning him in round six for the winner. Terry Rudge beat The Mighty Yankee, who was neither mighty nor American, but Ian Glasper from the North-East.

The final match that night saw the Belle Vue debut of a young wrestler from Warrington called The Dynamite Kid, who

3

was taking on veteran Kenny Hogan, with one fall needed to win. The youngster won the match in the second round, and went on to become one of Britain's best-ever wrestlers.

While Belle Vue was the main wrestling venue in the North, it was Croydon (after the Royal Albert Hall) that held that position in the South. Dale Martin put on a six-match spectacular on the 16th at Croydon, with three main events on the bill. Bert Royal, who had recently lost his British Heavy/Middleweight title to Steve Logan in Liverpool, took on Logan's tag partner, Mick McManus. Royal gained a semblance of revenge when he won by two falls to one in the fourth round. Croydon's favourite son, Steve Veidor, faced Klondyke Jake and found the big man too much to handle, losing inside four rounds. It was a result that saw Veidor's many fans, including the legendary Duchess, disconsolate. The third of the featured matches saw Giant Haystacks make short work of late-notice replacement Terry Rudge, beating him by two straight falls inside two rounds.

The first show of the season at the Royal Albert Hall on 24th September saw an intriguing tag match at the top of the bill. Kendo Nagasaki teamed with his manager Gorgeous George to take on the pairing of Steve Veidor and Tony St. Clair, who had replaced the unavailable Robby Baron. To the crowd's delight, George took a terrible beating, especially from Veidor. Once Nagasaki tagged in and had rescued George, the match ended after a little over twelve minutes, with Nagasaki getting a winning submission.

Two super/heavyweight contests were also featured, with Giant Haystacks making his Albert Hall debut, along with 'Terror of the North' Klondyke Jake. Haystacks made short work of his opponent, Lancashire heavyweight Pete Curry who, despite gaining a fall in the first round, was counted out in the second after being on the receiving end of a 'big splash'. Jake gained a notable victory over Count Bartelli, with submissions in the third and fourth round against Bartelli's fall in round two.

The rest of the evening saw Mike Marino defeat Sean Regan by two falls to one in the fourth round. John Naylor wrestled a one-fall-each draw over six rounds with Alan Serjeant in the opening match. The final bout saw two heavyweights making

4

their Albert Hall debuts, with Lee Bronson beating Essex campaigner Dave Freeman in the fifth round.

October

October began with the massive news that Les Kellett had given notice to Joint Promotions and would be leaving once he had completed that month's dates. Kellett was a complex character and while beloved by the fans for his unique style, it was a different story backstage. His actual age was something of a mystery, but he was in his sixties by then. With the top-of-the-bill spot for Joint Promotions in need of refreshment, an opportunity opened up for new blood to step up.

Wrestling was missing from World of Sport on the 4th as the Dunlop Masters golf tournament was shown at 4pm instead.

On the 11th, three bouts were broadcast from Southend on World of Sport, with the main match featuring Mick McManus against Catweazle. To McManus' fury, Catweazle opened the scoring in the second round, pinning his opponent with a folding press. McManus retaliated through liberal use of illegal tactics, which weakened Catweazle to such an extent that he was forced to submit in the fourth round by a single-leg Boston crab. The winner wasn't long in coming when Catweazle submitted again to the same move a minute or so into the fifth round to give McManus the victory.

The opening match saw Johnny Kwango take on Dave Freeman, with only one score needed to win. Freeman was making his TV debut and put up a good show before Kwango got the one fall needed to win in the fourth round. The show ended with a heavyweight match between Wayne Bridges and Steve Veidor, again with only one score needed to win. The match came to an unfortunate ending in the fifth round when an attempted flying tackle saw Bridges go out of the ring over the top rope. Bridges was unable to continue, but Veidor refused to accept the verdict so MC Mike Judd announced the decision would be a No Contest.

Southend was the venue again for wrestling on World of Sport the following week. The first match saw Count Bartelli take on Klondyke Jake. Referee Max Ward had a hard job keeping the match in order, as both wrestlers transgressed the rule book. At the start of the second round Bartelli was bleeding heavily from his forehead and Ward eventually gave public warnings to both wrestlers as things got out of hand. Eventually, Ward's patience was tested once too often and he disqualified Jake in the third round for a kick that sent Bartelli out of the ring.

The main match that week was another heavyweight bout, won by Mike Marino after his opponent John Elijah was unable to continue after submitting in the fourth round. The final contest that week saw Clive Myers defeat Steve Grey by the only fall needed to win in the fourth round.

Wrestling on the 25th came from Sheffield, where Kendo Nagasaki was once again in action. His opponent was the young Scottish heavyweight Bill Turner, who entered the ring in his kilt while Nagasaki, accompanied by Gorgeous George, entered to the usual jeers. Nagasaki finished off Turner with a Kamikaze Crash in the second round. The first match seen that week saw Bert Royal get the one fall needed, with a reverse folding press, to beat Steve Taylor in the fourth round.

Johnny Saint faced the heavier Keith Martinelli in the final match and gained an honourable one-fall-each draw. Martinelli opened the scoring with the first fall in round five. He reversed an attempted flying tackle from Saint into a body slam and pinned him with a cross press. Saint's equalising fall came in the sixth and final round with a lovely move in the opening seconds. Martinelli rushed out on hearing the bell, but Saint reversed Martinelli's throw into a reverse folding press, secured by a bridge.

Around the halls

It was a night full of action and controversy at the famous old Liverpool Stadium on 8th October, when the match between Big Daddy and Gil Singh was halted in the fourth round when the referee was knocked out of the ring. Daddy at this time was far from the beloved fans' favourite he would become later, and had already received two public warnings before the end of the bout.

The main event saw a tag match where Kendo Nagasaki teamed up with Giant Haystacks to take on Tibor Szakacs and Tony St. Clair. It was Nagasaki and Haystacks who won the match by two straight falls in just over eight minutes of contest.

Haystacks was in tag action again the next night at Belle Vue, when he teamed up with usual partner Big Daddy in the main event. Daddy and Haystacks, accompanied to the ring by their manager, 'Kangaroo Kid' Ken Else, faced opponents Honey Boy Zimba and Gil Singh. Daddy and Haystacks ran out easy winners by two straight falls in the tenth minute.

The rest of the show saw Bert Royal regain the British Heavy/Middleweight Title, defeating champion Steve Logan in his mandatory rematch. Logan got the first fall in the third round but Royal overcame the dubious tactics of the champion to equalise in the fourth round and secured the winning fall in the fifth. Johnny Saint won the Belle Vue Trophy when he beat rival Jim Breaks by two falls to one in the sixth round.

On an action-packed night, the remaining matches saw wrestling vicar Michael Brooks take on and defeat Blackjack Mulligan, who failed to beat the count in the fifth round. Mick McMichael beat newcomer Abdul Farouk by two straight falls in the third round.

There was an interesting article in the 18th October edition of TV Times, which asked: Does wrestling still grab you? The article stated that wrestling had held the hallowed 4pm slot on World of Sport for twenty years, as well as having a late-night midweek show, but that the grapplers' grip on the audience was weakening, with around a million viewers disappearing.

The ratings showed, the article said, that wrestling had an average of 8.5 million viewers each week in November 1970, but that this had dropped to an average of 7.5 million viewers. It went on to state that along with declining TV ratings, attendances at the local venues around the country were dropping away too.

Max Crabtree, the recently appointed managing director of Joint Promotions, responded by saying that wrestling had always been the whipping boy and that people loved to knock the sport. Crabtree claimed that attendances had been excellent

the finest 'baby faces' in the ring and was selling perfectly for Hayes before making the usual comebacks. Hayes received his final public warning at the end of the third round as Veidor bled from a mouth wound.

Hayes immediately went for Veidor's mouth as soon as the bell rang for the new round and the crowd grew more and more irate at his behaviour. It was Veidor who got the winning fall in the fourth round, though. After being thrown from the ring by Hayes, he pinned him with a double-arm nelson after re-entering the ring via a sunset flip over the top rope. The fans were on their feet celebrating as commentator Kent Walton noted that Hayes would be returning to the USA the following week. That would be the last time Hayes would appear on British TV screens until the end of the eighties, when he became part of the WWF shows broadcast on ITV.

Wrestling was missing from World of Sport on the 15th, when the Dewar Cup tennis tournament was broadcast instead.

Wrestling returned to World of Sport on 22nd November, at Gravesend in Kent. The first match saw Clive Myers take on Steve Grey with one score to decide the winner. After an excellent exhibition of lightweight wrestling, it was Myers who got the winner in the fifth round with a folding press.

The main match was of a different style, with Johnny Saint giving away plenty of weight to tackle Mick McManus. McManus got the opening fall in the third round with a reverse double-knee hold after plenty of weakeners, both legal and illegal. It didn't take long for Saint to equalise though, by pinning McManus in the opening minute of the fourth round with a superb counter into a double leg nelson secured by a bridge. Despite McManus' best efforts, Saint managed to hang on to secure an honourable one-fall-each draw at the end of the scheduled six rounds. The final contest that week pitched Steve Logan against Lee Bronson, who was pinned for the only fall needed to win in round three.

The second half of the Gravesend show was screened on World of Sport the following Saturday, the highlight being a match between Bobby Barnes and Johnny Kwango. Barnes continued his run of TV wins when he got the one submission needed to defeat Kwango in the fourth round. Bert Royal went

10

up to the heavyweight division to take on Johnny Yearsley in a match that ended in a one-each draw at the end of the scheduled six rounds.

Yearsley got the first fall in the second round before Royal equalised in the fourth. Yearsley thought he had got a winner in round five when he pinned Royal, but he'd done so with the assistance of a punch. Referee Max Ward, as eagle-eyed as ever, had spotted the foul move and told MC Bobby Palmer that the fall would be disallowed. Catweazle won the final match that week when he got the one fall required to beat Dave Freeman in the third round.

Around the halls

The departure of Les Kellett left a substantial hole in the bills, as the promoters, hiding behind the subject-to-change small print, struggled to find a suitable replacement. Kellett was booked for the Belle Vue show on 1st November, taking on Klondyke Jake, but in the end neither Kellett nor Jake appeared. Luckily, there were enough good matches that night, so they weren't missed.

Following his victory over Jim Breaks for the Belle Vue Trophy in October, Johnny Saint had a crack at Breaks' British Lightweight Title. Breaks opened the scoring with a submission in round four before Saint equalised in the fifth with a submission of his own. Despite both wrestlers' best efforts, neither were successful and at the end of the twelfth round it was a draw and Breaks retained his title. Big Daddy and Giant Haystacks were once again in tag action, that time taking on the team of Count Bartelli and Tony St. Clair. Despite Daddy and Haystacks' substantial weight advantage and their nefarious tactics, Bartelli and St. Clair won by two falls to one in the thirteenth minute.

The third main match saw Kendo Nagasaki take on fellow masked wrestler but the much lighter Kung Fu. Nagasaki was the winner when Kung Fu failed to beat the count in the fourth round. Bill Turner beat the unruly Bobby Graham by disqualification in the third round. Colin Bennett beat Kid Chocolate by two falls to one in the fifth round, while Bobby

11

Graham appeared again in the final bout of the evening and was defeated by El Olympico in round two by count out.

After a match between Kendo Nagasaki and Dennis Mitchell at Sheffield on 5th November ended with both wrestlers counted out, challenges were issued by both of them. The result was a tag match at the same venue on the 19th. Gorgeous George was once again forced to don his wrestling tights and boots to partner Nagasaki, while Mitchell partnered Phil Pearson, with the added stipulation that Martin Conroy would referee the bout.

Despite George taking a beating from Mitchell, he was rescued by Nagasaki and, to the fans' fury, Nagasaki and George got the winning submission in the sixteenth minute. The Royals were on the same show, but in singles action. Vic Faulkner beat Jim Breaks by disqualification in the sixth round while in an upset Bobby Graham beat Bert Royal by two falls to one in round five. Gil Singh beat Al Martin who failed to beat the count in the sixth round and Lee Sharron beat Terry Rudge, who was unable to continue for the sixth round.

The Native American, War Eagle, was in action at Croydon on 25th November, although Romany Riley had replaced his scheduled opponent, The Exorcist. In a heated encounter, War Eagle took the scalp of Riley by two falls to one in the fourth round. Kung Fu beat Bobby Barnes, who was disqualified in round four. Mike Marino and Steve Veidor wrestled a one-fall-each draw over four rounds, while Spencer Churchill beat Anglo/Russian Ivan Penzecoff by two falls to one in the fourth round. The other matches saw Johnny Czeslaw beat Dave Bond and Eddie Capelli beat Steve Grey.

November finished with that month's Royal Albert Hall spectacular, on the 26th. Harvey Smith, the legendary equestrian, was a surprise addition to the main event that night. Smith, infamous for his fall-outs with the showjumping authorities, had decided to try his hand at professional wrestling. In an interview for the Racing Post, he'd said that he was sick of riding horses and had chosen wrestling as something different to do. He confounded his critics, becoming a solid performer, with enough ability to beat his opponent at

12

the Albert Hall: Tally Ho Kaye, a fellow equestrian. Harvey Smith's wrestling exploits had even made the front page of the Daily Mirror back in February, when a bout with Jackie Pallo at Blackburn had got out of hand:

'There were no holds barred last night when Harvey Smith met Jackie Pallo in a wrestling match. The bout between Smith and Pallo turned into a furious roughhouse. The crowd screamed and shouted as Harvey and Jackie used fists, elbows, knees and feet. Referee Brian Crabtree was almost hurled out of the ring as he tried to separate them. And finally Harvey left the ring with a real shiner of a black eye. Afterwards, promoter Max Crabtree said 'I knew there was a bit of bad blood between them but this wasn't wrestling'.

The article was illustrated with a large picture of Smith and his black eye.

Not many sportsmen are good enough to hit the highest echelons in three different sports, but Harvey Smith was one of them, competing in the Olympics at showjumping, topping the bill at the Albert Hall as a wrestler, and as a trainer of a Grand National winner when he turned his hand to training racehorses with wife Sue.

War Eagle was also on the bill that night, and endured a tough battle with Johnny Yearsley. He came out on top at the last with the winning fall in the fourth round. Mick McManus lost his match against Kung Fu when he challenged the martial arts ace to an extra round after their match ended in a draw. Kung Fu took advantage and pinned McManus for a winning fall. McManus was still in the ring arguing with the officials when Mike Marino arrived for his match with Big Daddy. McManus viciously attacked Marino and opened up a cut over Marino's eye. Once McManus had been removed, the match with Big Daddy began and immediately Daddy targeted the cut, launching headbutts and punches at it. He even tried to bite it to worsen the cut before the match was stopped. Much to Daddy's disgust the bout was declared a No Contest, due to the interference by McManus. Mike Marino demanded an opportunity for revenge and stated he wished to take on both

McManus and Daddy in matches on the same night at the next Albert Hall show.

Steve Grey continued to impress when he beat Zoltan Boscik, who failed to beat the count in round five. Romany Riley beat Al Martin by two falls to one in the fifth round, and Ivan Penzecoff got the one fall needed in the third round to beat Billy Torontos in the show closer.

December

The month's first show on World of Sport was broadcast on the 6th from Solihull and featured another challenge from Big Daddy against Kendo Nagasaki. Nagasaki got the first score in the second round with his grapevine hold, causing Daddy to submit. Daddy equalised a minute or so into round three when he forced Nagasaki to submit from a neck-lift hold. The winner for Nagasaki came in the fourth round. Daddy had finally managed to pull Kendo's mask off, but he continued to wrestle and pinned Daddy for the winner a minute or so later.

Honey Boy Zimba beat Yorkshireman Floyd Craggs (also billed as Fat Boy Floyd) by count-out in the fourth round. A catchweight match saw Johnny Saint and Mick McMichael wrestle a one-fall-each draw over six rounds. McMichael took the first fall in round three before Saint equalised in the fifth round.

The second half of the Solihull show was screened the following Saturday. The main event was Jim Breaks' rematch for the European Lightweight Championship against Bobby Ryan, the man who had beaten him to take the title. Ryan retained the title, pinning Breaks for the winner in the fifth round.

Commonwealth champion Count Bartelli shared the honours with Pete Curry in a heavyweight match. Curry opened the scoring with a fall in round three before Bartelli evened it up in the fifth round. Alan Dennison's bout with Kung Fu ended in a No Contest after a referee bump in the third round, which saw the contest abandoned. Dennison threw Kung Fu, who accidentally caught referee Emil Poilve with his foot and winded him.

14

The pre-Christmas wrestling on World of Sport on the 20th came from Wythenshawe, on the outskirts of Manchester. Mick McManus took on Vic Faulkner, with the heavier man forcing Faulkner to submit in the fifth round for the winning score.

Pete Roberts ran out a two falls-to-one winner in round six in a hard-fought heavyweight match against Terry Rudge. The preliminary match featured Little Prince, who secured the one fall needed in the fourth round to beat Tally Ho Kaye.

On the 27th, World of Sport featured the rest of the bill from Wythenshawe. The main match saw another contest featuring Big Daddy and Kendo Nagasaki, this time in a tag challenge. The announced weight of all four wrestlers totaled more than 96 stone as Daddy was partnering Giant Haystacks and Nagasaki had paired up with Blackpool's Rex Strong. Strong fronted most of the offence in the match, which ended in a two straight falls win for Daddy and Haystacks in just over six minutes. During the match Nagasaki and Haystacks never came into contact, setting the scene for another feud, with Haystacks joining Big Daddy on Nagasaki's hit list.

Mark Rocco forced King Ben to submit in the third round to win, while Gil Singh beat Bobby Graham by disqualification in the fifth round to complete the wrestling seen on World of Sport for 1975.

Around the halls

Kendo Nagasaki seemed to be at the centre of controversy as usual for much of the month. At Banbury on 3rd December, he was booked to partner Gorgeous George in a challenge match against Mike Marino and Wayne Bridges. Once in the ring, George thought better of it and in the end Sid Cooper, who had already wrestled that evening, was called up instead. With Cooper outgunned by heavyweights Marino and Bridges, Nagasaki and his partner decided to simply leave the ring and leave Marino and Bridges the unsatisfactory winners.

The last show of the year at Croydon on the 9th had Nagasaki take on Lee Bronson as part of a double main event. Bronson was no match for Nagasaki and the Kamikaze Crash laid Bronson out in the third round, with no hope of the youngster beating the count.

The other main event was a super heavyweight tag challenge with Giant Haystacks and Klondyke Jake taking on Steve Veidor and Big Bruno. The match had come about following a show at the same venue on 28th October, when Veidor had beaten Jake in a fight to a finish. Haystacks and Jake won the match with a winning fall in the seventeenth minute.

The rest of the bill saw Johnny Kwango pin Bob Kirkwood in the fourth round for the only fall needed. Wayne Bridges beat Honey Boy Zimba by two falls to one in round four and Billy Torontos beat Dave Freeman in the third round.

The next night at Bath, Kendo Nagasaki was back in tag action and Gorgeous George was once again lined up to partner him. Their opponents were Big Bruno and Johnny Wilson, with the latter pairing snatching victory in a chaotic finish. Kendo seemingly got the winning fall over Wilson but the referee had taken a bump beforehand. He was unable to count and by the time the referee had come round, Bruno had covered George, and that was the fall that ended up counting. Despite George's best protests and insults directed at Bruno, the result stood.

At Wolverhampton on the 23rd, Nagasaki had two matches on the show. The first was a hair v mask match against Jarmain Singh. Nagasaki didn't take long to win, pinning Singh in round two to win. Gorgeous George, in something of a good mood, didn't insist on Singh having his head shaved, it being the season of goodwill and because Singh had been very brave challenging Kendo. Singh had a couple of inches of hair cut off instead, which actually resulted in a free haircut.

A slightly more difficult task came next, when Nagasaki would once again partner Rex Strong against Big Daddy and Giant Haystacks. Kendo and Strong proved the victors when their opponents were disqualified in the tenth minute.

1975 came to an end after an eventful few months.

championship time limit it was one score each. Davies had forced Bartelli to submit in the ninth round before Bartelli had equalised in the fourteenth round. Tony St.Clair gave weight and a beating to Mal Kirk on the same show albeit when Kirk was disqualified in the fourth round. Elder brother Roy was also victorious when he defeated Colin Joynson by two falls to one in the fourth round. Vic Faulkner won the night's other match again in the fourth round when he pinned Jim Breaks for the winner.

Kendo Nagasaki started 1976 with a challenge from Giant Haystacks on the 6th at Wolverhampton. Nagasaki won in round three when Haystacks was unable to continue. Also on the same show Jim Breaks defeated challenger Bobby Ryan in a defence of his British Lightweight Title. Breaks pinned Ryan for the winning fall in the fifteenth and final round.

Nagasaki again beat Haystacks on the 8th at Digbeth when Haystacks was counted out in round three. On the same night there was a chaotic main event at Nottingham between Big Daddy and Ray Steele. The referee for the contest was Tally Ho Kaye who was on Daddy's side throughout and delivered a fast count for Daddy's winning fall. Daddy's brother and referee Brian Crabtree then entered the ring and set about Kaye before reversing the decision much to his brother's anger.

More mayhem featuring the Crabtrees happened at Liverpool the next night. Tony St.Clair was leading Mark Rocco by one fall in round five when Rocco attempted to leave the ring and head back to the dressing room. He was carried back to the ring by St.Clair, Big Daddy and Brian Crabtree to continue the match and shortly after the restart was pinned by St.Clair for a two straight falls win. Kendo Nagasaki beat Giant Haystacks for the third time that week when again Haystacks failed to beat the count in round three. The rest of an excellent show saw Big Daddy knockout Rex Strong in the third round whilst Gwyn Davies defeated Mal Kirk by disqualification also in the third round.

Kendo Nagasaki made the journey to the south coast and Brighton on the 14th to take on The Mad Axeman in a mask v mask main event. It was Nagasaki who kept his identity secret when the Axeman failed to beat the count in the third round

21

after a Kamikaze Crash laid him out. Steve Veidor beat Mal Kirk by disqualification in the fourth round and Steve Logan beat Johnny Czeslaw who was unable to continue in the fifth round in other matches there that night.

Preston on the 20th saw another chapter of the Big Daddy and Kendo Nagasaki feud and naturally there was a chaotic ending. Nagasaki got the first score in the second round with a grape vine submission before Daddy equalised in the third when a neck lift forced Nagasaki to submit. It ended in the fourth round with Daddy pulling the mask off of Nagasaki who fled from the ring. The referee ruled that the verdict would be a No Contest. On the same show Tony St.Clair beat Mark Rocco who walked out of the ring in the sixth round and was counted out. Giant Haystacks forced Gwyn Davies to retire through injury in the fifth round whilst Jim Breaks beat Johnny Saint by two falls to one in round six.

The first Royal Albert Show of 1976 on 21st January saw the challenges to Mick McManus and Big Daddy by Mike Marino took place. The first match saw Marino take on McManus who had Daddy in his corner. For once Marino had the weight advantage and forced McManus to submit in the fourth round for the winner. Daddy was another matter though with his huge weight advantage. With the entire crowd willing him on Marino pinned Daddy with his trademark 'small package' in round three to win the match.

The other matches saw young heavyweights Lee Bronson and Johnny Wilson face each other with Bronson winning in the fourth round. Steve Veidor defeated reigning British Heavyweight Champion Gwyn Davies by two falls to one in the fourth round. Immediately afterwards Veidor demanded that Davies put his title on the line against him. Vic Faulkner wrestled a one fall each draw with Bobby Ryan over four rounds in a contest for those who enjoy pure wrestling. Mal Kirk beat Caswell Martin by countout in the third round whilst the evening ended with Johnny Kwango defeating Catweazle by the one fall needed.

At Hanley on the 24th there was a bloodbath in the match between Kendo Nagasaki and Giant Haystacks. Haystacks was leading from a submission in round two before his head was

22

split open in the third. With blood gushing everywhere the referee stopped the contest and decided to leave the decision as an open verdict. Also on the same show referee Brian Crabtree took on old foe Tally Ho Kaye and it was Crabtree to the crowd's delight who pinned Kaye in the first round to win.

The first Croydon show of the year was on the 27th with Kendo Nagasaki facing Count Bartelli in the main event. Yet again the Kamikaze Crash saw off another rival when Bartelli was unable to beat the count in round three after being the victim of it. John Kowalski beat Big Daddy who was disqualified in the third round. Clive Myers pinned Ricky Silver in round three to win their match. Steve Logan defeated Ivan Penzecoff by two falls to one in the fourth round. Tibor Szakacs wrestled a one fall each draw with Romany Riley whilst Pete Roberts beat John Kowalski who substituted for the missing Wayne Bridges.

February -

The first wrestling of the month on TV was another Wednesday late night show on the 4th. The two matches shown came from Brent Town Hall with Mick McManus beating Billy Torontos by countout in the fourth round in one of them. The other saw Lee Bronson beat Ivan Penzecoff by two falls to one in the round five.

Saturday's World of Sport on 7th February saw the second half of the Bradford bill shown. The main point of interest for not only grapple fans but casual sports fans was the first appearance on TV of Harvey Smith as a wrestler. Smith was carefully matched against Blackjack Mulligan who was the perfect opponent to showcase Smith with. A lively encounter saw Smith pin Mulligan in round three for the winner.

A heavyweight contest saw Ray Steele beat Mal Kirk who was disqualified in the sixth round. A clash of personalities between Liverpool's outspoken Kevin Conneely and Jeff Kaye was halted in the fifth round when Kaye couldn't continue. Conneely refused to accept the win in the circumstances so the usual No Contest verdict was the answer.

23

The final two contests from the Brent Town Hall bill was shown in the late night slot on the 11th. Johnny Kwango beat Sid Cooper by two falls to one in the fifth round whilst Giant Haystacks defeated Pete Roberts in the third round. Roberts was counted out after being slammed to the mat which was followed by a splash which left him with no chance of beating the ten count.

The wrestling on World of Sport on the 14th came from Southend and the usual three matches from there were shown. The highlight was Mick McManus taking on the heavier Tony St.Clair with McManus gaining the first fall in round two with a folding press following a punch that weakened his opponent. St.Clair didn't take long to equalise though when a double leg grab led to St.Clair pinning McManus with a folding press himself in the third round. St.Clair then retaliated to McManus' foul moves with ear grabs and jumps off of the ring apron. Unfortunately on the second of these moves St.Clair injured his leg and couldn't return to the ring before the count of ten finished. But referee Joe D'Orazio decided the result was that both wrestlers were counted out as McManus was lying prostate on the mat as he finished counting. MC Charlie Fisher tried to patiently explain the decision to McManus who had thought he was the winner.

A heavyweight match saw Steve Veidor pin Pete Roberts in round five for the one fall needed to win. Whilst a catchweight contest ended with Romany Riley pinning Robby Baron in the fourth round to win.

The midweek wrestling on the 18th featured two bouts from Solihull in the West Midlands. The first contest was at welterweight with John Naylor beating Colin Bennett with the one fall needed in the third round. The other match was a tag match with The Royals taking on The Dennisons, Alan Dennison and Sid Cooper. Bert Royal got the first score pinning Dennison in the eighth minute before Dennison equalised for his team making Vic Faulkner submit in the seventeenth minute. The end came in the nineteenth minute when Royal got the winning fall over Sid Cooper for another popular win for the brothers.

24

World of Sport on the 21st featured the other three matches from the Southend bill. The first match saw Johnny Wilson take on Steve Logan with the first fall etc. to be the winner. Perhaps stupidly Wilson delivered a forearm uppercut to Logan's mouth in the opening seconds with Logan retaliating with a punch. Logan was soon delivering his famed short range jabs to Wilson who had a 2st. weight advantage but was unable to take advantage of it. Logan got the winner in the third round after another short range jab had softened up Wilson and a bodyslam followed by a reverse double knee hold pinfall ended the match.

The main match of the afternoon saw the masked Kung Fu meet Mark Rocco and as MC Charlie Fisher introduced them commentator Kent Walton noted about the number of imposter Kung Fu's wrestling around the country. It had become a problem as a number of unscrupulous independent promoters put anyone in a mask and a judo suit and declared that their wrestler was Kung Fu. It didn't take long for Rocco to start the rough stuff but Kung Fu stunned his opponent with a knee to the jaw and a double handed chop. Again Rocco tried the rough stuff but a beautiful counter by Kung Fu saw him pin his opponent with a reverse folding press secured by a bridge in the third round. Rocco tested referee Joe D'Orazio's patience at times especially after receiving a final public warning in the fourth round with Kung Fu suffering from a nose bleed thanks to the punches from Rocco. Rocco finally got the equaliser in round five when he reversed an attempted flying tackle into a pile driver which weakened Kung Fu enough for the pinfall. The winner came in the final round when a riled up Kung Fu had removed his jacket as he lost finally lost his cool with Rocco's rule breaking. Rocco shoved Kung Fu through the ropes onto the floor outside before launching a dive through the ropes himself landing on Kung Fu who was still outside of the ring. Both wrestlers got back into the ring and Kung Fu landed a kick and a jab and pinned Rocco with a cross press to win a superb match.

The final contest that week was a heavyweight match between John Elijah and Count Bartelli which was a complete contrast to the previous match. With only one fall needed to win it was Bartelli who pinned Elijah in round three with a reverse double knee hold following a bodyslam to take the victory.

There was no midweek wrestling on TV that week so the following Saturday saw the next grappling broadcast. That week's wrestling on World of Sport came from Sheffield. The famed George Kidd should have been in the main event but he had announced his retirement so his place against Jeff Kaye was taken by Alan Dennison who was already at the hall for a different contest. Dennison won the match when he pinned Kaye for the only fall required in the fifth round. Pete Roberts beat Marty Jones by two falls to one in the fifth round with this match going on to be seen many times on TV over the next decade and never failing to disappoint. Jones had just returned from a successful tour of Mexico. Finally Tibor Szakacs took on Klondyke Jake who was disqualified in round three for illegal use of the fist.

Around the halls -

10th February saw another big night of action at Croydon with Steve Veidor defeating old rival Big Bruno by disqualification in the sixth round with the Southern Area Heavyweight Title on the line. Two more heavyweight matches saw Mike Marino beat Mal Kirk by disqualification in the third round whilst Ray Steele making a rare visit down south lost to Klondyke Jake. Steele submitted in the fourth round to lose by two to one after taking the lead with a fall in round two. Other matches saw Bobby Barnes wrestle a one fall each four round draw with Tony St.Clair whilst Johnny Wilson pinned Mel Stuart in the fourth round to win that contest.

Belle Vue opened its doors for the first time in 1976 after the famed Christmas circus had finished it's run. A suitably stacked card was arranged to entertain another packed house of five thousand or so. Belle Vue favourites The Royals were in action when they took on old rivals Mick McManus and Steve Logan in the evening's tag match. Despite conceding the opening fall in the ninth minute Bert and Vic won the match by two falls to one in the sixteenth minute.

26

That night also saw a bill at Bolton featuring Paul Luty who was better known in the ring as Nobby Garside. Garside was his stage name in the popular TV comedy show of the time Love thy Neighbour. Garside beat opponent Fat Boy Floyd who was counted out in the third round. Also on the bill was Harvey Smith who defeated his opponent Blackjack Mulligan by two straight falls in round five.

Kendo Nagasaki faced the challenge of Big Daddy at Liverpool Stadium on the 12th in a ladder match. Nagasaki won the match in the eighth minute but the feud was far from finished. The Royals defeated The Liverpool Skinheads, Terry O'Neill and Roy Paul. The other matches saw King Ben wrestle a one fall each draw with Little Prince and Dudley Cameron beat 'Angel Face' Bob Bibby with the winner coming in the fifth round.

The Royals were also in action the next night at Belle Vue when they took on Alan Dennison and Sid Cooper. The Royals won by two straight falls in just over eighteen minutes. Giant Haystacks beat Gwyn Davies who was disqualified in the third round. A special challenge match saw Jackie Turpin wear his boxing gloves to meet Tally Ho Kaye in a boxer v wrestler match. Turpin knocked out Kaye in the third round to win the contest. Jim Breaks beat Bobby Ryan when the 'Breaks' Special' saw Ryan submit in the sixth round. Billy Howes beat Al Shan by two falls to one in the fifth round and Marty Jones beat Alan Woods by two falls to one in the sixth to complete the night.

The March Royal Albert Hall spectacular took place on 24th March with the main event being a loser must unmask match between Kendo Nagasaki and the much lighter Kung Fu. Another packed to capacity crowd of five thousand saw an engrossing match in which Kung Fu gave Nagasaki plenty of trouble with his speed and slick moves. After taking the first fall in the third round Kung Fu found the 3st. or more weight advantage for Nagasaki eventually telling and in round four the Kamikaze Crash saw him laid out for the count of ten. As soon as he came to Kung Fu unmasked to reveal the handsome features of Northern Irish martial arts expert Eddie Hamill. The other main event match was a heavyweight tag challenge with the crowd favourites Mike Marino and Steve Veidor taking on the far from popular Big Daddy and Giant Haystacks. Marino and Veidor showed other heavyweights exactly how to take on the big men wiith their fast counters and team work bamboozling their opponents. The winning fall for Marino and Veidor came in the sixteenth minute to much excitement from the crowd.

Steve Veidor was an interested spectator as Gwyn Davies faced Pete Roberts. It had been announced Davies would defend his British Heavyweight Title against Veidor on the May Albert Hall show and Davies warmed up nicely for it defeating Roberts by two falls to one in the fourth round. Count Bartelli wrestled a one fall each draw over four rounds with Romany Riley. Mark Rocco beat Ricky Silver who was counted out in the fifth round and in the final bout Robby Baron beat Alan Serjeant.

Friday night on 26th March at Chatham saw an interesting match booked with Bobby Barnes facing Mark Rocco. Both wrestlers known for their explosive ring style as well as their liberal use of rulebreaking tactics. To the fan's in attendance astonishment both wrestlers wrestled entirely to the rules and instead showcased their wrestling skills. The match ended in a one fall each draw at the end of the four ten minute rounds. Rocco took the lead in round three before Barnes equalised in the fourth and final round. Someone who didn't wrestle within the rules on the same show was Giant Haystacks who was disqualified in the fourth round of the main event of the night against Tibor Szakacs.

The Saturday night show at Belle Vue the following night was advertised as a main event six man tag of Kendo Nagasaki, Gorgeous George and referee Karl Krammer against Big Daddy, Kung Fu and Daddy's brother and referee Brian Crabtree. In the end much to the fan's disappointment Brian was replaced by Jalman Singh and even worse the team of Nagasaki, George and Krammer won with the winning submission coming in the sixteenth minute. Showjumping star Harvey Smith continued to please the fans this time with a two straight falls win over Blackjack Mulligan in three rounds. Brian Maxine won an extremely bad tempered match with John

Naylor who walked out of the ring in the seventh minute and was counted out. Honey Boy Zimba beat Mark Rocco who was disqualified in round four and Roy St.Clair beat Tibor Szakacs by two falls to one in the sixth round.

March ended with Kendo Nagasaki in another chaotic match at Wolverhampton on the 30th when he took on Wild Angus as part of a four man tournament. Angus had recently returned from his worldwide travels and replaced injured Gwyn Davies to face Nagasaki in the first semi final. The match ended in round three when Nagasaki fled from the ring as Angus tried to unmask him and the decision was Nagasaki had been disqualified. The other semi final saw another masked wrestler, The Ringer take on Pete Roberts. Roberts was unable to continue due to injury in the fourth round so it was The Ringer who progressed to the final. The final didn't last long as Angus beat The Ringer who was counted out in the first round and unmasked as Lancashire heavyweight 'Beau' Jack Rowlands.

April -

The team match tournament from Nottingham was completed on World of Sport on the 3rd. The final three single's matches saw Kevin Conneely beat Brian Hunt by two falls to one in the fifth round. Bert Royal beat Terry O'Neill who was disqualified in the fourth round for punching his opponent. Fellow Liverpool Skinhead Roy Paul also lost in his match with Alan Dennison when he walked out in the fourth round. The six man tag finale saw Vic Faulkner, Alan Dennison and Bobby Ryan beat Jim Breaks, Phil Pearson and Tally Ho Kaye by three falls to two leaving the TV All-Stars winners by six points to one in the tournament.

The midweek wrestling on ITV on the 7th came from Leeds and saw Count Bartelli pin Roy St.Clair in the second round for the only fall needed to win. Alan Dennison wrestled a draw with Clive Myers in the other bout seen. Dennison's submission in round four equalised a fall by Myers in the third. The end came with the both wrestlers shoulders pinned to the mat in the fifth round so it ended honours even.

returned the favour when he pinned McManus in the seventeenth minute for the equaliser. When the bell rung to signal the end of the match after the scheduled twenty minutes it was still one fall each so the result was a draw. The third match saw Jim Breaks gain a two straight falls win over Maurice Hunter with a fall in the third round before forcing Hunter to submit in the fifth.

The final two bouts from the Leeds show were seen on the midweek ITV broadcast on the 21st. The first match was a heavyweight contest between Gwyn Davies and Giant Haystacks. Referee Ken Lazenby had his work cut out trying to keep order with each wrestler being issued with two public warnings as the second round progressed. Midway through the round Lazenby had had enough and disqualified the pair of them. The other match was a welterweight match between two of Kent Walton's favourite wrestlers, Jackie Robinson and John Naylor. At the end of the sixth round both wrestler had gained a fall apiece, Robinson in the second round and Naylor in the fourth so the result was a draw.

An action packed three bouts were shown from Woking on 24th April's World of Sport. The first was a teacher v pupil contest with Mike Marino tackling first year pro Lee Bronson. Bronson gave an excellent showing before Marino's experience told when he reversed a full nelson attempt to pin the youngster in round five to win.

The main match was a return challenge with Steve Veidor and Tibor Szakacs taking on Big Daddy and Giant Haystacks again. As soon as the bell rung Daddy and Haystacks targetted Szakacs with the usual barrage of belly butts and bodychecks before Veidor tagged in and received the same treatment. Daddy got the the first score in the fifth minute when a backbreaker saw Szakacs submit immediately. A throw from Szakacs on Daddy saw him nearly go out of the ring under the bottom ropes. As Daddy's legs dangled out of the ring Veidor tried to pull him out assisted by several enthusiastic fans before the security personnel aided by MC and former wrestler Charlie Fisher rescued him. The match descended into chaos when Veidor and Szakacs launched Haystacks into Daddy who was trapped in a corner before a punch from Daddy landed right into

Veidor's stomach. Referee Joe D'Orazio by now was having trouble keeping control of the match but when Haystacks broke up a cross press from Veidor on Daddy he decided enough was enough and disqualified both Haystacks and Daddy. The action hadn't ended as MC Fisher announced the verdict Szakacs landed several chops to Haystacks' chest whilst Veidor kicked Daddy in the face as he attempted to leave the ring. For sheer action, entertainment and crowd excitement it was a tremendous match whilst not one for the wrestling purist.

The other match shown was Mick McManus v Kung Fu and despite unmasking at The Royal Albert Hall the month before Kung Fu was wearing the mask again. McManus opened the scoring in the third round with his usual double leg grab followed by a folding press after several weakeners. Kung Fu equalised in the next round when a back hammer hold saw McManus submit instantly. McManus got the winner with a submission in the fifth round. The barefoot Kung Fu had injured his foot mistiming a kick and hit the corner post instead of McManus. After a couple of stamps on the injured foot McManus grabbed it and straight away Kung Fu submitted leaving him defeated on TV for the first time. He then took off his mask leaving Kent Walton to remark what a good looking fellow he was. McManus then grabbed the mask and put it on and as he did so Kung Fu then threw him around the ring for a spot of retaliation.

The wrestling on ITV for April ended on the 28th with one bout from Aylesbury shown on the Wednesday night. The match between Steve Logan and Pete Roberts ended in a competitive one fall each draw at the end of the scheduled six rounds. Logan got the first fall in the third round whilst Roberts pinned his opponent in the fifth to equalise.

Around the halls -

A couple of championship matches topped the bill of the latest Belle Vue spectacular on 10th April. In the first of them Bobby Ryan made a successful defence of the European Lightweight Title against former champion Jim Breaks. Ryan got the first fall in the fifth round before Breaks forced Ryan to submit with a 'Breaks' special' in the sixth round. Ryan reversed another attempt at the 'special' in the seventh to pin Breaks for the winner. The second title match saw Count Bartelli make short work of challenger Jamaica Kid in a defence of the Commonwealth Heavyweight Title. Bartelli won by two straight falls in only four rounds.

Two heavyweight matches on the bill saw in the first Pete Curry's match with Johnny Czeslaw end in a No Contest in the fifth round when Czeslaw was unable to continue. In the other a lively match saw Hans Streiger beat Ray Glendenning who failed to beat the count in the fifth round. Jackie Robinson beat Maurice Hunter by two falls to one in the fourth round whilst Catweazle and Kevin Conneely sent the fans home happy when they beat The Liverpool Skinheads by disqualification in the final bout of the night.

Giant Haystacks took on Kendo Nagasaki in the main event at Nottingham on the 15th with Nagasaki winning as Haystacks was counted out when he chased Gorgeous George from the ring. Jackie Turpin continued with his series of boxer v wrestler matches when he knocked out Tally Ho Kaye in the fourth round. The Royals were in single's matches to complete the bill. Bert Royal beat Roy St.Clair by two falls to one in the seventh round whilst Vic Faulkner beat Alan Woods by two falls to one in the sixth round.

Kendo Nagasaki was in action at Hanley on the Saturday night as part of a four man tournament consisting of Nagasaki, Giant Haystacks, Magnficent Maurice and Bob Abbott. The first semi final saw Abbott beat Haystacks who was disqualified in the second round whilst the other saw Nagasaki beat Maurice who was counted out in the second too. Nagasaki had an easy time of it in the final. Abbott was already severely weakened by Haystacks earlier and after receiving a Kamikaze Crash in round two was counted out leaving Nagasaki the winner.

It was Big Daddy's turn to take on Kendo Nagasaki at Croydon on the 20th with Nagasaki victorious in the fourth round when Daddy failed to beat the count. One the same bill Kung Fu beat Steve Logan by two falls to one in the fourth round. Bobby Barnes beat Spencer Churchill who was unable to continue in round five whilst Jon Cortez defeated Rajendra

Singh also in the fifth. A pair of one fall matches saw Clive Myers beat Joe Murphy and Johnny Czeslaw beat Ivan Penzecoff both in the fourth round.

The Undertakers tag team topped the bill Belle Vue in a tag match the following Saturday against Kung Fu and Little Prince. The Undertakers , Jonathan and Nathaniel, went down by two falls to one in just under nine minutes but refused to unmask following the defeat. The other featured match saw a battle of referees with the popular Brian Crabtree taking on the controversial Karl Krammer. Crabtree won by two falls to one in the fourth round. Wild Angus beat Beau Jack who was unable to come out for the fifth round through injury. Hans Streiger beat Honey Boy Zimba who was counted out in the fifth round. Marty Jones wrestled a one fall each draw with John Naylor over six rounds whilst Pete Curry and Roy St.Clair's match ended in round five when both were counted out.

A rare show was held on a Sunday night in London the next night at the famed Irish strongman Butty Sugrue's club Butty's in Kilburn. Big Daddy beat Tibor Szakacs in the fifth round with a back breaker hold seeing Szakacs submit. Irish veteran Joe Murphy beat Steve Grey by two falls to one in round six. Johnny Yearsley beat Lee Bronson who was counted out in the sixth whilst Johnny Kwango beat Sid Cooper who also failed to beat the count this time in the fifth round.

April ended with a show at Nottingham on the 29th with a return contest from the 15th between Kendo Nagasaki and Giant Haystacks. Nagasaki won the first match via count out and was victorious again this time when a badly cut Haystacks was unable to continue in the third round. Brian Maxine beat John Naylor who was counted out in the sixth round. Marty Jones beat local favourite Bob Abbott by two falls to one in round six whilst Colin Bennett beat Zoltan Boscik by disqualification in the fourth.

The final piece of news for April was the announcement that the May spectacular at The Royal Albert Hall would be a parade of the champions and would be filmed by ITV to be shown on World of Sport. The two main matches would see Steve Veidor finally get his shot at Gwyn Davies for the British

Heavyweight Title in a much anticipated contest. The other would see a tag challenge with Kendo Nagasaki teaming up with Gorgeous George to face Mick McManus and Steve Logan. The five other matches on the bill would see a British champion take on an opponent in non title matches. Not surprisingly the tickets sold out in rapid time.

May -

May started with a blank Saturday on the 1st with no wrestling shown on World of Sport. Despite it being FA Cup Final day ITV had decided that wrestling had no place in the schedule for the day which was most disappointing.

Just to make grapple fans even more angry the midweek show on 5th May was shown at past midnight in some regions like 12.15am for Granada viewers or 11.50pm in the ATV area. I doubt many stayed up so late as the two matches taped at Aylesbury hardly whetted the appetite. Johnny Wilson beat Lee Bronson by two falls to one in a heavyweight contest. In the other Johnny Kwango defeated Robby Baron by two falls to one as well.

Wrestling was back on World of Sport on the 8th with three bouts shown from Woking. This was actually filmed back at the beginning of November 1975 and had been forgotten about till now. The first match saw Zoltan Boscik beat Steve Grey by the only fall needed in the fifth round. A heavyweight contest saw the giant Klondyke Jake face the much lighter Romany Riley. Riley overcame the disadvantage to pin Jake with a folding press in the second round. As the match progressed Jake started the rough stuff and got a public warning from referee Joe D'Orazio in the fourth round. The ending came in the fourth when Jake sent Riley flying over the top rope. Riley had no hope of getting back into the ring before the count of ten had finished.

The other match was between Mel Stuart and Ivan Penzecoff. Only one score was needed to win and it was Penzecoff who got it in the fourth round. Stuart had been weakened from a throw to the outside of the ring and when he returned Stuart was slammed and covered with a reverse knee hold for the only fall needed.

The midweek wrestling that week was another late start with the programme starting just before midnight with another two matches from Aylesbury shown. In the first Kung Fu beat Sid Cooper who failed to beat the count after being kicked out of the ring by his opponent. In the other match Mike Marino beat the heavier Honey Boy Zimba by two falls to one.

Wrestling was missing from World of Sport again on 15th May as the England v Scotland football match was shown instead.

The midweek wrestling on the 19th came from the Plas Madoc Leisure Centre which was in Ruabon, a mile or so south of Wrexham in North Wales. This was one of the few times that the wrestling on ITV was shown from a venue outside of England. Another near midnight start saw Mick McMichael beat Jeff Kaye by two falls to one in the fifth round. In the second match Tally Ho Kaye beat Little Prince with the one fall needed coming in round three.

An England v Scotland tournament from Sheffield was shown on World of Sport on the 22nd In the first match Bill Ross for Scotland defeated England's Vic Faulkner in the fourth round. The second saw Kung Fu for England (technically Eddie Hamill was Northern Irish and lived in North Wales but such details never bothered anyone in wrestling) beat Tom Dowie who was disqualified for punching Kung Fu in the fifth round. The final match saw a win for England when Jim Breaks with two submissions in quick time in rounds five and six beat Len Ironside who had scored a fall in the second. England therefore won the tournament by two wins to one from Scotland.

The midweek show on the 26th came from Ruabon and featured the one contest which saw Bobby Ryan defend the European Lightweight Title against Johnny Saint. Bobby Ryan opened the scoring with a fall in the third round before Saint equalised in the fifth. That's how it ended with Ryan retaining the title as a result of the draw.

Football again replaced wrestling on World of Sport that weekend with the England v Italy international taking its place.

Around the halls -

May started with another match between Kendo Nagasaki and Big Daddy at Hanley but this time it was a lumberjack match with other wrestlers patrolling on the outside of the ring to prevent Nagasaki running away. It didn't matter as Nagasaki stayed inside the ropes throughout and was the winner with the deciding fall coming in the fourth round. Wild Angus who was back now from an extended tour of North America took on Count Bartelli on the same show and Angus won after three rounds of chaos.

The canteen at Bart's Hospital in London was an interesting venue for wrestling on 5th May. A packed crowd saw hospital worker Paul Darton team up with Steve Grey in the main event tag against The Roughnecks, Joe Murphy and Sid Cooper. Murphy and Cooper won with the winning fall coming after twenty minutes. Also on the show was Clive Myers who beat Peter Szakacs by two falls to one in the sixth round. A heavyweight match saw Johnny Yearsley wrestle a one fall each draw with Lee Bronson.

Kendo Nagasaki was involved in a wild main event at Belle Vue on the 8th when he faced Wild Angus in a ladder match. Nagasaki finally climbed up the ladder in just under seven minutes to grab the bag holding the money in a match that was pure mayhem from start to finish. Another match that ended in a chaotic fashion was Gwyn Davies against Giant Haystacks which ended with Davies being disqualified in the second round. A four man tournament saw Mick McMichael beat Jim Breaks in the first semi final and Johnny Saint beat Bobby Ryan in the second. Saint won the final by two falls to one in the fourth round. The car containing Steve Logan, Brian Maxine and Johnny Kwango failed to arrive at the venue so a couple of quick calls were made to replace them. In the first John Naylor beat Colin Bennett by two falls to one in the fifth round and in the second Honey Boy Zimba beat Ivan Penzecoff who failed to beat the count in round four.

Round two of the Kendo Nagasaki v Wild Angus matches took place at Wolverhampton on the 11th with Nagasaki again the winner. Mal Kirk had also returned from extensive world travels and his opponent Beau Jack took a pounding before retiring at the end of the fourth round. Kung Fu took on the heavier Johnny South on the same show and was victorious in round four.

A stacked show was on offer at Halifax on 13th May with hometown hero Big Daddy taking on Wild Angus. Angus tired of Daddy's non stop barrage of belly butts in the second round and walked away. Kendo Nagasaki had an easy night on the same show when he dispatched of opponent Jamaica Kid with the Kamikaze Crash in round three. Jim Breaks beat Bobby Ryan who was injured in the fifth round whilst a six man tag featured The Royals with Honey Boy Zimba who beat the trio of Magnificent Maurice, Tally Ho Kaye and King Ben.

That Saturday at Hanley saw Kendo Nagasaki and Wild Angus on the same side this time to take on Big Daddy and Count Bartelli. It was no surprise that the match was abandoned after eight minutes or so with all participants outside of the ring fighting on the stage.

Croydon fans on the 18th were left disappointed when Kendo Nagasaki failed to appear for his main event contest with John Kowalski. Nagasaki was replaced by Big Bruno who went on to defeat Kowalski with the winning submission in the fifth round. A battle of the big men saw Klondyke Jake beat Prince Kumali in four rounds. Romany Riley wrestled a one fall each draw with Johnny Kwango whilst Jon Cortez beat Brian Maxine by two falls to one.

Another loaded Belle Vue show happened on the 22nd with Big Daddy beating The Undertaker who he knocked out in the very first round. Mike Marino retained the World Mid/Heavyweight Title when he defeated challenger Count Bartelli by two falls to one in the twelfth round. Colin Joynson beat Magnificent Maurice in round five whilst Kevin Conneely's match with Jeff Kaye ended in a No Contest when Kaye was injured in the fourth round. The punters went home happy when The Royals with Johnny Saint beat Tally Ho Kaye, The Godfather and Blackjack Mulligan in a six man tag.

The main show of the month if not the whole year was at The Royal Albert Hall on 26th May with the ITV cameras and Kent Walton at ringside. Tickets had sold out instantly and on the night fans were hanging from the rafters for one of the best shows held for a long time. One of the main events was for the British Heavyweight Title over ten rounds with champion Gwyn Davies defending against Steve Veidor, or as Kent Walton described him the pin up boy of wrestling. After a quiet first round things started to liven up with Veidor receiving a forearm smash after referee Joe D'Orazio had called a break. Davies got his first public warning in the fourth for a punch as his weakeners began to have an effect. But it was Veidor who later on in round four got the first fall fooling Davies he was hurt before rolling Davies up for a folding press as the crowd went wild. The champion wasn't behind for long though as Davies got the equaliser with a back hammer submission in just over a minute of round five. Veidor nearly grabbed a winner in the sixth with a move similar to how he got his first fall, even Kent Walton was as excited as the crowd was but Davies kicked out at the count of two. D'Orazio gave Davies his final public warning after more use of his fist towards the end of the sixth but the weakeners especially on Veidor's wrist were having an effect. The end came in the seventh round with Veidor bleeding from the mouth , his wrist was giving him real problems and he looked a sorry sight. Veidor tried one last attack at the start of the round and landed a flurry of forearm smashes and kicks on Davies and even flinging the referee out of the way to continue his assault. Davies survived and threw Veidor over the top rope who on the way trapped his neck between the top two ropes and referee D'Orazio stopped the match in favour of the champion Gwyn Davies. It truly was a magnificent encounter between two top heavyweights and one of the matches of the year and easily rated as five star.

The other main match on the programme saw once again Kendo Nagasaki team up with Gorgeous George to face the challenge of Mick McManus and Steve Logan. As Kent Walton explained beforehand, McManus and Logan had sent a telegram to Nagasaki challenging him to get in the ring with his 'yakking manager'. The challenge was accepted and as MC Mike Judd introduced the teams it was McManus and Logan who heard the cheers of the fans in attendance for a rare time. George was bizzarely dressed in a white cat suit with an afro wig before he did a strip tease routine undressing to show his wrestling gear and removed the wig as their opponents waited patiently. Once the action started Kendo and Logan locked up to begin with and it was Kendo who got the upper hand in the early exchanges. Referee Max Ward showed a lot of leniency to the McManus and Logan team as they retaliated with plenty of foul moves. Nagasaki got the first fall on McManus with a reverse double knee hold after a straight jab to the throat had weakened him but he got a public warning as well for attacking Logan. Finally the moment the whole crowd and Kent Walton were waiting for happened when George was tagged in after Kendo had weakened Logan. George attempted a few attacks before quickly tagging out but soon returned once Logan was weakened again. It went wrong when Nagasaki failed to see McManus had been tagged in and both McManus and Logan went to town on the hapless George. George soon submitted from a neck hold applied by McManus but referee Ward was having a job keeping control. The action restarted with McManus attacking George but Nagasaki got the tag and returned to face Logan. The end came in the twelfth minute when Logan instantly submitted to Nagasaki's grapevine hold and maybe McManus and Logan regretted sending the telegram ? As Kendo and George celebrated the beaten McManus and Logan team had to swallow their pride and just to rub salt into their wounds they faced the long journey to Glasgow the next day to appear there that evening.

The rest of the show featured British champions in non title matches with Mid/Heavyweight number one Mike Marino having a tough test against Giant Haystacks. I'm not sure if there was any wrestling at all in the three rounds it lasted with eventually the referee's patience tested once too often and he disqualified the pair of them. Vic Faulkner beat Zoltan Boscik by the one fall needed in the fourth round. Bert Royal beat the much heavier Roy St.Clair again by the only fall needed in the fourth round. Jim Breaks and Jon Cortez had a lively battle with Breaks winning courtesy of a 'Breaks' special' in the fifth round. Finally Mick McMichael sent the fans home happy when he defeated middleweight maestro Brian Maxine in the third round.

May ended with Gorgeous George making another ring appearance , this time at Bradford when he tagged with Kendo Nagasaki at Bradford on the 31st. Their opponents were Big Daddy and Kung Fu and once again Kendo and George emerged victorious with a winning submission in the thirteenth minute. On the same bill the British Welterweight Title changed hands when Jim Breaks in his local hall relieved long reigning champion Vic Faulkner of his championship belt. In a rather heated and bad tempered match both wrestlers got two public warnings but it was Breaks who pinned Faulkner to win in the ninth round.

June -

The first wrestling on ITV for June was in the late night midweek slot on 2nd June with the last bouts from the Ruabon show screened. Only five of the six matches recorded were shown with a contest seeing Big Daddy beating Barry Douglas missing. The bouts on the 2nd were both at heavyweight and the first of them would have been better if it had been a two falls contest instead of just the one to win. Kendo Nagasaki took on reigning British Heavyweight Champion Gwyn Davies with Nagasaki pinning Davies in the third round to win. Of course Nagasaki was unable to make any title challenges as masked wrestlers were barred from any title contests. The second match saw Honey Boy Zimba take on Wild Angus who had replaced Steve Logan. Zimba got the first fall in round two which only served to upset Angus who equalised with a Boston Crab in the fourth round which was applied with such ferocity that Zimba was unable to resume for the fifth round.

Wrestling was missing from World of Sport that Saturday with the annual schoolboy's football match shown instead. There was no wrestling shown midweek either so grapple fans were left waiting till 12th June for the next wrestling seen on TV.

Southport was the venue for the wrestling on World of Sport that week with the usual three contests shown. The first match saw Jim Breaks with a two nil win when the 'Breaks special' saw opponent Mike Jordan submit for the winner. The main

46

event featured Mick McManus who would go on to be a regular at the bills recorded for World of Sport at Southport. McManus took on the crowd's favourite Catweazle and in a bout with both wrestlers receiving two public warnings it was McManus who pinned Catweazle for the winner in the fifth round. The final match that week ended prematurely when Maurice Hunter took an accidental fall from the ring in the fourth round and was unable to continue against King Ben. The sporting Ben refused to accept the win in the circumstances so a No Contest verdict was recorded.

There was no midweek wrestling shown that week as the ITV schedule was filled with a European Championship football match between Holland and Czechoslovakia. Boxing followed the football with highlights of the George Foreman v Joe Frazier heavyweight title fight from the night before.

The other three matches filmed at Southport were shown on the 19th June edition of World of Sport. A heavyweight match opened the show with Wild Angus taking on the colourful Magnificent Maurice who was making his TV debut. Angus used his superior experience and weight advantage to defeat Maurice with a winning fall coming in the fifth round. Marty Jones defied a bloody nose to pin Tally Ho Kaye in round five to win their contest. Finally Big Daddy met Roy St.Clair with St.Clair being knocked out in the second round courtesy of a spectacular double elbow drop from Daddy.

Wrestling was back in the midweek slot on the 23rd with a couple of matches from Hemel Hempstead broadcast. Mike Marino wrestled a one fall each draw with Steve Veidor over six rounds. Veidor got the first fall in the fourth round before Marino equalised in round five. In the other match Brian Maxine beat Ivan Penzecoff in a bad tempered match with the winning fall in round four.

There was no wrestling scheduled to be on World of Sport on 26th June as golf was meant to be shown in its place. The golf tournament though finished early so there was time for an unannounced bout to be shown. The match picked out was between Bert Royal and Johnny Saint recorded at Sheffield back in May and not shown yet. The contest ended in a six

47

round draw with Royal's final round fall negating Saint's fall in the third round.

The midweek wrestling on the 30th featured two bouts from Sheffield although not from the show recorded in May this year but from a show recorded back in May 1975. The first match saw the masked Exorcist beat Jeff Kaye who was counted out in the fourth round. The other match at heavyweight saw a six round draw with John Kowalski getting the opening fall in the third round before Tibor Szakacs equalised in round five.

Around the halls -

As with previous years once May had come to an end most of the inland city and town venues closed down for the summer and the focus was on the seaside venues. The weekly shows at Hanley continued though and on 5th June once again Kendo Nagasaki was involved in controversy. Nagasaki's opponent Wild Angus was disqualified when he lost his cool in the third round. Also on the bill was Big Daddy who beat Rex Strong by two falls to one in round four. It was noticeable on his brother Max Crabtree's shows that Daddy was now being booked more as a babyface and starting to hear the cheers of the fans.

Bobby Ryan made a successful defence of the European Lightweight Title at Wolverhampton on the 9th when challenger Johnny Saint was injured in the ninth round and unable to continue. On the same show Giant Haystacks' match with Gwyn Davies ended in the second round with the bout firmly out of control and a No Contest was the decision.

Haystacks was in action at Liverpool on the Friday night when he took on both Roy St.Clair and Pete Curry in a handicap match. It didn't matter as Haystacks made short work of both winning by knockout. Dynamite Kid continued to progress quietly up through the professional ranks with another victory over Kenny Hogan the same night with a two falls to one win in the sixth round.

The main event at Croydon on the 15th saw Brian Maxine defend the British Middleweight Championship against challenger Jon Cortez. Maxine kept a tight hold of the belt as a result of beating Cortez with the winning submission in the

48

sixth round. A heavyweight match saw Giant Haystacks defeat Wayne Bridges who was forced to submit in the fourth round to lose the contest. Northern raider John Naylor made a rare but winning appearance at Croydon when he pinned Steve Grey in round five to win their match. Romany Riley wrestled a one fall each draw over four rounds with Johnny Wilson whilst Roy St.Clair beat late notice substitute Mel Stuart who replaced Mark Rocco to complete the night.

A tag team tournament was featured at Liverpool on 25th June with six teams in competition. The first heats saw The Royals beat The Undertakers who were disqualified in the tenth minute. Alan Dennison and Mick McMichael defeated Kid Chocolate and The Godfather by two straight falls in just under ten minutes. The Liverpool Skinheads beat Jalmain Singh and Little Prince again by two straight falls in the seventh minute. The Royals won the semi final against Dennison and McMichael by two falls to one in the fourteenth minute to go through to the final against The Liverpool Skinheads. The Royals won the tournament when they defeated the Skinheads by two falls to one in the ninth minute. The evening's only single's bout was between Tibor Szakacs and Mark Rocco. Szakacs won when Rocco walked away in the sixth round after tiring of Szakacs' double handed chops to his chest.

The Royals had a rematch with The Undertakers the next night at Huddersfield with once again The Royals winning when both Jonathan and Nathaniel were counted out in just under thirteen minutes. Also on the show was Gwyn Davies who beat Giant Haystacks who was disqualified for refusing to break the hold after Davies submitted in the third round. Mick McMichael beat Mark Rocco who also was disqualified in the seventh round whilst Dynamite Kid continued to mount up his tally of wins against Kenny Hogan with another victory here.

The same night at Maidstone punters were disappointed when Kendo Nagasaki failed to show for his match against Wayne Bridges. Nagasaki was missing for over a week of bookings including a TV taping at Lincoln on 30th June. Not only did Nagasaki not turn up but neither did either of the wrestlers for the other main event turn up with both Big Daddy and Romany Riley missing. The old card subject to change etc.

49

clause came in handy as a rather put together at the last minute show took place. Wayne Bridges took on Mike Marino in the revised main event and gained a notable win when he defeated Marino by two falls to one in the fifth round.

The last Croydon show of the month on the 29th was headed by a tag match with The Royals taking on old rivals Mick McManus and Steve Logan. This time it was McManus and Logan's turn to celebrate when they won by two falls to one in the seventeenth minute. Two heavyweight matches were also on the bill with Klondyke Jake beating John Kowalski with the winning submission coming in the fifth round. Johnny Yearsley wrestled a one fall each draw over four rounds with Gordon Corbett. Another drawn match saw Johnny Saint and Mick McMichael share the spoils with one fall each whilst Rajendra Singh beat Dave Freeman by two falls to one in the sixth round.

July -

Wrestling was part of the World of Sport broadcast on 3rd July but it wasn't another session of freestyle wrestling as Kent Walton used to say each week to introduce the show. Instead highlights were shown of the 'War of the Worlds' contest between Muhammad Ali and Antonio Inoki as well as various undercard highlights featuring the likes of Andre the Giant. Three matches were shown in total , the aforementioned clash between Ali and Inoki plus Andre the Giant beating heavyweight boxer Chuck Wepner who was knocked out when thrown over the top rope in the third round. The other contest was a tag match for the WWWF tag titles with the champions The Executioners defending against Chief Jay Strongbow and Billy White Wolf. Strongbow and White Wolf won when their opponents were disqualified but under American rules the titles couldn't change hands on a disqualification.

The midweek wrestling that week came from Catford and insomniacs and wrestling fans were rewarded with an appearance from Kendo Nagasaki just before midnight. Nagasaki's opponent was former mentor Count Bartelli with Bartelli opening the scoring in the second round with a submission. It was all over in round three though with the

50

Kamikaze Crash from Nagasaki resulting in Bartelli being counted out. In the other match screened Cypriot Tony Costas' fall in round four was equalised by Steve Grey's fall in the fifth round of a six round draw.

Freestyle wrestling was back on World of Sport on the 10th with three bouts from Lincoln shown. The first of which saw Bobby Ryan face John Naylor with the first fall winning. It was Naylor who got the winner in round four when he pinned Ryan with a double arm over the top hold to win an absolute wrestling masterclass. The second match was the complete opposite with Bert Royal taking on the much lighter Sid Cooper. Royal won when Cooper failed to beat the count in the fifth round. The final contest that week and the main event saw another episode in the rivalry between Mark Rocco and Marty Jones. This was the third time they had been matched up on TV in recent times and it was obvious to all that their styles meshed perfectly. After the early exchanges Rocco turned to the rough stuff and referee Brian Crabtree gave him a deserved public warning in round three. Jones was soon in trouble after injuring his left shoulder on the corner post and Rocco targetted it with weakeners which paid off when Jones submitted from an arm lever in the fourth. Jones turned the tables with a superb reverse posting but an illegal follow up saw referee Crabtree give him a public warning. Jones got the equaliser in the sixth with cross press after a body slam on a weakened Rocco. The winner came in round seven with firstly Rocco getting a final public warning before Jones got the winner pinning Rocco with a double arm hold after a high knee to Rocco's jaw had nearly taken his head off. The crowd gathered round the ring to celebrate and Jones was now in pole position to compete for the vacant British Light/Heavyweight Championship. During the match Kent Walton mentioned Marty Jones' tremendous amateur pedigree as well as the youngster Dynamite Kid who Walton saw in a previous bout on the show. Unfortunately Dynamite's match wasn't shown until October so it made little sense to most viewers who had yet to see him wrestle live.

Giant Haystacks was the featured attraction on the midweek wrestling on 14th July taking on John Elijah from a bill recorded at Hemel Hempstead. Haystacks finished off Elijah in the second round when a bodyslam followed by a splash gave Elijah no chance of beating the count of ten. Brian Maxine pinned the heavier Ivan Penzecoff in the fourth round to win the other match shown that week. This would be the last midweek wrestling show to be seen regularly on ITV.

World of Sport that Saturday saw three matches broadcast that had been recorded at Woking back in April. Sid Cooper was back for the second consecutive this week and again taking on a heavier opponent, this time it was Robby Baron. Baron took advantage of his considerable height and weight superiority to win the match in the fifth round. The end came when Cooper was kicked out of the ring by Baron and failed to return before referee Joe D'Orazio finished his count of ten.

The next match saw a clash of Kent heavyweights with Wayne Bridges back from a long absence from the TV screens taking on Romany Riley. Bridges was billed as the Champion of Kent but no title was on the line in the match. Riley got the first fall in round two with a reverse double arm hold before Bridges equalised in the third with a cross press after a hip toss floored Riley. It was Bridges who won a slightly disappointing match in the fifth round when he pinned Riley with a reverse double arm hold after a flying headbutt had weakened him.

The final bout that week was another heavyweight match this time it was Klondyke Jake taking on John Kowalski. The match unfortunately only lasted a couple of minutes before it ended. A hip toss from Kowalski on Jake saw Kowalski injure his hand and he was counted out by referee Joe D'Orazio in less than three minutes of action.

The World of Sport shows on 24th and 31st July featured contests from the Royal Albert Hall bill in May. On the 24th it was headed by the title match between Gwyn Davies and Steve Veidor. The 31st show featured the tag match between Kendo Nagasaki and Steve Logan v Mick McManus and Steve Logan.

Around the halls -

July started with the sad news that Steve Clements had died in a car crash in Mexico. Clements the son of promoter Ted Beresford had gone abroad in the early seventies to make his name in America and claimed a version of the World Middleweight Title.

The summer holiday shows were by now in full swing and the country was still in the midst of a heatwave. One name missing from most of his bookings for the month was Kendo Nagasaki who had been laid low by a severe attack of vertigo. This was said to be a result of an ear injury sustained in a bout with Gwyn Davies. Going forward this would continue to be a concern for Nagasaki and result in more missed bookings.

Kendo Nagasaki was well enough to take his place in the main event at Belle Vue on 3rd July where he was partnering Rex Strong against the team of Giant Haystacks and Wild Angus. Again in a match with more chaos and mayhem than wrestling it would end in a disqualification with this time Haystacks and Angus thrown out by the referee after eleven minutes or so. Gwyn Davies successfully retained his British Heavyweight Title against Roy St.Clair in the main support. Davies got the first fall in the third round before St.Clair equalised in the fifth. During round six the referee took a bump and was unable to continue so the contest was stopped and Davies was still the champion. Marty Jones wrestled a hectic, fast paced one each draw with Mark Rocco over six rounds. A submission from Rocco was equalised by a fall for Jones in the fifth round and at the end of the final round the crowd demanded they meet again. Dynamite Kid continued his series of matches against Kenny Hogan with this time a two falls to one win in round five. The final match saw Jim Breaks beat Mick McMichael when the 'Breaks' special' saw McMichael submit in rounds five and six after taking the lead in the third round.

Croydon had another big show on the 13th with a rare handicap match as the top of the bill. Giant Haystacks took on both Wayne Bridges and Steve Veidor at the same time. Haystacks did have a special second in the form of Wild Angus but in the end Haystacks tired of taking on both men and walked out in the twelfth minute. A special challenge contest saw referee Max Ward take on Sid Cooper and it was Ward who had his hand raised in victory when Cooper was disqualified in the fourth round. Mark Rocco and Bobby Barnes wrestled an excellent one fall each draw over four rounds whilst Wild Angus beat Lee Bronson making the youngster submit in the fourth round. Romany Riley won a heavyweight contest against Bronco Wells by two falls to one in round five and to complete the evening Alan Serjeant beat Jim Martell by two straight falls.

Another big crowd flocked to Belle Vue on Saturday 17th July with a rare appearance from Mick McManus as the attraction. McManus faced the lighter Johnny Saint and in something of a surprise the normally mild mannered Saint was disqualifed in the fifth round after over doing the retaliation. Big Daddy who was now becoming a firm fan favourite on shows booked by brother Max Crabtree took on the masked wrestler The Ringer who had his manager the Kangaroo Kid with him. The match only lasted two rounds before the double elbow drop left the Ringer out for the count and he was unmasked as Phil Pearson. Kung Fu beat Tally Ho Kaye by two falls to one in the fifth round. Johnny Czeslaw beat Johnny South who was disqualifed in round four whilst Vic Faulkner beat Jim Breaks with a winning fall in the sixth. Catweazle sent the crowd home with a smile on their faces after beating Dave Shade in round five.

Kendo Nagasaki was back in action at the end of the month after recovering from his injuries but he only lasted for a couple of appearances before having to take time off again. Both dates he wrestled were in London, firstly at Wembley on the 26th when he took on Big Bruno. In a contest which was more of a brawl than a wrestling match with bothwrestlers receiving two public warnings. It was Nagasaki who was the victor with a winning submission in the fourth round. Each bout that night featured a wrestler from the Portsmouth area with Johnny Wilson wrestling a one fall each draw with Lee Bronson. Younger brother Peter lost to Johnny Kwango by two falls to one in five rounds. Wayne Bridges beat John Kowalski who was disqualified in the third round.

Both Kendo Nagasaki and Big Bruno were in action the next night at Croydon with Nagasaki this time taking on John Kowalski. Once again the Kamikaze Crash saw off another of Kendo's opponents with Kowalski unable to beat the count in the third round. Steve Veidor beat Big Bruno by two falls to one in round to six to successfully retain the Southern Area Heavyweight Title. Mick McManus beat the outgunned young Manchester based Mike Jordan who failed to beat the count in the third round. Spencer Churchill beat Dave Freeman by two falls to one in round three. Sid Cooper beat Ricky Silver by two falls to one in the fourth whilst Zoltan Boscik brought the curtain down on another Croydon season when he pinned Rajendra Singh in the third round of the show closer.

August -

The situation with the long dormant British Light/Heavyweight Championship looked to have been settled with the announcement that Marty Jones and Brian Maxine would compete for the vacant title on World of Sport on 7th August from Bedworth. Unfortunately on the day of the taping on the 3rd Maxine was injured and unable to compete so Jones was left to take out his frustrations on late notice substitute Alan Woods. Jones won the match when he dropkicked Woods out of the ring in the fifth round and Woods failed to return before referee Brian Crabtree completed his count of ten.

The opening match that week was an international heavyweight contest which saw Poland's Johnny Czeslaw wrestle a one fall each draw with Sierra Leone's Honey Boy Zimba. Czeslaw took the lead with a cross press following a backdrop in the fourth round before Zimba quickly equalised in the next round with a reverse double knee hold after a body slam.

The main event that week suffered from a last minute change too when Giant Haystacks didn't appear for the match against Kendo Nagasaki. Kent Walton noted after MC Martin Conroy's introduction that the match was different from what may have been advertised in the newspapers. Haystacks' replacement was Peter Stewart who gave Nagasaki a few problems before being counted out in the third round following a Kamakaze Crash.

The second half of the Bedworth card was shown on World of Sport the following week. There were no alterations to the advertised bill this week and the opener saw John Naylor take on and beat Colin Bennett by two falls to one in the fifth round. The second match featured Big Daddy who continued his transition to good guy when he knocked out 'Bully Boy' Ian Muir in round two.

The final match saw Wild Angus use his height and weight advantage to beat Beau Jack. Angus opened the scoring in the third round forcing Jack to submit. Jack quickly equalised with a fall in the fourth but wasn't level for long as Angus got the winning fall in the fifth round.

The Board of Control finally made their decision regarding the future of the World Lightweight Championship following champion George Kidd's retirement earlier in the year. It had been announced there would be a tournament and the thirty two top lightweights from all over the world would compete with the final eight remaining competing in eliminators held at Southport with the first two shown on World of Sport on 21st August. Now whether these earlier matches actually happened is a matter of conjecture as there is no record of them anywhere. The first eliminator saw two English wrestlers meet with European Lightweight Champion Bobby Ryan taking on Manchester's Jackie Robinson. It was Ryan who progressed in the tournament to the final four as a result of a winning fall in the sixth round. Johnny Saint was the next wrestler through to the final four when he defeated Scottish contender Bill Ross. It was an unfortunate ending to the match when Ross was unable to continue in the fourth round after a heavy fall from the ring. The sporting Saint wanted to refuse the win and have a rematch but MC Stan Rylands said due to the nature of the tournament Saint would have to accept the win.

The final contest that week was a special challenge match between Kung Fu and Tally Ho Kaye. Referee Brian Crabtree disqualified Kaye in the fourth round for refusing to wrestle, Kaye continually sat in his corner or ran away from his opponent.

The vacant World Lightweight Tournament continued on World of Sport the following Saturday. The first heat saw Pakistan's 'Little Prince' Mohammed Alam face Hungarian Zoltan Boscik. It was announced before the match started that

56

Alam had failed to make the lightweight weight limit of 11st. so would be unable to progress in the tournament if he had won. This was a stupid piece of booking as Alam was nearer 12 or 13st. and looked huge compared to a normal lightweight such as Boscik. The promoter's blushes were spared when Boscik won the match with two single leg Boston Crab submissions in quick order in round's four and five. The other heat again featured more daftness with somehow Irish job guy Tony Kelly beating a German opponent in Germany in the last round of the heats to go forward to meet Jim Breaks. Breaks himself had won in Germany too in the previous round or that is what Kent Walton told viewers. Kelly was making his TV debut and I doubt he was the best lightweight in his family let alone the world. There were far better lightweight wrestlers in the country who would have done the tournament justice than having Kelly in it. Breaks won with a 'Breaks' special' in the sixth round to join Boscik, Bobby Ryan and Johnny Saint in the final four. Kelly faded away just about straightaway from the grappling game and became more famous for having multiple convictions for driving whilst drunk in the Midlands. In the end he would serve six months in jail for driving whilst disqualified in 1979.

The other match saw Kenny Hogan making his first TV appearance which was against the flamboyant Magnificent Maurice who was wearing some fetching make up on his face. Maurice won the match with a straight neck lift hold which saw Hogan submit in the third round.

Around the halls -

Away from the shows on TV August was pretty quiet for much of the month with the ongoing heatwave now beginning to get on people's nerves. The first major show of the month happened on 14th August at Belle Vue with another tremendous card presented. The main event saw Kendo Nagasaki back from his injury lay off take on Giant Haystacks. Predictably the match ended in chaos and was abandoned in the second round with both wrestlers preferring to fight amongst the ringsiders than wrestle in the ring. Another match to end with it out of control was the opening contest. Not for the first or indeed the last time would a match between Mark Rocco and Marty Jones end with the referee being unable to restrain either of them and a No Contest was called. The contest between British Heavyweight Champion Gwyn Davies and his Mid/Heavyweight counterpart Mike Marino ended in a six round draw. Davies got the first fall in the fourth round before Marino got an equaliser in the sixth. Bert Royal's bout with John Naylor ended in a No Contest when Naylor was unable to continue in round six. Hans Streiger beat the crowd's favourite Count Bartelli who failed to beat the count in the third round. Finally in the last bout of the night Dynamite Kid took on Mike Jordan and it ended in round three when each wrestler's shoulders were pinned to the mat at the same time.

The only other newsworthy show of the month was again at Belle Vue on the 28th with another stacked card to look forward to. The main event was Vic Faulkner's mandatory rematch for the British Welterweight Title against the current champion Jim Breaks. To the packed crowd's delight Faulkner regained the title with a winning fall in the seventh round and so ended Breaks' three month reign as champion. Big Daddy was another to hear the cheers of the fans when he knocked out 'Bully Boy' Ian Muir in round four with the big splash. The masked martial arts exponent Iron Fist made short of work of Blackjack Mulligan who failed to beat the count in the third round. Behind the mask Iron Fist was Clive Myers who would wrestle as Myers for Dale Martin and then travel north to wrestle as Iron Fist under the mask for Best Wryton Promotions. Bert Royal made it a night to remember for the Royal Brothers when he beat loudmouth British Middleweight Champion Brian Maxine by two falls to one in the fifth round whilst in the show closer Bobby Ryan pinned newcomer Tony Barry in round two.

For most of 1976 the independent promoters flew under the radar with little news or publicity of their shows. One show that was newsworthy happened at one of Joint Promotion's main venues that of Wolverhampton Civic Hall and was held on 31st August. The main match featured Les Kellett who took on Jackie Pallo who were just about the two most recognisable wrestlers on the independent circuit at the time. The bout ended in the fifth round when Pallo was unable to continue after getting his head stuck between the ropes. Kellett refused to accept the decision so it ended as a No Contest. A championship match was billed and held as being for the British Heavy/Middleweight Title between champion Eric Taylor and challenger Pete Roberts. Taylor won when Roberts was unable to continue and a No Contest wasn't an option for a title match. Of course the official British Heavy/Middleweight Champion and Lord Mountevan's belt holder was Bert Royal. A heavyweight contest saw Pat Roach beat Bill Clarke by two falls to one in the sixth round whilst Jim Moza pinned Al Miquet in round two to win their match. Finally two novelty matches were on the show with The Borg Twins taking on the Wildman of Borneo in a handicap match with the twins winning in the third round. Sky Low Low won a midget's match beating Baby Brutus by two falls to one in round five to round off an interesting night's wrestling.

Sky Low Low and Baby Brutus, real names Bob and Dave, were only 19 and 17 respectively and came from Boston in Lincolnshire. They were featured in an article in The Sunday People earlier that year about not getting paid for their contests by their manager Bill Clarke aka King Kendo. Brian Dixon who booked the midgets for his shows through Clarke explained they can't expect the same money as proper sized wrestlers and were only ever in exhibition matches. One of the midgets, I'm not sure if it was Bob or Dave quit the grappling game shortly afterwards so Clarke had to resort to advertising for a replacement. He put an advertisement in his local newspaper The Spalding Guardian as well as being interviewed for the paper where he stated to would be applicants that there is no danger and wrestlers don't really hurt each other. Clarke added 'but don't say too much about that'.

September -

The first wrestling of the month on World of Sport on 4th September came from Catford and featured three rather low key bouts. There didn't seem to be a genuine main event calibre match across the whole six contests recorded. The first match on the 4th saw Jon Cortez pin Alan Serjeant in the second round to win. On next was a catchweight contest between Bert Royal and the heavyweight Romany Riley. Riley took the lead in the third round before Royal equalised in the fifth and that was the score at the end of the scheduled six rounds. Finally a heavyweight contest saw Steve Veidor beat Roy St.Clair by two falls to one in round five.

The other three matches recorded were seen the following week. Clive Myers won the opener when he pinned veteran Eddie Capelli for the one fall needed in the second round. Capelli was coming to the end of a career lasting thirty years and was a former British Welterweight Champion. Count Bartelli wrestled a one fall each draw with John Kowalski in the second match shown. Kowalski got the first fall in the fourth round before Bartelli got the equaliser in the next round. The last match saw Vic Faulkner with a weight advantage beat Steve Grey by two falls to one in the fourth round.

18th September's wrestling on World of Sport came from Castleford in Yorkshire with Mick McManus as the headline attraction. McManus took on Mick McMichael who had the capacity crowd firmly behind him. McManus pinned McMichael for the first fall in the third round before an equaliser for McMichael came in the opening minute of the fifth. After several weakeners in round six it was McManus who got yet another victory on TV when he forced McMichael to submit for the winner. Bill Ross from Scotland made a rare appearance in England as well as on TV but it was a winning one when he pinned Maurice Hunter in round four to win their bout. The final match saw another Scottish wrestler Tom Dowie in action who took on Mike Marino and it was Marino who won when Dowie was counted out in the fourth round.

There was no wrestling shown on World of Sport on the 25th as the Benson and Hedges International Golf Open tournament was on for most of the afternoon. With no midweek wrestling shown on TV anymore September proved to be a poor month for grapple fans watching at home.

60

Around the halls -

Kendo Nagasaki seemingly over his injury problems picked up a full time schedule again for September and was in action at Brighton on 2nd September for the final show of their summer season. Nagasaki beat Romany Riley who was counted out in the fourth round after being on the end of a Kamikaze Crash. Both of the Wilson brothers were in action as well with Johnny wrestling a one fall each draw with John Elijah over four rounds whilst Peter lost to Billy Torontos by two falls to one in the fifth round. Johnny Kwango beat Catweazle in a clash of personalities that had the crowd laughing throughout the match and Jon Cortez beat Sid Cooper with the winning fall in the fifth round.

Croydon opened their doors for another season on the 7th with another episode of the feud involving Giant Haystacks, Big Bruno, Steve Veidor and Wayne Bridges. The four met in a tag match with Haystacks and Bruno defeating Veidor and Bridges with a winning fall in the twenty first minute. Mick McManus met Mick McMichael over four rounds and it ended with each wrestler scoring one fall apiece. Robby Baron beat Rajendra Singh and Alan Serjeant beat Tony Costas each by the one fall needed. The final match saw Billy Torontos beat Hungarian Stan Karoly with the winner coming in the fourth round.

Saturday 11th September had another Belle Vue bonanza with a lumberjack match between Kendo Nagasaki and Giant Haystacks as the top of the bill. With other wrestlers from the bill surrounding the ring to prevent either wrestler escaping or there being any interference it didn't exactly work. The match was abandoned in the third round with Haystacks in front from a neck lift suspension hold to which Nagasaki had submitted to in round two. One of the lumberjacks Kojak Kirk jumped into the ring to attack Haystacks and Kirk was swiftly joined by Big Daddy who attacked Nagasaki. All hell broke loose and the only thing for the referee to do was to signal the end of the contest. Count Bartelli retained the Commonwealth Heavyweight Title when challenger Hans Streiger was disqualified in the fifth round in a particularly bad tempered

61

encounter. Kung Fu beat Alan Dennison by two falls to one in round five whilst three heavyweight contests completed the bill. Pete Curry beat Jim Moran by disqualification in the fourth round. Ray Steele beat Kojak Kirk who was disqualified in round two. Local favourite Roy St.Clair sent the fans home happy when opponent Ray Glendenning was knocked out in the fourth round.

At Hanley on the same evening there was a bizarre tag match with the team of Johnny Saint and Mick McMichael taking on the team of Catweazle and Tally Ho Kaye. With the score at one fall each Catweazle became tired of his partner's rule breaking and joined his opponent's whilst Kaye a minute of so later simply gave up and left the ring.

Sainsbury's employees at their main depot in Buntingford had a treat also on the same night with a Dale Martin show in their staff canteen. The Royals took on Johnny Czeslaw and Tug Holton in the main event with The Royals the winners in the eighteenth minute.

There was another show at Croydon on the 21st with The Royals in action but this time in solo matches. Vic Faulkner wrestled a one fall each draw with Johnny Saint over four rounds whilst brother Bert Royal lost to Steve Logan by two falls to one in the fourth round. Mark Rocco beat Kung Fu with a winning fall in the third round whilst Magnificent Maurice defeated Gordon Corbett by two falls to one in round six. Mike Marino beat the much heavier Klondyke Jake in round four whilst the evening ended with Roy St.Clair defeating Ivan Penzecoff by countout in the third round.

The first show of the season at The Royal Albert Hall took place on 22nd September and an interesting comment in Terry Needham's newsletter said 'How can Dale Martin charge £2.50 for this compared to the bills at Belle Vue ?' At the time you could get a ringside seat at Belle Vue for £1.50. It was a very sub par show for the Albert Hall and the crowd let their displeasure show at times. Steve Grey pinned Mike Jordan in the fifth round to win a lively lightweight opener. Mark Rocco who had recently been nominated to face Marty Jones for the vacant British Light/Heavyweight Title took on Johnny Kincaid in one of the main events. The match ended in the sixth round with Rocco leaving the ring in frustration at not being able to overcome Kincaid and as Rocco walked away the referee counted to ten. Magnificent Maurice was in the other main event but his originally billed opponent Steve Veidor was replaced by Count Bartelli. Maurice picked up a notable win when he won by two falls to one in the sixth round. Gordon Corbett wrestled a one fall each draw with Honey Boy Zimba over four rounds but a restless crowd started to jeer during the contest and a slow handclap rung out around the hall. Fans also got bored during the match between Johnny Wilson and Roy St.Clair which also ended in a draw with the slow handclap and booing ringing out at times. Fans were now preferring more action in their matches and two similar four round draws were too much for them to enjoy. The evening should have finished with a tag between two sets of brothers as The Royals were billed to take on Mick and Ricky Shannon from Kent. Ricky Shannon failed to appear for any of his booked appearances and was replaced at the Albert Hall by Jon Cortez. Cortez was in a bad mood throughout and persistently breaking the rules whilst the three others involved tried to have a wrestling match. In the end The Royals won in just under fifteen minutes with Shannon falling out with his partner.

Another big show took place the following evening but this time in Scotland at the Kelvin Hall in Glasgow. Promoter Peter Keenan was back with Joint Promotions and together they put on a spectacular card to open the season. Kendo Nagasaki took on and beat Gwyn Davies by two falls to one in the fourth round but Gorgeous George was no nearer getting the Board of Control to allow a masked wrestler to challenge for a British title. Local favourite Andy Robbins beat Kojak Kirk in round four whilst another Scottish wrestler Bill Ross upset Jim Breaks by beating him by two falls to one in the fifth round. Mick McMichael beat Kevin Conneely and a tag match saw Big Daddy and Giant Haystacks beat Roy St.Clair and Ray Steele.

The next night fans in Edinburgh had a great night of wrestling with Kendo Nagasaki topping the bill against Big Daddy. Nagasaki got the first score with a submission in the second round before Daddy equalised with another submission in the third. In a wild match Daddy managed to pull Nagasaki's mask off in the fourth round. Nagasaki fled from the ring minus the mask to leave Daddy the winner. Giant Haystacks easily beat the much lighter Roy St.Clair who was counted out after a splash in the third round. Jim Breaks had his revenge against Bill Ross after his defeat to him the previous night when he beat him with a winning fall in the fifth round. Mick McManus beat Mick McMichael by two falls to one in round five with surprisingly McManus wrestling within the rules throughout. Finally Ray Steele got an upset win when he defeated Kojak Kirk in the fourth round.

A double tag match main event was the highlight of the Belle Vue show on 25th September with perhaps not the strongest line up seen there. In the first tag match martial arts ace's Kung Fu and Iron Fist beat Scotland's Braw Lads with the winner coming in the thirteenth minute. The Braw Lads that night were actually Pete Ross and Phil Halverson and not the usual team of Bob Richardson and Jay Scott. Honey Boy Zimba teamed up with a rare visitor to Belle Vue in Johnny Kincaid to defeat Magnificent Maurice and Tally Ho Kaye who were disqualified in the eighteenth minute. Gil Singh won a hard fought heavyweight battle against Barry Douglas with a submission in round seven finishing Douglas off. Marty Jones beat Jeff Kaye by two falls to one in the sixth round whilst two characters in Kevin Conneely and Catweazle met in the final bout with the match ending in a No Contest in round five when Catweazle was unable to continue.

The Town Hall in Reading on the 28th saw the latest controversy involving Kendo Nagasaki and Big Daddy which was strange as this was a Dale Martin show and they normally frowned on such things. Big Daddy had won his match earlier in the evening beating Mike Marino who was unable to continue in the fourth round. After his shower Daddy was sat in the audience to see the main event which featured Nagasaki taking on Steve Veidor. In the fourth round Daddy entered the ring and the fans thought he was going to attack his old rival Nagasaki but instead turned on Veidor and attacked him instead. The contest was immediately halted with Veidor unable to continue and for once Nagasaki and Daddy left the ring as allies.

64

The truce lasted exactly one night as the next evening they were matched against each other at Banbury and both Nagasaki and Daddy were counted out in the fourth round for fighting outside of the ring.

October -

Grapple fans were left disappointed for a succesive week on 2nd October as the Dunlop Masters golf tournament replaced that weeks wrestling on World of Sport.

Wrestling was back on World of Sport on the 9th with the second half of the card taped at Castleford shown. The most notable happening about this week was the TV debut of the Dynamite Kid, his match taped at Lincoln back in June had yet to be seen. Since his ring debut a year or so ago Dynamite had been buried away at the bottom of the bill whilst he learnt his craft out of the spotlight. He had yet to appear at any Southern venue and was booked to take on suitable opponents to learn from such as Kenny Hogan. Not only was Hogan a regular opponent but he doubled up as Dynamite's driver and travelling companion too. Dynamite's opponent for the TV show was Hull's Pete Meredith and it was a winning debut with a two falls to one victory. Kent Walton made the most obvious comment when he remarked 'we will be seeing a lot more of the youngster in the future'.

The other two matches shown were both at heavyweight with Steve Logan defeating Tony Walsh in the fifth round by the usual two falls to one score. Roy St.Clair beat Ray Glendenning when Glendenning was disqualified in round four with the score one fall each.

The following week on World of Sport saw the two semi finals shown in the tournament to decide the new World Lightweight Champion. The first match of the show recorded at Wolverhampton saw Johnny Saint take on Zoltan Boscik with the Hungarian taking the lead in round three with his special 'three-in-one' hold seeing Saint submit Saint equalised in the fifth round with a submission hold of his own, he applied a surfboard and Boscik submitted from it. Even worse for Boscik he was unable to continue after the interval so Saint was the first wrestler through to the final to meet the winner of the second semi final. There was no winner though as the match between Jim Breaks and Bobby Ryan ended in a draw at the end of the scheduled six rounds. Breaks took the lead when a Boston Crab saw Ryan submit in the fourth round before Ryan equalised midway through the final round to leave Saint's opponent in the final to be decided. The other match that week was at the other end of the weight scale with Big Daddy taking on Eric 'Tubby' Hodgson who was making his first appearance on TV. Hodgson was also known as Vince Apollo and was under the mask of one of The Undertakers as well. Hodgson's debut didn't last long as he was knocked out in the second round after being on the receiving end of a big splash.

23rd October's wrestling from Wolverhampton on World of Sport saw a new British Light/Heavyweight Champion crowned when Marty Jones beat Mark Rocco to win the vacant title. Rocco took the lead with a fall in round four before Jones went onto equalise in the fifth round before Jones won the match when he pinned Rocco in the sixth. Kendo Nagasaki defeated British Heavyweight Champion Gwyn Davies when Davies was unable to continue in the fourth round with an injured knee. After the contest Gorgeous George presented a petition of over a thousand signatures demanding that Kendo Nagasaki be allowed to challenge for the British Heavyweight Title. The opening match that week between King Ben and Tally Ho Kaye came to a premature end when both wrestlers were counted out in the third round.

The last World of Sport of October on the 30th saw the Dynamite Kid in action again on a bill from Lincoln. This was the show that had been recorded at the end of June and saw Dynamite take on Alan Dennison. Dennison was still a villain at this time and at times he was described on the posters as being 'possessed of the devil'. Dynamite's slick and speedy moves were a perfect counter to Dennison's strength holds and an interesting bout came to an unfortunate ending. In the third round Dynamite missed a dive and landed throat thirst on the top rope and referee Brian Crabtree quickly called a halt to the contest. Surprisingly Dennison grabbed the MC's microphone and refused to accept the win and so it was deemed to be a No

Contest. The other main match should have seen Kendo Nagasaki take on Giant Haystacks but with Nagasaki absent through injury Gwyn Davies stepped in to take his place. Haystacks took the lead in the second round with a cross press after a hefty looking splash on Davies. Davies just about struggled to his feet for the start of round three but he managed to get an equaliser when he pinned the big man following a flying tackle. The end came in the fourth round when referee Crabtree disqualified Haystacks after he delivered two mighty splashes on Davies. The other match that week saw Tally Ho Kaye on TV for the second week running when he lost to Mick McMichael who pinned him in the fourth round for the winner.

Around the halls -

The Giant Haystacks/Big Bruno/Steve Veidor/Wayne Bridges feud at Croydon had another outing at the Fairfield Halls on 5th October. This time it was another tag match with two referees assigned to keep order which they did when they disqualified one of the teams but it wasn't Giant Haystacks and Big Bruno who were sent packing but Wayne Bridges and Steve Veidor. Veidor and Bridges eventually overdid their retaliation and were disqualified in the tenth minute of another highly controversial match that had the fans seething at the outcome. The opening match saw a very surprising result with King Ben (although he was billed for Dale Martin as Benny King) defeating the one and only Mick McManus by two falls to one in the fourth round. Tibor Szakacs beat John Elijah who was counted out in the sixth round whilst Robby Baron pinned Steve Grey in round five to win their match.

There was another controversial tag match involving Big Daddy and Kendo Nagasaki at Hanley on the 9th but this time Daddy and Nagasaki were partners. Their opponents meant to be Kojak Kirk and Bully Boy Muir but Muir was replaced by Gil Singh at the last minute. The match ended in a two straight falls win for Nagasaki and Daddy in just over eight minutes but it was marred with Kirk attacking his own partner to set up the winning fall.

67

At Belle Vue the following Saturday Nagasaki and Daddy were on opposing sides in a contest billed as 'the wildest tag match ever held' ! Nagasaki teamed up with Kojak Kirk whilst Daddy was back with Giant Haystacks. In a match that was hard to keep up with and the public warnings had no effect in stopping the amount of rule breaking happening. It was Nagasaki and Kirk who won with the winning fall coming in the thirteenth minute. The punters in attendance that night who had watched the wrestling on World of Sport that afternoon had a bonus as the rematch of the drawn lightweight tournament contest between Jim Breaks and Bobby Ryan contest was held. Originally a four man contenders tournament featuring all of the wrestlers who had made the semi final's of the World Lightweight Title tournament had been announced but this was then changed on the evening. With the rematch scheduled for unlimited rounds to ensure a winner it was Jim Breaks who went through to meet Johnny Saint for the vacant title when Bobby Ryan was unable to continue for the fourth round. Saint himself had a repeat of his semi final win when he defeated Zoltan Boscik in the fifth round when a surfboard hold saw the Hungarian submit. Gwyn Davies won a heavyweight contest against Gil Singh by two falls to one in round six whilst another heavyweight match saw Roy St.Clair defeat Ray Glendenning who was counted out in the fourth round.

For once Kendo Nagasaki heard the fans cheering for him on what was described as Kendo's greatest night at Liverpool on 29th October. Nagasaki was teaming with Count Bartelli to take on Big Daddy and Giant Haystacks with the packed crowd chanting for Kendo throughout the match. The match ended with Daddy and Haystacks disqualified after twelve minutes of mayhem and for once the crowd sat silent when George took the microphone at the end of the contest and addressed everyone in attendance.

The next night at Hanley though things were entirely different with Kendo Nagasaki partnering the Mighty Yankee who was a late replacement for Hombre Montana against Big Daddy and Giant Haystacks. Both teams entered the ring and as usual Gorgeous George took the microphone and he announced that three weeks ago on 9th October Big Daddy tagged with

68

Kendo and that is how he wanted it to be tonight. After much arguing Daddy agreed to the switch on the proviso that Nagasaki wrestled 'clean' in the contest. So the match started as Big Daddy and Kendo Nagasaki against Giant Haystacks and Mighty Yankee. After ten minutes Daddy attacked Nagasaki who had not adhered to the wrestling 'clean' stipulation and he was assisted by Haystacks who had yet to join in the match. The match was halted by the referee and Daddy announced afterwards he would never tag with Nagasaki again.

November -

November started with a blank Saturday on World of Sport for grapple fans on the 6th. Tennis was shown in it's place with the Dewar Cup tournament from the Royal Albert Hall screened most of the afternoon instead.

Luckily the wrestling on World of Sport from Bolton on the 13th was a special show with the final of the tournament to find the new World Lightweight Champion shown. It was Johnny Saint who became the new champion when he defeated Jim Breaks in the seventh round of a scheduled twelve rounds contest amidst much excitement from not only a capacity crowd but Kent Walton too. Breaks got the first score with his arm submission in the fourth round before Saint quickly equalised with a fall in the fifth. The end came in the seventh round when Saint pinned Breaks for the winning fall to become the new World Lightweight Champion and follow in the footsteps of George Kidd.

The opener that week saw Lee Thomas beat Hans Streiger who once again got himself disqualified. This time it was for punching his opponent in the third round. The final match that week was between Gil Singh and Ray Steele and it came to an early end in the second round when both wrestlers were counted out.

The wrestling on World of Sport the next weekend came from Croydon and the first match saw a brief glimpse of Zoltan Boscik beating Steve Grey. Boscik licking his wounds from his loss in the world title tournament pinned Grey in the fifth round. A heavyweight match saw Steve Veidor meet Midlander

Gordon Corbett who was making his TV debut. An interesting contest saw Veidor come out on top when he pinned Corbett with a folding press from the side in the fourth round. The main event was a tag match with the redoubtable duo of Mick McManus and Steve Logan taking on a team billed as the 'New Barons' consisting of Robby Baron and Alan Serjeant. McManus and Logan were a little too much for them to handle and Logan got the winning fall on Serjeant in the thirteenth minute to seal a two falls to one win.

World of Sport's wrestling the following week on the 27th came from Croydon again and Kendo Nagasaki featured in the top of the bill match. Nagasaki's opponent was Johnny Kincaid and this was his first appearance on TV for a while after a period of wrestling overseas. Before Nagasaki walked to the ring Kendo's theme rung out over the PA and then Gorgeous George and his charge made their way to the ring, George was looking particularly good in a light blue, sparkling jacket. Once Nagasaki's rituals had finished the action commenced and Kincaid went straight on the attack and in attempting to unmask Kendo sent him flying out of the ring. Kent Walton advised viewers watching on a colour television to look at Nagasaki's eyes which according to him were red. Whilst viewers studied Nagasaki's eyes Kincaid continued his attacks on them in a very lively first round in which referee Joe D'Orazio was having a job keeping control. D'Orazio's patience ended in round two with Nagasaki taking control through illegal tactics and Kendo got his first public warning. Kincaid got his first warning in the same round for attacking Nagasaki on the ropes and managing to pull the mask up over Nagasaki's mouth. Before the third round started Kent Walton told viewers in the interval between rounds that the petition to allow Nagasaki a chance to wrestle for the British Heavyweight Title had now reached twenty thousand. Walton thought that he should be able to have a title match if he could prove his British nationality and that he also behaved himself. The crowd went wild in the third round when Kincaid got the first fall after he pinned Nagasaki with a cross press following a neat side slam. The crowd's excitement didn't last long as in the fourth round the match ended. Nagasaki had split open Kincaid's head with a high knee and then Kincaid was counted out following a Kamikaze Crash. Straightaway Gorgeous George grabbed MC Bobby Palmer's microphone and threw out challenges to the likes of Big Daddy and Gwyn Davies. This was peak Nagasaki with his feud with Big Daddy and Giant Haystacks in singles and tag matches as well as with the aforementioned Davies. This was what got me interested in watching wrestling each Saturday and started the life long love of the sport.

The first match that week saw Count Bartelli taking on the powerful 'Bronco' Roger Wells who was another making a first TV appearance on the Croydon bill. Wells' power and rule breaking had Bartelli in trouble at times but it was the Count who won in round four when he slammed Wells after a posting and pinned his opponent with a reverse double knee hold. The third match saw Kung Fu tackling Sid Cooper who was booed as much on his way to the ring as Kung Fu was cheered. It was Kung Fu who emerged victorious in the fourth round when he pinned Cooper with a folding press after sending him head first into the corner post.

Around the halls -

2nd November saw the first of two appearances at Croydon that month for Kendo Nagasaki, the second would be the TV taping on the 16th. Nagasaki faced up to Mike Marino on the 2nd and once again he was victorious when he forced Marino to submit in the fourth round. Steve Veidor retained his Southern Area Heavyweight Title when challenger Big Bruno was beaten by two falls to one in the sixth round. An international heavyweight match between Tibor Szakacs and Sean Regan ended in a one fall each draw over four rounds. John Kowalski beat Bully Boy Muir who was disqualified in round five. To complete the evening there were two one fall matches with Johnny Kwango beating Robby Baron and John Elijah defeated Clayton Thomson.

An interesting card at Grays in Essex on the 8th saw a challenge match with no time limit between Mark Rocco and Steve Logan. It was Logan who the fans sided with and it was Logan who won after Rocco was disqualified in the nineteenth minute. On the same show Giant Haystacks beat Wayne Bridges who was counted out in the third round. Bridges who had got a fall in round two with a cross press after a flying tackle had no hope of beating the count of ten following a splash from Haystacks.

For once it was a rather low key show at Belle Vue on 20th November with quantity not quality on offer for once. Gwyn Davies beat Terry Rudge who was unable to continue in the fifth round in the nominal main event. Dynamite Kid beat Tally Ho Kaye by two falls to one in the fifth round. Ray Steele beat the Mighty Yankee who was disqualified in round four for refusing to break the hold after Steele had submitted. Roy St.Clair beat Colin Joynson in the sixth round whilst Johnny Czeslaw defeated Catweazle with a winning fall in the fifth round. Finally Gil Singh had two matches on the show defeating Jamaica Kid in the first and Magnificent Maurice in the second.

The final Royal Albert Hall show of 1976 took place on 24th November and once again Kendo Nagasaki and Big Daddy were to the fore. Unsurprisingly the match got totally out of hand and resulted in both wrestlers being disqualified in the fourth round. Magnificent Maurice finally got his hands on Steve Veidor but it ended in a loss when Veidor countered an onrushing Maurice for the winning fall in round five. King Ben had another victory over Mick McManus when he made McManus submit in the fourth round. As a result Ben was now made official challenger for the European Middleweight Title and a title match would be lined up for early 1977. New World Lightweight Champion Johnny Saint got the only fall needed in round five to beat Alan Serjeant with Saint receiving a tremendous reception from the crowd. The return of Steve Wright to British action and a match against Gil Singh failed to happen and his place against Singh was taken by Robby Baron. Baron made a decent effort against the far larger Singh but it was a losing one with Singh getting the winning fall in the fourth round. Tibor Szakacs made a return to the Albert Hall after an absence and the former Royal Albert Hall Trophy winner beat Ray Glendenning who was counted out after receiving one of Szakacs' back hand chops in round three. The crowd left happy when in the final match of the night Catweazle beat Sid Cooper who was pinned in the third round.

Rickmansworth near Watford was one of the usual Dale Martin venues and had shows there every month but the one on the 25th featured an interesting main event between Mick McManus and Johnny Kwango. The stipulation to the match was that there would be instant disqualification for Kwango if he headbutted McManus and the same for McManus if he used a forearm smash on Kwango. It was Kwango who lost when he finally used a headbutt on McManus in the fourth round after losing his cool with McManus' continual use of illegal tactics.

Promoters Best Wryton and the Liverpool Stadium owners had an interesting dilemma on the 27th, how to find a ladder capable of taking the weight of Giant Haystacks ? The main event was a ladder match between Haystacks and Kendo Nagasaki but the match ended with neither wrestler climbing the ladder but Haystacks being disqualified in the third round.

The month ended on the 30th at Croydon with yet another episode of the feud between Giant Haystacks and Big Bruno with Wayne Bridges and Steve Veidor. This time it would be a six man tag match with Haystacks and Bruno teaming up with Bronco Wells to take on Bridges and Veidor whose partner was none other than referee Max Ward. This time Bridges and Veidor with Ward got their revenge when they beat Haystacks, Bruno and Wells with a winning fall in the twenty second minute of a highly entertaining and exciting contest. Brian Maxine lost to the heavier Romany Riley in the fourth round much to Maxine's anger. Johnny Czeslaw defeated Billy Torontos by two falls to one in the fifth round whilst Sean Regan beat Ray Glendenning again by two falls to one this time in round four. Finally Johnny Kwango pinned Ivan Penzecoff in the sixth round to win their match.

December -

Three matches from Solihull featured on World of Sport on 4th December with a match between Bobby Ryan and Maurice Hunter kicking things off. Both wrestlers were based in Stoke-on-Trent so with local pride at stake there was an extra edge to

73

the match. It was Ryan who got the bragging rights when he pinned Hunter in the third round with a folding press for the only fall required.

The second contest saw Mick McManus take on the newly crowned World Lightweight Champion Johnny Saint in a catchweight bout. It was McManus who got the first fall with a folding press after a double leg grab in the second round. Saint equalised in round three with a flying tackle flooring McManus and Saint covered him with a cross press for the count of three. There was a rather curious ending to the match in the fourth round. Referee Brian Crabtree had turned his back on both wrestlers to instruct the timekeeper to announce a second public warning for McManus. Whilst he did Johnny Saint simply laid down on the mat and when Crabtree looked back he thought McManus had hit Saint and disqualified him. McManus complained to all and sundry about the unfairness of it and said over the microphone that the bloody referee was crooked. Saint responded to this by saying if he couldn't beat McManus fair and square he would never wrestle on TV again.

The final match that week saw Marty Jones wrestle Terry Rudge over six rounds with the first score to win. Rudge was a replacement for Steve Wright who had not appeared for the match. Despite the best efforts of both Jones and Rudge neither wrestler was able to pin or make his opponent submit within the scheduled six rounds so it ended in a rare no score draw.

The second half of the Solihull show was broadcast on World of Sport the following week with the main match featuring Kendo Nagasaki. Nagasaki's opponent this time was Colin Joynson who hadn't been seen on TV for eighteen months due to various overseas tours. The match ended in the third round with Joynson the latest victim of Nagasaki's Kamikaze Crash and Nagasaki was the winner by countout.

The opener that week saw an upset with the much lighter John Naylor beating Alan Dennison with the one fall needed in round four. The final match saw another win for Mark Rocco who this time defeated King Ben when he made him submit in the fourth round with a Boston Crab.

The last wrestling on TV for the year was on the 18th and the show on World of Sport came from Bolton. There was a

74

slightly different format this week with the team of 'The TV All-stars' comprising of The Royals and Dynamite Kid taking on Tally Ho Kaye, Blackjack Mulligan and Kenny Hogan. There would be three singles matches first before a six man tag to finish it off. The first match saw another impressive showing from Dynamite Kid this time against Tally Ho Kaye. Despite Kaye's best efforts with various nefarious moves Dynamite came back to win in the third round with a folding press.

The next match was between Bert Royal and Kenny Hogan and it was Royal who made it two nil to the 'All-stars' when he pinned Hogan with a folding press secured by a bridge in round two. The last single's contest featured Vic Faulkner against Blackjack Mulligan and Faulkner made it three nil to his team when he defeated Mulligan in the fourth round. The concluding six man tag ended in a four nil victory for the 'All-stars' when they beat Kaye, Mulligan and Hogan with the winning fall coming when Royal pinned Kaye with a reverse double knee hold in the seventh minute.

That was the end of wrestling on TV for 1976 with the following Saturday falling on 25th December and no World of Sport shown on ITV.

Around the halls -

The start of the month on 1st December saw a new tag team on show at Brighton with Magnificent Maurice teaming up with Bobby Barnes for a rather colourful duo. Barnes and Maurice had an impressive win when they beat The Royals by two falls to one in just under twenty minutes. Also on the show there was a match between Big Daddy and Wayne Bridges with Daddy winning in the fourth round but not before both wrestlers received two public warnings.

The final show of the year at Belle Vue before the Christmas break was held on the 4th. Kendo Nagasaki defeated Mike Marino when Marino was counted out in the fourth round following a Kam1kaze Crash. Big Daddy and Giant Haystacks were booked to wrestle the Three Assassins but on the night there were only two Assassins and Tony Walsh instead. The stipulation was that two Assassins were allowed in the ring at the same time but it wasn't said if that included Walsh too. An extra stipulation made it a no disqualification match but it didn't matter as Daddy and Haystacks won by two straight falls inside seven minutes. Johnny Saint followed up his world title win against Jim Breaks with another win against him on the show. Saint got the winning fall in the fifth round for a two falls to one victory. Jackie Robinson beat Dave Ramsden by two straight falls and Mike Jordan wrestled a six rounds, one fall each draw with King Ben.

Croydon's last show of the year was on the 14th with a stacked card to finish off with. Mick McManus had another match with Johnny Saint following their shenanigans on TV the previous Saturday. This time their was an inconclusive ending with the match ending in a draw over four rounds. McManus got the first fall in the second round before Saint equalised in round three. Even with both wrestlers totally forgetting the rules in the last round neither was able to get a winner. A tag match saw Honey Boy Zimba and Johnny Kincaid defeat Bully Boy Muir and Johnny Yearsley by disqualification. Steve Logan beat Gil Singh who was counted out in the sixth round. Ray Steele wrestled a particularly hard hitting draw with Mark Rocco over four rounds before Catweazle pinned Robby Baron in the fourth round to win that match.

Hanley's festive spectacular on the 18th saw Kendo Nagasaki taking on Big Daddy in a ladder match. Nagasaki won when he grabbed the money in the eighth minute to ensure that he and George had a prosperous Christmas.

There was another ladder match between Kendo Nagasaki and Big Daddy at Digbeth on 23rd December and again it was Nagasaki who was victorious. Kendo climbed the ladder in the ninth minute to grab the bag with the money in it and win the match.

As usual the immediate aftermath of Christmas saw only a few shows before the New Year. At Chelmsford on the 28th Mick McManus and Mel Stuart (replaced Steve Logan) suffered a defeat when they lost to the masked team of the Mad Axeman. At Bristol on the 30th there was a tag team tournament which should have featured Mick McManus and Steve Logan in it, this time it was McManus who was missing

76

and he was replaced by Sid Cooper. The final saw Johnny Kwango and Clive Myers beat Johnny Czeslaw and Johnny Yearsley who were disqualified. Kwango and Myers had beaten the Wilson Brothers earlier and Czeslaw and Yearsley had defeated Logan and Cooper.

With no shows booked for New Year's Eve that brought down the curtain on wrestling for 1976.

1977

January -

Grapple fans had a good start to the new year with the 1st falling on a Saturday so World of Sport was broadcast and it included three bouts from Woking. The highlight was a tag match featuring the team of Bobby Barnes and Magnificent Maurice taking on The Wilsons, Johnny and Peter. Barnes and Maurice were resplendent in their colourful robes with both sporting bleached blond hair. Kent Walton noted that Barnes hadn't been seen on TV for a while as he was building up his business near Maidstone. In the early stages both Barnes and Maurice were camping it up to the crowds delight until the Wilsons started to get on top and then the rough stuff started. Barnes pinned Johnny Wilson in the seventh minute for the first fall after a spot of double teaming had weakened Wilson. Maurice kissed his partner on the cheek as MC Mike Judd anounced the fall leaving lipstick on Barnes' face. Johnny Wilson got the equalising fall on Bobby Barnes after he had sent Barnes flying over the top rope following a dropkick. Barnes returned to the ring where he was slammed by Johnny and pinned with a reverse double knee hold in just about nine minutes. Maurice got the winner when Peter Wilson who had been weakened by a posting was easily pinned with a reverse double knee hold in the thirteenth minute.

The other main match that week saw Mick McManus tackling Robby Baron who perhaps was better known as Mick's chauffeur at the time. It didn't take long for McManus to start the rough stuff although Baron overdid the retaliation and got a public warning from referee Max Ward for using the closed fist. Baron got the first fall in round three with a beautiful counter on an onrushing McManus which resulted in a reverse double shoulder press. Despite Baron's best attempts for a two straight falls win over McManus it all went wrong in the fifth round when Baron mistimed a jump and injured his knee. Immediately McManus got an equalising submission with a single leg Boston and even worse Baron was unable to continue so McManus was the winner on a technical knockout.

The opening match was between Johnny Kwango and Ivan Penzecoff in a one fall contest. Kwango won when an excellent counter resulted in a cross press in the fourth round. An excellent week's wrestling which even the most hungover viewer would have enjoyed.

The second half of the Woking show was screened on World of Sport the following Saturday with two heavyweight contests featured. First though was a meeting of former British champions when former lightweight title holder Zoltan Boscik took on Alan Serjeant the former welterweight champion. Boscik won a very good technical match full of holds, counterholds and reversals and for once he was on his best behaviour. The end came in the third round with Boscik reversing a whip from Serjeant to pin his opponent with a folding press.

The first heavyweight contest was between the ever popular Steve Veidor and Johnny Yearsley. It didn't take long for Yearsley to start the illegal moves and in the second round got the first fall with a reverse double knee hold after Veidor had been weakened with a punch or two. Veidor finally got an equaliser in round four with a folding press after a double leg grab before the winner came in the fifth when Veidor reversed a posting to pin Yearsley with a side folding press. The other heavyweight match saw Tibor Szakacs face John Kowalski in a one fall match. Szakacs won the contest when he pinned Kowalski in the fourth round with a cross press.

The wrestling on World of Sport on the 15th came from Bradford with a match between Kendo Nagasaki and Giant Haystacks as it's centrepiece. Haystacks was first to the ring followed by Nagasaki as usual accompanied by Gorgeous George who had brought balloons with him which he threw into the crowd. After the introductions from MC Ron Denbrey who was making his TV debut and referee Brian Crabtree had issued his instructions the bell rang but not before Nagasaki threw the salt to the corners. Straightaway Haystacks was bludgeoning Kendo with forearms and belly butts as he brought his size advantage into play. Nagasaki retaliated with chops which had the big man on the mat and Crabtree gave Nagasaki a public warning for not breaking the hold. Kent Walton remarked in the interval between rounds that the heavily made up Gorgeous George used eleven different types of eye shadow. Meanwhile in Haystacks' corner a couple of fans had got into the ring to complain about Nagasaki's rule breaking. Whilst Crabtree dealt with them Nagasaki attacked Haystacks at the start of round two with illegal moves. Haystacks then delivered a couple of mighty forearms to Nagasaki followed by a splash but instead of pinning Kendo he tried to unmask Nagasaki. Haystacks used his strength to rip the mask from the top rather than lift it up and revealed the tattoo on Kendo's head before hoisting him overhead for a neck lift submission. Round three started with Nagasaki smashing away at Haystacks' forehead which eventually opened a large cut on it. Referee Crabtree had no option but to stop the match as blood poured down Haystacks' face and so Nagasaki won a very eventful contest in just under two minutes of the round.

The opener that week saw Dynamite Kid held to a one score each draw by the much more experienced Tally Ho Kaye. Dynamite equalised an earlier Kaye submission with a fall in the fifth round but was unable to get a winner in the time remaining. The final match of that week was between Mike Marino and Terry Rudge, Kent Walton reported that Rudge had wrestled a draw with the great Antonio Inoki whilst on a Japanese tour. Marino won this one with the winning fall coming in the fifth round.

The other three matches from the Bradford show were broadcast the following week on 22nd January. Suitably for Bradford a clash of Yorkshire based wrestlers opened the show with Doncaster's Mick McMichael taking on Hull's Jeff Kaye. It was McMichael who came out on top with the winner coming in round six for a two falls to one victory.

The main event was a heavyweight match between 'Beau' Jack Rowlands and the one and only Big Daddy. Daddy decided to behave himself this week and instead used his sizeable weight advantage to overpower Rowlands. The bout ended in the third round when Daddy's double elbow drop gave Rowlands no hope of beating the count of ten.

The other contest shown saw Brian Maxine's contest with Kung Fu end in a No Contest. Both wrestlers had scored one fall each but in round five Kung Fu accidentally injured his hand resulting in two dislocated fingers and referee Emil Poilve called a halt to the match. For once Maxine didn't accept the win and the No Contest verdict was a fair ending.

The last wrestling for January on World of Sport came from Croydon on the 29th. The usual three matches opened with an international catchweight contest between Hungarian Zoltan Boscik and the ever popular Billy Torontos. In a one fall contest it was Torontos who used his 4st. weight advantage to pin Boscik for the winner in the fourth round. Kendo Nagasaki was back on TV for the second time in the month when he took on the youngster Lee Bronson. Surprisingly it was Bronson who got the first fall when he pinned Nagasaki with a cross press following a flying tackle in the second round. It was to no avail as in the fourth round Nagasaki finished off Bronson with the Kamikaze Crash and once again Kendo left the ring victorious.

The last match of the week was another heavyweight contest this time with the first fall etc. winning with Steve Veidor meeting Roy St.Clair. After four solid rounds of action Veidor countered St.Clair and pinned him with a reverse double arm hold to win the bout.

Around the halls -

It was a rather quiet start to 1977 with things not really livening up till the second half of the month with the first show of the year at the Royal Albert Hall on 19th January. The main event would be between Big Daddy and Kendo Nagasaki and after the controversy of their last match at the Albert Hall back in November it would be fought as a lumberjack contest. Nagasaki won the match in the fourth round when Daddy was disqualified thanks to his tag partner Giant Haystacks attacking Nagasaki. The wrestlers patrolling the ring outside included various heavyweights like John Elijah, Lee Bronson and Mike Marino and even they had no hope of stopping Haystacks interfering. Daddy had a victory of sorts as he ripped off

81

Nagasaki's mask and Nagasaki fled from the ring with a towel covering his head.

After his win against Mick McManus in a non title match back in November King Ben had then demanded a crack at the European Middleweight Title held by McManus. The title match between the two was a featured attraction on a very good bill. Whilst giving a good account of himself Ben was unable to upset McManus and Ben found out McManus was a very different proposition in the big matches. The bout ended in the third round when the referee stopped the contest with Ben suffering from a badly cut head which saw McManus retain the title. Giant Haystacks defeated Irishman Sean Regan who was unable to continue in the third round after suffering a splash from Haystacks. A clash of styles but still an intriguing match saw Tony St.Clair defeat Kung Fu by two falls to one in the fourth round. Mal Kirk wrestled a very creditable one fall each draw over four rounds with Steve Veidor. Kirk's frequent overseas tours tended to rule him out of title contention for much of the time. The two preliminary one fall contests saw a scoreless six round draw between John Elijah and Lee Bronson which failed to engage the fans at times whilst Clive Myers pinned Tony Costas in the fourth round for the winner.

Liverpool saw yet another chaotic night on the 28th with Big Daddy being at the centre of it all. Mike Marino was wrestling Wild Angus and had just pinned Angus for the first fall in the third round. Daddy then entered the ring and attacked Marino which left the referee no alternative but to disqualify Angus. Daddy then took on King Kong Kirk in his scheduled match on the bill with this time the match ending in round four with both wrestlers counted out for fighting outside the ring.

February -

The second half of the Croydon taping was seen on World of Sport on 5th February with three interesting contests scheduled. First up was a heavyweight match featuring Mike Marino and Gil Singh which unfortunately ended early. Singh suffered a disclocated shoulder in the third round and the contest was stopped. Luckily Marino had expertise as a chiropractor and was able to manipulate Singh's shoulder back into place. Next up was Mark Rocco taking on Kung Fu which meant an eventful and exciting match. Once again both wrestlers went at it hammer and tongs from the first bell with Rocco getting a public warning in round three from referee Max Ward. Rocco took the lead with the first fall in the fourth round but Kung Fu equalised in round five with Rocco also getting his final public warning. Both wrestlers went all out for the winning fall in the sixth and final round but to no avail and it ended in a very exciting but hard fought draw. Finally that week Big Daddy easily disposed of another opponent when Johnny Czeslaw was counted out in the second round after a big splash.

The next two editions of World of Sport on the 12th and 19th came from a show recorded at Darlington. It featured a team match with the 'TV All-stars' taking on a team simply named 'The Rest'. The singles matches saw Bobby Ryan pin Blackjack Mulligan in round three for the first win for the 'All-stars'. The captain of the 'All-stars' Bert Royal took on the much heavier Ray Glendenning but still emerged the winner. Royal got the first fall in round two before Glendenning equalised when a backbreaker saw Royal submit in the fifth round. Royal got the winning fall in the sixth to make it two-nil to the 'All-stars'. The 'Rest' got their first win when Jim Breaks made Vic Faulkner submit in the third round from a 'Breaks' special'. Breaks immediately demanded a title match for Faulkner's British Welterweight Title. A brief glimpse was seen of Johnny Saint pinning Sid Cooper in round two to make it three-one for the 'All-stars'. Magnificent Maurice made it three-two when he defeated Catweazle when submissions in round's four and five wiped out an early fall from Catweazle in the second round. Alan Dennison opened up an unassailable four-two lead for the 'All-stars' when he defeated TV newcomer Gypsy Smith who was counted out in round two whilst outside of the ring.

Finally the tournament concluded with a six man tag with special rules in that there would be no public warnings but a sin bin would be utilised instead. Any wrestler deserving of a public warning would be forced to sit on a chair twelve feet from the ring for a period of a minute. The 'All-star's' trio of Vic Faulkner, Bobby Ryan and Johnny Saint beat Jim Breaks, Sid Cooper and Gipsy Smith with the third and winning fall coming in just under fourteen minutes. The only wrestler not to be sent to the sin bin during the match was Bobby Ryan whilst Breaks, Cooper and Faulkner served two periods in it.

It was back to more normal fayre on 26th February when the wrestling on World of Sport came from Brent Town Hall. The opening contest saw Clive Myers meet Alan Serjeant in an excellent wrestling match with Myers winning in round four. Myers pinned Serjeant with a double leg nelson following a sunset flip. Match number two saw Catweazle who was introduced by MC Bobby Palmer as the epitome of sartorial elegance take on Mick McManus. Catweazle had no chance of using his usual comedy stuff as McManus went straight on the attack and got a public warning in the second. Catweazle retaliated with attacks on McManus' ears to great effect and surprisingly got the first score when he forced McManus to submit from a reverse arm lift submission in round three. McManus wasn't behind for long though as he sent Catweazle flying from the ring early in the fourth injuring his knee. McManus scenting blood went for the weakeners on it and eventually forced a submission with a single leg Boston Crab. Unfortunately Catweazle was unable to continue and referee Joe D'Orazio had to signal the end to the bout and declared McManus was the winner.

The final contest that week was an international tag match with the Iron Curtain duo of Johnny Czeslaw and Ivan Penzecoff meeting the Indian team of Gil Singh and Rajendra Singh who were not related. Penzecoff got the first fall when he pinned the barefoot Rajendra with a cross press following a body slam. Gil Singh got the equaliser a couple of minutes later when he pinned Penzecoff after hip toss and it was Gil who got the winning fall when Czeslaw was pinned with a reverse double shoulder press in the eightheenth minute.

Around the halls -

A busy Saturday night on 5th February saw plenty going on with a scheduled Kendo Nagasaki against Big Daddy match at Huddersfield not taking place when Nagasaki failed to appear. It was replaced by a tag match with Daddy teaming up with Giant Haystacks against Gil Singh and Gwyn Davies. The match ended in the seventh minute with Haystacks refusing to wrestle and getting himself disqualified as he left the ring. Haystacks had already lost an earlier single's match on the same show when he was disqualified in the fourth round against Gwyn Davies.

Kendo Nagasaki was back from whatever ailed him at the weekend on the Monday night when he was at Wembley taking on Steve Veidor. Veidor gained a rare win over Nagasaki when he forced him to dash from the ring in the fourth round as he was about to be unmasked.

Belle Vue opened its doors for its first show of 1977 on the 12th with another attractive programme on offer. The main event saw Big Daddy defeat Mal Kirk who was disqualified in the third round for refusing to return to the ring. Marty Jones made a successful defence of the British Light/Heavyweight Title when he beat challenger Mick McMichael by two falls to one in the seventh round. Colin Joynson's match with Terry Rudge saw both fail to beat the count in the fifth round whilst another heavyweight match saw Wild Angus beat Roy St.Clair who was unable to continue in the third round. Finally a pair of catchweight contests saw Johnny Saint beat Alan Dennison and Hans Streiger beat Kung Fu.

Big Daddy under the booking of Max Crabtree for Best Wryton was already a firm crowd favourite and the formula that would be so successful going forward was being established. At Halifax on the 14th Daddy teamed with the much lighter Kung Fu against The Liverpool Skinheads with naturally Daddy and Kung Fu winning in just over ten minutes. On the same show Kendo Nagasaki and Giant Haystacks met in a ladder match with Nagasaki victorious in nine minutes or so.

Kendo Nagasaki was involved in another ladder match the next night at Wolverhampton where this time his opponent was

85

Wild Angus. Count Bartelli was brought in to act as referee in the hope of keeping some kind of control. Nagasaki was the winner when he climbed the ladder in just over four minutes. Giant Haystacks was also a winner on the same show when he flattened late notice substitute Barry Douglas in the round two. Tony St.Clair wrestled a hard fought six rounds draw with Colin Joynson in another contest on an excellent night's wrestling.

Croydon's grapple fans had a treat on the 22nd when Mike Marino defeated Kendo Nagasaki in the main event. Marino had just pinned Nagasaki in the fourth round after nearly unmasking him and as he attempted to finish the job Nagasaki fled from the ring back to the dressing room. The fans weren't so happy at the result of the tag match when Giant Haystacks and Big Bruno beat the team of Count Bartelli and Lee Bronson. Haystacks and Bruno sealed a two-nil win with a submission in the seventeenth minute. Steve Veidor beat John Kowalski with a winning fall in the fourth round whilst in another heavyweight match Romany Riley wrestled a one fall each draw with Johnny Wilson over four rounds. Finally Ivan Penzecoff defeated Catweazle in the fifth round by two falls to one.

Thursday 24th February 1977 was a special night for me as it was the first time I was able to go to see wrestling live. The half term school holiday had aligned perfectly with a Dale Martin show at The Dome in Brighton and I was able to persuade my Dad to take me. Having only seen the bouts on World of Sport it was fantastic to be able to see it all in person especially as Kendo Nagasaki was in the top of the bill match. My fascination with Nagasaki was purely from hoping to see him get beaten and be unmasked before finding out who was the person under the mask ?

Nagasaki's opponent that night was John Kowalski who had a size advantage which meant for nothing as despite Kowalski getting the first fall in the third round he would end up defeated. Nagasaki equalised in the fourth round and any hope of seeing him unmasked evaporated quickly in the fifth when Kowalski submitted again to lose the contest.

Also on the show was another wrestler who I had been impressed with on World of Sport and that was Big Daddy. Daddy was matched with fellow big guy Bully Boy Muir and seeing two 20st. wrestlers slam each other was most impressive to a thirteen year old at his first show. Daddy who was the crowd's favourite that night went on to win when Muir was disqualified in the fifth round.

The other bouts that night saw Count Bartelli wrestle a one fall each draw with Sean Regan over four rounds. Ivan Penzecoff beat John Elijah by two falls to one in round four whilst Mel Stuart defeated Ron Allcard with the winning fall coming in the sixth round. That saw me hooked and I couldn't wait for the next show there which the night's programme said would be on 7th April.

Kendo Nagasaki would be part of the next show at Belle Vue on the Saturday night when he faced the challenge of the much lighter Bert Royal. Nagasaki had a relatively easy time when Royal was counted out in the third round following a Kamikaze Crash. Colin Joynson was a late replacement to the evening's tag match when Wild Angus failed to appear. Joynson teamed up with Giant Haystacks to take on local favourites Roy and Tony St.Clair. The brothers notched up a notable win when they won by two falls to one in the fourteenth minute although the task was made somewhat easier when Haystacks was disqualified a couple of minutes earlier. Mark Rocco's continuing feud with Marty Jones went up a level when Jones jumped into the ring and interfered in Rocco's match with Gil Singh. The match was level with Rocco equalising Singh's fall in round two with one in the third before Jones interfered in the fourth round and the match was abandoned. Dynamite Kid defeated Jim Breaks by two falls to one in round six but immediately afterwards Breaks said it was a fluke and demanded a rematch. The other match that night saw Steve Logan beat Ian Gilmour with a winning submission coming in the sixth round.

March -

March started on World of Sport with the second half of the show recorded at Brent Town Hall on the 5th. The three matches didn't have any obvious main event and were just sort of there to fill that week's quota. First up was a heavyweight contest with Romany Riley taking on Johnny Wilson who hadn't yet discovered leopardskin for his trunks and wore plain white ones. With only the one fall needed for the win it was Riley who got it when he pinned Wilson with a folding press from the side in the early stages of the fourth round.

Next match saw Robby Baron face Brian Maxine, Maxine was wearing a yellow half leotard which looked like a child had scribbled all over it with a black pen. Amongst the things written on it was 'I am superstar', which didn't make any sense. Meanwhile Baron was clad in far more sensible blue wrestling trunks and once the action got started referee Joe D'Orazio had his hands full with Maxine up to his usual tricks. It was Baron who got the first fall though or thought he did but it turned out that Maxine had kicked out before the count of three. MC Bobby Palmer announced that the timekeeper had rung the bell prematurely and the fall was disallowed. Instead it was Maxine who got the first fall with a double arm nelson following a sunset flip in the second round. Baron wasn't behind long though as he got the equalised forty five seconds into round three with a folding press and there was no premature ringing of the bell this time. Brian Maxine won in the fourth when Baron fell for the handshake trick. Maxine offered his hand to Baron and instead of shaking it whipped him to the mat and pinned him for the winning fall.

The final contest saw Steve Logan meet Dave Bond with Logan conceding a couple of stones in weight to the younger Bond. An interesting match rather than a spectacular one saw Logan use his wrestling rather than rulebreaking to subdue Bond and win the match. The winner for Logan came in round three with a folding press after a nice take down had floored Bond.

The following week's wrestling on World of Sport came from Buxton in Derbyshire with three very good matches

88

scheduled to be seen. Tony St.Clair had been gaining weight and was now wrestling amongst the full heavyweights and he continued in the first match when he took on Colin Joynson. The far more experienced Joynson took the lead when a back breaker saw St.Clair submit in the fourth round. St.Clair came back with an equalising fall in the fifth and with no further score it ended in a draw.

The second bout saw Mick McManus meet John Naylor in a catchweight match. The heavier McManus had plenty of problems from the lighter but technically supreme Naylor and it was Naylor who got the first fall in round three. The match turned in the fourth round when Naylor got his foot trapped between the ropes and was left hanging from them. McManus straightaway started the weakeners when the bout continued and quickly extracted a submission from Naylor in the fifth. Unfortunately Naylor was unable to continue for round six so McManus was ruled the winner via a technical knockout.

Finally Big Daddy was in action but his original opponent Mal Kirk failed to show so local heavyweight Brian 'Buster' Hunt was summoned from his home to take his place. Kent Walton commented that Daddy had lost a stone in weight thanks to a diet of berries and nuts and was now a slim 19st.10lbs. Daddy didn't even break sweat as Hunt was counted out after just twenty five seconds of the first round after receiving a double elbow drop. At least Hunt didn't have far to travel home.

There was drama the following week on World of Sport with the second half of the show from Buxton shown on the 19th. Jim Breaks who had been having trouble making the 11st. lightweight title limit had demanded a shot at the British Welterweight Title after beating champion Vic Faulkner on TV earlier in the year. Breaks' wish was granted and it was the main event on that week's show. The match ended in controversy with incredibly Vic Faulkner disqualified and Breaks the new British Welterweight Champion. Faulkner had got the first fall in the third round but Breaks had equalised in the fifth with his special arm submission seeing Faulkner submit. During the interval Breaks rushed over to Faulkner and as he did so Faulkner punched him on the jaw and knocked him

89

clean out. There was no alternative but to disqualify Faulkner and so Breaks became the new champion.

The opener that week saw Gwyn Davies defeat Hans Streiger who was counted out in the third round whilst outside of the ring arguing with the crowd. Dynamite Kid beat Alan Woods in the final match when Woods who had already picked up two public warnings in the first two rounds trying to subdue Dynamite was counted out in round three.

March ended with a Dale Martin show from Walthamstow seen on World of Sport on the 26th. Kendo Nagasaki was the main attraction of the week and his opponent was John Kowalski. Despite taking the lead with a fall in round two Kowalski was not going to be the man to defeat Nagasaki and unmask him. Kendo equalised in round three with a special face bar submission before repeating it in the fourth round for the winner.

Dave Bond made a quick reappearance in front of the cameras when he was in that week's opening match with another tough assignment. This time Bond took on Mike Marino and despite his weight advantage Bond couldn't make it count. Marino got the winner with a fall in the third round shortly after Bond had been given a public warning for punching.

The final contest saw Clayton Thomson make a first appearance for quite a while after recovering from a spinal injury when he met Clive Myers in a catchweight contest. Myers pinned Thomson in the fifth round for the winning fall.

Around the halls -

Liverpool's grapple fans were left disappointed on 4th March when that week's advertised show at the Stadium featuring Kendo Nagasaki was cancelled with priority given to boxing instead. World Light/Heavyweight Champion John Conteh was defending his title there on the Saturday night against American Len Hutchins and it was decided that the wrestling had to be called off.

Nagasaki did get a chance to wrestle the next night when he defeated British Heavyweight Champion Gwyn Davies at

Hanley. After winning the bout by two falls to one in the fifth round Nagasaki once again had Gorgeous George press his claims for a title match. Big Daddy's match with Wild Angus on the same show never even got the chance to start as both wrestlers were already fighting before the bell rung. The referee had no alternative but to disqualify the pair of them.

The normally sedate Sussex coastal town of Worthing was anything but on the 8th. The Pier Pavilion was packed to capacity as a result of the main event tag challenge with the team of Steve Veidor and Robby Baron taking on Kendo Nagasaki and fellow masked wrestler The Mad Axeman. The crowd were wild throughout the contest and literally lifted the roof off when Veidor and Baron got the winning fall in the nineteenth minute of a frenzied match.

There was another packed crowd at Belle Vue on 12th March for their latest Saturday night spectacular. Vic Faulkner had a warm up for his forthcoming title match against Jim Breaks when he easily defeated Sid Cooper by two straight falls in four rounds. Kung Fu beat Johnny Yearsley who was disqualified in the fourth round for attacking Kung Fu after conceding an equalising fall. Mike Marino beat Ray Steele by two falls to one in the sixth round of a dour heavyweight match. Big Daddy beat late replacement Buster Martin who was counted out in the second round being the latest victim of the double elbow drop. Finally Catweazle was scheduled to take on Tally Ho Kaye but Kaye had been ruled out of the match. Kaye was unable to wrestle as he was injured when he went into the ring after the Kung Fu match earlier and Big Daddy came in as well and did a big splash on him. Catweazle therefore took on Magnificent Maurice who was bereft of an opponent when Leon Arras failed to appear. Catweazle sent the fans home or to the pub happy when he beat Maurice with the only fall needed in round two.

Wrestling was back at Liverpool Stadium on the 18th after the John Conteh fight and the chance for a bit of refurbishment. The cancelled main event from the 4th of Kendo Nagasaki against Kung Fu was rescheduled for this night but Nagasaki was ruled out through injury. Kung Fu had an easy night of it when he defeated a replacement masked wrestler called The

Outlaw by two straight falls. The Outlaw was then unmasked as Phil Pearson. Gwyn Davies won a particularly hard fought match against Wild Angus when the Scotsman was disqualified. Also on the same show young Bernie Wright made his pro debut when he lost to Kenny Hogan.

The highlight of the show at Croydon on the 22nd was a tag match between Mick McManus and Bobby Barnes who replaced Steve Logan. In the opposing corner was Johnny Czeslaw and Ivan Penzecoff and it was McManus and Barnes who won with the winning submission in the eighteenth minute. Other matches there that night saw Prince Kumali beat Ian Muir who was disqualified in round three. Tony St.Clair wrestled a one fall each draw over four rounds with Dave Bond. Colin Joynson beat Robby Baron by two falls to one in round six and Clayton Thomson beat Mel Stuart who was unable to continue in the fifth round.

After his so called fluke loss to Dynamite Kid at Belle Vue on 26th February at Belle Vue Jim Breaks had demanded a rematch. Breaks got his wish at the same venue on the 26th. Possibly Breaks should have kept his mouth shut as this time Dynamite went one better and beat him by two straight falls in four rounds. This time it was Dynamite's turn to demand a rematch and this time it would be for Breaks' British Lightweight Title. At the time Breaks was a double title holder with both the British Lightweight Title and the Welterweight Title in his possession and cynical ringsiders saw it as a convenient way to drop one of the belts. The main event should have been a cage match which would have been one of the first in this country between Kendo Nagasaki and Giant Haystacks. Unfortunately the injury problems and missed appearances were beginning to mount up for Nagasaki and in the end the match didn't take place. Nagasaki was replaced by a large masked wrestler called Great Bula who only lasted a couple of rounds before being knocked out by Haystacks. Bula was on the majority of occasions John Cox but others such as Phil Pearson also donned the mask to portray him. The rest of the bill saw Count Bartelli beat Brian Maxine who was disqualified in the fifth round. Johnny Saint beat Ian Gilmour by two falls to one in the sixth round and Terry Rudge's match with Hans Streiger ended with both counted out in round five.

The rivalry between Kendo Nagasaki, Big Daddy and Giant Haystacks finally came to an end at The Royal Albert Hall on 30th March. After various matches with different stipulations this would be a straight tag match with Nagasaki partnering Rex Strong against Daddy and Haystacks. Nagasaki and Strong emerged as the winners when their opponents were disqualified after fourteen minutes. Making his usual speech afterwards Gorgeous George was scathing in his criticism of Nagasaki's partner Strong and his contribution to the match. All three protagonists went their separate ways after the match, Nagasaki's career would end up being curtailed by injury and the remarkable unmasking ceremony in December. Big Daddy and Giant Haystacks as a tag team would have a high profile break up later in the year and set out on a rivalry that would be at the centre of British wrestling for over a decade going forward.

In the main support Mick McManus had to use all his cunning and experience to beat Tony St.Clair. McManus had been given a fall start to compensate for St.Clair's weight advantage and St.Clair had wiped that out with a fall in the fourth round. The winner came for McManus in round five with the help of a punch the referee didn't see and enabled him to pin St.Clair for the winner. A trio of heavyweight contests saw Prince Kumali's match with Gil Singh end in a draw at the end of the scheduled four rounds. Wayne Bridges defeated Johnny Yearsley with a winning fall in the fourth round whilst Mike Marino gave weight and a beating to Ian Muir with a two falls to one win in round five. Finally King Ben had an easy night of it when he beat Sid Cooper by two straight falls in the fourth round.

March ended with the news that Mick McManus would no longer be doing the booking/matchmaking for Dale Martin and Mike Marino would take over the role. Unlike the Best Wryton territory which had improved markedly under Max Crabtree Dale Martin remained mired in its sixties style presentation. Dale Martin insisted on still using ten minute rounds for a majority of contests and stipulation matches were very rare.

April -

Saturday 2nd April saw one of the two big Saturday TV sporting occasions of the year with the Grand National horse race being broadcast on BBC's Grandstand show. As usual the big race was front page news in that morning's newspapers with the legendary Red Rum going for his third win. ITV's idea to ensure that viewers switched back to World of Sport as soon as the race ended was to put the wrestling on early at 3.35pm instead of the usual 4pm start.

The early start on the 2nd saw four bouts scheduled to be shown and the first on the bill from Walthamstow saw Wayne Bridges take on Bully Boy Muir. Straightaway Muir was adopting the rough tactics and received a public warning in the first round for a punch to Bridges' stomach right in front of referee Max Ward. Muir received his final public warning in round two for another punch to Bridges' stomach before being disqualified in the third round. Stupidly Muir once again punched Bridges in his stomach right in front of Ward and was immediately sent back to the dressing room.

After the half time football scores it was back to Walthamstow for the rest of the show starting with a tag match. The team of Steve Grey and Alan Serjeant took on a strange pairing of Zoltan Boscik and Billy Torontos. The match was a last minute change from a billed singles match between Torontos and Grey and with Torontos at least 3st. heavier than the other participants the match didn't flow as it should. The first fall came when Boscik pinned Grey in the fifteenth minute before Grey returned the favour when he pinned Boscik for the equaliser five minutes later. The end came in the twenty fourth minute with a winning fall from Torontos on Serjeant.

The main match saw Mick McManus finally surrender his long unbeaten TV record when he was defeated by Tony St.Clair. St.Clair who was in receipt of a massive push up the card and was put over by McManus as part of it. McManus took the first fall in the second round before St.Clair equalised in the fourth round. St.Clair got the winning fall in round five to record a notable win amidst scenes of wild celebrations from the crowd. The final match that week saw Sid Cooper beat John

94

Hall by the only fall required in the fourth round but due to technical problems the contest wasn't screened.

The 'TV-All Stars' were back in action on World of Sport in a team match broadcast on the 9th and the 16th in show recorded at Leamington Spa. It was the same format with the six members of the All-Stars taking on the six members of the opposing team 'The Invincible Invaders' in single's matches.

The singles match saw captain Bert Royal take on local wrestler Tony Walsh and Royal won with a fall in round three which was the only part of the match seen on TV. Vic Faulkner's match with Maurice Hunter ended in the third round when Hunter fell out of the ring and was unable to continue. Faulkner didn't want to win in such a way so a No Contest verdict was recorded and no point scored. In the third single's contest Bobby Ryan defeated the heavier Tally Ho Kaye when a drop kick sent the country gentleman flying out of the ring. Kaye was unable to return inside the ropes before the count of ten so it was now two-nil to the All-stars. The Royals took on Kaye and Walsh in a tag match and an easy two straight falls win inside nine minutes made it three-nil.

Alan Dennison made it four-nil when he defeated Ian Gilmour by two falls to one with the winner coming in round six. Big Daddy took on substitute Al Martin who came in at short notice to replace John Cox. Daddy soon sent him packing when the double elbow drop knocked out Martin in the second round. Finally a clash of personalities saw little technical wrestling but plenty of laughs in the match between Catweazle and Leon Arras. Eventually Arras tired of being the butt of the jokes and was disqualified in the fourth round. That made it six-nil to the 'TV All-stars' and the 'Invincible Invaders' proved to be anything but.

Easter Monday was on the 11th and the Bank Holiday edition of World of Sport featured three bouts from a show recorded at Digbeth.

First match was a catchweight contest when Mark Rocco gave a hefty weight advantage to Gil Singh. Rocco got an early fall in the second round but was unable to keep up his non-stop attacks and conceded an equalising fall in the fourth round before Singh got the winner in the opening seconds of the sixth.

Marty Jones faced one of the leading contenders for his British Light/Heavyweight Title King Ben in a non title match. Ben showed he was up to championship class when he pushed Jones all the way but eventually lost in the sixth round. Finally a heavyweight contest saw Count Bartelli emerge the winner but only by disqualification when Terry Rudge overdid the rough stuff and was sent packing from the ring in round three.

The wrestling shown on World of Sport on the 23rd came from Hemel Hempstead with Mick McManus in the main event. McManus trying to bounce back from his recent televised defeat to Tony St.Clair took on another heavier opponent in Peter Wilson. McManus took out his frustrations on Wilson and following the usual leg weakeners gained a submission from Wilson with a single leg Boston crab in the third round. McManus quickly gained a second submission in seconds of the fourth round starting when another single leg Boston crab saw Wilson submit immediately.

The opener was an international catchweight match with Zoltan Boscik taking on Rajendra Singh with the normally barefoot Singh now deciding to wear wrestling boots. Boots or not it didn't make any difference as Boscik got the only fall needed to win in round four.

The final match saw a return between Wayne Bridges and Bully Boy Muir with hopefully this time Muir realising that closed fist punches are illegal. Bridges repeated his win when this time he pinned the giant Muir in the fourth round for the deciding fall.

The second half of the Hemel Hempstead show was seen on World of Sport on the 30th. The first match was a heavyweight contest between Blackpool's giant lifeguard Rex Strong and the popular John 'The Bear' Elijah. The match descended into fighting rather than free style wrestling with first Strong getting a public warning for over doing the rough stuff. Surprisingly Elijah then got a public warning for not breaking the hold and then Strong got his final public warning for punching his opponent. In the fourth round Strong tried referee Joe D'Orazio's patience once too often and after repeatedly attacking Elijah in the corner was disqualified.

A catchweight match between Brian Maxine and Ivan Penzecoff was joined at the start of the second round just in time to see Penzecoff take the opening fall. Maxine equalised in round four with a single leg Boston crab submission after Penzecoff had injured his knee. Maxine swiftly repeated the hold in the fifth round for a what was a routine win. The final match was another heavyweight contest with Johnny Yearsley taking on Lee Bronson with only one score needed to win. Despite Yearsley's rule breaking which saw referee Joe D'Orazio dish out two public warnings in the second round it was Bronson who won. In the opening seconds of round three Bronson reversed a throw off of the ropes to pin Yearsley with a folding press from the side.

Around the halls -

One of the differences with Mike Marino doing the booking for Dale Martin was the increase in the number of tag matches and April started with a plethora of them. On the 2nd at Maidstone a team of Tibor Szakacs and Lee Bronson took on the much lighter team of Brian Maxine and Gypsy Smith. Szakacs and Bronson won the match by two falls to one in seventeen minutes. Also on the card was a match between two notable rulebreakers with Bobby Barnes wrestling a one fall each draw with Johnny Yearsley with local boy Barnes having the crowd on his side.

A heavyweight tag match was the feature of the show at Croydon on the 5th with Pat Roach and Romany Riley beating Terry Rudge and Colin Joynson in the seventeenth minute of a hard fought contest. Count Bartelli beat Brian Maxine who was disqualified in the sixth round. Steve Grey beat Alan Serjeant by two falls to one in the fourth round and Bob Kirkwood defeated Tug Holton the same way. Finally Billy Torontos beat Sid Cooper by disqualification in the sixth round of a forgettable show and unfortunately this would be repeated in the next few months.

The same night at Worthing saw another tag match with the random pair of Dave Bond teaming with John Elijah to lose to another team paired up just for the night in Bobby Barnes and

Steve Logan. Local trier Tony Antonio had another appearance at Worthing and a losing one this time to Carl Heinz in the fourth round. Bout of the night saw Wayne Bridges wrestle a one fall each draw with mentor Mike Marino over four extremely good rounds.

The next night saw a special show at the White Rock Theatre in Hastings to mark it's 50th anniversary but apart from five matches instead of the usual four it was far from special. The main event surprisingly or not was a tag match which saw Johnny Kwango and Clive Myers beat Brian Maxine and Johnny Yearsley who were disqualified in the twentieth minute. Steve Logan wrestled a one fall each draw with Bob Kirkwood and Bronco Wells beat Ron Allcard in the fourth round with both matches over ten minute rounds. Joe Murphy beat John Hall by two falls to one in the sixth round and Stan Karoli beat John Hurley who was unable to continue in round four.

My second visit to a live show was again at Brighton on the 7th with this time Mick McManus topping the bill when he took on Catweazle. Catweazle picked up a creditable draw when an arm lever forced McManus to submit in the fourth and final round to equalise a fall conceded in round two. Steve Logan beat Bob Kirkwood with a winning submission in the fourth round as did Pat Roach who defeated Romany Riley in a similar fashion. Terry Rudge beat Johnny Czeslaw by two falls to one in the sixth round and Bobby Barnes beat John Hurley who for the second night running was unable to continue.

Saturday night's Belle Vue spectacular on the 9th saw Big Daddy and Kung Fu take on three opponents instead of the usual two in a tag match. It made no difference as Daddy and Kung Fu defeated Johnny Yearsley, Tally Ho Kaye and Masked UFO in the twelfth minute. Pat Roach was victorious against Mike Marino when he wore down the lighter man by tactics both fair and foul to win with a submission in round five. Colin Joynson beat Marty Jones who was counted out in the sixth round whilst Bobby Ryan beat fellow Stoke resident Maurice Hunter by two falls to one in the fifth round. Finally Johnny Czeslaw had an easy two straight falls win against the much lighter Blackjack Mulligan in round four.

A new face to the ring appeared at Wolverhampton on the 12th with the former bodybuilding champion John Holt appearing at his local hall. Holt had already appeared at Digbeth the previous Thursday against someone who would be a regular opponent going forward in Pat Patton and now made his debut in his hometown. Holt teamed up with none other than Dynamite Kid to take on Tally Ho Kaye and Tony Walsh in a tag match with Holt and Dynamite winning by disqualification in the tenth minute. Shortly afterwards Holt would change both his name and attitude and become Johnny England the loud mouth rule breaker with the fabulous physique.

Eastbourne has for a long time had the nickname of God's waiting room by account of the numbers of old age pensioners who move there in their later years. For them the highlight of their month and for others was the regular monthly wrestling shows at the Winter Gardens. The Winter Gardens was built in 1875 and is a beautiful listed building with a capacity of a thousand and usually filled for the likes of tea dances. On the 15th though it was a large crowd of around three hundred and thirty there for the wrestling and a heavyweight six man tag as the main event. The team of Big Bruno, Bronco Wells and Johnny Wilson were taking on Count Bartelli, Wayne Bridges and John Elijah. Like Worthing just along the Sussex coast from Eastbourne the crowds could get excited by the events in the ring and the atmosphere would get lively at times. Even so the events of 15th April took everyone by surprise and made the local TV news broadcasts and the local newspapers. The tag match was about five minutes in and Bruno had been thrown outside of the ring, suddenly a woman dashed from the crowd and stabbed him in his backside with a knitting needle. As people tried to see what had happened the woman fled from the building whilst Bruno was taken to the local hospital for an anti-tetanus injection and treatment. He was discharged later that evening and didn't suffer any lasting effects from his injury. After Bruno had been taken to hospital it was decided to restart the contest as a normal tag match with eventually Bartelli and Elijah beating Wells and Wilson inside seven minutes but all talk afterwards was about Bruno and an

99

unforgettable night. The venue manager afterwards told the Evening Argus that the assailant was known as a regular at the wrestling and her details were passed to the police. At the time of publishing the woman had not been aprehended and was still on the run.

It was not the first time Bruno had made the newspapers in Sussex as back in 1974 he had been fined £25 for plucking a palm tree from the gardens of the Royal Pavilion in Brighton. Police took a dim view of his excuse that he thought the 5ft. tree would make a nice present for his wife.

Bruno should have appeared the next night at Maidstone in another six man tag match but understandably decided to take the night off and let his wound heal.

Croydon's show on the 19th had a far better line up than it's previous one and plenty for those in attendance to enjoy. The Royals were in solo matches with Vic Faulkner beating Bobby Barnes who was disqualifed in the fourth round. Bert Royal meanwhile defeated the heavier Johnny Czeslaw by two falls to one in round six. Pat Roach took on Roy St.Clair who he beat in the fourth round whilst Steve Veidor was once again a winner at his home town venue this time beating Mark Rocco in the sixth round. The two preliminary contests saw Robby Baron pin Clayton Thomson in the fifth round and John Hurley defeat Tony Skarlo.

The fans that packed Belle Vue on 23rd April had two title defences to watch that night with a notable win in one of them. Dynamite Kid had finally persuaded Jim Breaks to put his British Lightweight Title on the line against him. With the crowd firmly behind him Dynamite won his first professional wrestling title when he pinned Breaks in the seventh round of a tremendous contest. Breaks took the lead in the fifth when his 'Breaks' special' arm hold saw Dynamite submit. Dynamite wasn't behind for long as he equalised in the next round before gaining the winner in the seventh to start great celebrations from everyone in attendance.

Tony St.Clair was not so lucky in his quest for the British Heavyweight Title the same night when his match against champion Gwyn Davies was halted in the fourth round with St.Clair unable to continue.

100

Other contests on the show which were overshadowed by the title matches saw John Naylor beat Alan Woods in round five. Jackie Robinson defeated Mike Jordan by two falls to one in the sixth round. Alan Dennison's match with Kid Chocolate ended in the fourth round when Chocolate was injured although a No Contest was called. Hans Streiger made short work of Pete Lindberg who was counted out in the second round.

At Hanley the same night saw a rare chain match in British rings with the Great Bula beating Count Bartelli in the sixth minute. Bula didn't fare so well the next night though when he was defeated by Big Daddy at Cleethorpes in the fourth round.

One of the notable things about the early days of the Mike Marino era at Dale Martin was the number of youngsters who started to appear and at Grays on the 25th Dino Skarlo was amongst the first of them. Teaming with father Tony they took on Sid Cooper and Peter Szakacs and won by two falls to one in the sixteenth minute.

May -

The City Hall in Sheffield hosted ITV's cameras for the wrestling seen on World of Sport on 7th May with The Royals in tag team action. Their opponents were Johnny Czeslaw and Ivan Penzecoff and it was The Royals who won when Bert Royal pinned Ivan Penzecoff for the winning fall in fourteen minutes.

An interesting heavyweight match was also shown between Pat Roach and Gwyn Davies with the coverage starting at the beginning of round five. That was just in time to see Roach get the first fall of the match. Davies equalised in the seventh when his arm suspension hold saw Roach submit and with neither wrestler able to get a winner the match ended in an eight round draw. The preliminary match saw Kung Fu pin Alan Woods in the third round for the only fall required.

Grapple fans were disappointed on the 14th when the Benson and Hedges International golf tournament was featured on World of Sport for most of the afternoon including the 4pm wrestling slot.

The FA Cup Final was on 21st May and after a blank year in 1976 wrestling was back on World of Sport as part of the show's build up. Three matches were shown at 1230pm from a show recorded at Southend with the highlight being Johnny Saint making a defence of his World Lightweight Title. Saint's opponent was the French based Moroccan Kader Hassouni and he had crossed the channel a couple of weeks beforehand to acclimatise and get used to the British style. An interesting rather than an exciting technical bout saw Johnny Saint take the lead in the third round with a side folding press after a smart reversal from him. Hassouni stunned the packed to capacity crowd though when he equalised in the fifth round pinned Saint with a double leg nelson after a sunset flip. Both wrestlers went all out for the winning fall in round six with Hassouni getting a two count from another double leg nelson before Saint got the winner. Saint had rolled himself up into the ball as perfected by George Kidd and when Hassouni grabbed Saint's arm the champion reversed it into the winning shoulder press. The crowd gave generous applause to both wrestlers as referee Max Ward returned the title belt back to Saint.

It wouldn't be Cup Final day World of Sport without Mick McManus in action and he took on Steve Grey in the first match shown. McManus had a 2st. weight advantage over his opponent and it showed as he employed all his usual foul tactics before pinning Grey with a reverse double knee hold in the third round for an easy win.

The final bout was a tag match with Kung Fu teaming with replacement Tony St.Clair to take on Colin Joynson and Romany Riley. Kung Fu's partner should have been Pete Roberts in their Kung Fu Fighter's team but Roberts had been delayed and was still wrestling in Japan. Kung Fu got the first fall when a couple of mule kicks had weakened Joynson and he pinned him with a shoulder press after a flying crucifix. Joynson returned the compliment when he got the equalising submission. Kung Fu had missed a dropkick and was then double teamed before Joynson put him in a back breaker which saw Kung Fu submit instantly. The winner came in the final minute St.Clair floored Joynson with a flying tackle and covered him with a shoulder press with only thirty seconds of the contest left.

The wrestling on World of Sport on the 28th came from Sheffield and was the second half of the show recorded there. It was important to note that the Sheffield Watch Committee (A watch committee was set up by the local authorities to preserve the peace amongst other duties) banned certain moves such as a back elbow, a straight arm lift and headbutts to the opponent's head so wrestlers had to be on their best behaviour. An international heavyweight match opened the show with Gil Singh defeating Johnny Yearsley with a winning fall coming in the fifth round. During the contest Kent Walton noted that Singh wanted a title match against Dara Singh for the Indian Heavyweight Title.

The new British Lightweight Champion Dynamite Kid faced the heavier Scotsman Ian Gilmour in the second bout with Walton informing viewers that Dynamite had beaten Breaks for the title back in April. Dynamite got the only fall needed to win when he pinned Gilmour in round four.

The last match that week saw Marty Jones taking on the much more experienced Steve Logan. Jones got the first fall in the third round before Logan equalised in the fifth. The match ended in round six when Logan was disqualified. Having already received two public warnings Logan stopped Jones from getting up off of the canvas and so was sent back to the dressing room in disgrace.

Around the halls -

Old enemies paired up at Croydon on 3rd May when Kendo Nagasaki teamed with Steve Veidor to take on Big Bruno and Steve Logan. It was Nagasaki and Veidor who won an entertaining but disorderly contest with a winning fall coming in the fourteenth minute. Kung Fu beat Mick McManus who left the ring in the third round having tired of Kung Fu's chops and mule kicks. The referee counted ten and then awarded the win to Kung Fu. Steve Grey's match with Clive Myers ended in the sixth round when Myers was injured but Grey refused to accept the decision. Johnny Kwango defeated Tug Holton by two falls to one in the fifth round before the final match of the evening saw Dave Bond beat Johnny Yearsley who was disqualified in the third round.

Count Bartelli had a free haircut at Hanley on the 7th as a result of losing a hair v mask challenge match against the imposing Great Bula. Bartelli failed to beat the count in the fourth round and afterwards the barber went to work with his clippers.

Big Daddy was the main attraction once again the following Saturday night at Belle Vue when he knocked out an opponent named King Kong in the the first round. Not much was known about Kong but he had been billed as The Maori on other occasions suggesting he came from New Zealand. A street fight challenge saw Kung Fu undress Tally Ho Kaye in the third round to win it. Roy St.Clair beat Mark Rocco who walked out of the ring in round five and was counted out. Johnny England made a first appearance at Belle Vue and a winning one when he defeated Pat Patton in the fifth round. Catweazle beat Steve Logan who was disqualified in the fourth round whilst Johnny Saint had an easy two straight falls win against the Gay One.

Croydon had yet another heavyweight tag match as the top of the bill on the 17th with Wayne Bridges and Lee Bronson wrestling a one fall each draw with Pat Roach and Romany Riley over the thirty minutes time limit. The other matches on an underwhelming show there saw Johnny Czeslaw defeated Bobby Barnes who was disqualified in the sixth round. Zoltan Boscik beat John Hurley by two falls to one in round five. Ian Muir knocked out Bob Kirkwood in the the fifth round whilst Mel Stuart was unable to continue against Brian Maxine for the start of round six.

The show at The Dome in Brighton on 19th May was much changed from the original line up but luckily the advertised Kung Fu v Mark Rocco main event took place. Fought over ten minute rounds Kung Fu took the lead in the second round with Rocco equalising in the third. The final ten minutes saw both wrestlers go all out for the winner but to no avail and an excellent match ended in a draw. Big Daddy took on substitute John Elijah in a match that was doing the rounds on Dale Martin shows. Daddy won with the winning fall in the fifth

104

round but Elijah gave as good as he got hoisting Daddy above his head on one occasion. Brian Maxine enfuriated the crowd with his foul tactics when he took on Johnny Wilson. Maxine's saw move which saw him rub his forearm against his opponent's throat in a sawing motion had the ringsiders howling abuse and I doubt many wanted the pictures Maxine handed out signed. Maxine won with a winning submission in round six.

Clayton Thomson wrestled a dull one fall each draw with Johnny Kwango over four rounds before deaf and dumb wrestler Harry Kendall beat Tug Holton by disqualification in round four. The whole evening had extensive coverage in the local Evening Argus as they were one of the few newspapers that took an active interest in the sport.

The same night at Sheffield Gwyn Davies made another successful defence of the British Heavyweight Title when he turned back the challenge of Pat Roach who was counted out in the fourth round.

The final show of the season at The Royal Albert Hall was held on 25th May and was by and large a dull affair. The only highspot was a six man tag match with The Royals joined by Johnny Saint to take on Mick McManus, Steve Logan and Brian Maxine. It was fought with the sin bin rules in operation with wrestlers sent there instead of receiving public warnings for misconduct. The team of McManus, Logan and Maxine were the winners with the fifth and deciding fall happening in just over twenty minutes of the match. The sin bin was particularly busy with Bert Royal having two visits there and ending up with a £10 fine for leaving it without permission.

The rest of the card was lacking in big names with no match on the show that hadn't been seen on Dale Martin's bills anywhere else. Colin Joynson wrestled a four round draw with Ed Wensor. Johnny Wilson beat Big Bruno who was disqualified in round four whilst another four round draw happened in the match between Steve Veidor and Pete Roberts. All three of the bouts were fought over the ten minutes round system which meant they tended to drag a little. Steve Grey continued to climb up the rankings when he beat Zoltan Boscik albeit by disqualification in the fifth round. A clash of personalities between Catweazle and Billy Torontos ended prematurely in round five when Torontos was counted out but Catweazle refused to accept the decision so a No Contest was recorded.

There was a sensation at Belle Vue on the 28th when Tony St.Clair dethroned Gwyn Davies to win the British Heavyweight Title. After their first title match ended in a No Contest Davies had generously gave St.Clair another chance at the belt. The match ended in confusion in the sixth round when an accidental low blow from Davies caught St.Clair who was unable to continue. The Mountevan's rules stated that the contest must end in a technical disqualification win for St.Clair and in Britain titles can change hands in such a way.

The rest of the card there that night saw Dynamite Kid have an easy win against Pete Evans who was counted out in the third round. Honey Boy Zimba beat the Highlander Sandy Scott who entered the ring in the full Scot's regalia by two straight falls in round five. Johnny Kwango defeated Sid Cooper by two falls to one in the fifth round before a tag match ended the night's programme. The Royals took on the masked duo of The Spoilers and beat them by two straight falls in the sixteenth minute. Afterwards both Spoilers were unmasked and revealed to be Johnny South and Al Martin.

A tag match was once again the main event at Croydon on the 31st with the team of Tony St.Clair and Lee Bronson defeating Mark Rocco and Gypsy Smith in just over twenty minutes. Big Daddy met Rex Strong in a clash of the super/heavyweights with nearly 50st. in the ring. Daddy saw off Strong with a big splash followed by a fall finishing it in the fifth round. John Elijah and Ed Wensor had a dull four rounds draw before Steve Grey notched up another good win beating Sid Cooper with the winning fall in the fifth round. Carl Heinz made a rare but winning appearance at Croydon when he defeated Mick Shannon again with the winner in round five.

That just about ended the season for most of the inland cities and town's venues for Joint Promotions. It was time for the coastal resorts to open up their doors for their summer events.

106

June -

Wrestling was missing from World of Sport on 4th June as the England v Scotland Home International football match was shown. The match ended in a rare win for the Scots and afterwards their over enthusiastic celebrations at Wembley made the front pages of the newspapers.

Luckily for grapple fans the normal Whitsun Bank Holiday at the end of May had been moved to the first Monday in June as part of the festivities for the Queen's Silver Jubilee. ITV broadcast wrestling from Digbeth on it's holiday sports show and three matches were shown at the early start of 1pm. The first match was a heavyweight contest between Ray Steele and Ali Shan. Steele equalised a fall from Shan in round three with a Boston Crab that saw Shan submit in the fifth as the bout ended in a draw.

Big Daddy knocked out Tony Walsh in the second round with the double elbow drop. A move which Walsh would be on the end of for many times over the next few years. Finally Kung Fu pinned Tally Ho Kaye in round three to win their match.

Wrestling was back in its normal 4pm slot on the 11th with three contests screened from a bill at Woking. The opening match saw Big Bruno take on one of his students in Johnny Wilson with the formidable Bruno getting the only fall needed to win in the third round.

Mark Rocco gave weight and a beating to Johnny Czeslaw when the Polish star failed to beat the count in the sixth round. Finally in another heavyweight contest Lee Bronson continued to impress when he took on Bronco Wells and defeated him with a winning fall in round four.

It was another blank Saturday for grapple fans on the 18th when the schoolboys football match between England and West Germany was shown on World of Sport instead.

To complete a rotten month there was no wrestling shown on World of Sport on the 25th also with the Uniroyal International golf tournament broadcast throughout the afternoon. Many wrestling fans put pen to paper to write to the newspapers to complain but it didn't do any good as the sport would continue to lose its slot on far too many occasions.

107

Around the halls -

The famous Tower Circus in Blackpool threw open its doors on 5th June to start another season of shows on a Sunday night there. An interestling match that night saw lightweight champion Johnny Saint take on the fully blown heavyweight Colin Joynson. Whilst Saint's speed and technical ability gave Joynson something to think about the match was halted in the fifth round when Saint couldn't continue. Sportingly Joynson refused to accept the decision so the verdict was a No Contest. Dynamite Kid defeated Tally Ho Kaye who was disqualified in round five and did a double duty when he also beat Alan Woods by two falls to one in the sixth round. Bert Royal beat the heavier Al Martin with a winning fall coming in round six.

The usual Friday night show at Liverpool on the 10th had a very surprising ending which didn't happen in the ring. It was announced that from following Friday on 17th June there would be new promoters who would be the locally based Wrestling Enterprises.

Mark Rocco had decided to curtail his pursuit of Marty Jones' British Light/Heavyweight Title for now and instead turned his attention to Bert Royal and his British Heavy/Middleweight Title. Rocco's actions were rewarded at Belle Vue on the 11th with a title match against Royal. Yet again a new champion was crowned with Royal unable to continue in the sixth round. Rocco joined the likes of Tony St.Clair, Marty Jones and Dynamite Kid as new British champions as the old guard were being phased out under the control of Max Crabtree.

Royal's brother Vic Faulkner had better luck though when he won his match against Jim Breaks on the bill to guarantee a title rematch against him. Faulkner had to win this match and he did with a winning fall in the fifth round. He would now get his rematch against Breaks for the British Welterweight Title which would be seen on World of Sport on 16th July.

The other matches that night saw Giant Haystacks defeat the mighty Samson Duval who simply walked away from the ring in the second round and was disqualified. Marty Jones won a very lively match against Colin Joynson with Jones getting a

108

deciding submission in the sixth round. With such a stacked programme Big Daddy's match was reduced to the walk out contest and it didn't last long. Daddy partnered Johnny Saint against The Liverpool Skinheads and they won with two straight falls in seven minutes.

Bert Royal had a rematch with Mark Rocco almost straightaway but it was in a non title match at Croydon on the 14th. Rocco repeated his win over Royal this time by two falls to one with the winner coming in round six. Once again Vic Faulkner had the better of things when he beat Mick McManus who was disqualified in the sixth round.

Wayne Bridges and Mike Marino wrestled another drawn match over four rounds but there was a certain tetchiness about Bridges' wrestling at times. Steve Veidor had his hands full in his match against Dave Bond. Veidor won with a winning fall in the fourth round but Bond gave him all he could handle and more and was beginning to become a foe to reckon with. The last match of the night ended early when John Kowalski was injured in the third round of his match with Pete Roberts. Roberts wouldn't accept the win so a No Contest was called.

The Liverpool Echo's headline announced on the 15th that 'Mitzi's back in town to boost the stadium'. The article stated that 'Professional wrestling starts a new lease of life at Liverpool Stadium on Friday with big names like Jackie Pallo and Mitzi Mueller on the bill and a new company promoting the show. Wrestling Enterprises, a Birkenhead based concern had taken over as the Stadium's regular promoters succeeding the Leeds based firm which ran shows until last week'. Top of the bill on the first show on 17th June was Mitzi Mueller who took on and defeated Lolita Loren whilst Pallo was in a tag match alongside son JJ against the team of Steve Haggetty and Bobby Barron.

New British Heavyweight Champion Tony St.Clair took on Kendo Nagasaki at Reading on the 21st and lost. St.Clair was counted out in the fourth round following a Kamikaze Crash and immediately afterwards Gorgeous George put St.Clair on notice that his man Kendo was coming after his title. Brother Roy St.Clair had better luck on the same show when he defeated John Kowalski by two falls to one in round six.

For Tony St.Clair and John Kowalski the Reading show was hardly the best way to prepare for their match at Belle Vue on the 25th. Kowalski had been designated the number one contender for the British Heavyweight Title and the match was signed for that night. An ill-tempered affair saw St.Clair retain the title with a winning fall in the fifth round but both wrestlers had received two public warnings as the match had threatened to get out of control.

A second title match on the same show saw Marty Jones defend his British Light/Heavyweight Title against Colin Joynson who had fought Jones in a non title contest on the last Belle Vue show. This time Jones was the winner and retained his championship with a two falls to one win in the sixth round. The rest of the programme consisted of a Battle Royale and a growing example of Max Crabtree using American ideas to update things this side of the pond. Dynamite Kid won the over the top finale throwing the likes of Tony Walsh, Tally Ho Kaye, Alan Dennison and Mike Jordan out of the ring on his way to the victory.

July -

After the multiple blank Saturdays on World of Sport throughout June wrestling returned on 2nd July with the second half of the bill recorded at Woking. It was a solid rather than spectacular show as Dale Martin shows tended to be at this time with a heavyweight match opening the programme. Roy St.Clair took on John Elijah with only one fall needed to win and with Elijah wrestling you know that there would be plenty of strength holds featured. Elijah got the winner when he reversed a flying tackle from St.Clair in the fourth round to pin him with a reverse double knee hold.

The second match was also at heavyweight with Rex Strong meeting Pat Roach and unlike the first contest sportsmanship was nowhere to be seen. Roach got the first fall in round three with a curious looking cross press following a crunching bodyslam. Both wrestlers received public warnings from referee Max Ward for punching before Strong equalised in the fourth with a cross press which was helped by another punch to

110

Roach's stomach. Strong received his final public warning for yet another punch before Roach got the winning fall. A riled up Roach lost his cool and following a posting pinned Strong in round five with the same bodyslam and cross press combo he got the first fall with. A curious final bout saw rulebreakers and sometime tag partners Zoltan Boscik and Sid Cooper take each other on. Both wrestlers were booed by the crowd as MC Fred Downes introduced them and the opening round saw both of them show off their excellent technical skills. Cooper soon reverted to rulebreaking and got a public warning from Max Ward and straightaway got another one for attacking Boscik before the bell for round three. The winner came in the third and it was for Boscik who pinned Cooper after a hip toss led to a cross press.

The wrestling on World of Sport on the 9th came from Leicester and the main event saw what was the first traditional Big Daddy type tag match featured. Daddy teamed up with the much lighter Bobby Ryan to take on 'Pork Chop' Mike Dean and Phil Pearson. Dean and Pearson got the first score when forcing a submission from Ryan after some dubious tactics had weakened him. Daddy got the equalising fall before the double elbow drop knocked out Pearson in the eleventh minute for a popular win. The cast would change over the years but the script would remain the same for Daddy's tag matches over the next fifteen years or so.

The opening match saw Dynamite Kid pin Tony Rowney in the third round for the only fall needed. Rowney was not a fan of Dynamite's dressing room pranks and would make his displeasure known at another TV taping later in the year. The final contest that week saw Johnny Saint defeat Alan Dennison who had now forsaken his crazy persona and had become a fan's favourite. Saint won by two falls to one with the winner coming in the sixth round.

The second half of the Leicester show was seen on World of Sport on the 16th and featured the long awaited return match for the British Welterweight Title between Jim Breaks and Vic Faulkner. As mentioned previously Faulkner had beaten Breaks at Belle Vue in June to secure his chance and he had brother Bert Royal in his corner for support. Referee Gordon Smith was

111

sure to have his hands full especially after the controversial ending to their first clash. Surprisingly though Breaks stuck to the rules in the early stages and it was Faulkner who was losing his cool. Faulkner got the first fall in the third round with a reverse double leg nelson for a folding press and the capacity crowd went crazy as did Kent Walton. Breaks got the equaliser in the fifth with once again a 'Breaks' special' seeing an opponent submit immediately. The end came in round six and like their first match it was controversial. Faulkner pinned Breaks with a folding press for the count of three but the problem was that Bert Royal was standing on the ring apron and had distracted Breaks. The crowd swarmed around the ring as Faulkner together with Royal celebrated as MC Brian Crabtree announced the win. The verdict did not stand though as Jim Breaks put in a complaint to the Board of Control regarding Bert Royal's interference. Quite rightly the result was quashed and it was announced the title would be held up until they had a third match.

The opener that week saw Count Bartelli meet Honey Boy Zimba with Bartelli getting the winning fall in the third round with a nice reversal from an attempted slam. Johnny England made his TV debut in the final bout that week when he took on Tally Ho Kaye. Kent Walton spent most of the match admiring England's physique but it was Kaye's experience that prevailed when he got the winner in round three with a double leg nelson after England had tried to trip him.

It was off to the seaside on 23rd July for the wrestling on World of Sport with three bouts taped at The Floral Hall in Southport. The first match saw Catweazle overcome the rulebreaking tactics of the heavier Jack Martin to pin him in the fourth round for the winner. Mick McManus took on the lighter Mike Jordan in the second match and McManus didn't really have to break sweat to win. Jordan was counted out in the fourth round following a nasty fall outside of the ring.

The final contest saw Tony St.Clair meet Colin Joynson and Kent Walton announced St.Clair was the new British Heavyweight Champion. Walton also remarked that he had heard Giant Haystacks was very unhappy that St.Clair was chosen for the title match and that Haystacks should be the leading contender now. St.Clair won the match with Joynson unable to beat the count in round six.

The second half of the show from Southport was shown on World of Sport the next weekend. A very good wrestling match between Marty Jones and John Naylor opened the show with Jones getting the winning fall in the seventh round.

The complete opposite of a good wrestling match happened in the second round with Big Daddy scheduled to take on Sandy Scott. Before the traditional wrestling bout started Daddy and Scott had a Cumberland and Westmoreland style match fought over the best of three throws. Daddy won that by two straight throws and then in the wrestling match he knocked out Scott in the second round following the double elbow drop. The final contest that week saw Dynamite Kid make short work of Blackjack Mulligan who was sent flying from the ring in the third round from a dropkick and failed to return before the count of ten.

Around the halls -

July saw the summer season of shows in full swing with wrestling held at an eclectic range of venues from the magnificent Tower Circus at Blackpool which I was lucky enough to attend that summer to The Oval at Cliftonville just up the seafront from the centre of Margate. The Oval was an open air bandstand where grapple fans could sit in deckchairs eating an icecream whilst watching their favourite wrestlers. Unfortunately the summer of 1977 was nothing like the one in 1976 and the inclement weather saw attendances at Cliftonville suffer greatly.

July also saw the kick off of the Big Daddy and Giant Haystacks feud when they started to be matched against each other in solo matches. The big televised break up had yet to be seen but at York on 7th July Daddy was very much pitched in the fan favourite mode with a top hat covered in glitter whilst the scowling, snarling Haystacks in the other corner could only ever be a villain. Daddy won their match that night when Haystacks was disqualified in the third round.

Giant Haystacks was in the feature bout at Belle Vue that Saturday on the 9th when he took on two opponents in a handicap match. It only took Haystacks a shade over three minutes to defeat both Mark Rocco and Phil Pearson who were both counted out. Bert Royal had demanded and got a match the same night against Jim Breaks. Once again Breaks' antics and tantrums saw Royal lose his cool and like brother Vic Faulkner before he too was disqualified. Dynamite Kid had an impressive victory against Steve Logan when he beat the much more experienced and heavier Logan by two falls to one in the fifth round. Johnny Saint defeated Mick McMichael whilst Pat Roach coasted to a two straight falls win against Count Bartelli to complete the evening's action.

At Maidstone the same night Dale Martin continued to introduce new faces and this time it would be youngster Mike Dean. Dean who in actual fact was the son of Wayne Bridges lost to Zoltan Boscik when he was forced to submit to Boscik's three-in-one speciality in the third round. Dean shortly after changed his ring name to Dean Brisco to avoid confusion with the Leeds based heavyweight also called Mike Dean. Fellow youngsters Dino Skarlo and Steve Kelly were matched against each other on the same show. Their bout ended in a No Contest when Skarlo was unable to continue in round four. Skarlo's father Tony was also in action when he lost to Steve Grey by two falls to one in the sixth round.

Dino and Tony Skarlo were also in action at Croydon on the 12th. Dino once again faced Steve Kelly as he would do for much of the Summer and Kelly picked up the win this time. Tony took on Sid Cooper and fared no better with Cooper gaining a winning submission in the seventh round. The main event saw old rivals Kendo Nagasaki and Steve Veidor team up once again at the Fairfield Halls to take on Big Bruno and Bronco Wells. Traditional wrestling holds were a rarity to spot in the match and it threatened to get out of control at times but in the end Nagasaki and Veidor won with a winning fall in the twelfth minute.

Two heavyweight contests completed the bill with Roy St.Clair and Wayne Bridges sharing the spoils at the end of the fourth round whilst Romany Riley beat Johnny Czeslaw who was counted out in round five.

On the independent circuit various shows continued to pop up here and there with the news of them hard to find at times. Sunday the 17th saw a show at the Beacholme Holiday Camp in Cleethorpes with the 1977 Women's Wrestling Trophy at stake between Sue Brittain and the Purple Angel. Brittain won the trophy with a winning submission in the fifth round before then taking part in a mixed tag match. Back in 1977 a lot of local authorities frowned on women's matches let alone mixed ones and it was very much of an underground scene. In the tag Brittain partnered Des Murphy to defeat Julie Gee and Terry McQueen with a winning submission coming in the eighteenth minute.

Just to add one more poke in the eye to their critics there was also a women's boxing contest on the same show with Vicky Montrose knocking out Kay Nolan in the fourth round to retain the BWA British Ladies Boxing Championship.

If grapple fans at the Lincolnshire resort preferred something more traditional that day Best Wryton ran their regular Sunday evening show at the Pier Pavilion. In action there was Dynamite Kid who beat Tally Ho Kaye by two falls to one in the sixth round. John Naylor defeated World No.1 Johnny Saint in a non title match and immediately issued a challenge for a chance at Saint's title. Marty Jones took on Ivan Penzecoff and won with a winning fall in the sixth round. Finally Honey Boy Zimba beat Blackjack Mulligan by two straight falls inside five rounds.

The next night , a few miles up the coast at Bridlington Dynamite Kid put the British Lightweight Title on the line against Kid Chocolate. Surprisingly to those present Dynamite was in something of a bad mood and resorted to rulebreaking tactics to see off the challenger. The winning fall for Dynamite in the eight round was greeted by much booing from the crowd. Also greeted by boos at Bridlington that night was Giant Haystacks but he suffered a rare reverse when he was disqualified in his match against Pete Curry.

Kendo Nagasaki was back at Brighton on the 20th to open the Summer season there against Steve Logan. For once Logan

115

heard the cheers of the fans but despite his best efforts and taking the first fall in round three it was a losing one. Nagasaki clamped on his grapevine with the arm bar on Logan's face in the fourth round for the equalising submission and swiftly followed up with the same move in the fifth for the winner. Vic Faulkner gained a popular win when he beat Sid Cooper with a winning fall in the seventh round. Tibor Szakacs defeated Bronco Wells who was disqualified in round six whilst Romany Riley pinned Robby Baron in the fourth for the winner. Finally Steve Kelly had a repeat win against Dino Skarlo with the deciding fall coming in the sixth round.

There was another stacked card at Belle Vue on 23rd July with Big Daddy beating Bronco Wells in the main event. Wells was unable to continue after a big splash from Daddy gained him an equaliser in the fourth round. Alan Dennison won a street fight when he undressed Tally Ho Kaye in the second round. John Naylor and Jackie Robinson wrestled a draw over six rounds. Finally a six man tag saw the team of Marty Jones, Kung Fu and Catweazle beat the trio of Tony Rowney, Ivan Penzecoff and Ed Wensor by two straight falls in the thirteenth minute.

The Beacholme Holiday Camp in Cleethorpes had another show featuring ladies action on the 24th with Vicky Montrose beating Lady Satan by disqualification in round six. Underneath the mask of Lady Satan was Sue Brittain. The Best Wryton show the same night down the road at the Pier Pavilion saw Big Daddy in tag action when he partnered Tony St.Clair against the team of Colin Joynson and Ron Allcard. Daddy and St.Clair won the match with a winning fall coming in the eleventh minute. Daddy was also involved in some controversy earlier on the same show when he attacked Tony Walsh. Walsh had been disqualified in his match with Jackie Turpin and continued to attack him. Daddy entered the ring to assist Turpin and a big splash on Walsh saw him taken to hospital with suspected broken ribs.

The Croydon show on the 26th saw another tag match as the top of the bill with Mick McManus partnering Joe Murphy instead of Steve Logan to face Johnny Kwango and Dave Bond. Despite being the lighter team McManus and Murphy won with plenty of help from rulebreaking tactics for a winning submission in the twentieth minute. An interesting heavyweight contest between Wayne Bridges and Pete Roberts ended in a draw at the end of the scheduled four rounds. Newcomer Gary Wensor, the younger brother of Ed, was now wrestling regularly for Dale Martin and beat opponent Reg Trood by two falls to one in the fifth round. Robby Baron beat Bobby Barnes who once again found himself disqualified whilst Alan Serjeant defeated Zoltan Boscik by two straight falls in the third round of the evening's final contest.

Kendo Nagasaki made somewhat of a rare trip north on the 30th to Hanley to take on Bert Royal in the main event. Nagasaki's matches through the summer had been sparse and most of them had been for Dale Martin in the south. The lighter Royal gave a good account of himself and got an early fall in the second round but following a Kamikaze Crash in the fourth Royal was counted out.

August -

The first wrestling on World of Sport for August came on the 6th from Southend and had been recorded back in May as part of the show that was seen on FA Cup Final day.

The first match was a heavyweight contest between Roy St.Clair and Johnny Wilson with Max Ward officiating. It came to an unfortunate ending in the fourth round when Wilson attempted a flying tackle but his momentum took him over the top rope. Not only did Wilson have a heavy landing outside of the ring but St.Clair dislocated his shoulder in the move and Ward called a halt to proceedings. As MC Mike Judd announced the verdict Max Ward attended to Roy St.Clair and put his shoulder back into its correct place. Judd announced the verdict would be a No Contest rather than the correct double knockout result due to the sporting nature of the contest.

The second match that week was anything but a sporting contest with Mark Rocco giving away weight to take on heavyweight Lee Bronson. It didn't take Rocco long to start the rough stuff with his continual attacks on the ropes or after a break. Rocco got the first submission in round three when a piledriver weakened Bronson's neck and Rocco quickly followed up with a reverse neck hold for the first score. Bronson got the equaliser in the fifth round when he delivered a reverse posting to Rocco and followed up with a cross press after a bodyslam. Both wrestlers went all out for the winner in the final round but to no avail and it ended in a really good six round draw. Rocco announced to Mike Judd that he was the moral victor as Bronson was at least 2st. heavier.

The final bout saw Brian Maxine take on Clayton Thomson with the first fall or submission the winner. Maxine was clad in a garish pink half leotard and luminous bright green socks showing above his boots whilst Thomson of course was wearing his kilt as he entered the ring. In the early stages Maxine was perplexed by Thomson's counters and Kent Walton considered his wrestling ability to be on a par with fellow Scotsman George Kidd. The contest came to an early end in round two when Maxine delivered a back elbow to referee Max Ward and he was instantly disqualified. Maxine was attacking Thomson on the ropes and as Ward tried to break them Maxine threw the elbow at Ward. Max Ward took his notebook out to make sure he recorded all of the details whilst Maxine then attacked MC Mike Judd. Kent Walton wasn't sure this was a good idea as he remarked Judd worked in the office for Dale Martin and wouldn't be keen on giving Maxine future bookings. That was also the final time Clayton Thomson was seen wrestling on World of Sport as his career was coming to an end.

Dynamite Kid made his debut for Dale Martin on the show seen on World of Sport on 13th August with the three matches recorded at the Picketts Lock Sports Centre in North London. Dynamite's opponent was the veteran Tony Skarlo who had been around since the early 1960's and hadn't been seen on TV for quite a while. Dynamite Kid got the winning fall in the third round of a solid rather than exciting clash when he pinned Skarlo with a folding press secured by a bridge. Skarlo wasn't quite the right opponent to showcase Dynamite's skillset with.

The main event that week saw the unpredictable Billy Torontos face Mick McManus with McManus shoving over his opponent before the first bell even rang. McManus got the first fall in round two with a reverse double knee hold following a bodyslam. Torontos tried to gain a foothold in the match in the third but each time he tried something McManus retaliated with his usual forearm jabs or full blown punches. McManus wrapped up a two straight falls win in the fourth round when Torontos was weakened by being thrown out of the ring. As with the first fall a bodyslam followed by a reverse double knee hold gave Torontos no chance of beating the count of three.

Finally that week it was tag team time with the team of Steve Grey and Alan Serjeant, Serjeant replaced an injured Johnny Saint, taking on Sid Cooper and Zoltan Boscik. Boscik announced that Saint wasn't injured but he was too scared to face him and then Cooper pointed out that Saint was also scared of him. With four great workers in the match it couldn't fail to be an excellent contest and the crowd loved it. Cooper got the first score with a single leg Boston after Grey had injured his leg when he missed a sunset flip in the tenth minute. The equaliser came a couple of minutes later when Grey pinned Cooper with a side folding press as Cooper showboated and played to the crowd. The match came to an end when referee Max Ward disqualified Boscik and Cooper as they attacked Grey in their corner with an enraged ringsider trying to attack them both from outside of the ring.

The TV cameras were at Morecambe for World of Sport's wrestling coverage on the 20th with a packed crowd of holidaymakers in attendance. The first match saw Johnny Saint take on John Naylor in a bout which turned out to be an exhibition of wrestling. With only one fall needed to win, it was Saint who pinned Naylor in round four for the victory but the crowd were generous in their applause for both wrestlers at the end.

Mark Rocco and Marty Jones took their rivalry to a new level in the second match shown. Both of them wrestled at 100mph with aerial attacks and moves off of the ropes followed by a surplus of rulebreaking for which both wrestlers received two public warnings. In the end the match was halted in the fifth round with it out of control whilst Jones had blood flowing from a bad nose bleed which started in the round before. The official verdict was both wrestlers were disqualified but those in

119

attendance and viewers at home couldn't wait for them to meet again in the ring.

The final match was a heavyweight contest with Gil Singh continuing to enhance his growing reputation when he pinned Count Bartelli in the fifth round for the victory.

The other three bouts from Morecambe were shown the following Saturday and they featured a rather strange main event with Mick McManus facing Zoltan Boscik. McManus did his best to stick to the rules but still managed to receive a public warning on his way to a two falls to one victory in round five.

Boscik's sometime tag partner Sid Cooper took on Bobby Ryan and despite Cooper's best attempts both legal and illegal Ryan won with a winning fall in the seventh round. The final match that week saw Dynamite Kid against the experienced Mancunian Jackie Robinson and in a hard fought contest Dynamite came out on top pinning Robinson for the winner in round five.

That was not the final wrestling of the month on ITV as the Bank Holiday Monday sports programme saw two matches from Harrogate broadcast. The whole Harrogate bill was advertised as a team match but by the time it was broadcast it was forgotten about which was good as the other part of the show wasn't seen until January.

The two bouts shown featured The Royals with Vic Faulkner taking on Tally Ho Kaye in the first of them. Faulkner won with the deciding fall coming in the fifth round. Brother Bert Royal took on the much heavier Honey Boy Zimba and despite conceding the weight pinned Zimba in round four for the only fall needed.

Around the halls -

August started much the way July ended with plenty of action at the coastal venues although a few of the city venues continued to hold shows. One of the them was Catford and on the 1st it saw a great tag match with Mark Rocco partnering Bobby Barnes to take on Johnny Kwango and Dave Bond. At times Kwango was having a job keeping up with the speed of the other three but he ended up on the winning side with Rocco and Barnes disqualified in the twentieth minute. The rest of the show though was on the poor side with yet another Dino Skarlo v Steve Kelly match which was won by Kelly. A rather dull match between Robby Baron and Bob Kirkwood ended in a four round draw whilst Sid Cooper beat Mick Shannon with submissions in both round's five and six.

Kendo Nagasaki and Gorgeous George with Nagasaki's injury woes seemingly over for now made an appearance at Belle Vue on the 6th. Nagasaki was matched with fellow masked wrestler Dr Death but he was far from a fearsome foe. The Doctor was counted out in the third round following a Kamikaze Crash and was unmasked as Yukon Billy. Pat Roach's match with Giant Haystacks quickly descended into a brawl and it was Haystacks who went too far and was disqualified in the second round. The Royals continued to lose major matches when they were defeated by Mark Rocco and Jim Breaks in a special tag challenge. A winning submission coming in the seventeenth minute continued to give Rocco and Breaks superiority over them.

With Johnny Saint still injured Steve Best took his place against Zoltan Boscik but was beaten when he was counted out in the fourth round. Tony St.Clair saw off the threat of old rival Colin Joynson with a winning fall coming in round six to complete an excellent night's wrestling at the Manchester venue.

The show at Catford on the 15th saw the Dale Martin debut for Mal Sanders, he was the latest of the youngsters being introduced by Mike Marino. Although losing his match against Steve Kelly he was by far the best of the young wrestlers that made their debuts at the time and Sanders went onto have a distinguished and long career in the ring.

The main event that night saw Mick McManus beat Reg Trood who was disqualified in the sixth round. McManus had successfully provoked Trood into losing his cool and he finally snapped in round six. Trood was coming to the end of his career as a wrestler and was considering other options.

Grapple fans at Brighton on the 17th felt short changed with only four bouts on the bill instead of the usual five but as things turned out three of them turned out to be very good matches.

121

The best of them was between Wayne Bridges and Mike Marino over four rounds with Bridges taking the lead in the second round. As Marino tried to get an equaliser Bridges went into an all out villain mode as he portrayed in the early eighties against Pete Roberts. Bridges would use the ropes to break any holds, complain to the referee about any perceived slight and it was an excellent match. No further score happened in the two rounds left and so Bridges won by dint of the fall he scored in round two.

Dave Bond must have been amongst the most improved wrestlers at this time and he battered Steve Veidor in their match much to the crowd's consternation. Veidor had no answer to Bond's aggressive style and only got the win from a disqualification verdict. Veidor had got an equalising fall in round four and Bond had attacked him during the interval and so was sent back to the dressing room in disgrace.

The third match saw heavyweight champion Tony St.Clair beat Colin Joynson who was counted out in the fifth round but Joynson's relentless pressure had given St.Clair no amount of problems.

Dynamite Kid teamed up with Big Daddy for the first time in the main event of the Belle Vue show on the 20th. Their opponents were Slim Gillan , a sizeable chap from Merseyside and Steve Logan but it was Daddy and Dynamite with the crowd's backing who won with the winning fall in thirteen minutes. Kung Fu took on 'Ring Gladiator' Tony Rowney in a mixed martial arts contest with Rowney counted out in the sixth round. Marty Jones defeated Pete Roberts in an excellent contest by two falls to one in round six. Bobby Ryan took on a full blown heavyweight in Johnny South and won when South was disqualified in the fifth round. Finally Alan Dennison faced Sandy Scott and won with submissions in round's three and four.

Kendo Nagasaki's injury problems were seeing him miss more and more matches and he failed to appear at Digbeth on the 25th for his match with Pat Roach. Kendo's replacement was another masked wrestler in the shape of the Great Bula. As Bula entered the ring Roach ripped off his mask to reveal him this time to be John Cox. Roach disposed of Cox in the fourth round when he was counted out following a 'Brumagen Bump'.

Giant Haystacks had a chance to press for a title match when he took on British Heavyweight Champion Tony St.Clair at Chester on 26th August. Haystacks ruined any hope of getting his opportunity when he was disqualified in the third round. Dynamite Kid beat the former Rugby League star Joe Doherty on the same show by two falls to one in round five. Jim Breaks pressed home his claims for a crack at Bobby Ryan's European Lightweight Title when he defeated him in the fifth round. A second 'Breaks' special' in the contest saw Ryan submit and Breaks loudly demanded Ryan give him a title match. Mick McManus defeated Catweazle with a winning submission in round five whilst John Naylor defeated the much heavier Marty Jones in the sixth round for an impressive victory.

September -

The new month on World of Sport started on the 3rd with a very good show recorded at Wolverhampton featuring a heavyweight knockout tournament. Before that though was a catchweight contest with Count Bartelli taking on Steve Logan. Bartelli got the first fall in the second round before Logan equalised with a fall in the fifth. It then got totally out of hand and resulted in both Logan and Bartelli being disqualified.

The four participants for the tournament were Big Daddy, Giant Haystacks, Tony St.Clair and Rex Strong. Strong was a late notice replacement for Canada's Bruce Hart who had been delayed on his journey and would turn up a few weeks later. The first semi final saw Big Daddy beat Rex Strong when Strong was knocked out in the third round following a double elbow drop. The second semi final was between Giant Haystacks and Tony St.Clair and it was St.Clair who got the first fall in the second round. It was all over in the third though when a splash from Haystacks left St.Clair with suspected cracked ribs and in no fit state to continue.

That meant the final was going to be Big Daddy v Giant Haystacks and the packed to capacity crowd at the Civic Hall couldn't wait for them to lock up. Unfortunately it ended in farcical scenes after about fifteen seconds when Haystacks left the ring not to return and was counted out. That left Daddy the winner of the tournament but for the fans in attendance and all those viewing at home were left disappointed.

The second half of the Wolverhampton show was seen on following Saturday's World of Sport with Kendo Nagasaki in the main event. Nagasaki's opponent was Marty Jones who was conceding plenty of weight to him but he put up a good fight. Jones took the lead in the second round with the first fall before Nagasaki got an equaliser in the fourth with a submission. Jones was forced to submit from a face bar hold with the grapevine before it was all over in round five when Jones took a heavy fall outside of the ring and was counted out.

The opener should have seen the Canadian Mountie take on Mike Marino but the Mountie was delayed arriving along with Bruce Hart so Sandy Scott took his place. For once Marino had a relatively easy task when he pinned Scott in the third round for the winner. The show ended with Jim Breaks defeating Jackie Turpin who submitted to a 'Breaks' special' in round three.

Wrestling was missing from World of Sport on the 17th when golf's Ryder Cup was shown on ITV instead.

Wrestling was back on World of Sport on the 24th with three contests from Picketts Lock shown. Once again Kendo Nagasaki was in the main event slot this time taking on Pete Roberts who was back from his various oversea's commitments. Round one saw both of them wrestle within the rules before it started to fall apart in the second. Referee Max Ward gave Nagasaki a public warning for attacking Roberts on the ropes and then Ward gave Roberts one for slamming Nagasaki's head on the ring apron. Surprisingly the first score of the match was a submission but it was Roberts who made Nagasaki submit from a single leg Boston crab in round three. The end came in the fourth round with Roberts attempting to unmask Nagasaki. Roberts just about had the mask off when he shoved Max Ward who was attempting to stop him. As Roberts argued with Ward he was hoisted over the top rope by Nagasaki and he took a heavy fall landing outside of the ring. Roberts had no chance of beating the count. As MC Mike Judd announced the verdict Gorgeous George stated that Roberts couldn't beat anyone let alone Nagasaki and then George went on a rant saying it was time Kendo had a title match against Tony St.Clair.

The first bout that week saw Bobby Barnes take on Johnny Kwango with the first fall or submission the winner. It didn't take long for Barnes to start his usual rough stuff and referee Max Ward gave him a public warning for attacking Kwango on the ropes. Kwango retaliated by messing up Barnes' immaculate blond hair before delivering a couple of head butts to the crowd's delight. A rather soft ending came in round two which saw Barnes do a double leg grab on Kwango and reverse it into a Boston Crab to which Kwango quickly submitted.

The final match that week was between Steve Veidor and the much lighter Mark Rocco, again with only one fall etc. needed to win. The action heated up in the second round and Max Ward had a job keeping order. Rocco got the first public warning for attacking Veidor whilst he was on the mat before Veidor got one for too much retaliation. Veidor then got a final public warning for attacking Rocco on the ropes before chasing him out of the ring. Max Ward had lost control of the bout by this stage and the bell to signal the end of round two saved him. Veidor got the winning fall in the third round when he got a folding press from the side as Rocco returned into the ring after being thrown out.

Around the halls -

The start of September saw the return of wrestling to most of the inland town and city venues with Mike Marino now settled in at the helm of Dale Martin. In his time as matchmaker Marino received plenty of criticism some fair, some unfair but he was trying to update a product that was still rooted in the previous decade. As seen in the summer months Marino had introduced many youngsters and had brought in even more for the Autumn but the problem was that whilst were all good technical wrestlers and had been trained well they had no name recognition so fans didn't know who they were. The thing that Marino did do well was make a big thing of tag teams and several permanent combinations were formed. The most controversial of these were the 'Caribbean Sunshine Boys' team of Johnny Kincaid and the renamed Butcher Bond. It's said in wrestling that the best characters are when they portray their own character tuned up to the maximum level which is what Kincaid and Bond did. From their swaggering entrance wearing their 'huggy bear' caps to everything they did in their matches it riled up the crowds to levels of heat not seen previously. I couldn't believe one night at Burgess Hill when I was there with my Dad and they were in the main event against the brothers, Romany and Chris Riley. The Martlets Hall was a small venue with the seats close to the ring and the crowd were packed in that night. As the match started an elderly gentleman sat in the front row reached into his carrier bag and brought out a bunch of bananas and started throwing them at Kincaid and Bond. They retaliated as the crowd got to close to them and kicks and punches were aimed at anyone trying to get into the ring. It was incredible looking back that someone decided to take bananas to a wrestling show but it happened at other sports too and this is late 1970's Great Britain summed up.

The Caribbean Sunshine Boys were booked to be in the main event of the first show of the new season at The Royal Albert Hall on 21st September but it was a bill devoid of excitement and a case of quantity not quality. Marino had booked eight matches for the bill but Terry Needham's comment in his newsletter summed up how he felt, he wrote one word which was rubbish !

Kendo Nagasaki was back at Belle Vue on the 3rd when he thought he had a match with Tony St.Clair. Injury ruled out St.Clair and his replacement was elder brother Roy who put up his usual good show before being counted out in the fourth round after a Kamikaze Crash. Johnny Saint defeated Zoltan Boscik by two falls to one in the sixth round with the same result as Gwyn Davies beat Gil Singh. On a rather underwhelming night Honey Boy Zimba beat Al Martin by two straight falls in round four and Tony Walsh who was introduced by his manager Fagan defeated Jackie Turpin who was counted out in the third round.

The Caribbean Sunshine Boys made their debut at Tunbridge Wells on 5th September taking on another newly formed team Ed and Gary Wensor. It was The Wensors who won when Kincaid and Bond were disqualified in the twenty third minute and it was how things would be going forward.

Johnny Kincaid reverted back to a favourite of the fans the next night though at Croydon when he was taking on Kendo Nagasaki. The match was short and sweet especially for Nagasaki when Kincaid was counted out in the third round following yet another Kamakaze Crash. The Royals were in singles matches on the same bill with Bert Royal taking on his nemesis Mark Rocco with the contest ending in a draw at the end of the four scheduled rounds. Vic Faulkner didn't fare so well against Mick McManus and lost when he was unable to continue in the fifth round. Steve Veidor gained another win at Croydon when his opponent Bully Boy Muir was disqualified in round five whilst the final match ended in a draw between Alan Serjeant and Gary Wensor.

Dynamite Kid defended his British Lightweight Title at Cleethorpes on the 11th against the former champion Jim Breaks. Dynamite took the lead with a fall in the fourth of the scheduled fifteen rounds contest. Breaks equalised in round seven when a 'Breaks' special' forced Dynamite to submit but as Breaks tried to follow up in the eighth round Dynamite countered and pinned him for the winning fall.

A better looking programme was on offer at Belle Vue on the 17th with once again The Royals resuming their feuds with Jim Breaks and Mark Rocco. There would be contests between Vic Faulkner and Breaks and Bert Royal and Rocco before a tag match between all of them. Royal pinned Rocco in the the third round and Breaks forced Faulkner to submit also in the third before The Royals won the tag with two straight falls in the twelve minutes.

Giant Haystacks took on Asian newcomer Ali the Wicked and overdid the rulebending and was disqualified in the second round. Kung Fu beat Alan Dennison by two falls to one in round five whilst Catweazle once again sent the fans home happy when he defeated Tally Ho Kaye albeit by disqualification in the fourth round.

127

Grapple fans had a choice at Blackpool the next night with the usual Sunday Best Wryton show at the Tower Circus and Worldwide Promotions having their show at The Casino down at the Pleasure Beach. The Royals were in action at the Tower with Mark Rocco again in opposition but this time partnered by Sandy Scott. Bert and Vic notched up the victory with a winning fall in the nineteenth minute. Billy Graham beat Johnny South who was disqualified in the sixth round. Alan Dennison wrestled a draw with John Naylor over six rounds whilst Catweazle defeated Blackjack Mulligan by two falls to one in the sixth round.

At the Casino the ladies were in action with Patti McGoohan beating Lolita Loren by two falls to one in the fifth round. Woody Waldo and Ian Gilmour took on the pairing of Bobby Barron and Steve Peacock who were disqualified in the twentieth minute. An imposter Kung Fu in a mask defeated Lee Sharron with a winning fall in round five and Al Miquet beat Ian Wilson by two falls to one in the sixth round.

The show at Croydon on the 20th featured a six man tag which had sin bin rules in operation. The team of Mike Marino, Steve Veidor and Roy St.Clair defeated Mr Big, Bully Boy Muir and Rex Strong in the nineteenth minute with plenty of visits to the sin bin for all of the participants. Johnny Saint beat Steve Grey in an excellent technical match by two falls to one in round seven. The other three matches saw newcomers in them to various degrees of success. Mal Sanders lost to Zoltan Boscik in round six. Steve Kelly beat Sid Cooper who was disqualified in the fifth round for attacking Kelly after scoring a winning fall. Rob Cody lost to John Elijah in round four, Cody was one of the fresh faces who didn't last very long in the grappling game.

As expected the first Royal Albert Hall show of the season on the 21st turned out to be disappointing and the consensus afterwards was that people wished they hadn't bothered going. The main event tag saw The Caribbean Sunshine Boys dominate their opponents Roy St.Clair and Johnny Wilson. Kincaid and Bond thought they had got a winning submission in the nineteenth minute but they ended up being disqualified for not breaking the hold when ordered to. The rest of the show was just dull and the advertised new masked star The Big Brute was 'Mr Big' Roy Parkes wearing a mask. Even with his manager Reg Trood the Brute wasn't the threat he claimed to be and despite winning his match against John Elijah nothing much more was heard of him. The younger Wilson, Peter, was also on the show taking on Steve Logan who beat him by countout in the third round. Johnny Czeslaw beat Brian Maxine who was disqualified in the fourth round for not releasing a winning submission in round four exactly as had happened in the tag. Johnny Saint beat Alan Serjeant by two falls to one in round six whilst Mick Shannon's match with Gary Wensor was halted in round five when both were counted out. The final two matches saw the youngsters make their Albert Hall debuts with the bout between Mal Sanders and Steve Kelly ending with another double countout in the fifth round. Dino Skarlo beat Tony White by two straight falls in the third round to complete the programme.

The only good thing was that the next show at the Albert Hall on 30th November would be a Silver Jubilee spectacular in aid of charity with the Duke of Kent in attendance.

There was a little bit of friction within Joint Promotions at Hoyland on the 23rd on a Relwyskow & Green show. Big Daddy was advertised in the main event against Gil Singh but on the night didn't appear and was replaced by Ray Thunder. The promoter's excuse for Daddy's no show was that 'Daddy will only wrestle for promoters who allow him to choose his own opponents'. Many took that to be a dig at Max Crabtree and the way he was booking Daddy for his shows for Best Wryton Promotions. At least the punters that night at Hoyland had their money's worth as the new main event of Marty Jones v Mark Rocco saw both wrestlers tear the house down with Jones winning in round seven by countout.

There was a similar problem for Relwyskow & Green the next night on their show at Knottingley. This time they had booked Marty Jones for that show but Best Wryton had booked him for their show at Hanley and that is where he wrestled. These sort of things weren't meant to happen with the booking meetings for Joint Promotions supposedly making sure each wrestler was booked only once each night.

It wasn't a good end to the month for Relwyskow & Green as their show at Leeds on the 29th collapsed into chaos through various no shows and travel problems. The bill had to be stitched together at short notice and Marty Jones ended up wrestling twice. Jones partnered Gil Singh in the main event tag against the masked Zebra Kid and Ray Thunder. This wasn't the original Zebra Kid from the sixties but a new masked star who was in fact Irish heavyweight Sean Regan under the mask. Regan was also a school teacher and in 1977 had moved from a school in Crawley to one in Lancashire but the problem was that his new headmaster didn't like one of his teachers being a wrestler. The solution was he became the Zebra Kid and he became a very decent character with his 'Atomic Drop' finisher but due to having to teach in the day he could only wrestle withing travelling distance of his school. The Leeds tag match saw Zebra Kid end up on the losing team when Jones and Singh got the winner in the sixteenth minute.

October -

October started with a blank screen for grapple fans on the 1st with World of Sport showing the Masters golf tournament instead.

Wrestling was back on World of Sport on the 8th with three bouts from Croydon shown. The first saw Steve Kelly making his TV debut against Mick Shannon. Kelly got the only fall needed in the second round when he reversed a folding press for one of his own secured by a bridge. Kent Walton sounded really excited as Kelly got the winner and MC Mike Judd announced it was a dream debut for Kelly.

The second contest was at heavyweight between Wayne Bridges and Ed Wensor, as Bridges made his way to the ring the Duchess gave him a kiss and presented him with a book. Seeing as she was wearing a t-shirt proclaiming her to be Steve's lady as in Steve Veidor and he was on the same bill too I just hope there was no jealousy between the two wrestlers in the dressing room. This was Wensor's TV debut but he had been wrestling for many years and was a regular on Devereux Promotions especially. Wensor got the first fall in the third

130

round before Bridges got the equaliser with an over the top rope shoulder press in the fifth. Bridges got the winner in the sixth round when a flying tackle floored Wensor and he was pinned with a cross press.

The final match of the week was a tag with the Caribbean Sunshine Boys making their first TV appearance as a team taking on the Kung Fu Fighters team of Kung Fu and Pete Roberts. Incredibly as Mike Judd introduced Kincaid and Bond some of the crowd were applauding them and cheering but they wouldn't be doing that by the end of the contest. It didn't take long for the Sunshine Boys to start to break the rules and referee Max Ward gave a public warning to Kincaid for attacking Roberts who was on the mat. Bond got the first score when he forced Kung Fu to submit from a curious looking move when he was hoisted upside down. Kung Fu got the equaliser in the twelfth minute when he pinned Bond with his over the top shoulder press move. Kincaid was furious claiming his partner's shoulders weren't pinned to the canvas for the count of three. The final session started with Max Ward having a job keeping control of the bout and he gave Bond and Kincaid a final public warning for double teaming Roberts. Roberts then got a public warning for breaking up a fall attempt on Kung Fu and immediately got a second one for doing the same thing. By now it was total mayhem as the crowd were getting involved and Ward finally disqualified the Sunshine Boys as they attacked Kung Fu in one of the corners. As Mike Judd entered the ring to announce the decision the fighting continued between the two teams as the crowd surrounded the ring wanting to attack Kincaid and Bond. One foolhardy fan threw one of the second's water bottles at Kincaid which hit him and Kent Walton remarked as Kincaid chased the fan that he would be in trouble and would have his leg broken if Kincaid caught him. It was total and utter chaos at ringside but it made absolutely brilliant viewing as well as one of the best tag matches ever seen on TV.

Unfortunately it was a one and done for the Caribbean Sunshine Boys as they weren't allowed as a team to wrestle on TV again with the ITV authorities frowning on such misbehaviour.

Things were a little more staid the following week on the 15th when the wrestling on World of Sport featured three bouts from Skegness. The first match saw King Ben take on Little Prince who was replacing Johnny Saint. Saint was still recovering from an ankle injury which had needed fifteen stitches. Ben pinned Prince in round four for the only fall required to win.

The second contest was for the 'Skegness Holiday Challenge Trophy' and would be fought for by Big Daddy and Colin Joynson. It was Daddy who won with a deciding fall coming in round four and a splendid trophy made its way back to Halifax with Daddy. The final match of the week saw Dynamite Kid beat Tally Ho Kaye who was unable to continue in the fifth round.

The second half of the show from Skegness was seen the following week with the opening match seeing Bobby Ryan beat Jackie Robinson by two falls to one in the sixth round.

Count Bartelli bit off far more than he could chew when he took on Giant Haystacks in the second match that week. Bartelli managed to get the opening fall in round two but it wasn't long into the third round that Haystacks scooped him up, slammed him onto the mat and flattened him with a mighty splash. Bartelli had no chance of beating the count of ten and the St.John's Ambulance medics were called into the ring to scrape him up off of the canvas and take him back to the dressing room.

Finally it was tag team time with The Royals facing an interesting duo of Jim Breaks and Alan Dennison. Bert Royal got the first fall pinning Breaks in the ninth minute before Breaks equalised when he made Faulkner submit from a 'Breaks' special' in the fifteenth minute. The winner came in the eighteenth minute when Faulkner pinned Dennison.

The Royals were on World of Sport the following Saturday as well as part of three bouts shown from Chester. This week their opponents would be Mick McManus and Steve Logan and the result at the end of the twenty minute time limit was a draw. Logan got the first fall on Bert Royal in the fourteenth minute before Royal returned the favour with an equalising fall on Logan in the eighteenth minute.

132

A clash of the champions saw British Heavyweight Champion Tony St.Clair take on Heavy/Middleweight No.1 Mark Rocco in what was a very lively encounter. Rocco got the first fall in round three before and equaliser from St.Clair in the fourth. The end came in the fifth round when Rocco was counted out and St.Clair was the winner.

The preliminary match that week saw a mix of personalities with the funny man Catweazle facing the straight laced John Naylor. Despite Catweazle's antics it was Naylor who won with a winning fall coming in the third round.

Around the halls -

1st October saw the latest Belle Vue spectacular in the form of a team match. The 'Belle Vue All-stars' would take on a team captained by Steve Logan. Dynamite Kid pinned Fat Boy Floyd in the second round to win the first match. Tony St.Clair beat Steve Logan who was counted out in the third round before Johnny Saint beat Mal Cartwright in the second. Baron Donovan got a victory for Logan's team when opponent Marty Jones was unable to continue in round two. Mike Jordan beat Steve Best before Big Daddy wrapped up the singles matches when he knocked out Tony Walsh in the first round with the double elbow drop. The concluding tag match saw Marty Jones and Dynamite Kid beat Baron Donovan and Brian Hunt by two straight falls in seven minutes.

Instead of being part of the Belle Vue team as usual The Royals were down at Maidenhead with Bert Royal beating Johnny Kwango by two falls to one in the sixth round whilst Vic Faulkner beat Zoltan Boscik with the deciding fall coming in round seven.

The same night saw The Caribbean Sunshine Boys in action at Maidstone and it would have been lively enough without the opposition containing that venue's local hero Romany Riley. Luckily Riley and his partner John Elijah won the match when Johnny Kincaid and Butcher Bond were disqualified after fifteen minutes. Once again the crowd took exception to the tactics of Kincaid and Bond and trouble at ringside involving them was now happening on a regular basis.

If the action wasn't lively enough the main supporting contest that night saw Mark Rocco take on Kung Fu and it was Kung Fu who came out on top with a winning fall in the sixth round.

Once again Blackpool saw two tournaments on the next night with Best Wryton featuring Big Daddy at the Tower Circus. Daddy took on the masked Dr Death who he beat in the fourth round. Dr Death was then unmasked as John Cox. The best match of the night saw Marty Jones beat Dynamite Kid by two falls to one in the seventh round. Johnny Saint defeated Alan Woods with a decider coming in round six whilst Dynamite Kid appeared again in the final contest against Alan Dennison. Dennison's booked opponent Catweazle failed to appear so Dynamite stepped in but it was Dennison who won in the fifth round.

At the Casino a ladies match saw Paula Valdez defeat Lolita Loren by two falls to one in the sixth round. Red Indian Billy Whitecloud beat Bobby Barron who was counted out in round four whilst Kevin Conneely beat Monty Swann by two falls to one in round six. The other match saw a masked Kung Fu take on Ian Wilson who replaced the advertised Baron Donovan. With Donovan now wrestling for Joint Promotions it seemed he didn't want to upset his new employers and wrestle on the independent circuit as well. Donovan made do with sitting amongst the fans watching the action instead. Kung Fu won in the sixth round and naturally it wasn't Eddie Hamill under the mask but Al Miquet.

There was all manner of confusion at Bradford on the 3rd with Big Daddy topping the bill against Dr Death again. As Daddy waited in the ring two Dr Deaths walked to it both claiming to be the real one. The only conclusion was that Daddy would take them both on with the first Dr Death being knocked out in the first round with a double elbow drop. The second Dr Death then entered the ring accompanied by 'Angel Face' Bob Bibby and manager Charlie the Gent before the trio decided that discretion was the better part of valour and they all departed before the bell rang.

Whilst that was all knockabout good fun there was some excellent wrestling on the bill there that night with a technical masterpiece between Johnny Saint and Dynamite Kid the highlight. In a surprise it was Dynamite who got the deciding fall in round six to win.

The Big Brute popped up again at Reading on the 4th and repeated his Royal Albert Hall win over John Elijah. As it was a Dale Martin show naturally there was a tag match on the bill as well with Steve Grey and Tony Skarlo defeating the Roughnecks, Joe Murphy and Sid Cooper.

The final show of the season at the Tower Circus, Blackpool was on the 9th and a pretty low key end to the season there. Bert Royal beat Mark Rocco who was counted out in the sixth round whilst brother Vic Faulkner took on Tally Ho Kaye and beat him by two falls to one in the sixth as well.

Les Kellett had been busy on the independent circuit since leaving Joint Promotions and on the 10th he was at Ossett where he faced up to the challenge of the giant Klondyke Bill. Kellett won when Bill was disqualified in the fifth round whilst a ladies match on the show saw Cherokee Princess beat Rusty Blair by two falls to one in the sixth round.

Bobby Ryan lost the European Lightweight Title to Jim Breaks at Wolverhampton the next night. Ryan's two year reign as champion came to an end in the fifth round when he was injured and unable to continue. Pete Roberts defeated Marty Jones by two falls to one in the sixth round and Alan Dennison undressed Tally Ho Kaye to win a Street Fight on the same show.

Kendo Nagasaki was still missing quite a few scheduled bookings in October and once again failed to appear at Bath on the 12th. His replacement on the show was the Big Brute and he beat Johnny Kincaid who retired injured in the fifth round. It was a bit weird as on some shows Kincaid was causing mayhem as part of the Caribbean Sunshine Boys and on others was being cheered. The Royals were also there and Bert Royal beat Sid Cooper who was disqualified in round five whilst Vic Faulkner defeated Zoltan Boscik with the winning fall in the third round.

An ultra rare tag match which was wrestled within the rules throughout took place at Brighton the next evening. Not only was there no rule breaking but it ended in a thirty minute time limit draw with The Royals getting the first fall in the twenty fourth minute and opponents Johnny Saint and Mick Mason equalising in the twenty seventh minute. For those there who preferred something more action packed Kung Fu beat Mark Rocco by two falls to one in round six in the main supporting match on the show.

Kendo Nagasaki was fit to face Kung Fu in the main event at Belle Vue on the 15th and he wasn't extended to win with Kung Fu being counted out in the third round following a Kamikaze Crash. Tony St.Clair took on Giant Haystacks and the match ended in a No Contest in the fourth round with it out of control. Pete Roberts beat Ray Steele in a dull heavyweight contest and King Ben defeated Little Prince in a scrappy preliminary bout. John Naylor beat Kenny Hogan by two straight falls in the final match of a show that was far from the best seen there.

The Big Daddy v Giant Haystacks feud was doing great business and they had another match at Bradford on the 17th. Haystacks was the winner of this one when Daddy was counted out whilst outside of the ring and failing to return in time. Two monsters fighting it out have drawn money since the start of time, Max Crabtree knew this and booked Big Daddy and Giant Haystacks accordingly. A small guy taking on a giant has always done business at the box office since David first took on Goliath. What fans didn't want to see was a giant like Big Daddy taking on a smaller wrestler in a wrestling match full of headlocks, chin locks and bearhugs which is exactly how Dale Martin booked him against the likes of John Elijah on their shows.

The Croydon show the following night featured another tag match as the top of the bill and it ended in a thirty minute time limit draw. Sid Cooper and Zoltan Boscik got the first fall in the sixteenth minute before Steve Grey and Mal Sanders equalised with a fall in the twentieth minute of a highly entertaining match. Tony St.Clair beat Lee Bronson with a winning fall in the fourth round with Romany Riley getting a winner in round five in his bout against Bully Boy Muir. John Elijah and Johnny Wilson wrestled a draw over four rounds and Ivan Penzecoff beat Brian Maxine who was disqualified in the fourth round in the other bouts.

An excellent show at Bedworth on the 28th saw the team of Kung Fu and Pete Roberts repeat their TV win over the Caribbean Sunshine Boys when once again Johnny Kincaid and Butcher Bond were disqualified in the eighteenth minute. Big Daddy was booked properly in his match with Mr Big which ended with Mr Big disqualified in the third round of a brawl. Fans had a dilemma who to support in the match between Mark Rocco and Steve Logan and in the end there was no winner to cheer as it ended in a four round draw. The final two matches saw the youngsters in action with Steve Kelly beating Dean Brisco who was unable to continue in the fifth round whilst Mal Sanders won against Dino Skarlo in round four.

It was noticeable that since the start of September that attendances were down for Dale Martin which meant that profits were declining too which raised concerns for the cartel in charge. One of the problems was that Mike Marino with his booking of tag matches everywhere was adding two extra wrestlers to the payroll each show and like the Bedworth show not only was there a tag match but four singles matches too. A venue like Bedworth would normally have four matches and eight wrestlers to pay, on the 28th there were twelve wrestlers to pay for no discernible increase in takings at the box office. The decline in attendances would continue for Dale Martin shows apace as fans stopped due mainly to the lack of familar faces wrestling on them.

29th October was a busy night up and down the country with shows everywhere with Belle Vue the highlight. Giant Haystacks took on Tony St.Clair in a non title match and once again pressed his claims for a title match after beating him. St.Clair was counted out in the third round, after mistiming a flying tackle St.Clair was slammed to the mat and flattened by a splash. The Undertakers should have been in action against The Royals but instead of Jonathan and Nathaniel turning up it was Tubby Hodgson and Bob Abbott instead. As it was Hodgson and Abbot who normally portrayed them it might well have been a case of them forgetting their costumes. The Royals didn't care who they faced and in a typical Royal's style tag match they won by two straight falls in ten minutes.

A rather lacklustre rest of the bill saw Steve Best beat Johnny England who was disqualified in the fourth round. Alan Dennison's match with Bobby Ryan ended in a No Contest in round three when Ryan was injured and Brian Maxine beat Johnny Saint in the fifth round.

Elsewhere that night at Hanley Count Bartelli beat Tally Ho Kaye in a chain match whilst John Naylor won a Battle Royale there. Big Daddy was at Maidenhead and as it was a Dale Martin show his bout with John Elijah was a dull wrestling match which Daddy won by two falls to one in the fifth round.

Kendo Nagasaki missed his scheduled match at Bradford on the 31st against Pete Roberts but he had an interesting replacement in Bruce Hart. Hart had finally arrived in this country for a tour and his first match would be against Roberts. The match ended in a No Contest in the fifth round when Hart was injured and Roberts refused to accept the win. Dynamite Kid won a Battle Royale on the show when he eliminated the likes of Sid Cooper, Tally Ho Kaye, Kid Chocolate and Bobby Ryan to win.

November -

The second half of the show recorded at Chester was shown on World of Sport on the 5th and it was a show full of fireworks. The first match would have been a top of the bill on any other week with Johnny Saint and Jim Breaks meeting again. For once Breaks kept his temper in check and used his skills which were rewarded when he pinned Saint for the only fall needed in the third round.

The main event was a super heavyweight showdown with Big Daddy taking on Giant Haystacks. Daddy got the first fall in the first round before the match was abandoned in round two. Referee Dave Reese was trapped between both wrestlers as they charged at each other and was knocked unconscious. The match had to be halted as Reese was taken to hospital and the Daddy v Haystacks rivalry went up to another level.

Finally that week Dynamite Kid defended his British Lightweight Title against Tally Ho Kaye. Dynamite got the first fall in the second round before Kaye got the equaliser in the fifth when an arm lever saw Dynamite submit. Dynamite pinned Kaye in the seventh round for the winner and Bruce Hart came into the ring to make the presentation of the belt to him.

A Dale Martin show from Aylesbury was shown on World of Sport the next weekend with the first match seeing Johnny Kincaid take on Johnny Wilson. Kincaid's tag partner Butcher Bond was in his corner to give support wearing an 'I'm with Kincaid' t-shirt. Kent Walton noted in the first round about Kincaid's change of attitude and that he was a very dangerous man now. Kincaid started the rough stuff in the second round with referee Max Ward giving Wilson a public warning for retaliating with a punch. Kincaid then got a public warning for not breaking a hold whilst on the ropes. Ward gave Kincaid a final public warning in round four for not breaking on the ropes again but shortly after he pinned Wilson with a folding press for the only fall needed.

The second match was between Kung Fu and Mark Rocco and as expected the action went from 0-100mph pretty quickly. Rocco got his first public warning in round two from Max Ward for attacking his opponent on the mat. Kung Fu got the first fall in the third fall pinning Rocco with a cross press after a high back drop had floored him. Rocco finally got an equaliser in round five with a reverse double knee hold following a side slam. The end came in the sixth and final round with Rocco standing outside the ring on the apron when Kung Fu launched a suicidal looking flying tackle on him. Both wrestlers went flying off of the ring landing amongst the ringside seats and neither wrestler could beat the count so it ended in a double knockout.

The final bout of the week saw Steve Kelly in action although he was introduced by MC Fred Downes as Tony Kelly before Downes quickly corrected himself. Kelly took on Zoltan Boscik. Facing Boscik was a lot different from his first TV match against Mick Shannon for Kelly and he had no answer to Boscik's experience. The winner came in the third round when

Boscik put Kelly in his 'three-in-one special' and the youngster submitted instantly.

Another of the youngsters made his TV debut on World of Sport on the 19th with Mal Sanders taking on Steve Grey. The match was the first of three from Aylesbury and the first fall etc. would be the winner. The contest was an interesting one with Sanders not showing any sign of inexperience but it was Grey who got the win reversing a double leg nelson for a folding press in round four.

The second contest saw the other half of The Caribbean Sunshine Boys in action with Butcher Bond facing Tony St.Clair. As with Kincaid's match the previous week with Bond in his corner now Bond had Kincaid seconding him. Before the match Kent Walton had to correct comments he had made about St.Clair and him refusing to give Giant Haystacks a championship match. Walton apologised to him and said St.Clair welcomed the challenge of any heavyweight at any time.

As the second round started St.Clair landed a couple of slaps to Bond's face and who retaliated with a punch to St.Clair behind referee Max Ward's back. St.Clair did the same with a punch to Bond which Ward spotted and gave him a first public warning. In the interval between round's two and three Walton announced the details of the Royal Albert Hall show on 30th November which would be seen on TV that same evening. Bond got his first public warning in the third round for not breaking on the ropes as this happened a fight broke out at ringside after a fan had tried to get involved. All manner of mayhem was going on by the timekeeper's table with fans trying to attack Johnny Kincaid who was giving as good as he got in return. With everyone distracted by events outside of the ring Bond got the first score when he forced St.Clair to submit from a neck lift. St.Clair got the equalising fall in the fifth round with a cross press after bodyslam had weakened Bond. With one round left it was all to play for and straightaway St.Clair went looking for a winner and sent Bond flying over the top rope but as St.Clair attempted a flying tackle Bond deliberately dropped him legs astride the top rope. Max Ward immediately called for the bell and MC Fred Downes' voice went up an octave or two as he announced Bond was disqualified. Downes then told Bond that Ward was putting his name in his notebook and even worse not only was his name in the book but his purse money would be witheld.

The final match that week featured Big Daddy who arrived in the ring with 'We shall not be moved' playing on the PA and wearing a glitter covered top hat. His opponent was John Elijah and as it was a Dale Martin show unfortunately it would be a wrestling match rather than Daddy destroying him in a round or two. The bout was strength holds followed by a handshake with Daddy condescending at times towards the much lighter Elijah. Daddy got the winner when a big splash on Elijah led to a fall in round three.

The final wrestling for November on World of Sport was on the 26th and came from Bradford with the MC George Mitchell making his first appearance on TV. The first contest was a local derby between two Yorkshiremen in King Ben and Phil Pearson. Pearson had stepped in at short notice to replace Pat Patton but it was Ben who came out on top with a winning fall in the fourth round.

Local favourite Alan Dennison took on Mick McManus in that week's main event with the rough stuff and rulebreaking starting as early as the first round. McManus got his first public warning during the opening round and got his final one in round two as did Dennison who got his first warning in that round. Dennison went in front when he forced a submission out of McManus with his raised double arm speciality hold. McManus quickly equalised in the fourth round with Dennison claiming foul play by his opponent. Dennison completely lost his cool and he couldn't be calmed down so the match was abandoned and the verdict announced as a No Contest.

Finally that week Dynamite Kid gained another impressive victory when he defeated the much heavier and more experienced Steve Logan. Dynamite got the winning fall in the fourth round and it seemed at the time the sky was the limit for the talented youngster.

141

Around the halls -

November started with the details of the Silver Jubilee show at The Royal Albert Hall and the main event would be not only for the British Welterweight Title between Jim Breaks and Vic Faulkner but the winner would receive the William Hill Silver Jubilee Trophy too.

Surprisingly or not the show at Croydon on the 1st featured another tag match as the main event. Mick McManus and Joe Murphy took on Vic Faulkner and Johnny Saint and they wrestled a thirty minutes time limit draw. The rest of that night's show was dire and would be an indication of how poor some of the Dale Martin shows were becoming in terms of star appeal and decent matches. Gypsy Smith and Mel Stuart's match ended in a one fall apiece draw at the end of the four rounds. Tony Costas beat Billy La Rue by two falls to one in the fourth round. Catweazle defeated Red Kane with a winning fall in round five before Paul Duveen beat Bobby Barnes who was disqualified in the fourth round. Truly awful.

Just for comparison the same night at Solihull saw an action packed show full of excitement. The match between Pat Roach and Pete Roberts ended with both wrestlers disqualified in the sixth round with the contest out of control. The main event there saw Big Daddy and Lucky Gordon defeat Giant Haystacks and Rex Strong with a winning fall in the ninth minute.

Big Daddy and Giant Haystacks were in tag action again at Hanley on the 5th with Daddy this time teaming with Tony St.Clair whilst Haystacks was with Rex Strong again. Daddy got the winning fall on Strong in the ninth minute following a big splash with Haystacks disqualified a minute or so before for attacking St.Clair. An exciting and eventful contest saw Pete Roberts beat Mark Rocco by two falls to one in the sixth round. Jackie Turpin sent the fans home happy that night when he knocked out Gay One in a boxer v wrestler contest.

Jackie Turpin and Gay One opposed each other the following Saturday at Belle Vue with the match stopped in round four. Turpin had put his boxing gloves on and proceeded to knock his opponent out cold once again. A lot of wrestlers

142

backstage would say that was the least the vile Al Vippond aka Gay One deserved. A catchweight contest saw Johnny Saint defeat the Canadian visitor Bruce Hart by two falls to one in the fifth round of an excellent technical match. Pat Roach beat Roy St.Clair with a winning fall in round six whilst the rest of the programme featured a team match. The concluding six man tag saw Big Daddy, Catweazle and Mike Jordan defeat The Outlaw, Tally Ho Kaye and Phil Pearson.

What would have been a highly interesting tag match with Big Daddy partnering Bruce Hart to take on Kendo Nagasaki and Mark Rocco failed to happen when Nagasaki failed to appear. The contest at Crewe on the 21st went ahead with The Outlaw partnering Rocco instead with Daddy and Hart winning in twelve minutes.

Jim Breaks beat Alan Dennison in the main event of the show at Belle Vue on the 26th. Once again Dennison's infamous temper let him down and he was disqualified in the fifth round after losing control. Kung Fu beat Mark Rocco when he was counted out in the fourth round whilst Bert Royal warmed up nicely for his impending title match with Rocco defeating Johnny Czeslaw by two falls to one in round six. Pat Roach knocked out Colin Joynson in the fourth round of their match whilst Dynamite Kid went over old ground when he beat Kenny Hogan who failed to beat the count in round four.

Grapple fans in North West London had a treat with shows at Brent Town Hall in Wembley on consecutive nights on the 27th and 28th November. The Sunday night card was a charity spectacular but it ended early. The main event was a tag match between Johnny and Peter Wilson against Johnny Czeslaw and Ivan Penzecoff and it was about five minutes in when the lights went out. A power cut had occurred and the match had to be abandoned and everyone was forced to leave the venue.

There was no power cut there the next night and the main event tag went ahead as booked although Mike Jordan and Mick Mason might have wished there was. Jordan and Mason took a twenty minute beating from Mick McManus and Steve Logan before losing in straight falls.

The show at Croydon on November 29th again featured a tag match with Johnny and Peter Wilson facing Sandy Scott and Gypsy Smith. The brothers won with a winning fall coming in the nineteenth minute. It was another poor undercard which saw Wayne Bridges beat Caswell Martin by two falls to one in six rounds. Mal Sanders defeated Red Kane with the winning fall coming in the fifth round. Phil Rowe beat Joe Murphy who was disqualified in the fourth round whilst the best bout of the night saw Steve Grey defeat Mike Jordan by two falls to one in round five.

The best show of the year and the most important one was at The Royal Albert Hall on 30th November with the Duke of Kent amongst other dignitaries sat at ringside and over £5000 was raised for the Queen's Silver Jubilee Appeal. Despite what Kent Walton had said no matches were shown on TV that night but two were broadcast the following Tuesday on 6th December. The main event between Jim Breaks and Vic Faulkner was shown as was the tag match. Breaks and Faulkner finally ended their near year long battle for the British Welterweight Title when Breaks won decisively. For once it wasn't a 'Breaks' special' that made Faulkner submit but a single leg Boston Crab. In round six Faulkner had injured his knee avoiding a posting and Breaks quickly seized his opportunity to extract the winning submission.

It wasn't a good night for the Royals with Bert Royal failing in his attempt to regain the British Heavy/Middleweight Title back from Mark Rocco. Rocco won by two falls to one in the sixth round . The tag match saw Kung Fu and Pete Roberts take on and defeat Mick McManus and Tally Ho Kaye with a winning fall coming in the seventeenth minute. Dynamite Kid made his Albert Hall debut and it was a winning one when he pinned Steve Grey in the third round. Wayne Bridges defeated Mike Marino with the only fall required in the fourth round. Two more heavyweight matches completed the show with Tony St.Clair defeating Colin Joynson who was counted out in the fourth round whilst Big Daddy knocked out Sandy Scott in the third following a double elbow drop.

November came to an end and with it a lot of the more familiar names having left Joint Promotions and especially for Dale Martin even more youngsters and newcomers were being featured. Those that had departed included John Kowalski,

144

Robby Baron, Alan Serjeant and perhaps surprisingly Steve Veidor who had crossed over to the independent circuit.

December -

The first World of Sport for December on the 3rd saw the second half of the Bradford show screened. The preliminary match saw Bobby Ryan defeat Johnny England by two falls to one in round six with England's posing and flexing his incredible physique angering the fans.

A tremendously hard fought heavyweight battle between Pat Roach and Gwyn Davies topped the bill that week. Davies had stepped into replace Ray Steele in a rare case of the substitute match being better than the original. Roach was fired up from the start and received a public warning in round two before getting the first fall in the same round. Davies got an equaliser in the fourth round with Roach getting his final public warning as well. The match ended in the fifth round when referee Brian Crabtree disqualified Roach after he kicked Davies between his legs and left him writhing in agony on the canvas.

The final match saw another replacement in action with Tony Rowney taking the place of Brian Maxine against Kung Fu. Kung Fu won in the second round when Rowney was thrown outside of the ring and didn't return before the end of Crabtree's count of ten.

Wrestling was back in it's midweek slot on the 6th with coverage from the Silver Jubilee Appeal show at The Royal Albert Hall broadcast. Jim Breaks beating Vic Faulkner for not only the British Welterweight Title but the William Hill Silver Jubilee Trophy was seen alongside the tag match with Kung Fu and Pete Roberts beating Mick McManus and Tally Ho Kaye.

Three matches from a Dale Martin show at Hemel Hempstead were shown on World of Sport on the 10th. The preliminary contest saw a piece of unoriginal matchmaking with Clive Myers facing Steve Grey. This was a match seen regularly on Dale Martin shows and would still be seen on TV a decade later. Despite some neat holds, counterholds and reversals it was a case of familiarity breeding contempt with it all seen before. The end came in round four with Myers attempting a hip toss too near the ropes and Grey went flying over the top rope closely followed by Myers. Both had a heavy landing and referee Max Ward counted them out as they lay at the feet of the fans sat at ringside.

The second match was a return contest between Tony St.Clair and Butcher Bond after Bond's disgraceful behaviour which saw him disqualified a month or so ago on World of Sport. Max Ward was in charge again and it didn't take long for matters to start getting out of hand. Ward issued public warnings to both Bond and St.Clair in the second round before St.Clair got the first fall in round three. St.Clair got another warning in the fourth before Bond got a final warning in the fifth as Ward struggled to keep things in check. Bond equalised with a neck lift suspension which saw St.Clair submit in the fifth round leaving one round left for either to get a winner. It was St.Clair who got the win but in an unsatisfactory way with Bond counted out whilst he was outside of the ring. Bond was furious but the result stood.

The final match of the week saw another rare sighting of Dynamite Kid in a Dale Martin ring where he took on Jim Breaks. The first notable thing was the size of Dynamite compared to Breaks and how big Dynamite was now. It didn't take Breaks long to start the underhand stuff as he tried to counter the speed of Dynamite including one throw which saw Dynamite nearly land on Kent Walton's table. Ward gave Breaks a first public warning in round two for dissent as he shouted at the referee for not taking a submission attempt seriously. With only one score needed for the win it came in round three and it was for Dynamite Kid whose nose was bleeding heavily at the time. As Breaks tried a 'Breaks' special' it was blocked by Dynamite and after a shoulder wrench he pinned Breaks with a folding press. Afterwards MC Mike Judd said to Breaks that Dynamite would make a great British Welterweight Champion to which Breaks replied 'Two words - Not good enough !'. Jim Breaks was a brilliant wrestler as well as a superb entertainer in the ring and made a brilliant challenger for up and coming wrestlers like Dynamite Kid.

It was back to Hemel Hempstead the following weekend for another three bouts seen on World of Sport. The opening match

146

that week saw Bobby Barnes take on and defeat Peter Wilson. In the third round Barnes forced Wilson to submit from a Boston Crab for the only score needed to win.

The second match marked a sad occasion with it being Roy St.Clair's final match before he retired. St.Clair had had a stellar career both as a single's wrestler and in tag matches with younger brother Tony and it was a shame to see him bow out. Unfortunately he couldn't go out as a winner in his match with Wayne Bridges when he was unable to continue through injury in the sixth round.

The final contest of the week was another heavyweight match with Pat Roach meeting Lee Bronson with once again Roach dishing out the rough stuff from the start. Bronson could hardly get a look in as Roach launched attack after attack both legal and illegal. Referee Peter Szakacs issued public warnings in both round's one and two to try and control Roach without success and in round three Roach got the one submission needed for the win. Perhaps stupidly Roach refused to break the hold and instead of celebrating a win found himself disqualified by Szakacs.

Christmas Eve in 1977 fell on a Saturday and luckily for grapple fans wrestling was shown on a truncated edition of World of Sport. The show had somewhat of a different feel about it with comedian Eric Morecambe hosting it alongside Dickie Davies. The wrestling came on at 2.30pm and featured two matches from Wolverhampton with a super/heavyweight tag match as the top of the bill. Big Daddy would team up with Tony St.Clair to take on arch nemesis Giant Haystacks who partnered Detroit Donovan. Donovan had moved on from Baron to being supposedly named after where he was from, in actual fact Donovan was from Merseyside and wrestled as Bill Bennette for numerous years in the past. Even in the early days of the Daddy and Haystacks rivalry the matches didn't last long and if it went past ten minutes you were lucky. This match just about lasted that time before Daddy knocked out Donovan with a double elbow drop to finish things. St.Clair got the first fall in the fourth minute when he pinned Donovan. Haystacks was then disqualified in the eighth minute after launching a splash from the ropes on St.Clair before Daddy ended the contest two minutes later.

The other match was a clash of styles and personalities with the crowd's favourite Catweazle defeating Tally Ho Kaye. Catweazle pinned Kaye in the second round for the first fall in the second round before Kaye equalised in the fourth with a submission. Kaye immediately got a winning submission in round five or thought he had but referee Dave Reese disqualified the unruly horseman for not breaking the hold.

The last wrestling of the year shown on World of Sport on New Year's Eve featured one of the most sensational events in the sport of not only that year but many a year. It didn't involve any actual wrestling but there were still three bouts on the programme. Dynamite Kid made a quick TV reappearance in the opener when he defeated Kid Chocolate with a winning fall coming in round three.

There were two main events that week with in the first Kung Fu taking on Steve Logan. Logan got the first fall with his forearm jabs weakening his opponent sufficiently so he could pin him in the third round. Kung Fu got the equalising fall in round four before the match ended in the fifth round with Logan disqualified. Logan punched Kung Fu right in front of referee Brian Crabtree who had no hesitation in immediately sending Logan back to the dressing room.

The other main contest saw Bert Royal gain some sort of revenge when he defeated Mark Rocco in a non title match. Rocco had gone in front with a fall in the third round before an equaliser from Royal came in the fourth. Royal then threw Rocco over the top rope in round five and Rocco was still outside of the ring arguing with all and sundry as referee Crabtree finished the ten count.

The wrestling that week was hugely overshadowed though as millions had tuned in to see the ceremonial unmasking of Kendo Nagasaki.

It came as a shock to every grapple fan when it was announced that Nagasaki would voluntarily unmask in front of the TV cameras and everybody had their own theory as to why he was doing it. The most popular theory was that he was having to unmask so he could get his match with Tony St.Clair

148

for the British Heavyweight Title. The other one which made sense was that he was retiring through the injuries that had caused him to wrestle infrequently in the past three months or so and it was a ceremonial retirement celebration. Nagasaki said in his autobiography that he wished to step away from wrestling to get into show business and by unmasking it would make a big occasion out of it. The ceremony started with Gorgeous George clad in a blue robe and Nagasaki in his usual ring gear accompanied by a couple of accolytes. George then made a speech explaining what was going to happen and why it was happening. Kendo then knelt down whilst George performed the unmasking in front of a stunned crowd. Most people had an inkling of what he looked like but it was still a shock to see him without the mask in the ring. The mask was then put in a tray, set on fire and with it came the end of an era.

Around the halls -

One of the things that grapple fans hated was when promoters ran shows in the same town on the same night as happened at Cleethorpes on 4th December. Best Wryton had run at the Pier Pavilion there every fortnight on a Sunday night for a long time and lined up a bill with a chain match between Alan Dennison and Tally Ho Kaye heading it. Wrestling Enterprises then announced that they were holding a show on the same night at Bunny's Place nightclub which was half a mile or so away up the road from the Pier Pavilion. The Wrestling Enterprises' bill had the ladies wrestling with Mitzi Mueller taking on Lolita Loren and Adrian Street facing Terry Jowett in the other main event. A few days before the show Best Wryton announced an extra bout for their show and it would be Big Daddy versus Giant Haystacks in a singles match which totally saw off the threat from the opposition. On the night a packed crowd saw the contest between Haystacks and Daddy end in a No Contest after Haystacks used nefarious means to get an equalising fall in the second round. Alan Dennison beat Tally Ho Kaye in the chain match in the sixth minute. Tony St.Clair beat Colin Joynson by two falls to one in the sixth round. Honey Boy Zimba defeated Don Michaels with

149

the winning fall coming in round five whilst Jim Breaks beat Pete Ross who was unable to continue in the third round.

Dynamite Kid challenged Jim Breaks for the European Lightweight Title at Buxton on the 7th. Dynamite got the first fall in the fifth round before Breaks equalised with a 'Breaks' special' in the sixth but was subsequently disallowed as Breaks had hold of the ropes. Breaks quickly went for the 'special' again at the start of round seven and forced Dynamite to submit once more. But Breaks had again used the ropes for assistance and with Dynamite unable to continue the match ended and a No Contest was the result. On the same show, in what was described in the weekly newsletter as the bout of the week, Ray Steele beat Mark Rocco who walked out in round six with the score one fall each.

The last show of the year at Belle Vue before the Christmas shut down was on the 10th and featured a twelve man heavyweight knockout tournament. The first round matches saw Colin Joynson who was a substitute for Kendo Nagasaki beat Steve Logan. Gwyn Davies beat Rex Strong. Big Daddy beat the useless Hillbilly Hell-on. Hell-on billed as from the USA was actually from Burnley and was one of the guys who put up the ring at shows for Best Wryton. Tony St.Clair beat Ivan Penzecoff. Giant Haystacks beat Gwyn Davies and finally Detroit Donovan beat Lucky Gordon. The next round saw St.Clair beat Joynson before Daddy was disqualified against Donovan. Haystacks was then disqualified against St.Clair leaving the final to be Tony St.Clair against Detroit Donovan which St.Clair won when Donovan was counted out in the first round.

Grapple fans in the Reading area had a treat on 13th December when the brand new Hexagon Theatre finally opened and wrestling was one of the first shows put on there. Suitably Dale Martin put on a spectacular to mark the occasion with an excellent tag match in the top of the bill slot. Pete Roberts and Kung Fu took on Mick McManus and Mark Rocco with McManus and Rocco getting the first fall in the twenty fifth minute. Kung Fu and Roberts equalised in the twenty eighth minute and the thirty minutes time limit was up before either team could get a winner. Big Daddy beat Detroit Donovan by

150

two straight falls in the third round in the chief supporting match. Zoltan Boscik defeated Chris Bailey by two falls to one in the sixth round. Bailey was making a comeback after a couple of years away from the ring. Brian Maxine beat Gary Wensor who was unable to continue for round six after submitting in the fifth. Steve Grey and Clive Myers wrestled a four round draw to complete an excellent night's wrestling. Going forward the Hexagon Theatre would be the scene of many great shows as well as numerous shows recorded for TV.

There was a tournament at Leeds on the 15th to decide the No.1 contender for Johnny Saint's World Lightweight Title. With Dynamite Kid as one of the participants he was the clear favourite to win but in a huge upset he fell at the final stage when he lost to Al Miquet. Dynamite was unable to continue through injury in the fourth round so it was Miquet who sealed the chance to challenge Saint for his title. Johnny Saint was on the same show keeping a watchful eye on the tournament before defeating Kenny Hogan by two falls to one in the fourth round.

Mark Rocco made a successful defence of his British Heavy/Middleweight Title at Hanley on the 17th. Rocco turned back the challenge of Kung Fu who was a fall in front when he was counted out in the fifth round. The other title match on that show was cancelled when Marty Jones failed to appear for his match with Count Bartelli for the Commonwealth Heavyweight Title. Bartelli took on Ivan Penzecoff instead and had an easy two straight falls win in the fourth round.

Mark Rocco had a busy weekend with another defence of the British Heavy/Middleweight Title at Cleethorpes on the next night. This time the challenger was Dynamite Kid. It was a step up too far for Dynamite and he was forced to retire at the end of the fifth round with Rocco retaining his title once again.

After a couple of days off for the Christmas celebrations wrestling recommenced on 27th December and for me a trip to Worthing. As with the tag match involving Kendo Nagasaki earlier in the year ,this time there was another capacity crowd in attendance for another tag challenge. This time it was the Caribbean Sunshine Boys taking on the team of Mike Marino and Wayne Bridges and the fans were red hot for it. Kincaid

151

and Bond went in front from a submission in the eleventh minute before an equaliser came two minutes later. Marino and Bridges got the winning fall in the seventeenth minute and the crowd there literally lifted the roof off of the building and to a man were on their feet celebrating. Worthing is an unlikely place to be a hot bed of professional wrestling but it has always had a lively and knowledgeable crowd and even in the post TV days always drew good numbers. Many of the big names in wrestling have appeared there over the years including Davey 'Boy' Smith on his British Bulldog tour in 1994 and even the ex WWE star Daniel Bryan in 2003.

There was a bizarre tournament at Hanley on the 30th with Big Daddy, Giant Haystacks, Tony St.Clair and Butcher Bond competing in it. The draw for the semi finals pitched Daddy against Haystacks and St.Clair against Bond. The first semi final in the ring was the Daddy v Haystacks match but they then had an argument over who would referee. In the end it was decided St.Clair would referee the first round and Bond would do the second. St.Clair gave Haystacks two public warnings before the first bell had rung and Daddy got the first fall with a big splash in the first round. Bond took over officiating duties for round two and after giving Daddy a public warning proceeded to disqualify him leaving Haystacks as the winner. Tony St.Clair then defeated Butcher Bond in the other semi final when Bond was counted out in the fifth round. St.Clair won the final when Haystacks walked out at the end of round two. St.Clair had just pinned him with a cross press following a flying tackle and instead of continuing Haystacks went back to the dressing room.

As well as the tournament there was an excellent tag match on the show with Bobby Ryan teaming up with Dynamite Kid to take on Mick McManus and Steve Logan. Ryan and Dynamite notched up an impressive win with the deciding fall coming in the fourteenth minute.

Whilst Best Wryton continued to put on good shows each night that drew the fans in it wasn't the same with Dale Martin. The Mike Marino reign as matchmaker wasn't proving to be a success and attendances were dwindling rapidly and changes would need to happen in 1978.

152

1978

The first two wrestling shows of the year on World of Sport both came from bills taped many months before which suddenly resurfaced.

The show on the 7th came from Harrogate and was recorded back in August. The opening bout saw Bobby Ryan pin Zoltan Boscik in round five for the only fall needed to win.

A rematch happened in the second contest with Catweazle taking on John Naylor. The match ended in round two when Catweazle was unable to continue because of a head injury. Naylor refused to accept the decision so a No Contest was the verdict.

The final match of a lacklustre programme that week saw Johnny Saint meeting Alan Woods. Woods surprisingly took the lead in round two when he forced Saint to submit from a single leg Boston Crab. Saint equalised with a fall in the fourth round before quickly following up with the decider in the fifth.

The wrestling shown on World of Sport on the 14th came from Croydon and had been filmed at the start of October. The opening match saw a TV debut for Gary Wensor when he took on Peter Wilson. The end came in the fourth round with neither wrestler able to beat the count of ten.

The second match saw Mike Marino replace the advertised Kendo Nagasaki to face Scotland's Sandy Scott. Marino took the lead with the first fall coming in the third round before Scott equalised in the fourth with a single leg Boston Crab making Marino submit. Marino quickly turned the tables though and pinned Scott for the winning fall in round five.

The final match saw another TV debutant Phil Rowe tackle Steve Veidor with only one score needed to win. Veidor was ambushed on the way to the ring by the Duchess who gave him a kiss which must have made his night and presented him with flowers. Rowe depending on who introduced him was either from Middlesbrough or South Africa. Rowe started to mix the wrestling with some rough stuff which incurred referee Peter Szakacs' wrath who gave him a public warning in round three. Veidor also got a public warning in the third for overdoing the retaliation. The winner came in round four when Veidor got the only fall needed with an over the top shoulder press.

Three bouts from Hemel Hempstead were shown on World of Sport on the 21st with the opener seeing Mal Sanders taking on Zoltan Boscik. Boscik was a far tougher opponent than the various youngsters and newcomers Sanders had been facing in the early months of his career. Sanders showed up nicely in the opening round and a half before Boscik started bending the rules to overcome the youthful exuberance of his opponent. Referee Max Ward gave Boscik a public warning in the second round for attacking his opponent whilst on the mat. The inexperience of Sanders showed in round three when he missed a dropkick and after a couple of knee weakeners he instantly submitted from a nasty looking leg hold.

The second contest saw a rare TV appearance from Jeff Kaye and he was matched up with none other than Mick McManus. Before the introductions from MC Mike Judd began Tony St.Clair came into the ring to announce that he had signed a contract for a match with Johnny Kincaid to be seen on TV on a future date. Surprisingly Kaye got the first public warning in the opening round for a punch to McManus' stomach in retaliation to several he had got from his opponent. The first fall of the contest came in round two and went to Kaye. He pinned McManus with a double leg nelson following a sunset flip. McManus got his first warning in the third round for attacking Kaye whilst he was on the ropes with a sly punch also thrown in the move. Kaye retaliated with an illegal ear hold whilst trying to put McManus into a sleeper. McManus got his second public warning in the fourth round for another attack on Kaye whilst he was on the ropes whilst Kaye got his second warning in round five for another punch in clear view of referee Ward. Whilst the official was giving the public warning McManus reversed a run from Kaye and sent him flying out of the ring between the ropes. Kaye suffered a shoulder injury as he landed and was unable to continue so McManus was perhaps a fortunate winner.

154

The final match of the week was between Bobby Barnes and Ivan Penzecoff with the first score being the winner. The only fall needed to win came in the fourth round with Barnes getting it. Barnes had punched Penzecoff as he attempted to slam him and then it was an easy cover via a cross press for the winner.

Three great matches featuring eight heavyweight wrestlers were seen on World of Sport on 28th January from a show recorded at Preston. Interestingly Kent Walton set a quiz for the viewers at home and asked them what was the total weight of the eight wrestlers in action that week ? The winner of the quiz would get to have lunch with her favourite wrestler and the lady who won chose to have it with Catweazle. The correct answer was 165st13lbs. The first match saw Pat Roach who more or less wrestled within the rules defeat Colin Joynson with the third and deciding fall coming in the sixth round.

The main event saw Big Daddy and Giant Haystacks once again square up to each other in a tag match. Daddy with his now regular partner Tony St.Clair whilst Haystacks teamed up with 'Hillbilly' Albert Hell-on, the Tennessee native or in the real world from Burnley. Haystacks saw hardly any time in the ring as Daddy got the first fall on Hell-on in the fourth minute before St.Clair got the winner a couple of minutes later pinning Hell-on for a two straight falls win. Haystacks had already left the ring and headed back to the dressing room before the winning fall and that would be a recurring theme as the months went on.

Finally that week Ray Steele took on King Kong Kirk with Kirk losing by disqualification. Referee Brian Crabtree had already given Kirk two public warnings to no effect and in the end disqualified him in round four

Around the halls -

Pete Roberts had a terrible start to 1978 when he suffered a broken leg in an accident at his home. Roberts had beaten Bronco Wells in the opening match at Maidstone on their usual Saturday night show on the 7th and made his way back home to Chatham. He had showered and put his dressing gown on ready for bed when there was a disturbance at the bottom of his

155

neighbour's garden. His wife asked him to go and see what was going on and as he made his way down his garden in the dark Roberts fell and broke his leg. The injury would keep him out of the ring for the best part of five months and see the end of his tag team with Kung Fu.

Jim Breaks made a successful defence of the European Lightweight Title at Bradford on the 9th when he defeated the challenger John Naylor. Naylor was unable to continue for the sixth round with an arm injury caused by a 'Breaks' special' in round four. Dynamite Kid continued to impress especially so on the Bradford bill where he beat Mark Rocco by two falls to one with the winner coming in the fifth round.

Giant Haystacks and Pat Roach were involved in a bloodbath during their match at Solihull the next night. Roach had got a fall in the first round but due to him and Haystacks both bleeding badly the match was stopped and a No Contest called.

After winning the lightweight contenders tournament at Leeds back in December Al Miquet got his championship match there against Johnny Saint on the 12th. Unfortunately for Miquet it was a losing one when he was unable to continue in the sixth round so Saint retained again.

Big Daddy and Giant Haystacks continued their feud at Hanley on the 14th with another tag match. This time Daddy partnered Bobby Ryan whilst Haystacks teamed up with Steve Logan. Haystacks and Logan went ahead through a submission on Ryan in the fifth minute before an equaliser came in the eighth minute. Haystacks then did his regular disappearing act and went back to the dressing room and left Logan alone to take the winning fall from Daddy.

The first show at The Royal Albert Hall for 1978 was on 18th January and it was a poor show, probably the worst ever seen there. The only saving grace was the proposed main event tag with The Caribbean Sunshine Boys going up against The Kung Fu Fighters in a repeat of the match that caused all the controversy on TV back in October. With Pete Roberts injured all he could do is sit at ringside and watch Kung Fu partner Caswell Martin instead. Martin had none of the charisma or understanding that Roberts had with Kung Fu and it showed in

156

the match. Johnny Kincaid and Butcher Bond won by two falls to one in the nineteenth minute but the contest was bereft of the heat usually seen in Kincaid and Bond's matches.

The main supporting feature was a six man knockout tournament with Brian Maxine, Phil Rowe, Romany Riley, Johnny Czeslaw, Johnny Wilson and Lee Bronson competing for the prize. The first round heats saw Lee Bronson get the winning fall in the third round against Phil Rowe to progress to the next round. Johnny Wilson beat Johnny Czeslaw when Czeslaw was unable to continue in the third round to go through. The final heat saw both Romany Riley and Brian Maxine eliminated when their match descended into a fight and both of them were disqualified. The result of that was the tournament went straight into the final where Lee Bronson beat Johnny Wilson by two falls to one in the fifth round. It's strange how so often a six man tournament would end in such similar circumstances. Anyone would think it was planned !

More newcomers featured in the other two matches on the night. Mick Mason wrestled a four round draw with Leon Fortuna who was making a comeback after a few years out of the ring. Chris Bailey took on Ray Neal and Neal didn't make much of an impression losing by countout in the second round. All in all an embarrassment to the venue and for the few customers who bothered to attend, a waste of money.

Drama occurred at Sheffield on the 19th when bad weather caused disruption to the scheduled bill there. Magnificent Maurice, Ivan Penzecoff, Bobby Ryan, Mike Bennett, Boy Blue, Dave Shade and Gwyn Davies all failed to appear. MC Arthur Green had to entertain the expectant crowd whilst phone calls were made and locally based talent asked to drop everything and come to the City Hall. By 8pm enough wrestlers were there to start the eight man tag with the team of Marty Jones, Gil Singh, Steve Best and Mickey Gold beating the team of Ray Thunder, Ron Allcard, Jackie Robinson and Johnny Peters by fifteen points to eight in a match lasting 60:36. Gwyn Davies finally made it to Sheffield by 9.20pm so his billed match against The Viking went ahead and Davies won when The Viking was disqualified in the fourth round.

There was a surprise ending to the main event tag at Blackburn on the 20th when Big Daddy and Tony St.Clair were disqualified in their match against King Kong Kirk and Colin Joynson. Daddy and St.Clair had already received two public warnings when they were sent back to dressing room in the twelth minute. Dynamite Kid won a knockout tournament on the same show beating John Naylor and then Alan Dennison in the final.

Tony St.Clair made a successful defence of his British Heavyweight Title at Wolverhampton on 31st January. St.Clair defeated the challenger King Kong Kirk in round four to retain his belt. Dynamite Kid added the name of Mick McManus to his growing list of big name wins when he got the winning fall against him in the fifth round.

The end of January saw the news emerge that Mike Marino had lost the job of booker/matchmaker for Dale Martin. The Marino era had not been a success at the box office and the powers that be decided to act. In a move few saw coming it was announced Max Crabtree would take over the booking for Dale Martin as well as Best Wryton and basically run all of Joint Promotions apart from Relwyskow & Green. Some changes were made instantly such as ten minute rounds being consigned to history as were things like announcing weights of wrestlers in the programmes. Another thing Crabtree did was to scrap some shows that Marino had already booked especially the next Royal Albert Hall show scheduled for March and Crabtree put his own matches on the show.

February -

There was a massive upset seen on World of Sport on the 4th when Dynamite Kid beat Jim Breaks to win the British Welterweight Title. It was obvious that Dynamite had outgrown the lightweight division and had set his sights on the welterweight crown. In the match recorded at Preston Breaks didn't go down without a fight after Dynamite got the first fall in the third round. The 'Breaks' special' forced an equalising submission for Breaks in the sixth round but that was as good as it got. Dynamite trapped Breaks in a surfboard hold in round

158

seven and Breaks held out for so long he suffered a rupture but in the end Breaks had to submit. Dynamite Kid was now the British Welterweight Champion as well as still holding the lightweight belt but he quickly relinquished the lighter title. It seemed at the time that nothing would stop Dynamite in his rise to the top of British wrestling and as for Breaks he had to spend several weeks on the sideline recovering from his injury.

The opening match that week was between Mick McManus and Johnny Saint and it ended in a No Contest in the second round. Saint had placed McManus legs apart on the top rope and referee Emil Poilve had to stop the bout with McManus in agony. The show ended that week with Alan Dennison taking on Tally Ho Kaye in a lively match. Dennison was the winner when Kaye was counted out in the fifth round when he was thrown out of the ring and failed to return in time.

The wrestling seen on World of Sport on the 11th came from Aylesbury and saw something of a novelty with Mick McManus joining Kent Walton as co-commentator. The opener saw a TV debut for Mick Mason against fellow youngster Steve Kelly. Mason was the son of one of the Dale Martin ring crew and by the end of the month had disappeared from the game without trace. Kelly won the match when he pinned Mason in the third round.

Mike Marino took on Butcher Bond in the main event. Bond opened the scoring in the fourth round when a neck lift saw Marino submit. Marino came back strongly in the fifth and won the match when Bond was outside of the ring arguing and was counted out by referee Max Ward.

Another heavyweight match closed the show with Johnny Czeslaw getting the only fall needed to beat Romany Riley in the fourth round.

The second half of the show from Aylesbury was shown on World of Sport the following Saturday. The first match was between Brian Maxine and Gary Wensor with Maxine entering the ring wearing a crown and robe and underneath the usual garish pink and yellow half leotard. Straightaway Maxine went on the attack ending with him getting a public warning from referee Max Ward in the first round. Once again Mick McManus was on co-commentary and he told viewers that

Maxine was far too experienced for the boy Wensor. McManus was proved right when Maxine forced Wensor to instantly submit from a knee hold in round two for the winner.

The main event was the long awaited match between Tony St.Clair and Johnny Kincaid. Kincaid was in command in the early stages of the bout helped by a bit of rulebreaking. Kincaid got a public warning from Max Ward in round two when he attacked St.Clair whilst he was on the canvas. Mick McManus was impressed by both wrestlers and saying they were moving around like welterweights. It was Kincaid who got the first score in the third round when St.Clair landed heavily from a back drop. Kincaid applied a Boston crab and St.Clair had no choice but to submit from it. Kincaid got his second public warning in round four after refusing to break a hold with McManus telling us that Kincaid was stupid taking a risk of being disqualified. St.Clair finally got the equaliser in the fifth round when he pinned Kincaid with a cross press following a hip toss. St.Clair quickly followed up with the winning fall in round six with a flying tackle flooring Kincaid and a cross press was enough for the winner. This was a tremendous contest between two excellent wrestlers.

After all the heat of the main event the final match featured a change of styles and some comedy as Catweazle who had recently been named 'Britain's best dressed wrestler' took on Sid Cooper. Mick McManus told viewers that Cooper had two loves of his life , wrestling and Leeds United and if you wanted to get on his bad side then say something nasty about Leeds. It didn't take long for Cooper to start the rough stuff and he got two public warnings in the second round as Catweazle's antics left him looking the fool. Cooper once again found himself being disqualified as he punched Catweazle straight in the stomach right in front of Max Ward in the third round.

The wrestling seen on World of Sport on the 25th was a rare Relwyskow & Green presentation in front of the cameras. The show recorded at the Clifton Hall in Rotherham had the usual three bouts shown but some new and returning faces on it to add to the interest.

The opener saw Mike Bennett who was making a welcome return to the small screen and the former TV Trophy winner

160

had a tough match against Vic Faulkner. It was Faulkner who won when he pinned Bennett for the only fall needed in round four.

The next match shown was a heavyweight contest between Gil Singh and TV debutant The North Man. The North Man was also billed as The Viking and hailed from Merseyside and had wrestled for quite a while overseas and on the independent scene. The bout quickly got out of hand and descended into a brawl as early as round two and referee Ken Lazenby was dishing out public warnings without any effect. The match was totally out of control in the third round and Lazenby decided to call a halt and disqualify both wrestlers.

The last bout of the week was a tag match with unfortunately Pete Roberts unable to appear so Mick McMichael was drafted in to partner Kung Fu. Their opponents were the much heavier duo of Rex Strong and Ray Thunder who were not known for their wrestling finesse. It was Thunder who got the first score when he made McMichael submit from a backbreaker in the seventh minute. The match had to be paused after ten minutes when Ken Lazenby was hurt and couldn't continue to officiate. Luckily Count Bartelli who was on the other half of the show had his referee's licence and was called from the dressing room to take over the officiating. Once the action restarted Kung Fu was able to get an equalising fall when he pinned Rex Strong in the twelfth minute. Strong rather overdid his protests about the fall and actually punched referee Bartelli who instantly disqualified him. Therefore the winners were Kung Fu and Mick McMichael maybe a shade fortunately but less fortunate was Rex Strong who faced a hefty fine and a lengthy ban for his apalling behaviour.

Around the rings -

Although Max Crabtree had taken over the booking of Dale Martin's matches most of February still had the remnants of Mike Marino's bills on offer and it wasn't until March that things would noticeably change. Big Daddy was wrestling for Dale Martin for the first week of the new month but he was still being billed and used as a wrestler unlike for Best Wryton where he was the 'Mams and Dads favourite' superhero. Daddy was at Rickmansworth on the 2nd where he had another wrestling match with John Elijah with the deciding fall in the fifth round. Wayne Bridges had a heated encounter with Johnny Kincaid on the same bill with Kincaid refusing to lock up with Bridges. Everytime Bridges attempted to put a hold on him Kincaid would go for the ropes and escape. Eventually Kincaid left the ring and was counted out in the fourth round for a facile victory for Bridges.

The best match of the night saw Kung Fu and Mark Rocco once again lock horns to batter each other for the six rounds the contest lasted. Kung Fu got the first fall in round three before Rocco quickly equalised in the fourth. Rocco got the winning fall in round six but carried on attacking Kung Fu and ended up being disqualified. The final match of the night saw Steve Logan beat the overmatched Jim Martell by two straight submissions in four rounds.

The Caribbean Sunshine Boys were still raising hell on every tag match they were booked in with more and more involvement from fans at ringside. On the 7th they were at Hemel Hempstead and went down by two falls to one to Mike Marino and Lee Bronson but Kincaid and Bond's days as a team were coming to an end. The problems were beginning to mount up for them as the back office staff were facing more and more complaints from venue's about their behaviour and the subsequent crowd disturbances.

Al Miquet got another chance at Johnny Saint's World Lightweight Title on the 9th at Leeds after his chance was thwarted by injury in his attempt in January. Saint retained with a two falls to one win with the decider coming in the sixth round. Also on the show was a six man tag with the trio of Mick McMichael, Jeff Kaye and Tony Borg beating the team of John Naylor, Bobby Ryan and Mike Jordan in the thirty second minute.

Mark Rocco and Kung Fu were back in opposing corners at Chester the next night with this time Rocco's British Heavy/Middleweight Title at stake. Rocco retained the belt when the match was stopped in round seven when Kung Fu was unable to continue through injury. The other featured match on that bill saw The Royals defeat Detroit Donovan and Ron Allcard by two straight falls in less than ten minutes of action.

The Caribbean Sunshine Boys made their only appearance outside of the Dale Martin area on the 18th at Hanley. Johnny Kincaid and Butcher Bond were just as unpopular there as they were everywhere down south and it didn't help that their opponents were crowd favourites Tony St.Clair and Mick McMichael. Kincaid and Bond thought that they had got a winning submission in the eighth minute but it was ruled out for illegal interference leaving St.Clair and McMichael to get a winning fall a minute later.

A new face from South Africa that of Bull Schmidt appeared in the middle of the month. One of Schmidt's initial matches was against Big Daddy at Banbury on the 15th and it wasn't a good experience for Schmidt as he was knocked out in the fourth round following a double elbow drop.

Big Daddy got his hands on The Caribbean Sunshine Boys at Bedworth on the 17th when he partnered Colin Joynson against them. After ten minutes of action both inside and outside of the ring Daddy and Joynson got the deciding fall with a big splash from Daddy sealing the win.

Wrestling returned to Belle Vue on the 18th after the Christmas and New Year's break with another fine show. The main event was a tag with Giant Haystacks and King Kong Kirk taking on Gil Singh and Ray Steele. Singh and Steele found the weight disadvantage too much to overcome and after a splash from Haystacks the match was stopped in the eleventh minute and a win for him and Kirk. Kung Fu used his speed and martial arts moves to outfox the heavier Steve Logan and beat him by two falls to one in the fourth round. Marty Jones went back over old ground when he defeated Colin Joynson with a winning fall in the sixth round. Johnny Saint pinned Alan Dennison for a winning fall in round five in their match whilst Dynamite Kid easily defeated Tally Ho Kaye winning in by two straight falls in the fourth round.

Giant Haystacks and King Kong Kirk had much tougher opponents at Digbeth on the 23rd when they faced up to Big Daddy and Tony St.Clair in the main event. The first score was a submission for Haystacks and Kirk in the sixth minute before a quick equaliser for Daddy and St.Clair. Haystacks did the now usual disappearing act leaving the ring in the ninth minute leaving his partner Kirk to take a big splash from Daddy on the way to the winning fall for Daddy and St.Clair.

The same night at Leeds there was a contender's tournament for the winner to challenge Tony St.Clair for the British Heavyweight Title there. The first round heats saw Count Bartelli beat Hillbilly Hell-on, The Viking beat Pete Curry, Pat Roach knocked out Rex Strong and Ray Steele beat Beau Jack. Roach won the first semi final when he forced a submission from Bartelli in the first round. Steele won the second semi final when The Viking was disqualified in round three. The final saw action from the first bell with Steele getting the first fall in the opening round before Roach hit back with falls in the second and third to guarantee his title match against Tony St.Clair.

The end for The Caribbean Sunshine Boys happened on the 27th when they finally imploded amongst more ugly scenes after a bout at Catford. They had lost their match against Mike Marino and Lee Bronson and once again it kicked off outside of the ring. The incident made the national newspapers and under the headline of 'Tag duo gave me the old one two' The Sun reported that burly ex-policeman Vic Bowen really copped it when he told The Caribbean Sunshine Boys what he thought of their tag wrestling performance. He finished up in hospital after a ringside punch up with the tag men Dave 'Butcher' Bond and Johnny Kincaid.

Other reports said that Bond had kicked Bowen under the chin which was followed up by a punch from Kincaid. Bowen was taken to hospital where he had to have seven stitches inserted in his wound. Bowen's wife was quoted as saying they intended to sue them both for assualt and it had put her off going to wrestling for life. Mike Judd who was MC there that night said he gathered that the fan was holding onto Bond's legs and the wrestler simply retaliated.

That was it for Max Crabtree , Johnny Kincaid was sacked on the spot although Butcher Bond did keep his job that was the end of The Caribbean Sunshine Boys. Whilst they were only a tag team for six months or so their impact is still remembered by those lucky enough to have seen them wrestle.

Not only was Crabtree having to deal with the fall out over the Sunshine Boys but he was also getting ready for the relaunch of Dale Martin Promotions under his control. The relaunch would happen at The Royal Albert Hall on 15th March and see the Big Daddy 'We shall not be moved' era begin. Before he could concentrate on that Max Crabtree had to scrap the bill Mike Marino had proposed which summed up his spell in charge. Marino had intended an all heavyweight card including a tag match with Wayne Bridges partnering Prince Kumali against Bronco Wells and Beer Barrel Brannigan. Brannigan was from Merseyside and had just moved over from the independent circuit and his calling would be as an overweight cannon fodder in Big Daddy's matches and not top of the bill at the Albert Hall. As with most of Marino's bills some matches would be excellent such as booking himself against King Kong Kirk on the Albert Hall show whilst some would be dreadful and you have to wonder the thinking behind putting Dusty Miller v Rob Cody on a show there with very few fans having a clue who they were.

Max Crabtree went all in with the 15th March show teaming up Big Daddy with Dynamite Kid against Giant Haystacks and King Kong Kirk in the main event. Haystacks hadn't been seen on Dale Martin shows for the best part of a year and Dynamite had been seen even less. Mike Marino would make a rare defence of his British Mid/Heavyweight Title against Terry Rudge and the beginning of Steve Grey's well deserved push to the higher echelons of the bill would start with a match against Jim Breaks.

March -

The first wrestling of the month on World of Sport was on the 4th and was the second half of the show recorded at Rotherham. The opening bout that week was an interesting clash of old school in Bert Royal and new in Marty Jones. Jones had about a stone in weight advantage but was unable to defeat Royal and the match ended in a draw. Royal opened the scoring with the first fall in round four before Jones equalised in the fifth round. The second match was a rather dull heavyweight contest in which Barry Douglas pinned Ray Steele in round three for the only fall needed for the win.

The final match that week should have been John Kowalski against Bronco Wells but the car bringing the pair up from Hampshire went missing. A replacement bout was quickly set up between Count Bartelli and Ivan Penzecoff. Bartelli won the match in the fourth round when a fearsome reverse chop sent Penzecoff flying out of the ring and he was unable to return inside the ropes before referee Ken Lazenby had completed his count of ten.

A Dale Martin show was seen on World of Sport on the 11th with the second half of the Hemel Hempstead show filmed in January shown. First match of the week was a heavyweight contest with the now departed Johnny Kincaid taking on Sandy Scott. The bout got off to a flyer with Scott attacking Kincaid right from the first bell and throwing him out of the ring. As soon as Kincaid got back inside the ropes then Scott kicked him back out over the top rope as Kent Walton wondered what was going on. Kincaid was soon on top with the help of punches that referee Max Ward failed to spot. Scott nearly got the only fall needed when Ward distracted Kincaid which was only foiled by a rope break. Kincaid was furious by this and gave Ward a mouthful of dissent as well as complaining to Walton at his ringside table. Kincaid got a public warning in the second round for dropping Scott onto the top rope from a body slam. A weakened Scott was then easy meat for Kincaid to get the winning fall from. A side suplex from Kincaid led to a cross press in the final seconds of round two for the one fall needed. It would be many years before we got to see Johnny Kincaid on the small screen again.

The second match was a catchweight contest with the much heavier Colin Joynson who had just returned from a successful tour of Germany meeting Kung Fu. After a couple of rounds of feeling each other out Kung Fu dished out a bodyslam to Joynson and followed up with a reverse double knee hold to pin him for the first fall. Joynson took exception to this and as Kung Fu tried to shake his hand Joynson bodychecked him instead. Max Ward gave him a public warning and as soon as the bell rang for the fourth round Joynson continued to try and rough up his lighter opponent. Kung Fu retaliated and got a public warning from Ward after attacking Joynson who was trapped between the ropes. Joynson finally got his equaliser after weakening Kung Fu with a combination of postings and backbreakers and when he trapped him in a Boston Crab Kung Fu had to submit. The match ended in the final round of six when Joynson was disqualified. He draped Kung Fu upside down in the corner and proceeded to kick him in the stomach. Max Ward was having none of that kind of behaviour and sent him back to the dressing room in disgrace. This was another excellent match between two very underrated wrestlers who always entertained.

The last match was completely opposite and was for grapple fans who liked technical wrestling from wrestlers with a smile on their faces. Johnny Saint faced Vic Faulkner in a one fall match but the match ended in round three without a score happening. In quite a scrappy ending Saint clearly missed an attempted dropkick on Faulkner but Faulkner still took the bump and went outside of the ring between the ropes. In doing so Faulkner made sure to trap his foot between the bottom two ropes and the match ended with Faulkner unable to continue. Naturally a No Contest was the decision.

Another Dale Martin show this time from Walthamstow was seen on World of Sport on the 18th with not the most impressive line up of bouts. The opening match was a heavyweight contest when Bronco Wells made the most of a 6st. weight advantage to defeat Ed Wensor. Wells got the winner in round three when he forced Wensor to submit from a single leg Boston Crab.

Another heavyweight contest was on next between Wayne Bridges and Lee Bronson. The score was a fall apiece in round five when Bronson hurt his back on the ringpost and was unable to continue. Bridges refused to accept the win so a No Contest was recorded.

The final match of the week saw Steve Grey continue his climb up the lightweight rankings when he beat Zoltan Boscik. Boscik started to rough Grey up from the start and got a public warning in the first round. Boscik got the first score in round three when he made Grey submit from his 'three-in-one' special before another public warning came his way in round four as he tried for a winner. Grey rallied in the fifth round and got an equalising fall before quickly following up with a winner in the next round for an impressive win.

A cracking show from Nottingham was seen on World of Sport on the next week with Dynamite Kid challenging for the European Welterweight Title as the highlight. Dynamite's opponent was the veteran French champion Jean Corne who had held the belt for quite a while. The match was fought over the championship duration of fifteen rounds and it was the champion Corne who got the first fall in the fifth round. Dynamite finally got an equalising fall in round eighth when he pinned Corne to even the match up. The winner came in the tenth and was a carbon copy of the way Dynamite beat Breaks to win the British Welterweight Title. Dynamite put Corne into a surfboard and forced him to submit and thus become the new European Welterweight Champion. An impressive achievement by the youngster but things were happening behind the scenes that would see the championship become vacant and the champion depart for Canada.

The opening contest was a hard fought catchweight contest with Marty Jones pinning King Ben in the opening minute of the fifth round for a two falls to one win. The other match was perhaps a tad farcical as Big Daddy took on King Kong Kirk. Kirk spent most of the time arguing rather than wrestling and actually left the ring at one stage to take advice from Giant Haystacks who was at ringside. Whatever Haystacks told Kirk it was a waste of time as Daddy got the winning fall in round two. Daddy pinned Kirk afer delivering a big splash on his rival.

Easter Monday fell on 27th March so grapple fans had a bonus with three matches shown on the holiday edition of World of Sport. The coverage came from Reading and the first time the TV cameras had filmed wrestling at The Hexagon. The opening contest saw Johnny Kwango defeat Steve Logan. Kwango had just equalised Logan's opening third round fall in round five when Logan lost his cool and attacked Kwango.

Referee Peter Szakacs had no hesitation in disqualifying the 'Iron man' and awarding the victory to Kwango.

Second match was for those who enjoy a wrestling match with Johnny Saint taking on Mick McMichael in a catchweight contest. Saint got the first fall in the third round before McMichael equalised in round five. Saint defied the weight disadvantage when he pinned his opponent in the sixth round to win the match. Finally Bruiser Muir rather overpowered Johnny Wilson by foul means as well as fair and after sufficient weakeners forced Wilson to submit in the third round from a reverse bear hug hold for the only score needed.

Around the halls -

Max Crabtree had a busy start to the month with rebooking shows following the demise of The Caribbean Sunshine Boys as well as changing some of the Mike Marino booked bills that were awful.

Johnny Saint successfully defended the World Lightweight Title at Digbeth on the 2nd when he defeated Jim Breaks. Saint got the deciding fall in round eight to once again thwart Breaks' chances of adding the World title to his European one.

The same night at Sheffield there was a contenders tournament with the winner getting a title match against Saint on their next show there. The first round heats saw wins for Jackie Robinson against John Naylor, Mike Bennett who defeated Steve Best, Tony Borg who beat Pete Evans and Mike Jordan against Dave Ramsden. Bennett beat Jordan in one semi final and Borg defeated Robinson in the other. The final ended prematurely when Borg and Bennett were counted out in the first round so the tournament had to be decided by a toss of a coin which Borg won.

There was another main event tag match for the team of Giant Haystacks and King Kong Kirk at Belle Vue on the 4th but this time they faced the challenge of Big Daddy and Tony St.Clair. Predictably there was very little actual wrestling in the match and plenty of rulebreaking which saw both Daddy and Haystacks disqualified in the seventh minute. This left St.Clair to take on Kirk alone and it was St.Clair who got the winner when he pinned Kirk in the twelfth minute.

Kung Fu once more came up short when he had another shot at Mark Rocco's British Heavy/Middleweight Title. Kung Fu took the first fall in the fifth round before Rocco's relentless pressure took its toll and the referee called a halt in round six with Kung Fu unable to continue.

The other matches on the Belle Vue card saw John Naylor beat Ray Thunder who was disqualified in the third round. Mike Jordan defeated Jeff Kaye by two falls to one in the sixth round and Honey Boy Zimba beat Barry Douglas who was counted out in round five.

There was another Big Daddy and Tony St.Clair v Giant Haystacks and King Kong Kirk tag match on the 6th at Bradford. This time there was drama before the start when Haystacks landed a splash on St.Clair's legs leaving him unable to compete in the match. Neither was Haystacks able to wrestle in the match though as he was disqualified for this evil act leaving it as a Daddy v Kirk solo match which Daddy won when he pinned Kirk via a big splash in two minutes. Fans there who were viewers of World of Sport would see the exact same thing happening again in the match screened on FA Cup Final day.

Max Crabtree's first show at The Royal Albert Hall on the 15th was not only a success in the ring with six top notch matches but a success at the box office too with a full house in attendance. The main event tag of Big Daddy and Dynamite Kid against Giant Haystacks and King Kong Kirk was won by Daddy and Dynamite when a big splash flattened Kirk for the winning fall in the tenth minute. Haystacks had earlier got the first score when he forced Dynamite to submit from a suspended neck lift before Daddy equalised in the eighth minute. The most surprising thing about the match was seeing Dynamite Kid give the huge Kirk a torrid time with his speed and skillful moves. This saw the take off for the Big Daddy era of British wrestling and some things would never be the same again.

The rest of the show at the Albert Hall saw some great action as well as plenty of blood. Mike Marino made a successful defence of his British Mid/Heavyweight Title when the challenger Terry Rudge was forced to retire in the eighth round. Rudge had given Marino far more trouble at times than the champion could handle but with blood streaming from a suspected broken nose Rudge was forced to quit. The now No.1 contender for the British Heavyweight Title Pat Roach was given a brisk workout by Colin Joynson in their bout but in the end Roach's class showed and Joynson was counted out in the fourth round. One of the contenders for the now vacant British Lightweight Title Steve Grey recorded a fine win when he defeated former champion Jim Breaks. After ten years on the circuit Grey had become something of an overnight sensation and by dint of his two falls to one win over Breaks he became favourite to be the new lightweight title holder. Wayne Bridges recorded an easy victory over the South African Bull Schmidt with a two straight falls win in the fourth round. Unfortunately Schmidt was to suffer a heart attack during a match later in the month and had to return home prematurely. Once again Catweazle was in the final contest taking on Sandy Scott. A lively match ended early in round three when Scott was injured but Catweazle refused to accept the win so a No Contest was called.

There was more drama at Sheffield on the 16th with wrestlers arriving late or in some cases not at all so another show there had to be rebooked at short notice. Luckily the main event took place as scheduled with Johnny Saint defending the World Lightweight Title against Tony Borg. Saint notched up another successful defence by way of a two falls to one win in the sixth round.

The Belle Vue show on the 18th felt a little bit below par compared to the last few bills there with a tag match involving The Royals in the top of the bill slot. The Royal's opponents were Butcher Bond and Detroit Donovan and once again Bert and Vic were victorious. Bond was disqualified in the fifteenth minute leaving Donovan to wrestle alone and he was pinned a couple of minutes later.

The imposing Zebra Kid continued his run of victories when Lucky Gordon was the latest victim of his 'Atomic Drop' finisher. Gordon was counted out in the third round and the

171

Zebra needed to be tested against some of the heavyweights at the top of the division. Mike Marino's match with The Viking resembled more of a brawl than a wrestling contest and it ended with both of them disqualified in the fifth round. The other two matches on the Belle Vue bill saw Jim Breaks beat Mick McMichael via a 'Breaks' special' in round six and Bobby Ryan pinned Johnny England in the fifth round for the winning fall.

Giant Haystacks was up to his old tricks at Hanley on the same night in the main event. Haystacks once again teamed up with King Kong Kirk to take on an impressive duo of Pat Roach and Gwyn Davies. As was now a regular event Haystacks was disqualified before the first bell to leave Kirk wrestling alone and being pinned after a couple of minutes of the contest.

Giant Haystacks for a change actually had to wrestle the next evening at Cleethorpes. This time he would compete against two opponents in a handicap tag match with Honey Boy Zimba and Alan Dennison being the lucky duo. The match ended in the ninth minute when Zimba was flattened by a splash and wouldn't have beaten a count of ten minutes let alone ten seconds. Big Daddy was also in action there when he took on King Kong Kirk in an all-in rules match with only a knockout to win. Daddy won but not via a clean knockout as the fans in attendance wanted but when Kirk was counted out after leaving the ring in the eighth minute.

The Big Daddy roadshow rocked up at Croydon on the 21st in front of another packed crowd as Daddy's 'TV All-stars' took on a team captained by Mark Rocco. In the singles matches Kung Fu beat Sid Cooper who was counted out in the fourth round. Bert Royal defeated Mark Rocco with a winning fall in round five. Bobby Barnes was disqualified in his match with Vic Faulkner in the fifth round. Wayne Bridges beat Terry Rudge who was unable to continue in the third round. The final singles match saw Big Daddy knockout The Mask with a double elbow drop in the first round which left the TV All-stars with a five-nil lead going into the six man tag. Daddy, Royal and Kung Fu rounded off a whitewash with a winning fall coming in the tenth minute against Rocco, Cooper and the

Mask. Just for his pains the Mask was unmasked as Barry Douglas.

North London fans were not to be denied as the Big Daddy roadshow rolled into town at the Picketts Lock Sports Centre on the Friday of that week when Daddy's 'TV All-stars' faced a far greater threat from a team captained by Giant Haystacks. The five singles matches saw Vic Faulkner beat Mark Rocco in the fourth round. Brother Bert Royal also won when he pinned Barry Douglas in round three. Captain Big Daddy defeated King Kong Kirk who was disqualified in the second round. In a true David v Goliath battle Kung Fu who was something like 30st lighter than his opponent Giant Haystacks came out on top when Haystacks was disqualified in round two. Steve Grey continued the rout when he defeated Sid Cooper by three straight falls after Cooper continually demanded another chance. The TV All-stars completed a six-nil win when Daddy and Grey beat Kirk and Cooper in the seventh minute.

Big Daddy continued his tour of London when on the Saturday night he was part of a bill at The Seymour Hall in central London. It had been well over a year since Dale Martin had promoted there but they decided to put on an Easter Spectacular on 25th March. Daddy wouldn't be in a tag match but as part of a four man tournament with the other three participants being Giant Haystacks, King Kong Kirk and Butcher Bond. The semi finals conveniently kept Daddy and Haystacks apart and in the first Bond beat Haystacks who was disqualified in round two. Haystacks kept on attacking Bond after pinning him for the only fall needed and it was a severely weakened Bond who progressed to the final. Daddy beat Kirk in the other semi final when the former miner was counted out in the second round. The final was a non event with the referee stopping the contest in the opening minute with Butcher Bond clearly unable to wrestle so the tournament winner was Big Daddy.

There were four other matches on the Seymour Hall bill with none of them whetting the appetite that much. Leon Fortuna beat Brian Maxine who was disqualified after refusing to break what would have been a winning submission in the fifth round. Steve Grey wrestled a six round fast paced draw with Clive Myers. Steve Logan beat Tim Fitzmaurice who failed to beat the count in the fourth round whilst Johnny Kwango's match with Catweazle was stopped in round five when Catweazle was injured. Kwango refused the decision so it ended in a No Contest. This was the final show from Dale Martin at the venue but the independent promoters were back there on 10th April for a knock out tournament. Eight international heavyweights would participate for the right to challenge Bruno Sammartino for his WWF title, which was of course nonsense. The contestants would be Steve Veidor, Tibor Szakacs, Sucha Singh, Majid Ackra, L'Ange Blanc, Giant Klondyke, Crusher Mason and The Outlaw.

Easter Sunday saw a holiday show at The Tower Circus in Blackpool with Giant Haystacks in the main event. Haystacks took on Tony St.Clair and he was disqualified at the end of the third round for attacking his opponent after St.Clair had got an equalising fall. Johnny Saint defeated Tally Ho Kaye with the deciding fall coming in round five. Colin Joynson and Marty Jones had another of their hard fought battles with this time Joynson coming out on top by two falls to one in the sixth round. Ray Steele notched up a creditable win when he beat King Kong Kirk by two falls to one with the winner in round five.

Bert Royal won the prestigious Preston Silver Trophy on the 31st at the Lancashire venue. Royal defeated Steve Logan by two falls to one in round five to add another honour to those he already held. Count Bartelli defeated the Zebra Kid in round three when the masked man was disqualified. Another heavyweight who was disqualified was The Viking who was sent packing in round four of his match with Ray Steele.

The rest of the Preston show comprised a knockout tournament with Tally Ho Kaye beating King Ben in one semi final and Vic Faulkner defeated Bobby Ryan in the other. Faulkner beat Kaye by disqualification in the third round to win the tournament to complete a successful evening for The Royals.

The effect of the down turn of business for Dale Martin under Mike Marino was illustrated in the East Kent Times and Mail which covered the Thanet area. They reported that the

174

promoters for the first time in many years would not be putting on wrestling at the Margate Winter Gardens for the next two months and hadn't revealed their plans for the summer either. In the end Thanet Council's leisure committee agreed to underwrite the summer season of wrestling at The Oval in Cliftonville. Dale Martin were unwilling to continue with the shows there unless they were guaranteed £300 for each show. The 1977 summer season of wrestling at The Oval was a washout due to bad weather and Dale Martin now received the financial guarantee they wanted to carry on for 1978. The Entertainments Manager told the newspaper that there had been a change in Dale Martin's southern area booking agents and that the shows for the summer were likely to be more attractive and draw larger crowds.

April -

World of Sport on the 1st featured the second half of the show from Leicester and the start of the tournament to crown the new British Lightweight Champion. Dynamite Kid had relinquished the lightweight belt after winning the welterweight version and a four man tournament was set up. The first semi final featured Jim Breaks taking on the man who had recently defeated him at The Royal Albert Hall, Steve Grey. Breaks opened the scoring in the third round when once more the 'Breaks' special' forced a submission from an opponent. Grey wasn't behind for long and equalised with a fall in round four. Yet again Breaks' temper let him down and in round five he punched Grey right in front of referee Brian Crabtree who disqualified him on the spot.

The second semi final saw Bobby Ryan meet John Naylor for the right to face Grey in the final. Ryan got the first fall in the fourth round before Naylor equalised in the fifth and neither was able to get a winner in the final round. This was obviously a problem with the final due to be taped on April 5th at Blackburn to be shown on World of Sport the following Saturday. It was announced that a rematch would be held the same evening ,1st April, at Hanley.

175

A great week's wrestling was finished off by a title match with Mark Rocco defending the British Heavy/Middleweight Title against the former champion Bert Royal. Rocco proved once and for all that he was a league above Royal who was unable to withstand the ferocity of Rocco's attacks. Rocco got the first submission in the third round after severely weakening Royal's arm. Royal did bravely battle back to get an equaliser in round four but that was his swansong. The match was stopped in the interval between round's four and five by referee Dave Reese with Royal's arm too badly injured to allow him to continue.

The aforementioned rematch between Bobby Ryan and John Naylor at Hanley for the right to fight Steve Grey for the vacant lightweight title failed to happen but it was Ryan who got the nod for the title match.

The contest for the vacant British Lightweight Title was part of an entertaining programme from Blackburn and shown on World of Sport the following Saturday. The opening bout saw the No.1 heavyweight contender Pat Roach mark time waiting for his title opportunity by meeting Ray Steele. Steele pinned Roach for the first fall in round three but that only served to anger him and in the end Steele was unable to continue in the fifth round with an injured knee. This win ensured Roach got his title match against Tony St.Clair on a forthcoming TV bill to be recorded at Nottingham later in the month.

Steve Grey finally got his hands on a championship belt when he defeated Bobby Ryan to win the British Lightweight Title vacated by Dynamite Kid. Grey was one of the most improved wrestlers of the past year and was rewarded with this push to the top end of the card. Ryan actually got the first fall in the round two before Grey equalised in the fifth round. Grey quickly followed up with the deciding fall in the sixth to win a richly reserved British Lightweight Title.

The final match was something of a farce with a handicap match seeing Giant Haystacks take on both Sandy Scott and Lucky Gordon at the same time. Scott was first to be flattened in the third minute by a splash following a body slam and Gordon followed the same way a minute later.

It was back to Blackburn for the second half of the show recorded there on World of Sport on the 15th. This week's wrestling was a three-a-side team match with a six man tag finale. Big Daddy captained one team with Kung Fu and Kid Chocolate against a trio captained by Mick McManus who had Tony Walsh and Tally Ho Kaye on his team. All three singles matches were one fall etc. and in the first Mick McManus overcame Kung Fu with a winning fall in the third round. McManus' team made it two-nil when Tally Ho Kaye forced Kid Chocolate to submit from a single leg Boston Crab in round four. Big Daddy finally got a win on the board for his team when he pinned Tony Walsh in the first round following the usual big splash.

The concluding six man tag saw McManus open the scoring when he repeated the single leg Boston Crab on Chocolate and made him submit in the fourth minute. Daddy equalised when he knocked out Walsh following a double elbow drop in the fifth minute and Kung Fu wrapped up the win when he pinned Tally Ho Kaye in the seventh minute. So the team match ended up in a two-two draw and it made another entertaining week's grappling on the small screen.

The wrestling on World of Sport on the 22th came from Nottingham and despite Kent Walton saying the Tony St.Clair v Pat Roach bout would be for St.Clair's British Heavyweight Title it was actually a non title match. This was lucky for St.Clair as he lost a bruising encounter to a fired up Roach when he was unable to continue in the fifth round. St.Clair was in front from a fall in the third round when Roach hoisted him aloft and finished him off with the 'Brumagen bump'. This was where Roach simply dropped his opponent face first onto the canvas and very few could continue after it.

Once again Mick McManus was co-commentator for the show and in the opening match he saw Johnny Saint give Alan Dennison a 3st. weight advantage and still pin him in the third round for the winner. The final match saw Dynamite Kid take on veteran Ken Joyce who was making something of a comeback. Joyce had only been seen in recent times on his own Devereux Promotion's shows and had been persuaded to make a full time return to the Joint Promotion's roster. The wily

Joyce gave Dynamite many problems in the ring to solve during the contest but in the end Dynamite got the deciding fall in the fifth round of an intriguing battle.

The second half of the Nottingham show was seen the following week on World of Sport with the regular three bouts broadcast. The opening match was announced as being a final eliminator for the World Mid/Heavyweight Title held by Mike Marino and the title match would be seen in June. Both Rudge and Joynson were well known for their no nonsense wrestling and it showed during an extremely competitive contest. Rudge went ahead with a fall in the fourth before a quick equaliser for Joynson came in the fifth. With only one round left to find a winner both wrestlers went all out for the win but unfortunately in doing so both of them went flying out of the ring. Neither of them was able to get back in time to beat the count of ten from referee Dave Reese. It was an inconclusive ending and the title match contender was left to be decided. In the end there was no title match with Mike Marino for either of them but Colin Joynson did in time get a televised World Mid/Heavyweight Title contest when he unsuccessfully challenged Marty Jones in 1988.

Lee Bronson faced the unenviable task in the second match shown when he faced a man who weighed twice his body weight in Giant Haystacks. Bronson managed to topple Haystacks with a flying tackle and cover him with a cross press in round two for the first fall. That was as good as it got for him, another attempt at a flying tackle in the third round found Haystacks waiting for him. Haystacks slammed Bronson to the mat and flattened him with a splash that had those in attendance wincing and referee Gordon Smith stopped the match immediately.

The final contest that week saw The Royals gain a new honour when they captured the Silver Challenge Trophy. An enjoyable tag match saw them defeat the team of Mark Rocco and Tally Ho Kaye with the winning fall coming in the sixteenth minute when Vic Faulkner pinned Kaye.

Around the halls -

April started with the news that the now unmasked Kendo Nagasaki was going to make his comeback and would do so in a match to be recorded for TV at Croydon on 18th April. Many thought they would never see him wrestle again after the ceremonial unmasking back in December but yet again Nagasaki confounded everyone. Not only would Nagasaki's return would be on the Croydon show but also Big Daddy and Giant Haystacks would meet in a tag match to be shown on the FA Cup Final day World of Sport in May. Not surprisingly tickets sold out in an instant and there were many disappointed fans on the 18th who turned up without a ticket and were unable to buy one on the door. During the show Kent Walton remarked that over five hundred fans had been turned away which shows something of the demand for tickets that night.

Inside the ring April opened with an impressive bill at Belle Vue on the 1st with Big Daddy and Giant Haystacks there. Daddy was part of a two versus three tag match when he partnered Kung Fu against Mark Rocco, Tony Walsh and Tally Ho Kaye. Despite the advantage of the extra man it made no difference and it ended in the seventh minute with Walsh knocked out by a double elbow drop.

Haystacks was part of a heavyweight knockout tournament alongside Zebra Kid, Bronco Wells and Beau Jack. Zebra Kid beat Wells in the first semi final making him submit in round three for the winner. Haystacks was in one of his uncontrollable moods and found himself disqualified in the second round of his match with Beau Jack. The final was something of a non event with Zebra Kid winning in the opening minute when he knocked out the weakened Jack with an Atomic Drop.

After his many unsuccessful attempts at Mark Rocco's title in the heavy/middleweight division Bert Royal moved up in weight on the Belle Vue card for a non title match with champion Marty Jones. Royal fared no better against Jones The match was stopped in the sixth round when Royal was injured and unable to continue. The only consolation was that Jones refused to accept the win and a No Contest was called instead.

The other match that night saw Johnny Czeslaw defeat Sandy Scott by two falls to one in round six.

The giant Guyanese Prince Kumali made a comeback to the ring on the same night when he took on Wayne Bridges at Maidstone. Kumali had been missing for over a year and made a winning return when he defeated Bridges with the decider coming in the fifth round. Mike Marino should have faced Bull Schmidt on the Maidstone card but Schmidt had been forced to return home by illness so Marino was forced to take on Beer Barrel Brannigan instead. Marino won without too much fuss in the fourth round.

The show at Croydon on the 4th featured a tag match with the winners advertised as meeting Big Daddy and Tony St.Clair at the same venue on the 18th for a televised match. It didn't take a genius to work out beforehand that it would be the team of Giant Haystacks and Bruiser Muir and not Mike Marino and Wayne Bridges who would be back there in a fortnight's time. The strange thing was that it was Marino and Bridges who won when Haystacks and Muir were disqualified in the ninth minute. In wrestling there is no logic and stipulations are there to be ignored so it was Haystacks and Muir who wrestled on the next show.

Another match on the Croydon show had the same stipulation advertised with the winner of the Clive Myers v Steve Grey bout meeting Jim Breaks on the 18th April show. This time it did work out as advertised with Grey defeating Myers by two falls to one in round six and he went on to wrestle Breaks as scheduled. The rest of the Croydon show on the 4th harked back to the dark winter days of the Mike Marino era with Zoltan Boscik beating Tony Skarlo who couldn't continue in the fourth round. Chris Bailey defeated Chris Riley who was unable to beat the count in round four whilst Johnny Kwango v Gary Wensor ended in a No Contest in the fourth round when Wensor was unable to continue.

One of the immediate benefits of Max Crabtree's takeover of Dale Martin was the amount of northern based wrestlers who were now coming to wrestle down south on a regular basis. The week commencing the 3rd was a good example with Giant Haystacks, Mark Rocco, The Royals, Kung Fu and notably

Dynamite Kid all being booked by Dale Martin for the week. On the other hand though when these wrestlers were not available for Dale Martin there was a distinct lack of headliners or top stars and Mick McManus was just about the best of them. Throughout 1978 there was a lopsided look to a lot of venue's bills, one week the card would be brilliant with four or five matches to savour and the next time it would be hard to find a main event on the programme.

The Royals were involved in single's matches at Brighton on the 5th with Bert Royal having another match with Mark Rocco in the main event. This time Royal managed a victory with a winning fall coming in round five but without the TV cameras in attendance or his title at stake Rocco didn't exactly go all out to win. Vic Faulkner had a crowd pleasing and humorous match with Catweazle which ended in round five when Catweazle couldn't continue.

The other matches at Brighton saw Brian Maxine defeat the Masked Outlaw who quickly left the ring in round five when Maxine unmasked him. A lot of ringsiders recognised him without the mask on as Phil Rowe and he was back in the dressing room before the referee completed the count of ten. Mike Marino beat Butcher Bond who was disqualified in the fifth round and Mal Sanders got the winning fall in the third round to defeat Chris Bailey.

Amazingly Big Daddy and Giant Haystacks met in a ladder match at Chester on the 7th with the question was there was a ladder strong enough to take the 30st. weight of Haystacks ? It was Daddy who climbed the ladder to grab the money after only a couple of minutes and it wasn't a match to satisfy the fans. The Zebra Kid chalked up another victim of his 'Atomic drop' finisher when he knocked out Marty Jones with it in the third round. Despite his impressive record as the masked man it was Sean Regan's outside commitments that stopped him from becoming the bigger attraction that he deserved to be.

The Zebra Kid was back in action on the 9th at Cleethorpes but his defeat by disqualification to Sandy Scott was overshadowed by the main event tag match. For once bitter enemies Mark Rocco and Marty Jones put their differences aside to team up to take on Dynamite Kid and Bert Royal.

181

Those lucky enough to be in attendance reported an excellent match which was won by Dynamite and Royal with a winning fall in the fourteenth minute.

There was another ladder match between Big Daddy and Giant Haystacks scheduled at Wolverhampton on the 11th but this time the ladder was not up to scratch. Early on the match had to be abandoned when Haystacks broke the ladder so after a bit of quick thinking a tag match was arranged instead. The match between Mike Marino and The Viking on the bill had yet to happen so Marino joined Daddy to take on Haystacks and The Viking in the replacement match. Again Haystacks had left the ring before the match ended which happened in the ninth minute when The Viking was pinned for the winning fall.

On an excellent show that night Dynamite Kid moved up to middleweight to challenge Mick McManus for his European Middleweight Title. As usual with his cherished title at stake McManus went up a gear and retained the belt when the match was stopped in round eight with Dynamite Kid unable to continue.

Dynamite Kid was fully recovered in time for his match with Jim Breaks at Belle Vue on the 15th. Dynamite was a tad fortunate to get the win that night. Breaks had forced him to submit from the 'Breaks' special' in round five for what should have been the winner. Breaks though refused to release his hold despite the referee instructing him to and instead of celebrating a win was disqualified. The other main event at Belle Vue saw Pat Roach continue his pursuit of Tony St.Clair and his British Heavyweight Title. Their rivalry was becoming very intense and that continued with this match. St.Clair went ahead with a fall in the third round but the match had to be stopped in the fourth. Both wrestlers were bleeding heavily from head wounds and any semblance of a wrestling match had long been forgotten.

A more traditional heavyweight match on the card saw Gwyn Davies defeat Colin Joynson by two falls to one in round five. Johnny Saint had his work cut out in his bout with Zoltan Boscik and he finally came out on top with a winning fall in the fifth round. The final match of the night saw Catweazle beat Sid Cooper by two straight falls in four rounds.

182

On the same night at Hanley Mark Rocco and Marty Jones decided to give their strange alliance another go against local favourites Count Bartelli and Bobby Ryan. In another heated and thrilling match it was Bartelli and Ryan who won with a deciding fall in the fifteenth minute to wild celebrations from the fans there that night.

Dynamite Kid got another chance at Mick McManus' European Middleweight Title at Edinburgh on the 21st. Unfortunately it ended the same way with Dynamite injured in the seventh round and McManus retaining his title. Shortly afterwards the news emerged that Dynamite Kid had given in his notice to Joint Promotions and would be departing for Canada at the end of the month.

There was another match between Pat Roach and Tony St.Clair at Hanley the next evening and another wild brawl ensued. The match had to be abandoned in round five with things totally out of control. Kung Fu defeated Brian Maxine on the same show when Maxine left the ring and was counted out. Maxine had got fed up being on the receiving end of Kung Fu's chops and mule kicks and decided he had had enough.

Pat Roach finally got a championship match against Tony St.Clair at Wolverhampton on the 25th. But Roach fell short in the match despite getting a first fall in the seventh round. St.Clair equalised in the tenth round and at the end of the championship time limit of twelve rounds it was one fall apiece. St.Clair retained the British Heavyweight Title and a frustrated Roach was left waiting for another championship opportunity. Another heavyweight match on the bill saw The Zebra Kid knockout John Elijah in the fifth round when the 'Atomic drop' gave Elijah no chance of beating the count.

Dynamite Kid had his final British match for the time being on the 26th when he beat Ivan Penzecoff at Banbury. He was scheduled for another couple of matches at the end of week tagging with Big Daddy but left early for Canada on 28th April. The man who replaced him in the tags was Sandy Scott who shortly left Britain himself to go to Canada and wrestle there. Scott didn't have the success that Dynamite Kid had in Calgary and was last heard of emptying dustbins there.

Dynamite Kid had been scouted by Bruce Hart on Hart's British visit the previous winter and with Hart suitably impressed he organised the contract for Dynamite to leave the UK to wrestle for Hart's father Stu's Stampede Promotion based in Calgary. Most of Dynamite's recollections in the book Pure Dynamite are incorrect about this time of his career. On arrival in Calgary and acclimatised to his surroundings Dynamite's first match for Stampede was on May 19th in a tag match where he partnered Bruce Hart against Norman Frederick Charles III and John Foley.

With Dynamite Kid departed his newly won European Welterweight Title was left vacant and the belt went back to the continent. The British Welterweight Title was also stripped from him with Dynamite unable to fulfil his title defence obligations but it would take over a year to crown a new champion.

There was another of night of Relwyskow & Green's strange bills at Sheffield on the 27th with a strong contingent from the south as well as wrestlers not seen anywhere else for a while. Locally based deaf and dumb wrestler Alan Kilby made a very infrequent appearance as a late substitute for Pete Curry and it was a winning one too. Kilby beat Phil Rowe by two falls to one in round six. Kid Chocolate had a similar result when he defeated Johnny Peters in the sixth round. The main event tag match saw Mike Marino partner Bob Abbott against Hans Streiger and Rex Strong. Marino and Abbott won with the deciding submission coming in the eighteenth minute. Honey Boy Zimba was another late replacement, this time for Bull Schmidt to take on John Elijah. Zimba despite showing signs of overeagerness which resulted in a public warning in round five came out on top in the same round with a winning fall. Finally Steve Best defeated Bob Bibby who was counted out in the fourth round.

April ended with another Belle Vue show on the 29th which saw Kung Fu get another match against Mark Rocco for the British Heavy/Middleweight Title. Kung Fu lost again when Rocco retained the belt courtesy of a winning submission in the seventh round. Wayne Bridges was booked to wrestle the winner of the Pat Roach v Tony St.Clair match on the previous

184

Belle Vue show but as that ended inconclusively Bridges was forced to step aside for a rematch. This time there was a winner with Tony St.Clair winning in the fifth round but he was incredibly lucky. Roach had spent the whole of the contest attacking his opponent and actually pinned St.Clair for the winning fall. Roach's temper let him down though and he was unable to control himself. Roach carried on attacking St.Clair despite having won and it ended with him being disqualified. Alan Dennison won his match against Ray Thunder when the Anglo-Canadian was disqualified in the fifth round. Jackie Robinson won the only decent wrestling match of the night with a winning fall coming in round six against local rival Mike Jordan. Finally The Royals faced a new combination of Blackjack Mulligan and Ivan Penzecoff but they were easily beaten by two straight falls in the fifteenth minute.

May -

Grapple fans had a bonus on the 1st with the new May Day Bank Holiday on that date which meant there was an extra helping of wrestling shown on the holiday World of Sport. Two matches were shown from Reading and the first featured Dynamite Kid taking on Sid Cooper. Dynamite was now happily settled in Calgary and this was his last match seen on British TV for well over a year. He went out in suitable style with a two straight falls win in four rounds against Cooper who was unable to cope with the range of skills displayed by Dynamite.

The other match screened was another tag match for The Royals taking on opposition including Mark Rocco. This time Rocco partnered Ray Thunder in another hectic contest. Rocco got the first score when he forced Vic Faulkner to submit in the tenth minute before Rocco let his partner down when he was disqualifed in the twelfth minute. Rocco punched Faulkner right in front of referee Joe D'Orazio and was immediately sent back to the dressing room. Thunder was left to carry on alone and soon he was pinned by Bert Royal for the equaliser in the fifteenth minute before the winner came the same way for Royal two minutes later.

185

The 1978 FA Cup Final was on the 6th with World of Sport on air at 1200pm for the build up to the big match between Arsenal and Ipswich. Three matches were broadcast at 1235pm from the bill taped at Croydon in April. First up was a match between Kung Fu and Mick McManus and as part of his introductions MC Mike Judd announced that Kung Fu had now formed a new tag team with none other than Kendo Nagasaki. Kung Fu went straight on the attack from the first bell hurling McManus around the ring before a few punches from McManus on the blind side of referee Peter Szakacs evened things up. The match continued with McManus doing his best to slow the pace of it down. By now Szakacs must have missed at least five punches before he finally spotted one and gave McManus his first public warning right at the end of the first round. McManus got his final warning as early as the second round for kicking Kung Fu out of the ring under the bottom rope but Kung Fu rallied with a straight fingers jab to the throat which was followed by Kung Fu's signature reverse folding press for the first fall. McManus started the third round with his usual forearm jabs to the stomach before barely beating the count of ten from a reverse spine drop. McManus was lucky not to be disqualified as he continued the illegal moves before again he barely beat the count from another of Kung Fu's trademark kicks to his throat. McManus finally got the equaliser in round four when Kung Fu submitted from a curious looking neck hold which was more him being strangled by McManus with his own judo suit. Then the mayhem commenced with McManus refusing to break the hold when suddenly Kendo Nagasaki appeared in the ring wearing a cape and dark glasses and proceeded to attack McManus. Nagasaki threw McManus from the ring and he quickly ran back to the dressing room. Mike Judd announced that referee Peter Szakacs had decided the match verdict would be left open. Nagasaki then went back to the dressing room to try and make McManus return to the ring but to no avail and that was the end of the bout.

The main event was a tag team challenge between Big Daddy and Giant Haystacks with Daddy partnering Tony St.Clair and Haystacks teaming up with Bruiser Muir. As soon as Daddy entered the ring he squared up to Haystacks before

186

Mike Judd made the introductions and then there was chaos. As referee Max Ward issued his pre-fight instructions to the teams Haystacks complained there was something wrong with the tag rope in Daddy's corner. As Ward and Daddy went to check the rope Muir knocked St.Clair to the floor and Haystacks landed a splash on St.Clair's legs. Referee Ward ordered Judd back into the ring to announce that Haystacks had been disqualified and with St.Clair unable to wrestle it turned into a Daddy v Muir one fall to win match. After some shoulder checks and forearm smashes to start the match Daddy threw Muir to the floor. Daddy followed up with a big splash before he covered Muir with a cross press for the winning fall. Mike Judd had to explain to the audience what had happened and even Kent Walton was confused. Those in attendance including me were very disappointed with the lack of a proper match. This was a repeat to what was happening in tag matches involving Daddy and Haystacks around the country in the few weeks previous to this show and all it meant was fans were left feeling ripped off. There was no obvious pay off to this as the solo match wouldn't happen for another three years and if there had been a big match that summer it might have made more sense.

The final match saw Jim Breaks take on new British Lightweight Champion Steve Grey over six rounds with the winner facing Johnny Saint for Saint's world title. Breaks was quickly into his stride although for a change he was wrestling mainly within the rules for the first couple of rounds. The third round saw Breaks do his usual trick of getting Grey's arm in a backhammer hold before 'accidentally' trapping it in the ropes. Grey's arm was weakened enough for Breaks to place it in his 'Breaks' special' to extract an instant submission from his opponent. Breaks went straight on the attack in round four to try and get a winner from the hold again but Grey reversed it for an over the top folding press for the equaliser. The final two rounds saw Breaks try any trick he could do to get a winner but Grey refused to submit from another 'Breaks' special' and in the end neither wrestler could get a winner. The match ended in a draw but when Mike Judd announced the decision he failed to mention who would go forward to wrestle Johnny Saint.

The second half of the show from Croydon was seen on World of Sport the following Saturday afternoon with viewers eager to see the first appearance of Kendo Nagasaki wrestling without the mask on. Nagasaki's opponent for his comeback was the much heavier Bronco Wells but Kendo didn't waste any time in seeing off the threat from Wells. After a couple of nasty looking straight finger jabs to the throat in round two Nagasaki got the first score when he made Wells submit from the grapevine with face bar hold. As soon as the third round started Nagasaki was right onto Wells and quickly made him submit from the same hold for an impressive win.

The opening match that week was a clash of personalities with Bobby Barnes meeting Catweazle. The first couple of rounds saw Catweazle's usual antics upset Barnes especially when his elegantly styled hair was ruffled. There was no score in the contest till the fourth round when Barnes took the lead with a folding press after dishing out several weakeners including a clear punch to Catweazle's stomach. Barnes was issued with a first public warning during the interval and Kent Walton could only think it was for the punch earlier. Catweazle fought back in round five and in the end pinned Barnes with a folding press after tripping Barnes as he came off the ropes. It was Barnes though who won the match when he reversed an attempted pinfall attempt to pin Catweazle with a double arm hold. It was an excellent contest between two great wrestlers.

The final match of the week was between Johnny Czeslaw and Brian Maxine who entered ring clad in his usual robe and wearing his crown. Maxine got the first fall in round two pinning Czeslaw with a reverse double knee hold after a bodyslam to the mat. Maxine went all out for the win in round three and incurred referee Peter Szakacs' anger to such an extent he was given two public warnings during the round. Czeslaw was so upset by this he tried to bring a chair into the ring to attack Maxine with but he was persuaded by Szakacs to leave it outside. Maxine then attacked Czeslaw with his 'sawing' move which only angered Czeslaw and the crowd even more. Finally Czeslaw got back into the bout in round four when he got the equaliser with a folding press after stopping Maxine in his tracks with a reverse chop. There was drama in the fifth round when Czeslaw accidentally chopped referee Szakacs in the corner after Maxine ducked. Maxine pinned Czeslaw taking advantage of the situation but Szakacs was in no fit state to count the fall. Maxine tried to revive the referee and as he did so Czeslaw took advantage and after another chop floored Maxine Czeslaw pinned him with a folding press. Maxine was absolutely furious and complained vociferously to Mike Judd who told him to put up his belt against Czeslaw if he wanted a rematch.

That was an excellent week's wrestling on World of Sport which was lucky as that was it till the holiday special on Bank Holiday Monday 29th May. On the 20th the England v Scotland football match was shown and on the 27th the schoolboy's football match between England and Scotland was on instead of wrestling.

The wrestling on the Bank Holiday World of Sport on the 29th was shown at the unlikely time of 440pm and featured three matches from a bill recorded at Preston. The first of which was a replacement for the advertised match between Kung Fu and Alan Woods. To mine and other Kung Fu fan's immense disappointment Kung Fu had handed in his notice to Joint Promotions at the end of April and had left the organisation. Instead of Kung Fu v Woods viewers saw Mal Sanders defeat Chris Bailey. Sanders pinned Bailey in the third round for the only fall needed to win.

The main event was a rematch between Pat Roach and Tony St.Clair and this time Roach finally got a win against his opponent albeit in a non-title match. St.Clair was unable to continue in the sixth round and once again Roach pressed his claims for a long awaited title match.

The final match shown was another lively meeting between Jim Breaks and Steve Grey. Breaks took the lead in the third round with a 'Breaks' special' forcing Grey to submit before Grey equalised with a fall in the fourth. The match was still all square going into the final round when Breaks thought he had pinned Grey for the winner whilst Grey thought he had pinned Breaks. In fact both wrestlers shoulders were on the mat for the count of three so the result was a two-two draw.

Around the halls -

The big news to start May was the final show of the season at The Royal Albert Hall would be back to the days of a showpiece spectacular with a very strong proposed programme. It was said in the Wrestling Scene newspaper that there were plans for Andre the Giant to wrestle in the main event, nine years after his last appearance. Unfortunately those plans didn't come to fruition neither did a rumoured appearance of Kendo Nagasaki in the ring happen. Instead like the previous year's May show a six man tag would be the main event. Unlike 1977's match this would be far more appetising with the team of Big Daddy, Leon Fortuna and Kung Fu taking on Giant Haystacks, Mick McManus and Steve Logan. With a defence of the World Lightweight Title by Johnny Saint against Steve Grey as the main supporting contest it was no wonder tickets sold out for the night.

Steve Grey had an opportunity before the big Albert Hall match to win the title but he came in overweight for the contest at Croydon on the 2nd. Grey must have been kicking himself for not watching his weight as he defeated Johnny Saint with a winning fall coming in the ninth round. Also on the show that night was a successful evening for The Royals in solo matches with Vic Faulkner beating Steve Logan who was counted out in the fourth round. Brother Bert Royal notched up another win against Mark Rocco in a non title match when Rocco frustrated in his inability to beat Royal walked away in round five and was counted out. The rest of the show comprised of a knockout tournament but unfortunately there was no winner. The final was between Butcher Bond and Terry Rudge with both wrestlers totally ignoring the Lord Mountevan's rules in favour of a closing time bar brawl the referee abandoned the contest in the fifth round and disqualified both of them.

Sid Cooper's big mouth got him into bother and in the end a completely new look at Bristol on the 4th. Cooper had taken exception to referee Max Ward's partiality in a previous match at the venue and challenged Ward to a match against him. Just to add a bit of spice to the match Cooper demanded it be a hair versus hair match and as he was so confident of winning he gave Ward a one fall start. It didn't take Mystic Meg to foresee what would happen and in round four Ward pinned Cooper to win the match. A barber was called into the ring who proceeded to shave Cooper's head and to his credit he took it well and adopted the skinhead look for the rest of his wrestling career.

The Big Daddy and Giant Haystacks roadshow was travelling the nation most nights of the week with the same dodgy finishes whether in tag matches or solo contests. At Hastings on the 5th in a tag Haystacks walked away from the ring before the end of the match leaving partner Steve Logan to be the victim of the big splash from Big Daddy. The following night a few miles down the coast at Eastbourne Daddy and Haystacks were part of a knockout tournament. The semi finals saw Daddy beat Lee Bronson with a fall coming in round two whilst Haystacks destroyed his opponent John Elijah and ended up being disqualified in only the first round. Elijah was in no fit state to wrestle in the final and Daddy came to the ring to suggest that Haystacks take Elijah's place and wrestle him instead. After a few shoves and a bit of argy bargy Haystacks left the ring chased by Daddy to never return and yet again leave a crowd disappointed.

The same night at Hanley Pat Roach had another title match against Tony St.Clair and once again Tony St.Clair retained the British Heavyweight Title. This time it was a result of an incredibly tough twelve rounds draw with Roach taking the lead in round eight before St.Clair equalised in the eleventh round.

Belle Vue had another super show on the 13th with Big Daddy and Giant Haystacks on view but in separate bouts. Daddy was in tag team action with now regular partner Bobby Ryan taking on Bruiser Muir and Steve Logan. Muir did the walk out trick in the tenth minute leaving poor Logan alone to take the winning fall from Daddy a minute or so later. Haystacks took on the Zebra Kid and it was the Zebra Kid who kept his unbeaten record and identity intact when Haystacks was disqualifed in the first round. Johnny Kwango defeated the now bald Sid Cooper by two straight falls in the opening match whilst Johnny Saint took on and beat Jim Breaks with a winning fall in round seven. The final match saw Steve Grey beat the Gay One in round three but no doubt most punters would have left by then to get a bus home or get a pint before last orders. If you could be charitable about such a person as Al Vippond the one thing you could say was at least he could wrestle and whoever had trained him had done a good job.

Kendo Nagasaki made another appearance at Croydon on the 16th but his planned tag team with Kung Fu had fallen apart following Kung Fu's departure from Joint Promotions. Nagasaki's partner was Dean Brisco against the team of Bronco Wells and The Viking. Apart from an early submission by Brisco things went pretty much to form and two quick falls from Kendo saw him and Brisco victorious in the fourteenth minute. Apart from the tag match the rest of the show was distinctively average. Veteran Irishman Joe Murphy beat the lively leprechaun Tim Fitzmaurice who was counted out in the fifth round. Caswell Martin replaced Brian Maxine who should have been in a rematch against Johnny Czeslaw and the match ended in a No Contest when Czeslaw was injured in round four. Mal Sanders cemented his growing reputation when he defeated Zoltan Boscik by two falls to one in the fifth round and Wayne Bridges beat Johnny Wilson with a winning fall coming in round six.

Kendo Nagasaki was in action at one of his local venues , the Civic Hall in Wolverhampton on the 23rd. Nagasaki took on The Viking who simply couldn't handle Nagasaki's aggression and after conceding a fall to Kendo in round two decided to walk away in the third round. Mark Rocco should have had another match with Kung Fu but instead Rocco took on replacement Pat Patton instead. Rocco's relentless attacks were far too much for the inexperienced Patton to handle and he was beaten by two straight falls inside four rounds. Perhaps the most interesting match on the show was buried away in the small print with two youngsters facing each other. In one corner was Bernie Wright who had made his debut in 1977 and in the other was Dave Smith a rather skinny sixteen year old from Warrington making his Joint Promotions debut that night. The contest ended in a one fall each draw but it was doubtful any in attendance there would have realised the significance of the occasion. Smith of course would go on to become one of the best known wrestlers produced in this country as the 'British

Bulldog' but in 1978 it was baby steps for Smith for the first few months with matches against Wright the norm as he learnt his trade.

Two title matches formed the main events at Belle Vue on the 27th and once again Pat Roach failed when he challenged Tony St.Clair for the British Heavyweight Title. As per the match at Hanley previously in the month this one again ended in a one fall each draw at the end of the twelve rounds. This time it was more of a wrestling match but Roach still failed to get a winning fall when it mattered and St.Clair's equalising fall in the eleventh round ensured he kept hold of his coveted title. The other title match saw Johnny Saint defend his World Lightweight Title against Steve Grey. Grey found out that he may be able to defeat Saint in non title matches but with the title at stake it was a different matter. Saint pinned Grey in the ninth round for the winning fall and Grey returned home that night with much to think about before his next title match with Saint the following week. The rest of the show wasn't that interesting with Bert Royal beating Butcher Bond who was disqualified in the fourth round. Vic Faulkner got a winning fall against Alan Woods in round six whilst Kid Chocolate defeated Johnny England who was disqualified in the third round.

Kendo Nagasaki had his first contest unmasked against Giant Haystacks at Hanley on the 27th when they opposed each other in a tag match. Nagasaki's partner was Bobby Ryan whilst Haystacks tagged with Steve Logan. With little in the way of recognised wrestling holds it was a riotous match with the crowd lively throughout the ten minutes the bout lasted. Nagasaki and Ryan won with Haystacks walking out and Logan being counted out. Dave Smith had another outing as a professional on the show with once again Bernie Wright as his opponent. The result again was a one fall each draw at the end of the scheduled six rounds.

There was a mammoth twelve man knockout tournament at Croydon on the 30th with wrestlers of all weight divisions invited to take part. On the night it turned into an eleven man tournament with Ray Thunder failing to show up. The trophy went to Tony St.Clair who received a bye in the first round before defeating Pete Roberts and Bert Royal to take his place in the final against Mark Rocco. Rocco had taken care of Billy Torontos and Vic Faulkner on his way to the final but it was one match too far with St.Clair pinning Rocco in round two for the winner.

May ended with the final Royal Albert Hall of the season on the 31st but with no Kung Fu for the main event it saw the welcome return from injury of Pete Roberts to take his place. Roberts with Big Daddy and Leon Fortuna defeated Giant Haystacks, Mick McManus and Steve Logan with a winning fall in the ninth minute to the fan's delight. Steve Grey once again failed in an attempt to beat Johnny Saint for the World Lightweight Title but this time luck was not on his side. Grey took the lead with a fall in the sixth round before an equaliser from Saint in the eight. In the tenth round of an excellent wrestling match with another five rounds to go the contest ended with both wrestlers failing to beat the count.

There was not a dull match on the programme with the opening contest seeing Vic Faulkner take on Bobby Barnes who was a late replacement for Ray Thunder. Once more Barnes' temper got the better of him and he was disqualified in the sixth round. Brother Bert Royal also got a victory when he beat Mark Rocco although fortuitously. Rocco was unable to continue in the fifth round from a bad cut on his forehead. Jim Breaks defeated fellow Yorkshireman Alan Dennison with a winning fall coming in round five whilst Tony St.Clair recorded a victory against Pat Roach when Roach walked out in the fourth round and was disqualified.

June -

The wrestling on World of Sport on the 3rd came from Walthamstow and a show recorded back in March. This explained why Kung Fu was part of the coverage despite him leaving for the independent circuit at the end of April. Kung Fu teamed up with The Royals to take on The Liverpool Skinheads and Blackjack Mulligan in a team match.

The single's bouts saw Vic Faulkner beat Roy Paul with a winning fall in the third round. Brother Bert Royal beat the other Liverpool Skinhead Terry O'Neill by pinning him in the third round. Kung Fu completed a clean sweep in the solo matches when he defeated Blackjack Mulligan again with a winning fall in round three.

The six man tag finale saw The Royals and Kung Fu complete a four-nil whitewash with a rather easy two straight falls win in just over five minutes. Neither of The Liverpool Skinheads would be seen on TV again and they shortly departed for the independent circuit and it would be nearly four years before Kung Fu was back on the small screen.

The wrestling on World of Sport on the 10th came from Catford and despite the World Cup in Argentina being in full swing a full programme was shown at 4pm. The coverage this week featured not only a four man knockout tournament but also a heavyweight contest as a bonus. The tournament's prize was to be named the number one challenger for Marty Jones' British Light/Heavyweight Title and receive a title match to be televised from Chester later in the month.

The participants in the tournament were Mark Rocco, Butcher Bond, Clive Myers and Leon Fortuna and it was Rocco and Fortuna who contested the first semi final. It was fair to say that the much lighter Fortuna was totally out of his depth against a wrestler like Rocco. Rocco was soon over powering his opponent by fair means but also plenty of foul ones too. Mick McManus was back co-commentating and noted at the end of the first round that Rocco had got the easiest semi final and it was proved right in the second round. Firstly Rocco got a public warning from referee Max Ward for attacking Fortuna whilst he was in a corner before weakening him with a couple of back elbows. Rocco then reversed a flying tackle attempt from Fortuna into a piledriver which left him with no chance of beating Ward's count of ten. Afterwards Fortuna had to be taken to a local hospital suffering from a suspected concussion.

The other semi final between Clive Myers, who was now billed as Iron Fist and wearing a colourful judo style outfit, and Butcher Bond promised to be a lot more competitive. Bond used his considerable weight advantage in the early stages to try and subdue the lightning quick Myers but once this failed he resorted back to his usual rule-breaking. Max Ward gave Bond a public warning in the second round for continually attacking

Myers whilst he was on the mat. Every time Bond got on top Myers would rally with kicks and chops which would stop Bond in his tracks. Eventually Bond's frustration at these moves told in the third round when he punched Myers right in the stomach after receiving more chops. Referee Ward instantly disqualified Bond and Myers went through to the final.

Before the final there was a heavyweight match shown between Colin Joynson and Pete Roberts. In a hard fought match it was Joynson who took the lead with the first fall in round four. After a posting had weakened Roberts, a knee drop from Joynson enabled him to cover Roberts for the count of three. Roberts showing no ill effect from his recent injury woes battled back to get an equaliser in the final round. Roberts rolled up Joynson for folding press from the side for the match to end in a well deserved draw for each wrestler.

Finally it was time for the tournament final with Mark Rocco the hot favourite to beat Clive Myers to ensure he got the title match against Marty Jones. Myers was still suffering the effects of his bruising match against Butcher Bond but still shocked Rocco by taking the first fall in the first round. After taking a couple of chops Rocco seemed to somersault to the mat where he was pinned by Myers. Rocco was furious and attacked Myers as he celebrated for which he received a deserved public warning from Max Ward. Rocco went all out for an equaliser in the second round but Myers gave as good as he got and McManus noted that he had never seen Myers wrestle so well. It couldn't continue though as finally Rocco got on top in the third round. Rocco delivered a back elbow as Myers came off of the ropes which sent him back between the top two ropes. Myers suffered a heavy fall and viewers knew it was bad as Kent Walton let out his trademark 'Ay, ay, ay' comment whenever such an event occurred. There was no chance of Myers being unable to continue so it was Rocco who would be the challenger for the British Light/Heavyweight Title.

There was only time for one bout to be shown on World of Sport on the 17th with the World Cup Finals from Argentina, the Swedish Grand Prix and athletics as well as the usual ITV 7 horse racing also being featured. At least the match was a dandy with Tony St.Clair defending his British Heavyweight

Title against persistent challenger Pat Roach from a show recorded at Chester. With only twenty five minutes of broadcast time alotted at 430pm the match was joined in round five with Roach having already received a public warning from referee Brian Crabtree in the fourth round. Roach went in front when he got the opening fall in the seventh round and his relentless attacks was causing St.Clair no end of problems. St.Clair finally managed to get an equaliser in the tenth round and with two rounds left the title was up for grabs. Unfortunately the match descended into a brawl with St.Clair receiving a public warning in the eleventh round as did Roach and the contest went into the final round with the score still one fall each. It was St.Clair who won the match in the twelfth round when Roach was knocked from the ring and he was unable to return inside the ropes before referee Crabtree had completed his count of ten. Tony St.Clair was still champion and was now ready to move onto other challengers and a certain unmasked Kendo Nagasaki. Nagasaki's manager and spokesman Gorgeous George had remarked there was no rule now forbidding Kendo from being able to challenge St.Clair for the title.

There was no wrestling shown on World of Sport on the 24th with the Rawlings International tennis tournament shown in its place.

Around the halls -

June saw the traditional start of wrestling at the coastal venues but it was noticeable for 1978 that some places were starting the season later and some venues who ran twice weekly would only have wrestling on once a week. The growing popularity of holidays on the Spanish Costas and other Mediterranean resorts were having an effect on the usual week at the British coast.

Punters at Wolverhampton on the 6th had a treat with the main event seeing Kendo Nagasaki square up to Giant Haystacks. The unmasked Nagasaki had become something of a fan favourite and his fans were rewarded with a win when the match was stopped in the interval between round's one and two with Haystacks unable to continue. Another treat on the same

197

bill saw Mark Rocco take on Marty Jones and this time it was Rocco who beat his nemesis. Both wrestlers threw everything bar the kitchen sink at each other but it was Rocco who won when he made Jones submit in the fifth round.

The perils of holding wrestling tournaments at outdoor venues in an English summer were illustrated when rain forced the cancellation of the show at Great Yarmouth on the 7th. Unfortunately heavy rain before the start forced fans to miss out on seeing Giant Haystacks take on The Royals and Mark Rocco wrestle Pete Roberts.

There was a noteable debut in the pro ranks the next night at Digbeth with the former three time British National Judo Champion Chris Adams had his first match. Adams was a member of the 1976 Olympics judo squad but never actually competed at the games whilst younger brother Neil went on to win a silver medal at both the 1980 and 1984 Olympics.

Adams had been shown a few moves and holds by fellow Leamington Spa resident Tony Walsh before his debut but in his early contests relied on his judo training to get him through. As a nod to his judo roots Adams wore a judogi for his matches as well as wrestling barefoot and it wasn't long until he was paired up with the similar styled Clive Myers as the 'Martial Arts Fighters'. Adams' opponent at Digbeth was Tally Ho Kaye who was perfect for a novice to wrestle and Adams made a winning start with Kaye disqualified in the fifth round.

There was a welcome return to this country on the 10th at Belle Vue of Johnny Eagles. Eagles who had departed from Britain to wrestle in the USA at the start of the seventies had returned for a brief holiday and managed to fit in the bout at Belle Vue. Eagles' opponent was Colin Joynson. In a surprise it was Joynson who won courtesy of a fall in the fifth round. The main event there that night was a tag match which promised mayhem galore with Kendo Nagasaki partnering Pete Roberts who had replaced the billed Kung Fu. They would take on Giant Haystacks and Mark Rocco who had struck up a fearsome partnership recently. Naturally the match descended into anarchy. With all matter of action going on both inside of the ropes and outside of them it was hard to keep up with the action but Rocco was disqualified in the ninth minute.

Haystacks decided he didn't want to take on both Nagasaki and Roberts alone so he accompanied his partner back to the dressing room to forfeit the match.

The other three matches on the show saw Tally Ho Kaye's bout with John Naylor end with both of them failing to beat the count in the fifth round. Alan Dennison put up a good show before falling to defeat in the sixth round to the much heavier Marty Jones. The final match of the night saw the Zebra Kid make short work of Ivan Penzecoff and he finished Penzecoff off with an 'Atomic drop' in the second round.

Great Yarmouth's grapple fans were luckier with the weather on the 14th when their show went ahead as scheduled with no problems from rain. Unfortunately the line up was not nearly so good as the previous week's cancelled show with this week Tibor Szakacs beating Steve Logan in the main event. Szakacs had recently returned to the ring after a hiatus of well over a year and the former Royal Albert Hall trophy winner was as popular as ever. Unfortunately time had taken its toll and Szakacs had aged tremendously in his absence and it was a shame seeing such a great wrestler trying to defy 'Old Father Time'.

There was something of a shock at Chelmsford on the 20th when The Caribbean Sunshine Boys reappeared in the main event tag against Tibor Szakacs and Wayne Bridges. It was a surprise after all the problems that they had caused him that Max Crabtree had booked them back as a team. Disappointingly for their fans this was a one and done with Johnny Kincaid back on the books for only a short while. Szakacs and Bridges were the winners of the match with the winning fall coming after fifteen minutes with no sign of any improvement in Kincaid and Bond's behaviour in the ring.

There was a huge Summer spectacular at Reading on the 23rd with a star studded programme on offer which ensured a capacity crowd to see it. Big Daddy and Giant Haystacks were still battling each other up and down the country in tag matches with various partners and it was the same at Reading. On the evening both of their advertised partners though were replaced with Mal Sanders teaming with Daddy instead of Leon Fortuna and Tony Walsh taking over from Tally Ho Kaye to tag with

Haystacks. Again Haystacks pulled the walking out of the ring trick after Daddy had equalised an earlier submission from Haystacks on Sanders. This left Walsh to carry on alone and a minute or so later in the ninth minute he saw stars after receiving Daddy's double elbow drop for another Big Daddy win. Mike Marino took on Mark Rocco on the show in a clash of styles and it was Marino who won. Rocco was disqualified in the fifth round for attacking Marino after pinning him for an equalising fall. Tony St.Clair defeated Colin Joynson in one of their regular meetings with a winning fall coming in round six. Johnny Czeslaw beat Johnny Kincaid who once again saw himself on the wrong end of a disqualification verdict in the fifth round. The final match of the night saw Billy Torontos and Catweazle send the fans home with a smile on their faces with a mixture of comedy and wrestling which the unpredictable Torontos won in round five.

Compared to the previous Belle Vue show on the 10th the one there on the 24th felt underwhelming in comparison. The main event featured a tag match with The Royals beating a thrown together team of Butcher Bond and Clive Myers by two falls to one in thirteen minutes. Jim Breaks recorded a win against Johnny Saint with a winning fall in the fifth round and straightaway was demanding another chance at Saint's title. Mal Sanders beat Blackjack Mulligan who was disqualified in the fourth round and Mick McMichael defeated Billy Torontos by two falls to one in round six. Ray Steele's match with Gil Singh came to an early ending when both were counted out in the fourth round.

The show at Croydon on the 27th saw Kendo Nagasaki in the main event spot and where Nagasaki appeared there tended to be chaos, controversy and mayhem in large doses. Nagasaki's opponent was Mark Rocco which heightened the expectations of the fans as these two were never involved in a dull match. Nagasaki went ahead with the first fall coming in the second round. Rocco then threw a chair from outside into the ring with which Nagasaki proceeded to hit him with on his head. Rocco suffered a badly cut forehead and the match was halted. After discussions an open verdict was declared.

The opener saw Tibor Szakacs take on fellow veteran Big Bruno and it was Szakacs who won with Bruno disqualified in the fourth round. Mike Marino's clash with Pete Roberts was boiling up nicely with the score one fall each when Roberts was injured in round six. Roberts was unable to continue but sportingly Marino refused to accept the win so a No Contest was declared. Match number four on the night was a heavyweight contest between Wayne Bridges and Romany Riley with nothing untoward happening until the fifth round. Bridges was a fall ahead when suddenly Bruiser Muir appeared in the ring to try and attack Bridges forcing the match to be stopped. Muir was scheduled to be in the night's final contest taking on Terry Rudge so after a quick conversation a tag match was decided to be the best option. Bridges teamed with Rudge against Muir and Riley with Bridges and Riley winning by two straight falls in the tenth minute.

There was a treat for all grappling fans with the announcement that the legendary Billy Robinson was returning to Britain at the end of June for a month or so and would be fitting in several matches in the time. Disappointingly most of Robinson's bouts were on Relwyskow & Green Promotions' shows with only one for Best Wryton at Belle Vue and a televised match for Dale Martin. Robinson took on the rather overmatched Pete Curry at Morecambe on the 29th with Robinson winning from a submission in round three and a fall in the seventh round. It was a guarantee that Curry would be in pain for a few days afterwards having been stretched all over the ring. Robinson was at Leeds the following night when he took on local favourite Gil Singh. Robinson again won with a winning fall in the seventh round but Singh at least had the honour of pinning Robinson in round five for an equaliser.

July -

July should have started without any wrestling shown on World of Sport on the 1st with the Sun Alliance World Match-Play golf tournament scheduled for the 4pm slot. Grapple fans who were watching were lucky as the golf finished early so there was time for a spot of wrestling and one match from the

201

recent Chester show broadcast. The contest was between Mick McManus and Johnny Kwango with McManus winning with a fall in the fourth round.

Another three bouts from Chester were seen on World of Sport the 8th with three entertaining matches shown. The opening contest was the bout that really ignited the feud between Mark Rocco and Marty Jones although it was a non-title match conflicting what was said during the Catford tournament on 10th June. Rocco was straight onto the attack and got public warnings in both rounds two and three from referee Brian Crabtree before he pinned Jones in the fourth round for the first fall. Jones equalised in the fifth round as the pace went to a frantic level with both wrestlers searching for a winning fall. In the seventh round Rocco was outside the ring and in a move seldom if ever seen before in a British ring Jones dived out of the ring at full speed between the ropes and smashed into Rocco. The impact saw both wrestlers suffer a clash of heads and Brian Crabtree had no option but to call the match off.

The second match saw Big Daddy face the equally imposing Big Bruno with the first fall winning. It was Daddy who got it when he pinned Bruno in round two with a big splash following a bodyslam.

The final bout of the week was something of a novelty with Giant Haystacks taking on both of The Royals in a handicap tag match. It didn't end well for Bert and Vic who were totally out of their depth in such a contest. In the fifth minute Haystacks flattened Faulkner with a splash. There was no hope of Faulkner beating the count and all Bert Royal could do was help his brother back to the dressing room.

The wrestling on World of Sport on the 15th featured the usual three matches from a show recorded at Bedworth. The first of which was a brief glimpse of Bobby Ryan pinning Johnny England for the only fall needed to win in round four. The second of the contests was a heavyweight clash with Gwyn Davies making a welcome return to the TV screen to tackle Wayne Bridges. The contest had to be paused in the second round as referee Brian Crabtree suffered an injury but he was ok to continue for round three much to everyone's relief.

Davies took the first fall in the fourth round before Bridges battled back for an equaliser in the fifth. With only a round left there was no time for either wrestler to get a winner so the decision was a well regarded draw.

The main match saw Jim Breaks and John Naylor compete for The Bedworth Civic Hall Trophy with Mick McManus named as special referee for the bout. Breaks took the lead in the third round with a 'Breaks' special' seeing Naylor submit. Naylor came back to equalise with a fall in the fourth after which Breaks did something incredibly stupid. Whilst protesting about the validity of Naylor's pinfall Breaks hit McManus who disqualified him. This left Naylor the proud winner of The Bedworth Civic Hall Trophy and Breaks now facing a challenge in the ring from McManus.

Chris Adams made his TV debut on World of Sport on the 22nd on the second half of the show taped at Bedworth. It was some going for Adams and rare for any wrestler to be shown on TV within a month of turning professional. Adams had shown up well in his first month and just to make sure everything went ok with the contest he was matched with Tally Ho Kaye who would make sure Adams looked good in the match. Adams indeed did make a good impression for one so inexperienced but it was a losing one as a Boston Crab in round three saw him submit to Kaye.

The main match of the week saw Kendo Nagasaki meet Pete Roberts with Nagasaki booked as a 'good guy' in his matches since he unmasked. There was always something of the night about Nagasaki though and an unpredictability whenever he wrestled. Before the start Gorgeous George made his usual introduction but instead of being booed those in attendance for a change listened to him. The first round saw both wrestlers exchange holds and counters but even in this round Nagasaki was slow breaking on the ropes and referee Brian Crabtree was keeping a keen eye on proceedings. The match livened up in the second round with Nagasaki warned by Crabtree for being too early when attacking Roberts who was on the mat. Roberts responded by reversing a throw off of the ropes to pin Nagasaki following a hip toss for the first fall. Nagasaki couldn't believe it and wandered about the ring with his hands covering his ears like he was having a meltdown. Whatever it was effecting Nagasaki he completely lost the plot in the third round and attacked Roberts unmercifully and ended up getting two public warnings from Crabtree. Roberts responded by attacking Nagasaki outside of the ring amidst scenes of violence rarely seen on World of Sport's wrestling coverage. Referee Crabtree was having a job controlling the contest and was lucky Nagasaki didn't attack him as Crabtree constantly tried to physically intervene and break the wrestlers up. The match came to an end in the fourth round when Nagasaki reversed a flying tackle from Roberts and purposefully threw him over the top rope. Roberts suffered a heavy landing at ringside and Brian Crabtree ruled Nagasaki the winner by countout. As MC George Mitchell announced the decision Gorgeous George grabbed Mitchell's microphone to deliver another speech and this time boos and jeers drowned out whatever he was trying to say. That wasn't the end of the matter though as when the coverage ended and went back to the World of Sport studio the presenter Dickie Davies told viewers that the decision had been reversed. Following an investigation by the Board of Control after viewing the footage they had determined it was an illegal move by Nagasaki and that Pete Roberts was now deemed to be the winner.

The third and final match of the week was a heavyweight match between Terry Rudge and Gil Singh and whenever they fought it never disappointed. In a hard hitting match it was Rudge who took the lead in the fourth round when he pinned Singh with a cross press following a bodyslam. Singh fought back in the fifth round and got an equalising fall with a cross press after flooring Rudge with a hip toss. The bout came to an unfortunate ending in the final round when Rudge suffered a nasty looking injury. With both wrestlers going all out for the winning fall Singh threw Rudge who landed on the top rope and was unable to continue. Singh refused to accept the decision so George Mitchell announced it would be a No Contest.

The wrestling on World of Sport on the 29th was the second half of the Catford show seen in June. The first contest was a clash of personalities and styles with Billy Torontos taking on Johnny Kwango. Mick McManus was again doing co-

commentary alongside Kent Walton and I'm not sure he appreciated the sportsmanship between the two wrestlers. There was a little bit too much comedy according to Kent Walton in the match instead of wrestling. It was Kwango who won with a folding press coming in the third round. Coverage of this match recently turned up on the BBC as part of a documentary on the 1981 New Cross arson attack. Kwango's son-in-law was one of the victims of the fire.

The main contest of the week was a return challenge match between Brian Maxine and Johnny Czeslaw after Czeslaw had won their first encounter shown in May. Czeslaw had been unable to train down to the middleweight weight limit so couldn't challenge for Maxine's middleweight title as originally planned. Maxine took the lead in the second round with a soft looking fall. He pinned Czeslaw with a reverse double knee hold after a couple of jabs to the stomach and Kent Walton sounded particularly bored as he called it. Maxine got a public warning from referee Max Ward in the third round for a punch on Czeslaw before Maxine started the 'saw' which initiated a slow handclap from the crowd. Czeslaw came back with an equalising fall in round four with a folding press after a back chop had stunned Maxine. It was Maxine who won the contest though with a winner in the fifth round. Maxine caught Czeslaw with a forearm coming off of a posting and folded him up for the winning fall. Maxine then grabbed MC Fred Downes' microphone and started ranting at the crowd whilst Czeslaw exacted some sort of revenge with a punch to Maxine's jaw that left him rolling around the ring. The St.John's Ambulance staff were called to attend to him and Maxine's proposed music tour of Nashville was left in jeopardy.

Last but not least Mal Sanders took on Sid Cooper with Cooper getting his usual warm welcome from the Catford crowd. Sanders once again impressed in the bout despite Cooper using all his usual tricks. It was Cooper though who took the lead in round four when he forced a submission from Sanders via a Boston Crab. Sanders wasn't behind for long though as he pinned Cooper with a double leg nelson in just forty two seconds of the fifth round. Sanders got the winning fall in round six when he reversed a Boston Crab attempt by

205

Cooper into a folding press for a popular win especially amongst the young ladies at ringside who came forward to offer their congratulations.

Around the halls -

Most of the action in July happened at the coastal resorts but an interesting show at Picketts Lock on the 7th saw both Kendo Nagasaki and Big Daddy on the show. Nagasaki's opponent was Pete Roberts and in another bad tempered contest betweent the two it was Nagasaki who won with Roberts counted out in the fifth round. Big Daddy was in tag action with his partner Mal Sanders against a masked duo known only as The Assassins. Sanders was injured in the sixth minute and unable to continue so Daddy carried on alone and defeated both Assassins in the tenth minute with double elbow drops to seal the win. Afterwards Daddy unmasked them to reveal Banger Walsh and Dusty Miller who quickly rushed back to the dressing rooms.

Both Kendo Nagasaki and Big Daddy were also on the bill at Belle Vue the next night. At Belle Vue Nagasaki squared up to Mark Rocco with Nagasaki winning when Rocco was disqualified in the third round. Daddy was again in a tag match with teenage newcomer Dave Smith teaming up with him for the first time to take on The Outlaw and The Destroyer. The contest ended in the seventh minute with another Daddy double elbow drop finishing off an opponent but both Outlaw and Destroyer managed to flee before being unmasked. Chris Adams made a victorious debut at Belle Vue when opponent Sid Cooper was disqualified in the fifth round. Marty Jones defeated Ray Steele with a deciding fall coming in round six whilst Brian Maxine came out on top against Mick McMichael who was counted out in the fifth round.

With British wrestling's popularity riding on the crest of a wave and interest at its highest level for years the Gaumont Cinema chain signed a contract with Joint Promotions to show wrestling at their venues up and down the country. The first show of the new contract was held at the Gaumont State

Cinema in Kilburn, North London which was a beautiful art deco building with its iconic 20ft. tower outside.

A packed crowd was at the four thousand capacity venue on the 14th for a Dale Martin show which was worthy of anything shown at the Royal Albert Hall. The main event saw Kendo Nagasaki meet Giant Haystacks in a solo match for the first time since Nagasaki was unmasked. Fans in attendance weren't let down with two rounds of violence with Nagasaki taking the first fall in the second round. Both wrestlers were bleeding profusely from head wounds and Haystacks decided he didn't fancy carrying on anymore and walked back to the dressing room with those there shouting for more.

The rest of the show was a team match with a squad captained by Big Daddy taking on one captained by Mick McManus. The singles matches saw Mark Rocco beat Jackie Turpin by submission in round three. Bert Royal beat Mick McManus who was disqualified in the fourth round. Colin Joynson pinned Pat O'Sullivan in the third round. Big Daddy knocked out Banger Walsh in the first round and Butcher Bond beat Dean Brisco who was counted out in the third round.

The six man tag finale saw Daddy, Royal and Turpin beat Rocco, Walsh and Bond by two straight falls in eight minutes.

Billy Robinson was continuing his tour of mainly northern coastal resorts and turned up at Morecambe on the 20th where defeated Rex Strong by two falls to one in the fifth round. Chris Adams was on the same show and he beat Blackjack Mulligan with a winning fall in round five.

Kendo Nagasaki was at Cardiff the next evening in the main event tag partnering Kid Chocolate against Mick McManus who had reformed his old team with Steve Logan. Despite McManus and Logan's best endeavours it was Nagasaki who got the winning fall in the eight minute to complete a two falls to one win. The rest of the show was a knockout tournament with the winner receiving the 'William Hill Trophy'. The first round heats saw Mark Rocco beat Chris Adams who submitted in the third round. Marty Jones pinned John Elijah in round three. Brian Maxine beat Billy Torontos who was counted out in round three and Bert Royal beat Alan Dennison with a winning fall in, yes round three. The first semi final saw Marty

Jones beat Mark Rocco who was disqualified in the second round. Unfortunately Jones was injured and couldn't continue so the final was deemed to be Bert Royal v Brian Maxine and Royal won it with a winning fall in the second round.

The long awaited homecoming for Billy Robinson to Belle Vue was on the 22nd and his opponent would be Pat Roach. Roach was certainly fired up for the contest and for once was not taking it easy. Roach got public warnings in both round's two and four as he got stuck into Robinson although at times their styles didn't mesh and things got a little messy. Robinson continued with his ground based offence and eventually got the first fall in the fourth round. Roach equalised in the fifth before the deciding fall went to Robinson in round six. It was by no means a classic and Billy Robinson would finish off his tour the following Wednesday which would be the final time Robinson would wrestle in Britain.

The second main event on the Belle Vue saw Giant Haystacks once again take on The Royals in a handicap match with once again the same result. This time Bert and Vic managed to get a fall in the ninth minute with a nice bit of double teaming enabling the pin but three minutes later the match ended with them both unable to continue.

The other matches on the programme saw Johnny Wilson beat Big Bruno who was disqualified in the fourth round. Jim Breaks defeated Johnny Saint with a winning fall in round five and Mike Jordan beat Kid Chocolate by two falls to one in the fifth round.

Kendo Nagasaki teamed up with Mal Sanders at Bletchley the same night to take on a new team of Steve Logan and Butcher Bond. Nagasaki got the winning fall in the ninth minute for a two falls to one victory.

It was surprising after the shenanigans the previous month that the management of the Fairfield Halls in Croydon allowed another match between Kendo Nagasaki and Mark Rocco at their venue. But they did and on the 25th Nagasaki and Rocco met in a ladder match. There was no chairs used or blood appearing in the match but at times the ladder was a handy weapon to use. Nagasaki eventually used the ladder to grab the bag of money held above the ring in the seventh minute to win the contest. In a slight surprise on the Croydon bill Wayne Bridges beat Pat Roach in a battle from the first bell. Bridges got a fall in round five to win and propel himself right into contention for the British Heavyweight Title. Clive Myers beat Mal Sanders by two falls to one in round six of the best wrestling match on the show. Lee Bronson won a bad tempered match with Romany Riley who was counted out in the fifth round whilst Steve Grey beat Tim Fitzmaurice by two straight falls in the closing bout of the night.

The French Legionnaires tag team made a welcome return to this country on the 28th to take on The Royals at Bristol for the European Tag Team Trophy. Unfortunately Vic Faulkner was injured and unable to compete so his place against Albert Sanniez and Claude Roca was taken by Steve Grey. Even without brother Vic Bert Royal was still victorious with a winning fall coming in the sixteenth minute of a tag match that was the polar opposite of some of the heavyweight tag matches seen in the past few months. The rest of the show comprised another knockout tournament which seemed to be presented at most venues around the time. The ten participants was reduced to nine with Steve Grey being put in the tag match so Mal Sanders received a bye in the heats. Mark Rocco was the winner when his opponent in the final Mal Sanders was unable to continue in round four.

Big Daddy captained his 'All-stars' team in a tournament at Hanley the following evening against a team captained by Giant Haystacks but this time it was Haystacks who was captain of the winning team. Mark Rocco beat Chris Adams who was counted out in round three. Johnny Wilson beat Big Bruno who was disqualified in the sixth round. Giant Haystacks flattened Count Bartelli in the third round and won by countout. Marty Jones beat Mike Jordan who was unable to continue in the fourth round. Big Daddy and Chris Adams beat Mark Rocco and Bronco Wells with Wells walking out in the third minute and Rocco a minute later for a farcical ending to the match. Haystacks' team therefore won the match by three-two although the match quality left a lot to be desired.

Chris Adams was challenged to a judo match at Cleethorpes on the 30th by none other than Marty Jones. They first had a regulation wrestling match which Jones won when he forced Adams to submit in the third round. Adams had his revenge in the judo match when he beat Jones in the first to throw his opponent three times. Big Daddy was also on the show when once again Banger Walsh was on the receiving end of the double elbow drop and was knocked out in the second round.

August -

St.Albans was the venue for the wrestling shown on World of Sport on the 5th and it turned out to be an unmissable show. The preliminary match saw Catweazle take on Chris Bailey in a definite clash of styles as well as personalities. Catweazle was the winner in the third round when Bailey mistimed a dive and went out of the ring between the ropes. He injured his knee on landing and referee Max Ward called the bout off and declared Catweazle the winner.

The main event was a return match with Marty Jones who sported an afro perm taking on Mark Rocco after the inconclusive ending in the match shown from Chester. Both on TV and live around the halls I never saw a dull match between these two and this one was an absolute classic. The first round saw both wrestlers feel each other out with Rocco using his impressive wrestling skills most of the time. It didn't take long though for Rocco to lose his cool and right at the start of round two he was attacking Jones who was on the mat before Jones responded with a couple of arm drags to floor his opponent. Max Ward was having difficulty keeping the bout under control as both wrestlers were using moves and tactics that were not in the Lord Mountevans' rule book but Ward didn't see the need to issue a public warning to either. It was Rocco who got the first fall in round three with a reverse double knee hold from a bodyslam after a kick to Jones' head had stunned his opponent. Rocco couldn't wait for the next round to start whilst Jones sat on the bottom rope in the corner wanting a few extra seconds to recover but it was Jones who quickly drew level. First Jones delivered an upside down posting to Rocco before Rocco sent Jones flying with a stupidly high back drop. Jones retaliated with the same move that sent Rocco even higher before flooring him with a flying tackle. With Rocco on the mat Jones covered him for the count of three and an equaliser. Max Ward delivered his first public warning in round five to Rocco for throwing Jones over the top rope by his hair and straightaway Jones got one for doing the same thing. The action was by now crazily intense and some of the moves done were incredible and way ahead of their time. It was Rocco though who got the winning fall in round six when Jones missed an attempted flying tackle and hit the ropes instead. Rocco was quick to capitalise, he bodyslammed Jones to the canvas and covered him with a reverse double knee hold to win a spectacular match. It had to be given a five star rating.

That wasn't the end of things though as when MC John Harris announced the result Rocco grabbed the microphone and told everyone it was time for him to challenge Jones for his British Light/Heavyweight Title. Jones responded by saying he would train down to the Heavy/Middleweight weight limit and make it a title v title match. Rocco accepted the challenge and the match was on ! That still wasn't the end though as when Rocco went to leave the ring with his title belt on his shoulder Jones rather unsportingly attacked him from behind damaging the belt. A furious Rocco slammed the belt to the mat and told Jones he would pay for it in his blood. Rocco said the belt was two hundred years old and when he had finished with Jones he would look two hundred years old ! Absolutely fantastic entertainment for those there and those watching on TV.

Keeping the crowd at boiling point the final contest was a tag match with Mick McManus and Steve Logan taking on the newly formed 'Martial Arts Fighters' team of Clive Myers and Chris Adams. Adams was already on TV for the second time in less than two months as a professional wrestler. McManus and Logan looked on with disdain as Myers and Adams did a karate workout before the first bell rang and they preferred to do the old fashioned moves done behind the referee's back. It was Myers who got the first fall of the match in the fifth minute when he floored McManus with four chops before covering him with a folding press. For a time that looked to be the only fall happening in the twenty minutes time limit bout but with two minutes or so to go McManus finally managed to get an

211

equaliser. McManus and Logan had targeted Adams and with the help of plenty of double teaming weakening him McManus put Adams in a single leg Boston which saw him submit. Despite McManus and Logan going all out for a winning submission Adams managed to survive and it ended in a draw.

A blank weekend for grapple fans on the 12th with wrestling missing from World of Sport with the Benson and Hedges International Open golf tournament shown in its place.

Wrestling was back the following week with the annual show from Southport shown. The three matches shown were in a team tournament format with the other three shown the following week. Big Daddy once more captained the 'TV All-Stars' against Mick McManus' 'Mighty Men' with just six solo matches and no tag finale.

The first match saw Tony St.Clair tackle Ted Heath who had recently returned back home after an extended time in North America. St.Clair's weight advantage was too much for Heath to overcome and a fall in the sixth round sealed a two falls to one victory for St.Clair.

Next up was Big Daddy who took on and knocked out Butcher Bond in the second round with the double elbow drop.

The last match that week saw old rivals Johnny Saint and Jim Breaks meet again. Saint got the first fall in round two before Breaks equalised in round five. As Breaks celebrated his fall Saint punched him flush on the jaw which saw referee Dave Reese disqualify him instantly. Breaks nursing an injured jaw was also disqualified as Reese deemed him to have provoked Saint.

The team match continued on World of Sport on the 26th with the other three bouts in the tournament shown. Vic Faulkner won the opening contest with a victory against the much heavier Ray Thunder. Faulkner overcame a 4st. weight disadavantage to pin Thunder in the sixth round for a two falls to one win.

The second match saw what was the beginning of the passing of the torch with Mick McManus taking on Mal Sanders. Sanders had impressed everybody since his pro debut a year or so ago and was now ready for the next step. After giving Tony St.Clair a clear win on TV in 1977 to propel him to

212

the top of the bill and the British Heavyweight Title, McManus was now ready to do the same for Sanders. Sanders won the bout by two falls to one in the fourth round and it was announced that Sanders would now challenge McManus for his European Middleweight Title. In one of those strange things that happens in wrestling the title match was actually taped a week before the Southport show on 2nd August so many already knew the outcome of that before the initial bout was fought.

The final contest in the team tournament saw Bert Royal defeat Alan Woods by countout in round five when Woods was thrown out of the ring and wasn't able to return in time. Therefore the final score in the tournament was a five-nil win for the 'TV All-Stars'.

The last wrestling seen on TV for August came on the 28th with a Bank Holiday edition of World of Sport showing three matches from a bill recorded at Preston back in May. The main event saw Big Daddy partner Bobby Ryan to defeat Bruiser Muir and Steve Logan by two falls to one in a normal Daddy tag match. John Naylor defeated the heavier Alan Dennison with a winning fall in round seven.

The most interesting match shown was Kendo Nagasaki tackling the much heavier Rex Strong. With only one score needed it wasn't going to last long and Nagasaki won in round two. Nagasaki seemingly hypnotised Strong and took him to the mat with a flying tackle before pinning him with a cross press.

Around the halls -

August carried on with most of the action still happening at the coastal resorts but Joint Promotions were capitalising on Big Daddy's increasing popularity by running shows with him on at larger than usual halls. One such show was at Woking on the 5th which was a Saturday at the larger Leisure Centre rather than the normal Centre Halls. A packed crowd were in attendance to see the main event tag with Daddy and Steve Grey beating Giant Haystacks and Butcher Bond. Haystacks was still pulling the walking away trick and it was left to Daddy to pin Bond following a big splash in the eleventh minute for the winning fall.

The same night at Belle Vue saw a twelve man tournament featuring wrestlers of all weights competing for the trophy prize. On the night the number of participants was reduced to eleven when Dusty Miller and Jack Armstrong didn't turn up. Jack Armstrong had only made his debut in May for Dale Martin but was being pushed by Max Crabtree as the 'next big thing' in the heavyweight ranks. Armstrong had already been featured on a front cover of the programme as well as already having his picture on advertising posters which was unprecedented for a newcomer. Unfortunately Armstrong had a dark side to him which saw him firstly remanded in prison before being sentenced to a severe amount of time in jail for armed robbery. Dusty Miller was billed as 'The singing dustman' in a gimmick that not surprisingly didn't last long. There was only one replacement available who was a new name to the Belle Vue crowd in that of The Resister. The Resister wore a mask and a few fans in attendance may have recognised him as it was Ted Heath beneath the hood. The first round heats saw Marty Jones pin Alan Woods in round three. Colin Joynson pin Count Bartelli also in round three. Brian Maxine's match with Alan Dennison ended with both disqualified in the third round. John Naylor beat Johnny England who was counted out in round three. Bobby Ryan pinned the Gay One in the first round.The Resister received a bye to the next round. The semi finals saw Marty Jones get a winning fall in the third round to beat Colin Joynson and Bobby Ryan beat The Resister who was disqualified in the second round but Ryan was unable to continue in the tournament. This left Jones v John Naylor as the final and it was Jones who won and went home with a nice trophy for his mantlepiece.

There was a curious tale that week involving Chris Adams. Adams was doing his first week of wrestling for Dale Martin and it was also my first time watching him wrestle live that Wednesday at Hastings. As was usual I got an autograph ,had a brief chat and I found him to be a really friendly guy unlike some other wrestlers. Friday night I was at Bognor Regis and Chris Adams was on the bill there as well and to my delight he recognised me outside and was curious about the number of shows I went to. The problem with Adams being at Bognor Regis was that the same day he should have been at Leamington Spa magistrates court answering a charge of criminal damage. An intoxicated Adams was showing a friend some of his newly learnt wrestling techniques when he took a flying dropkick at a car and caused some damage. He appeared before the magistrates the following week where not only was he fined £25 with £10 compensation for damaging the car but he was also fined £10 for breaching bail and not appearing there the previous Friday. Adams' excuse was that he was coming back from wrestling at Penzance on the Thursday when his car broke down and he hitched a lift instead to London. He claimed to have notified the court on the Friday morning of his inability to attend the court but the presiding magistrate told him he could have made more effort. Adams' solicitor claimed that he earnt £40 a week from wrestling and so the escapade cost him more than a weeks wages.

The second spectacular at Gaumont Cinema in Kilburn was on the 18th with a top notch programme on offer for another packed crowd. The main event was a follow up from the first show there with Kendo Nagasaki and Giant Haystacks meeting again but now in a tag match with Nagasaki partnering Tony St.Clair to take on Haystacks and his partner Mark Rocco. The match lasted a short but violent five minutes and ended with Haystacks and Rocco disqualified. The rest of the show comprised of a knockout tournament with eight wrestlers this time competing for the prize. The first round matches saw Bert Royal get the winning fall in round four to beat Bobby Barnes. Steve Logan force a submission from Catweazle in the third round. Clive Myers pinned Johnny Czeslaw in the third round and Brian Maxine beat Steve Grey who was counted out in round three. The first semi final ended with both Maxine and Royal fighting in the orchestra pit rather than the ring. They were both counted out in the third round so the other semi final turned into the final in which Myers beat Logan by two straight falls inside three rounds.

After a week at the south coast resorts Big Daddy returned north to wrestle at Belle Vue on the 19th in a six man tag challenge. Daddy teamed up with The Royals to take on Giant Haystacks, Beer Barrel Brannigan and Banger Walsh. Faulkner was was unable to continue after submitting in the fifth minute before Haystacks disappeared a minute later. He was joined by Brannigan who walked out in the tenth minute to leave Walsh to take the losing fall when he was pinned by Daddy following a big splash in the thirteenth minute. Dave Smith had another match with Bernie Wright on the show with Smith winning by two falls to one in round six. Marty Jones and Mark Rocco had another of their highly exciting matches which ended in a one fall each draw at the end of the scheduled six rounds. Clive Myers' contest with Steve Grey ended in a No Contest in the eighth round when Grey was injured. The final bout of the night also ended inconclusively when Jackie Turpin tired of Tally Ho Kaye's antics and knocked him out from a punch which landed flush on Kaye's chin. The referee took pity on Turpin and ruled it a No Contest because of Kaye's earlier rulebreaking provoking Turpin.

The Gaumont Cinema in Southampton had their first spectacular on the 25th with a capacity crowd in attendance to see Big Daddy in the main event. Daddy and Mal Sanders beat Giant Haystacks and Mark Rocco by two falls to one in the contest.

Kendo Nagasaki's return to the ring as an unmasked wrestler came to an end by the end of August with him missing all of his bookings leaving a lot of fans disappointed. Even with all the wacky angles such as the hypnotism stuff which would make an unwanted return a few years later. Wrestling without the mask made Nagasaki lose that unique something the masked man had. With the retirement of Nagasaki just as they had filmed a challenge by him to wrestle Tony St.Clair for the British Heavyweight Title it seemed an inopportune time to walk away. Nagasaki and George always danced to their own tune and that was it from them till Kendo reappeared with the mask back on in the early eighties.

September -

Davey 'Boy' Smith as he was now billed made his World of Sport debut on the 2nd in a show taped at Huddersfield. His opponent was Bernie Wright who he had wrestled a few times around the halls before this bout. It was introduced by MC Neil Soden as a special teenage contest to be wrestled over three minute rounds. Both wrestlers were unrecognisable from their later years but you could see in the early exchanges that they had been trained really well. Wright got the first fall in the third round with a neat reversal for a shoulder press. Smith equalised in round five with a well executed victory roll into a pinfall. The match ended without further score and this was an excellent match for two wrestlers so inexperienced who could have froze in front of the TV cameras.

The opening match saw Tally Ho Kaye face the former boxer Jackie Turpin with Brian Crabtree as referee for the contest. Kaye got his first public warning from Crabtree for attacking Turpin on the canvas in round two before receiving a second in round three for not breaking the hold whilst on the ropes. The illegal tactics did their job though as shortly after Kaye forced Turpin to submit from a Boston Crab. Turpin was quickly on level terms though with an equaliser in the fourth round when he reversed an attempted Boston Crab into a double knee hold to pin Kaye. Unfortunately MC Soden's microphone had packed up so he had to shout out the announcement of the fall. The contest ended in the fifth round when referee Crabtree disqualified Kaye after he had dropped Turpin onto the ropes before posting him. Luckily Soden's microphone was working so he could announce the decision and Kaye could protest that he hadn't done anything wrong.

The second contest saw Kid Chocolate tackle Johnny England who insisted on limbering up with some posing before the contest could begin. Chocolate got the first fall in the second round rolling up England into a side folding press as he caught England by surprise. England came back to equalise in the fourth round with an arm lever hold which saw Chocolate submit to. The hold had injured Chocolate's wrist and he was forced to retire on his stool giving England the win. Sadly Kid

217

Chocolate aka Alain Bardouille died as I was writing this book in September 2021.

All six wrestlers then competed in an over the top rope Battle Royale finale. First out was Wright followed by Chocolate whose injured wrist hindered his attempts to stay in. Turpin made a spectacular exit, flying over the top rope as Kaye ducked. This left Kaye, England and young Smith. Smith was quickly thrown out as the other two teamed up on him. Kaye was the winner when he double crossed England who was posing by the ropes thinking he had shared the win with Kaye. Kaye threw England over the top rope to claim the prize and England had learnt a lesson about trust.

The perils of taping the wrestling too early for World of Sport was perfectly illustrated on the 9th September broadcast. The three bouts shown were from the other half of the Huddersfield show recorded. The opening contest was between Kendo Nagasaki and Colin Joynson with only the one fall or submission needed to win. Nagasaki was back to being the rulebreaker and attacked Joynson when he was on the ropes and Kendo was losing his cool already in the first round. Referee Emil Poilve was surprisingly lenient as Nagasaki kicked Joynson out of the ring under the bottom rope as Nagasaki continually flouted the rulebook. Joynson gave as good as he got at the start of the second round but his attack didn't last long as Nagasaki delivered straight finger blows to his throat. Nagasaki then got the winner from the grapevine hold with the face bar to which Joynson submitted instantly. Gorgeous George grabbed the microphone from MC Neil Soden and repeated his claims for Nagasaki to be allowed to challenge Tony St.Clair for the British Heavyweight Title. Luckily Tony St.Clair was there to answer the challenge and entered the ring and told George to 'Put up or shut up, anywhere ,anytime'. George accepted the challenge on behalf of Nagasaki and it looked at the time as the match was on. Unfortunately by the time this was shown on World of Sport Nagasaki had retired and the championship match was never held.

The main event of the afternoon saw Mick McManus defend his European Middleweight Title against Mal Sanders who had recently beaten him on a bout seen on TV on 26th August.

After a couple of rounds of wrestling in which Sanders was giving as good as he got a frustrated McManus started with the tricks in the third round. Referee Brian Crabtree gave McManus a public warning in that round for showing dissent which was very rare. McManus weakened Sanders with plenty of forearm jabs with the odd punch thrown before bodyslamming him to the mat and covering him for the first fall in round five. McManus got his final public warning in the sixth round for kneeing Sanders as he was on the mat and Sanders was a sorry sight as he now bled from a cut on his forehead. Sanders found renewed energy in the seventh round to get back on level terms when he stunned McManus with a dropkick before covering him with a cross press following a bodyslam. The match ended in controversy in round nine with McManus disqualified by referee Crabtree after he had thrown Sanders over the top rope. Sanders had attempted a flying tackle but in doing so had gone too near the top rope and McManus had used Sanders' impetus to dump him out of the ring. Kent Walton thought that McManus was the winner as Sanders couldn't continue but MC Soden said that Crabtree had disqualified McManus as it was an illegal move. As titles could change hands on a disqualification this meant Sanders was the new European Middleweight Champion. An incensed McManus took the microphone and ranted that it was never a disqualification and Sanders had been counted out but the result stood and McManus had successfully passed the torch onto Sanders.

The other bout seen on an eventful afternoon saw Jim Breaks once again face Johnny Saint in front of the TV cameras. It was Saint who went in front with the first fall in the third round when he pinned Breaks with a folding press secured by a bridge. Breaks went on the attack with several arm weakeners which culminated in Saint submitting from a 'Breaks' special' in the fifth round. Saint's left arm had been severely injured by the move and he was unable to continue which left Breaks the winner.

The wrestling seen on World of Sport on the 16th was the second half of the show taped at St.Albans in July and featured the only TV appearance of Billy Robinson on his visit home. Robinson's opponent was Lee Bronson who endured a rather painful wrestling lesson for the four rounds that the bout lasted. Robinson pinned Bronson for the first fall in round three with a folding press secured by a bridge after a nasty looking suplex had weakened Bronson. The winner for a two straight falls win for Robinson came in the fourth round when he pinned Bronson following a double arm suplex.

Another heavyweight match was on next with Wayne Bridges taking on Giant Haystacks. As usual Haystacks stalled in the opening minutes of the first round, arguing with the crowd and referee Max Ward before eventually locking up with Bridges. Haystacks got a public warning for continually knocking Bridges off of the ring apron as he tried to clamber back into the ring at the end of round one. Haystacks went ahead in round two with a single leg Boston Crab after he had delivered a splash to Bridges' legs. Round three saw referee Ward give Haystacks his final public warning for continually kicking Bridges' legs whilst he was on the canvas before Bridges retaliated with a couple of flying headbutts. Bridges then floored Haystacks with a flying tackle and managed to cover him with a cross press for a count of three and the equalising fall. The match unfortunately came to a premature end in the fourth round when Bridges attempted to lift Haystacks and they both collapsed to the canvas. A ring board had then broken when such a hefty weight had landed on it. Referee Ward was forced to stop the match which left MC John Harris to announce the result was left open.

The final contest saw Bobby Barnes face Steve Grey with the ring luckily repaired in time for it to start. Grey upset the heavier Barnes with a folding press in the third round with Barnes complaining that his feet were through the ropes. Barnes reverted to the dirty tricks in the fourth round getting a public warning from Max Ward. Barnes got an equaliser in the fifth round when Grey submitted from a backbreaker after several postings had weakened his spine. Grey was the winner though when Barnes was disqualified in the sixth. As Barnes tried to put Grey in an aeroplane spin hold he knocked the referee flying. Although it looked accidental Ward disqualified him.

The wrestling seen on World of Sport on the 23rd contained one of the best bouts I've described in this book or in my previous one The Saturday Afternoon War. This was the title v title match between Mark Rocco and Marty Jones but before that contest in the show recorded at Woking there was the usual preliminary bout to see. This week it was a catchweight match between Clive Myers in his now familiar 'Iron Fist' outfit and the much heavier Romany Riley. Myers took the lead with a fall in round two with a cross press after a double arm suplex had floored Riley. Riley didn't like this and began the rough stuff in the third round to try and subdue his much speedier opponent. Referee Peter Szakacs gave Riley a public warning for kneeing Myers in the head whilst he was on the floor. Riley got a final warning from Szakacs in the fourth round when he kicked Myers out of the ring. The weakeners did their trick as later in the round Riley got an equaliser when he pinned Myers with a cross press after slamming him to mat. Myers though recovered to come back strongly in the fifth delivering several chops before dropkicking Riley over the top rope. Riley was counted out by Szakacs but was unhappy about the way he lost and challenged Myers to an arm wrestling match. MC Bobby Palmer was in the process of telling the audience that Myers was off to Kansas City to compete in the World Arm-Wrestling Championships when Riley said he could beat him at that sport. A table and a couple of chairs were hastily brought to the ring and not surprisingly Myers defeated Riley. Romany Riley sadly passed away shortly before this book was published.

After that entertaining opener it was time for the much anticipated title v title match with Mark Rocco putting the British Heavy/Middleweight Title on the line against Marty Jones who was putting up his British Light/Heavyweight Title. There was a rare show of sportsmanship between the two as they shook hands after referee Joe D'Orazio had delivered his pre-match instructions. The first round saw both Rocco and Jones feel each other out with some basic holds but it wasn't long till the action started to heat up. Surprisingly in the first couple of rounds both of them stuck to the rules and D'Orazio had a quiet time of it but that didn't last. At the end of the second round Rocco slammed Jones across the top rope which injured Jones' knee and as soon as the third round started Rocco targetted it. Jones broke the leg hold Rocco had used by kicking him over the top rope and on landing the ringsiders let Rocco know how they felt about him. Rocco got his first public warning in round four for a punch to Jones' stomach as the bell rung for the end of the session. Jones overcame the injured knee which was troubling him to get the first fall in the fifth round when he caught Rocco with an over the top double arm shoulder press and pinned him for the count of three. Rocco hit back straightaway in round six with an equaliser after a minute of the round. After a failed attempt at a cross press Rocco tried a double arm suplex and pinned Jones to leave the match perfectly poised at one fall each. The match came to a dramatic ending in the eighth round when Rocco was backdropped out of the ring by Jones and was counted out lying on the floor at ringside. Marty Jones now held both the British Light/Heavyweight Title and the British Heavy/Middleweight Title but not for long as he gave the heavy/middleweight belt back to MC Bobby Palmer. Jones stated he wished to remain the British Light/Heavyweight Champion and so the British Heavy/Middleweight Title was declared vacant.

After all the drama of the previous match there was a change of emphasis in that week's final bout with Johnny Czeslaw taking on Billy Torontos with only one fall needed to win. Czeslaw got the win when he pinned Torontos following a bodyslam in the third round.

The Woking show was the final time MC Bobby Palmer would announce in front of the TV cameras although the second half of that show would not be seen till January. Another departure amongst the MC ranks was that of Mike Judd who also left his position in the back office at Dale Martin. There were rumours of financial irregularities going on and soon after Judd departed and he was never heard of or seen again. John Harris was promoted to lead MC for Dale Martin although he had problems with his personal life which forced his departure a couple of years later.

There was another dramatic week of wrestling seen on World of Sport on the 30th with three bouts coming from Digbeth. Digbeth was probably the best small hall to watch wrestling in Britain with the crowd close up whether they were on the stage, up in the balcony or sat around the ring.

The first match saw Honey Boy Zimba take on Ray Thunder with Thunder in front from a fall in round two when coverage began during the fourth round. The unruly Thunder was giving Zimba plenty of problems with plenty of rough stuff which gained him a public warning in the fourth round from referee Dave Reese. Thunder got his final public warning in the fifth round for kicking Zimba whilst he was on the canvas but Zimba retaliated with a face first knee drop. Zimba then pinned the weakened Thunder with a double knee press after slamming him to the mat. It didn't take long for Zimba to get the winner with another body slam followed by the same double knee hold used to pin Thunder for a two falls to one victory.

The main event was a tag match which saw Big Daddy and Giant Haystacks meeting once more. Daddy was billed with newcomer Jack Armstrong although Kent Walton insisted on calling him Dave Armstrong. Perhaps Walton got confused with the great Dave Armstong, the Choppington Chicken who was one of the top heavyweights in pre and post-war Britain ? Unfortunately Armstrong was still in custody so unavailable. He was replaced by Gary Wensor whilst Haystacks was teaming with Big Bruno. It was rather a strange match only lasting a second or two under seven minutes and neither team getting a public warning. Wensor took quite a pasting from Bruno and then Haystacks in the first couple of minutes before eventually making the 'hot tag'. After three belly butts from Daddy on Haystacks who then fled from the ring and tagged in Bruno. A belly butt sent Bruno flying and he was knocked to the ground and covered with the help of a big splash from Daddy for the first fall. Haystacks attempted to return to the dressing room but was stopped by Daddy whilst in the ring Bruno delivered another beating to Wensor before getting an equaliser with a neck lift submission. The shock win happened a minute or so later when Haystacks slammed Wensor to the mat and landed a huge splash on him. As Kent Walton remarked Wensor will never move from that and finally Haystacks had a win over Big Daddy on TV. That would have been the ideal opportunity to build to a singles match between Daddy and Haystacks which would have drawn a huge crowd as well as a lot of money. It didn't happen though and it would be nearly three years till they finally fought in their major singles match with arguably the rivalry way past its sell by date. After that and in the further ten years of wrestling being shown on ITV Daddy never tasted defeat again in a televised match winning against a myriad of opponents some good, some bad and some absolutely rotten.

The week's coverage ended with a drawn match between Bert Royal and Brian Maxine. Royal went in front in the third round with a pinfall before Maxine equalised in the fifth with a single leg Boston Crab submission.

Around the halls -

September saw the start of the new season at the inland venues as well as the last shows from the seaside halls. Kendo Nagasaki should have been at Belle Vue on the 2nd to take part in a knockout tournament alongside Tony St.Clair, John Cox and Gwyn Davies. Not only was Nagasaki missing but so was Davies with Pat Roach and Beau Jack taking their places. The first semi final saw Tony St.Clair pin John Cox in round three and the other saw Pat Roach defeat Beau Jack by making him submit in round two. The final was held with a ladder match stipulation and it was St.Clair who climbed up the ladder to grab the money in five minutes. Mark Rocco had another excellent match with Marty Jones on the bill and it was Rocco who won when he made Jones submit in the fifth round for the win. Johnny Czeslaw beat Ray Thunder who was counted out in round six whilst Honey Boy Zimba beat the Masked UFO by two straight falls in round's three and four. UFO was unmasked afterwards to reveal him to be Brian Hunt.

With the retirement of Kendo Nagasaki there was a chance for someone else to challenge Tony St.Clair for the British Heavyweight Title and at Croydon on the 5th it was Wayne Bridges who stepped up to the mark. Bridges pushed St.Clair all the way in a tremendous match with Bridges getting the first fall in the seventh round before St.Clair equalised in the tenth. At the end of the scheduled twelfth round it was still one fall each and St.Clair had held onto his title by the skin of his teeth in a match that thoroughly engrossed those in attendance. Also on the bill Mick McManus took on Clive Myers in a two part challenge. Firstly McManus beat Myers in a wrestling match with a fall in the second round before Myers gained revenge in a judo match winning by two clear throws. Bobby Barnes beat Tony White who was counted out in the seventh round. Ken Joyce beat newcomer Johnny Risco by two straight falls in four rounds whilst once more Catweazle sent the crowd home happy in the finale when he beat Pat O'Sullivan in the third round. O'Sullivan had made his debut for Joint Promotions earlier in the year and was best known as a regular substitute on a show that was missing a billed wrestler. I used to imagine Pat sat at home by his phone every lunchtime waiting for a call from the Dale Martin office telling him where he needed to be that evening if they were a wrestler short.

Tony St.Clair rekindled his rivalry with Pat Roach at Hanley on the 9th when Roach took the place of Kendo Nagasaki. A very bad tempered brawl ended in the fifth round when Roach ran out into the street outside to escape from St.Clair. Bobby Ryan also had a popular win with a two falls to one victory over the irritating Johnny England.

It was announced that for the third consecutive show Big Daddy would headline the card at The Royal Albert Hall when it opened its doors for the first programme of the new season on the 27th. With the announcement of the first show came the news that because of overwhelming demand they would go back to monthly programmes starting in January 1979.

The next Kilburn show was on the 15th and it was hindered by several no shows and changes to the advertised bill. Not surprisingly it failed to live up to the first two shows there with a disappointing night's wrestling on offer. The matches saw Romany Riley beat Count Bartelli by two falls to one in the fifth round. Johnny Kwango beat Gay One by two straight falls in the fourth round. Wayne Bridges defeated Pat Roach by two falls to one in round five. Butcher Bond beat Billy Torontos with a winning submission in the fifth round. The makeshift team of Steve Grey and Chris Adams beat Mick McManus and Steve Logan who were disqualified in the eighteenth minute. The easiest way to kill a venue was illustrated at Kilburn that night.

There were similar changes to the card at Belle Vue the next night with alterations to two of the three advertised main events. Giant Haystacks was booked to wrestle Ray Steele but Steele was replaced at short notice by Bill Blake. Blake was flattened in the first round with a splash from Haystacks and carried from the ring unable to continue. The Royals were slated to wrestle another team of brothers, in fact they were twins, Dai and Emlyn Tremorgan. The Tremorgans had wrestled a couple of dates for Joint Promotions but had decided to return to the independent circuit by the time of the Belle Vue show. The Royals therefore faced a makeshift team of Lucky Gordon and Pete Evans who were beaten by two straight falls in the fifteenth minute. The other main event saw Big Daddy flip Banger Walsh over his shoulders and land the double elbow drop on him in the first round to knock Walsh spark out. Bobby Ryan beat Johnny England who was disqualified in the sixth round. The rest of the card saw a four man tournament culminating in an over the top rope Battle Royale. Alan Dennison pinned Kid Chocolate in the third round whilst The Resister beat newcomer Tom Rigby with a fall in the second round. Rigby had made his debut earlier in the month and had a similar pedigree as Chris Adams as a highly decorated judo exponent. Rigby would be renamed shortly afterwards as Ringo Rigby. Alan Dennison won the over the top rope finale in under three minutes to complete another entertaining night's wrestling there.

Big Daddy made his first appearance of the new season at Croydon on the 19th when he partnered Bobby Ryan in the main event tag against The Masked Assassins who were accompanied by their manager The Kangaroo Kid. Ryan who was making an ultra rare appearance for Dale Martin made it a winning one when they beat the Assassins by two falls to one. Billy Torontos beat Sid Cooper who was counted out in the third round. Pat Patton defeated travelling companion Johnny England with a winning fall coming in round six. Butcher Bond beat John Elijah by two falls to one in the sixth round and Jack Armstrong pinned Steve Logan in the third round to win their bout.

226

There was yet another capacity crowd at The Royal Albert Hall for the first show of the season there on 27th September. The advertised main event of Big Daddy and Mal Sanders taking on The Tremorgan Twins had to be changed with Daddy and Sanders now facing The Masked Invaders. The Invaders were a team that were hurriedly put together to plug the gap and it showed in the match. Daddy and Sanders had an easy night of it with a two straight falls win in six minutes. Daddy managed to unmask the lighter Invader after the match before he could flee and revealed him to be Phil Rowe. The bigger Invader managed to get away with the mask still on but to seasoned ringsiders it was obvious that it was the burly, Blackpool lifeguard Rex Strong trying to conceal his identity.

Chris Adams made his Albert Hall debut in the main support as part of the 'Martial Arts Fighters' team alongside partner Clive Myers. In something of a terrible mismatch they were booked to take on Giant Haystacks in a handicap tag match. Haystacks outweighed both men's total weight by over 10st. and it showed once Adams got too close to the big man. Haystacks clubbed Adams to the floor and landed a splash on him that saw Adams counted out. His partner Myers wisely decided not to carry on alone so Haystacks ended up with an easy win.

Mick McManus got his hands on Jim Breaks in a match after their disagreement at the Bedworth show seen on World of Sport back in July. To nobody's surprise it ended up with both of them disqualified in the third round. Ted Heath made an Albert Hall return after a long absence but it was a losing one when John Naylor beat him by two falls to one in round six. After his defeat of Mark Rocco Marty Jones now eyed up another champion's belt and faced heavyweight number one Tony St.Clair in a non title match. Unfortunately Jones was injured in the fifth round and St.Clair refused to accept the win so a No Contest was recorded. Finally Billy Torontos rounded off another great night's wrestling when he got the only fall needed to beat Chris Bailey in the third round.

Young Dave Smith's career had somewhat stalled due to his education commitments and his appearances were being carefully managed. Smith was able to fit in a bout at Chester on the 29th when he faced a tough task against John Naylor. Naylor gave Smith a thorough schooling on the way to beating him by two straight falls in the fifth round. Big Daddy was in the main event tag there partnering Jackie Turpin to defeat Rex Strong and Banger Walsh inside less than eight minutes. An intriguing match up saw former judo stars Chris Adams and Ringo Rigby meet in a wrestling bout with Rigby winning with a submission in the fourth round. Afterwards Adams asked for a judo match and he defeated Rigby by three throws in just over a minute.

Jim Breaks had yet another chance to win Johnny Saint's World Lightweight Title on the 30th, this time at Belle Vue. Yet again though Breaks lost, this time his temper causing him to lose by disqualification. Saint took the first fall in round nine before Breaks equalised in round eleven. Despite receiving two public warnings Breaks didn't heed them and in the twelth round he was disqualified. A rather average programme was on offer with Chris Adams beating Tally Ho Kaye who was disqualified in the fourth round. Billy Torontos beat Sid Cooper who was counted out in the fourth round. Steve Grey beat Mike Jordan with a deciding fall coming in round five and finally Alan Dennison took on Pete Ross who was injured in the second round and Dennison refused to accept the decision.

October -

There was no wrestling shown on World of Sport on the 7th with the Dunlop Masters golf tournament on instead.

The wrestling on World of Sport the following Saturday featured the second half of the Digbeth show. Unfortunately without the advertised main event which should have seen Jim Breaks challenge Johnny Saint for the World Lightweight Title. It was reported that Saint had been in a car crash on the way to the venue and instead of wrestling he was sat at ringside with his arm in a sling. Breaks therefore took on replacement Kid Chocolate instead. The coverage commenced in round two and within a minute or so Breaks got the first fall with a folding press although Breaks had his legs on the rope to enable it. Saint pointed this out to the referee Dave Reese so MC Brian

Crabtree announced the fall was disallowed and to make it even worse Reese dished out a public warning to Breaks as well. It didn't matter as Breaks soon went with the arm weakeners in the third round and it wasn't long till Chocolate submitted but from an arm lever instead of the usual 'Breaks' special'. Chocolate tried to rally in round four but wasn't able to get an equaliser and Breaks went onto a two nil win when Chocolate submitted from a 'Breaks' special' in the fifth round. Luckily Johnny Saint showed great powers of healing and was able to make his booked appearance at Lincoln the next night. The opening match that week was a rather dull contest between Johnny Wilson and Mel Stuart in which Wilson pinned Stuart for the only fall needed in round three.

Marty Jones faced Tony St.Clair in the revised main event with another chance for Jones to press his claims for a heavyweight title match after his injury ruined the Albert Hall contest between the two. Facing a full blown heavyweight like St.Clair who had a 2st. weight advantage was a lot different for Jones than taking on opponents at his own weight. Jones did surprise St.Clair though taking the first fall in round three with an over the top folding press after he reversed an attempted monkey climb. St.Clair wasn't behind for long though when he got an equalising fall in round four with a superb reverse double arm shoulder press as Jones attempted a hip toss. The winner came in the sixth round when the wrestlers clashed heads and it was St.Clair who recovered the quicker to pin Jones with an over the top folding press. This was an excellent contest between two brilliant wrestlers.

Golf replaced the wrestling on World of Sport for the second time in the month on the 21st with this time the European Open being seen as the priority.

Wrestling was back on World of Sport the next Saturday though with an interesting show from Walton-on-Thames broadcast. The centrepiece of the week's show was a rematch although it was a non-title bout between Mick McManus and Mal Sanders. Without the title at stake the bout lost a bit of its significance and the opening round was pretty even with both wrestlers keeping to the rules. McManus started the second round weakening Sanders with the usual forearm jabs but

Sanders countered with a neat whip into a wristlock before an overexcited Sanders attacked McManus whilst he was on the ropes. The first fall came in the second when Sanders reversed a posting, a quick leap over McManus before an over the top folding press secured Sanders the fall. McManus lost his cool in round three as Sanders attacked his ears for which McManus made vociferous complaints to referee Max Ward. Ward gave McManus his first public warning in that round for a sly punch to Sanders' stomach as he tried a flying tackle. The Mayor of Elmbridge who ran the Leisure Centre was shown in the interval watching the match intensely but the bout barely lasted another few seconds. The bell sounded to start the fourth round and McManus charged across the ring and caught Sanders flush on the jaw with a forearm smash. Sanders collapsed to the floor and was counted out by referee Ward to give McManus his revenge but not his title back. As MC Fred Downes made his announcement McManus grabbed the microphone and launched a tirade of abuse at Sanders which was mainly drowned out by boos from the crowd but McManus did demand a title match which was now fully deserved.

The rest of that week's show saw The Martial Arts Fighters team of Clive Myers and Chris Adams take on Butcher Bond and Bobby Barnes in solo matches and then a tag. Adams took on Barnes in the first solo match with Adams still showing great potential as a pro wrestler for someone so new to the game. Adams had adopted the mule kick as one of his moves and it soon upset Barnes when he received a couple. Barnes' greater experience soon told though and in the third round he got the only fall needed to win when pinned Adams. The problem was that referee Max Ward missed the punch that Barnes delivered to Adams before he was able to pin him with a folding press.

The second solo bout followed with Bond facing the much lighter Myers. Myers bamboozled Bond in the early stages with his lightning speed and chops but Bond hit back with clubbing blows which soon sent Myers to the canvas. Bond ended the second round with a crafty move when he pulled Myers' headband across his eyes so Myers couldn't see. Myers wandered about the ring sightless whilst Bond attacked him from all angles and was only saved when the bell rung to end the round. Myers showed his anger when he removed his jacket at the start of the third round to show he meant business and straight away attacked Bond with kicks and chops. The end came a minute or so later when Myers launched a dive whilst Bond was trapped on the ropes. Bond anticipated the move and tried a reverse and he sent Myers flying over the top rope with a hip toss. But Bond went flying over the rope too and they landed in a heap at ringside. Neither of them was able to get back inside the ring before Max Ward's count of ten finished so a double countout was the decision.

The tag match finale ended the week's show with once again the speed and moves of the Martial Arts Fighters impressing in the early stages of the bout. Barnes soon changed things when he threw Myers over the top rope to land on Kent Walton's table at ringside. It was Myers though who got the first fall in the sixth minute when he pinned Barnes after a straight fingers jab to Barnes' throat halted his momentum. This only made Barnes and Bond intensify the rough stuff and Bond turned an attempted backbreaker into just throwing Adams over the top rope to the floor outside. Max Ward signalled the end of the contest and Fred Downes announced that for failing to wrestle to the referee's instructions Ward had disqualified both Barnes and Bond.

Around the halls -

October saw the end of two fine careers when both Mike Marino and Tibor Szakacs retired from the ring. Szakacs' comeback had lasted about six months and it was obvious age had caught up with him when watching his matches. Marino had been seen less frequently since losing the booking job at Dale Martin and persistent injuries seemingly saw him forced to retire from the ring. Surprisingly Marino made a comeback eighteen months or so later when like a lot of wrestlers the lure of the game proved too much to ignore.

The show at Croydon on the 3rd saw a Battle Royale advertised with such matches unheard of before Max Crabtree took over at Dale Martin. The solo matches saw Steve Grey beat Mel Stuart with a winning fall in the fifth round. Tibor Szakacs won a rough match against Bronco Wells pinning him in round five. Mal Sanders defeated Brian Maxine with a deciding fall in the fifth round. Mark Rocco beat Johnny Saint who was unable to continue after submitting in the fourth round. Count Bartelli won when Big Bruno was disqualified in round four. Before the over the top rope match it was announced that both Saint and Szakacs were unable to compete in it through injury whilst Bruno and Maxine were barred due to their disgraceful behaviour. The match was won by the lightest wrestler left in, Steve Grey.

Wrestling was back at Kilburn's Gaumont Cinema on the 13th with an interesting looking show. The main feature was a heavyweight knockout tournament with the contestants being Big Daddy, masked wrestler The Ringer, Banger Walsh and Lucky Gordon. Gordon replaced the advertised Jack Armstrong who was back in trouble with the law and missing his appearances again. The tournament matches didn't last long with the first semi final won by Walsh who forced Gordon to submit in the second round. Daddy saw off the Ringer with a fall in the first round after a big splash flattened the masked man. Before he left the ring he was unmasked as Phil Rowe. Daddy not surprisingly won the final when he once more knocked out Walsh with a double elbow drop in round one.

Wrestling fans were catered for with a lightweight clash of champions with World No.1 Johnny Saint facing British title holder Steve Grey. Grey once more pressed his claims for another world title match when he defeated Saint with a winning fall in round six. An international heavyweight clash saw Honey Boy Zimba pin Ray Thunder for the deciding fall in the sixth round and a similar result saw Pete Roberts beat Lee Bronson. The other match saw Catweazle defeat Tally Ho Kaye who was disqualified in the fourth round.

Mark Rocco got another chance to win Marty Jones' British Light/Heavyweight Title at Belle Vue the next evening. Rocco once again fell short when it mattered and Jones retained his belt when the match was stopped in round nine with Rocco unable to continue through injury. Rocco's submission in the seventh round was equalised by a fall for Jones in the eighth before the match came to its early ending.

There was a curious ladder match on the show with Alan Dennison clambering to the top of the ladder in five minutes to beat The Resister. The Resister aka Ted Heath was of course Dennison's partner in The Dennisons' tag team before Heath departed for the USA. The rest of the programme saw Pat Roach easily defeat Beau Jack who was counted out in the fourth round courtesy of a 'Brumagen Bump'. Clive Myers beat Steve Logan who was disqualified in the fifth round and finally Dave Smith bit off more than he could chew when the youngster took on John Naylor. Naylor was far too experienced and knowledgeable for him and Naylor gave Smith another wrestling lesson before the contest was stopped in the fourth round with Smith unable to continue. Naylor refused to accept the win so a No Contest was the decision.

One of the best lightweights of recent times Johnny Kidd made his pro debut on the 21st at Salisbury. Kidd who was trained by Ken Joyce was called in as a late notice replacement with the show hit by non-appearances to take on Tony Skarlo. Unfortunately it was a losing debut with Kidd being pinned by Skarlo for the only fall needed for the win. Kidd's career in the pro ranks was a bit slow to take off and he wasn't seen on TV till 1981 but he was one of the British wrestlers who managed to keep the sport going in the dark days of the late 1990's when nobody was much interested in it and his reminisces have greatly helped with both of my books.

Once again a match between Johnny Saint and Jim Breaks topped the bill at Belle Vue, this time on the 28th. The contest wasn't a title match but was scheduled for the twelve round title limit. In the end the bout only lasted four rounds with the contest brought to end at the end of the fourth round. Breaks had just secured an equalising fall when Saint lost his cool with Breaks' cheating and a brawl broke out so the match was abandoned. Tony St.Clair beat Butcher Bond by two falls to one in the fifth round of a bad tempered heavyweight match. Bert Royal gave weight and a beating to Ray Thunder with a winning fall coming in round six. Catweazle beat Blackjack Mulligan who was counted out in the fourth round whilst Mike

233

Jordan beat Tally Ho Kaye who was disqualified in the third round.

At Hanley there was mayhem galore on the same night with naturally Mark Rocco at the heart of it. Local favourite Bobby Ryan was on the bill booked to take on The Resister but as they waited for the bell to start the match Rocco and Marty Jones entered the ring and attacked Ryan. Ryan was injured by the assault and the match with The Resister had to be cancelled. Jones who was something of a hate figure at the Potteries venue was teaming with Rocco in the main event tag against a team of Pete Roberts and Honey Boy Zimba. Rocco and Jones continued with their bad behaviour in their own match and ended up being disqualified in the twelfth minute.

October finished with two title matches at Croydon on the 31st with Steve Grey defending his British Lightweight Title against Jim Breaks. Despite Breaks taking the lead with a 'Breaks' special' in the sixth round Grey battled back to retain his title in the ninth round. An equalising fall in the eight round for Grey was quickly followed by a winner in the ninth for another successful title defence.

The other title match saw Brian Maxine defend his British Middleweight Title against European kingpin Mal Sanders. Sanders attempt to add the British belt to his European one ended in the seventh round when he accidentally caught Maxine with a low blow and was disqualified on technical grounds. Croydon newcomer Ringo Rigby saw off Blackjack Mulligan by two straight falls in the third round. Zoltan Boscik recorded an impressive win beating Alan Dennison with the deciding fall in the fifth round. Johnny Czeslaw beat Tally Ho Kaye who was counted out in the fifth round of a lively encounter.

November -

The British winter of 1978/79 is commonly known as 'The winter of discontent' as a result of the number of industrial disputes and strikes that had a great effect on the population. Grapple fans bore the brunt of a lot of it and it was quite common to switch on the TV on a Saturday afternoon and see a blank screen due to industrial action. The regional TV stations that were not affected on the 4th saw the second half of the Walton-on-Thames show on World of Sport. The programme was devoted to a six man knockout tournament with an interesting line up of contestants who were Mark Rocco, Alan Dennison, Steve Grey, John Naylor, Tally Ho Kaye and Johnny England who replaced the advertised Vic Faulkner. The first of the first round heats which were all fought over a twenty minute time limit with only one fall needed to win saw Grey take on England. As usual England took the first minute or so to flex his impressive physique whilst Grey waited patiently. Grey overcame the weight disadvantage and the strength of England to pin him in the eighth minute for the winner. Grey took England to the mat for the count of three as once again England was posing for ringsiders and Grey pinned him with a flying crucifix.

The second of the heats saw Rocco face Dennison in a particularly heated match with Rocco suffering a particularly nasty landing on the top rope in the early stages. Dennison ducked as Rocco attempted a dropkick and he landed legs astride the top rope. Rocco writhed on the floor in agony but Dennison was unable to take advantage. It was Rocco who got the winner when he reversed Dennison's arm submission move with help from the ropes and gave him a forearm smash to the head. Dennison was out on his feet and Rocco slammed him then followed up with a reverse double knee hold for the count of three in the eighth minute.

The final heat was between Kaye and Naylor with Kaye employing all his usual tricks to try and subdue his fellow Lancastrian. Most of Kaye's moves were on the illegal side and referee Max Ward gave him a public warning for kicking Naylor whilst he was on the mat. The match ended in the fourteenth minute with Kaye disqualified. Naylor missed an attempted flying tackle and got his left ankle trapped between the top two ropes. Whilst Max Ward and the seconds tried to extricate Naylor from the ropes Kaye did his best to continue to attack his opponent. Referee Ward disqualified Kaye but unfortunately Naylor was forced to forfeit his place in the semi final as his ankle was too injured for him to continue.

Therefore the final was now Rocco v Grey which would be fought over the traditional rounds system and the best of three falls etc to decide the winner of the trophy. Rocco was on top from the start and got the first fall in the second round as he reversed a flying tackle from Grey into a piledriver which was quickly followed by another to enable Rocco to pin Grey with a reverse double knee hold. Surprisingly Grey was back on level terms in round four with an equalising fall. This time a flying tackle worked for Grey and he floored Rocco and covered him with a cross press for the count of three. Grey wasn't level for long as Rocco turned up the heat and slammed him to the ropes a couple of times to weaken his legs. Straight after Rocco grabbed Grey's leg and applied a single leg Boston Crab from which Grey submitted instantly. Rocco was presented with a beautiful trophy and a bouquet of flowers as his prize.

Fresh from winning the tournament on the 4th Mark Rocco received more good news when he was named as one the eight contenders who would fight for the vacant British Heavy/Middleweight Title. Rocco now had his chance to regain the title he lost to Marty Jones but it wouldn't be easy. The first two matches were shown on World of Sport the following week from a bill recorded at Rotherham. Bobby Barnes took on Mal Sanders in the opening contest and all the first round heats would be fought over ten rounds. It didn't take long for Barnes to start his usual rough stuff and rulebreaking. Referee Ken Lazenby gave Barnes a public warning in round four before issuing him a final warning in the fifth. The tactics worked as Barnes got the first score in round five with a submission when Sanders was forced to submit from a figure four leglock. Sanders got back into the match in round seven when he finally got the equalising fall. Three rounds were left and all to play for but Barnes suspect temperament let him down again. Barnes threw Sanders through the ropes onto the floor outside in the eighth round. As Sanders tried to re-enter the ring Barnes knocked him back to the floor. Lazenby decided enough was enough and disqualified Barnes leaving Sanders the first wrestler into the semi finals.

Before the second heat there was brief coverage of a catchweight bout between Mike Jordan and Kid Chocolate.

Chocolate took the first fall in the second round before Jordan equalised with a fall in the fifth. During round six Jordan took a heavy fall from the ring through the ropes onto the floor at ringside. The match was stopped but Chocolate refused the win and insisted a No Contest was the decision.

The second heat promised to be a cracker with long time British Middleweight Champion Brian Maxine moving up a weight to challenge for another title just as he had done in 1971 when he had moved up from welterweight. Mick McManus stood in Maxine's way and it was certain referee Ken Lazenby would have his work cut out to keep order. The first public warning went to McManus at the start of round three but it did the trick as he pinned Maxine shortly after for the first fall. Maxine wasn't behind for long as he equalised in fifty seconds in round four but it was McManus who progressed when he surprised Maxine in the fifth round and rolled him up for the winner. McManus thus joined Sanders in the semi finals to be joined by the two winners from next week's show.

It was back to Rotherham for the wrestling on World of Sport on the next Saturday for the other two first round heats in the tournament for the vacant British Heavy/Middleweight Title. The first heat was a bit of surprise with Chris Adams taking on Ringo Rigby who was making his TV debut. It was asking a lot for two inexperienced wrestlers to be able to put a match together worthy of being seen on World of Sport. Kent Walton told viewers that after the first fall the contest would be fought under judo rules although it was not clear why this would be. Rigby got a public warning in round three for a clear kick to Adams' groin area and Walton hoped Rigby wouldn't turn out to be that kind of wrestler. Adams quickly recovered and pinned Rigby with a folding press after a sunset flip from the top of the corner post. Now things got a little strange with the rules going forward would be both of them wearing judo jackets and the winner would be the first to throw his opponent three times. Kent Walton seemed a bit confused by all of this and noted that Adams was already ahead by one fall which didn't seem to count anymore. Anyway it didn't matter as Adams quickly threw Rigby to the mat three times to win this strange match and be the third wrestler into the semi finals.

The second match that week was a lightweight contest between World No.1 Johnny Saint and Jackie Robinson who wasn't seen on TV as much as his talents warranted. It was sad to hear that Robinson passed away during the writing of this book (July 2021) and he will be greatly missed by all his former colleagues and family. Coverage started at the start of round three and it wasn't long until Saint got the first fall. Saint went through his repertoire of tricks before pinning the confused Robinson with a folding press. Robinson did his best to get an equaliser but it wasn't to be and Saint went on to a two straight falls win in round five. Robinson fell for the outstretched hand trick offered by Saint and was quickly pinned with a cross press for the winning fall.

The final heat for the vacant title tournament was between two former champions with Mark Rocco taking on Bert Royal with the stakes high for both of them. Fred Dineage standing in for Dickie Davies told viewers the match was scoreless as we joined coverage at the start of round four. Royal wound up Rocco with a couple of slaps to his face in round five and Rocco retaliated with three punches followed by a kick which got him his first public warning from referee Ken Lazenby. Rocco who had been controlling his temper so far was now beginning to let loose with the rough stuff and made Royal submit at the start of the sixth round with a neck stretch hold. Rocco went all out for the win and soon got a final warning as he attacked Royal on the ropes with punches. Royal now lost his cool and sent Rocco flying with a couple of monkey climbs and followed by slaps to Rocco's face. Royal went crazy when Rocco tried to take a chunk out of his shoulder with a bite which Lazenby didn't spot. Royal finally got the equalising fall in the ninth round when he pinned Rocco with a reverse double knee hold after slamming him to the mat. With one round left it was all to play for but neither wrestler could get the deciding fall. The bell sounded to signal the end of the tenth round and with the score level MC Mark Green announced there must be a winner. Kent Walton thought it would go to sudden death extra time but Green said it would now be down to a toss of a coin to decide the winner. Rocco called it correctly so he was the final wrestler into the semi finals but it was terribly unfair on Royal to be eliminated in such circumstances.

The first semi final of the tournament was seen on World of Sport on the 25th from Catford and it would be between Mark Rocco and Mal Sanders. The match started and continued at a real fast pace with both wrestlers at the top of their form. Every time Rocco seemingly got on top Sanders would fight back and send Rocco flying from a backdrop or something similar. Tempers were soon fraying with Rocco kicking Sanders after the bell sounded to end round two and he received a stern, private warning from referee Peter Szakacs. Rocco did get a public warning in the third though for attacking Sanders who was on floor. As the bout progressed Rocco started to bust up Sanders with his natural weight advantage and his all out attacks weakening him. A combination of headbutts and forearm smashes to Sanders' face from Rocco led to Sanders bleeding from the nose as the match went into round five. The first score came in the fifth and it went to Rocco when he reversed a flying tackle from Sanders into a piledriver and followed up with a neck stretch which saw Sanders submit. Sanders managed to get back into the match in the sixth round much to the crowd's delight. He back dropped Rocco from a posting and followed up with a flying tackle from the top of the corner post. Sanders quickly covered Rocco with a cross press for the count of three and he was level. The end came in the eighth round and the winner was Rocco. Rocco threw Sanders over the top rope from a monkey climb to floor outside. A quick posting for Sanders when he got back into the ring and then straight into a Boston Crab saw Sanders submit and Rocco was the first wrestler into the final.

The rest of the show that week comprised of a first for World of Sport with a super/heavyweight tag knockout tournament. The four teams competing for the prize saw nearly 2500lbs of prime British beef in the ring. Or as Kent Walton described it 'All that meat and no potatoes !'. Big Daddy was back partnering Tony St.Clair after the Digbeth debacle with Gary Wensor which saw him suffer a first televised loss to Giant Haystacks. Haystacks stuck with Big Bruno as his partner and was confident of a second victory. Rather making up the numbers were Bruiser Muir and Bronco Wells and the other team of Wayne Bridges partnering Lee Bronson. The first semi final saw Haystacks and Bruno take on Bridges and Bronson. Bridges and Bronson's total weight only just matched the weight of Haystacks who was looking bigger than ever and he even dwarfed his partner the far from small 20st. Bruno. Surprisingly Bridges and Bronson put up a good show considering and even went in front when Bridges pinned Bruno in the ninth minute. Bridges weakened Bruno with a headbutt before a flying tackle floored Bruno and Bridges covered him in a flash with a cross press. That was as good as it got as Haystacks and Bruno's weight advantage began to tell and once Haystacks started on Bronson with weakeners the end was nigh. Haystacks didn't go for a big splash but put Bronson into a mighty bearhug and the submission was instant to bring the contest level in the twelfth minute. Bronson didn't get a chance to tag in Bridges and the match was over when he submitted from a Boston Crab applied by Bruno in the fifteenth minute.

The second semi final saw Muir and Wells wait patiently whilst Daddy and St.Clair made their entrance to the sound of 'We shall not be moved' coming from the venue's speaker system. Daddy and St.Clair coasted to a two straight falls win in nine minutes. St.Clair did all the work in the early minutes before Daddy finally tagged in after four minutes or so had gone. Daddy sent both Muir and Wells flying out of the ring following some hefty belly butts before St.Clair was tagged back in. St.Clair got the first fall when he headbutted Muir in his stomach and grabbed his legs to pin him with a folding press in the eighth minute. A minute or so later it was all over when Daddy clubbed Wells to the mat and followed up with a big splash for the winning fall.

After two entertaining semi finals the crowd at Catford and viewers were looking forward to the final but once again there was a rotten ending. Haystacks and Bruno's second came running to the ring to tell MC John Harris that they had thrown in the towel and wouldn't wrestle Daddy and St.Clair in the final. It was laughable to treat fans in such a way and it didn't mean a thing or draw money in the future.

240

Around the halls -

The position of number one contender for Tony St.Clair's British Heavyweight Title was finally filled when it was announced that Giant Haystacks would meet St.Clair for the belt at The Royal Albert Hall on 22nd November. With the departure of Kendo Nagasaki and the failure of Pat Roach to capitalise on numerous title opportunities it made sense to give the big man his chance.

Clive Myers had a rare opportunity to win a title on the 4th when he challenged Brian Maxine for his British Middleweight Title at Maidstone. Sadly Myers was unable to get his hand's on Maxine's treasured belt as a result of the bout being stopped in the eleventh round with Myers unable to continue. There was some cheer for the fans at Maidstone that night though when their local favourite Romany Riley beat Big Bruno who was counted out in round four.

Big Daddy and Giant Haystacks were at the centre of more controversy at Belle Vue on the 11th when their tag match had to be abandoned. Daddy and partner Bobby Ryan were taking on Haystacks and Big Bruno. Daddy had given his team the lead with a fall in the first minute before Haystacks had flattened Ryan in the seventh minute to level things up. Daddy fought on alone but not for long as the match ended after a referee bump which saw Haystacks and Bruno walk back to the dressing rooms to leave the ending announced as an open verdict. There was plenty of action in the other bouts with Marty Jones getting the better of Mark Rocco in a chain match that threatened to get totally out of hand. Johnny Czeslaw beat Bronco Wells who was disqualified in the sixth round. Johnny Wilson completed the battalion on view from Portsmouth when he lost to Ray Steele with a winning fall in the seventh round. Jackie Robinson completed the list of winners when he beat newcomer Eddie Riley by two straight falls in round four.

On the same night at Hanley Pat Roach once again was unable to get the better of Tony St.Clair in a championship match when he was disqualified in the tenth round. The bout was nicely poised with St.Clair's fall in round seven equalised by one for Roach in the ninth round. The end came when Roach who had already had two public warnings failed to heed the referee's warning and was disqualified.

Johnny Kidd made his first appearance that night at the Potteries' hall and made it a winning one when his opponent Blackjack Mulligan overdid the rulebreaking and was disqualified in the fourth round.

Giant Haystacks finally got his large hands on a championship belt when he defeated Tony St.Clair at The Royal Albert Hall on 22nd November. Haystacks had long demanded a chance to wrestle for the British Heavyweight Title and when it finally came he made it count. For once Haystacks just about wrestled within the rules and concentrated on using his immense bulk to wear down St.Clair with a combination of strength holds and bludgeoning blows. Despite a brief period in the fourth round when St.Clair got the first fall it was all Haystacks on the attack. At the end of the fifth round Haystacks had landed a splash across St.Clair's legs and the bell saved the champion but only temporarily. Referee Max Ward stepped in as the bell rang for the start of round six and deemed St.Clair was in no position to continue and stopped the contest. Giant Haystacks was the new British Heavyweight Champion and there was only one problem in that the title belt didn't go anywhere near being able to go around his vast waist so he left the ring with it slung over his shoulder instead.

Also on the bill was a match which featured the two top contenders for the heavyweight title in Pat Roach and Wayne Bridges. Both had received title opportunities against St.Clair and hadn't been successful so were now looking for another chance press their claims against the new champion. The match over a twenty minute time limit rather than traditional rounds saw both wrestlers frequently lose their cool especially Roach. Roach got the first fall in the tenth minute before an equaliser from Bridges in the fifteenth. Shortly after this Roach's temper got the better of him and he was disqualified by Max Ward.

The rest of the programme featured a team match with a squad captained by Big Daddy taking on one captained by Mark Rocco. The singles matches saw Bert Royal pin Sid Cooper in the third round for the winner. Bobby Ryan beat Tally Ho Kaye with the winning fall in round four. Steve Grey who surprisingly had been picked by Rocco for his team justified it when he beat Clive Myers with a fall in the fourth round. Captain Rocco made Mal Sanders submit in the second round to make the score two-two. Big Daddy beat Bruiser Muir who decided to walk out in the first round and Honey Boy Zimba made it three-three when he pinned Johnny Czeslaw in the third round. The six man tag finale saw Daddy joined by Sanders and Czeslaw to beat Rocco, Cooper and Muir with a winning fall in the sixth minute to seal a four-three win for Daddy's team.

Saturday 25th November saw the first (and last) British Festival of Wrestling which was held at Digbeth Civic Hall in the centre of Birmingham. The day was split into two parts with afternoon events such as a meet and greet with Big Daddy, Giant Haystacks would send a sworn statement which would be a declaration of war and a fans forum compered by Brian Crabtree. Other events in the afternoon would be an arm wrestling challenge, displays, competitions and prizes galore !

The evening would feature a wrestling show which included a six man tag for the TV Stars Wrestling Magazine trophy. The event was put on by the Joint Mitchell Organisation which was George Mitchell who also was an MC on World of Sport shows and his wife Alison. They published numerous magazines around this time all containing heavily kayfabe articles and branched out with the festival.

Sadly I was unable to attend being only fourteen at the time and a trip to Birmingham for the day was not affordable. Those who did attend deemed it to be a success with the opening ceremony performed by Count Bartelli. Clive Myers took on all-comers at arm wrestling whilst long queues of fans formed to meet Big Daddy to have their photo taken with him. Kendo Nagasaki sent one of his ring costumes for fans to see and there was even a message sent from Canada by Dynamite Kid to the fans in attendance.

The evening's wrestling saw Banger Walsh beat Chris Adams who was counted out in the fifth round. Ringo Rigby beat Gay One by two straight falls in round five and Jackie Turpin defeated Johnny England who was disqualified in the fifth round. Adams, Turpin and Rigby won the TV Stars

Magazine Trophy when their opponents, Walsh, Gay One and England were disqualified in the eighth minute.

The usual regular Saturday night Belle Vue show was also held on the 25th but it wasn't one of the better bills there. Bert Royal beat Jim Breaks in the main event when Breaks was disqualified in the fifth round. Tony St.Clair had yet another match with Pat Roach which saw Roach counted out in round five. Honey Boy Zimba beat Tally Ho Kaye who was counted out in the fourth round. Barry Douglas made a welcome return albeit a losing one when Gil Singh beat him by two straight falls in the fifth round. Finally John Naylor defeated Alan Woods who was disqualified in round three.

December -

The second semi final in the heavy/middleweight title tournament was seen on World of Sport on the 2nd when the other half of the Catford show was broadcast. The opening match was a curious clash of styles between Steve Grey and Billy Torontos. Grey took the lead in round two when he rolled up Torontos from the side for a folding press. Torontos equalised with a fall in the fourth round with a nicely executed folding press but it was Grey who won in the fifth when he pinned Torontos with yet another folding press.

The main bout of the week was Mick McManus facing Chris Adams with the winner facing Mark Rocco in the final of the vacant British Heavy/Middleweight Title Tournament. Adams was still wrestling barefeet with knee length tights instead of regular wrestling gear as sported by McManus. It didn't take long for McManus to start the rule breaking but Adams retaliated with chops before he targetted Adams' ankle which didn't have any protection. McManus got his first public warning from referee Peter Szakacs in the second round for pulling Adams' hair. It was Adams who surprised many when he got the first fall in round four when he fooled McManus who was expecting a straight fingered jab, instead Adams grabbed his legs and pinned him with a folding press. This only infuriated McManus and he delivered his usual forearm jabs before getting his final public warning for attacking Adams

244

who was on the canvas. McManus got his equaliser in round six after he continued to attack Adams with moves both legal and not so legal. Adams picked up McManus and went to deliver a bodyslam, as he did so McManus punched him in his stomach and Adams collapsed to the floor. McManus grabbed his left arm and applied an arm lever to which Adams submitted to almost instantly. As McManus celebrated MC John Harris announced that McManus was disqualified as Szakacs had seen the punch so it would be a Rocco v Adams final for the vacant title.

The final match saw Sid Cooper take on former boxer Jackie Turpin in a lively encounter. As usual Cooper was up to all his tricks behind referee Szakacs' back and went ahead with a fall in the second round. Unfortunately for Cooper it was disallowed as Szakacs had spotted that his feet were on the ropes. It was Turpin who got the first legitimate fall in round four when he pinned Cooper with a flying crucifix as he argued with the crowd at ringside. Cooper continued to wind his opponent up in the fifth round with his antics which was a bit stupid and he paid a heavy price for it. As Cooper came off of the ropes Turpin delivered a left jab to his stomach followed by a right hook to Cooper's jaw which knocked him out and both of which were totally illegal. Referee Szakacs had no option but to disqualify Turpin. Cooper therefore gained a rare win in front of the TV cameras but he looked a sorry sight as his second tried to revive him.

Sadly during the writing of this chapter in July 2021 the news came out that Sid Cooper had died. He was the wrestler's wrestler and one of the greats of British wrestling in the thirty years or so he was entertaining fans night in and night out. That penthouse suite in Soho will be a lonely place right now without Sid residing in it.

Wrestling was missing from World of Sport on the 9th when the Davis Cup Final tennis match between USA and Great Britain was shown in its place.

The final of the tournament to decide the vacant British Heavy/Middleweight Title was shown the next weekend as part of three bouts recorded at Blackburn. As part of the changing scene the regular referee for title matches in the north Brian

Crabtree was replaced by a rookie in Alan Simpson from Newcastle. Instead Crabtree was MC for the show and he introduced the two finalists Mark Rocco and Chris Adams and it was hoped Simpson would be able to control the pair of them. Rocco was overwhelming favourite to win the match and reclaim the belt he had lost three months before. Adams though had improved in leaps and bounds and the packed crowd were firmly behind him. Rocco didn't take long to start roughing up Adams and continued even as the bell sounded to end the first round. Rocco's father Jim Hussey was at ringside and looked on approvingly as his son carried on the attacks in round two. Referee Simpson was far too lenient on Rocco and allowing his illegal moves without warning and even letting punches go without sanction. Finally Rocco got a first public warning in round four and not before time as he kneed Adams who was lying on the canvas. Hussey whispered some advice to his boy in the interval between round's four and five and whatever he said worked as Rocco got the first fall in the fifth round. Rocco caught Adams coming off of the ropes with a powerslam and easily pinned him with a reverse double knee hold for the count of three. It seemed Rocco was on his way to winning back his title but surprisingly Adams rallied in round six and came back into the contest. Adams reversed an attempted bodyslam from Rocco and managed to pin him with a double leg nelson for the equalising fall. Jim Hussey was quickly on his feet to give Rocco a pep talk whilst Adams with blood coming from his nose celebrated. Kent Walton was getting increasingly excited during the seventh round and when it seemed Adams had got the winning fall Walton nearly exploded with excitement. Unfortunately Rocco had his feet on the ropes and the fall was disallowed. After that scare Rocco didn't mess about and in the eighth round following a couple of weakeners he secured the winner when he made Adams submit from a neck stretch and Rocco had regained his beloved Lord Mountevan's title belt.

The other two matches shown that week were somewhat overshadowed by the main event. The opener saw Alan Dennison take on the much heavier Ray Thunder and beat him with the only fall needed coming in the third round. The final match was between Steve Logan and Johnny Czeslaw with surprisingly Logan adhering to the rules most of the time. Logan was relying on his forearm jabs and other strength holds to weaken Czeslaw. Czeslaw got the first fall in round four before Logan's weakeners finally told in the fifth round. Czeslaw submitted from an arm lever and unfortunately he was unable continue in the contest giving Logan the win.

The pre-Christmas edition of World of Sport on the 23rd had another attempt at getting Big Daddy and Giant Haystacks to wrestle each other. It would be a rematch of sorts of the tag knockout tournament final that didn't happen at Catford with Daddy and Tony St.Clair taking on Haystacks and Big Bruno once more.

Before that though the opening bout on a show recorded at Aylesbury saw Clive Myers take on Banger Walsh who was more often those days seen in the opposing corner in Big Daddy tags. It didn't take Walsh long to start breaking the rules and he got a public warning from referee Joe D'Orazio in round two for punching Myers in the face. Myers retaliated in the best way possible by pinning Walsh following an awkward double arm suplex. Walsh got his final warning for attacking Myers between the interval of round's three and four. The tactics worked for Walsh as he got the equaliser in round four when Myers submitted from a straight arm lift. It was Myers though who won the match with a curious ending in the fifth round. Myers sent Walsh over the top rope with a kick to the back of his head landing onto Kent Walton's ringside table. Walsh clambered back into a ring where Myers landed a dropkick and a rather botched attempt at going over the top rope from Walsh. Finally Myers did dropkick Walsh over the top rope where he crashed onto the table again. D'Orazio didn't count and told Walsh to get back into the ring but he seemed to signal to the referee he didn't want to so Myers was the winner.

For once there was no trickery in the main event and the tag match with Big Daddy and Tony St.Clair taking on Giant Haystacks and Big Bruno took place. The early stages saw St.Clair take on Bruno with Bruno's strength equalled by St.Clair's speed. It wasn't long till Bruno was joined by Haystacks to double team the much lighter St.Clair and an attempted cross press from St.Clair was stopped by Haystacks.

247

Finally Haystacks tagged in and he was followed by Daddy and a battle of belly butts quickly ensued. Haystacks didn't stick around for long and quickly tagged Bruno back in. Daddy threw Bruno to the floor and landed a big splash on him followed by a cross press for the first fall in the fifth minute. St.Clair came back into the ring and after some early success on Bruno it was Haystacks' turn to come back into the match. St.Clair tried a flying tackle but he was easily caught by the big man who then slammed him to the mat. Haystacks then landed a splash right across St.Clair's legs in a replica of the move that had cost St.Clair his title at The Royal Albert Hall. St.Clair just about managed to get to his feet but was grabbed by Haystacks who forced a submission from a single leg Boston in the seventh minute. Of course St.Clair had to restart the contest with Haystacks and it looked like he had pinned Haystacks with a cross press for the winner. Unfortunately Daddy had assisted when he had shoved Haystacks over and referee Max Ward disallowed the fall. It didn't matter in the scheme of the things though as soon as the bell rang for the restart Haystacks rushed across the ring to attack St.Clair but instead Haystacks was met by a forearm smash from Daddy which felled him. St.Clair covered Haystacks in an instant and Ward counted three for the winning fall. I have no idea why that fall was allowed and the other one wasn't with similar interference. Despite enquiries to the Board of Control no definitive answer was given to the reason why. Daddy and St.Clair celebrated as 'We shall not be moved' played over the PA whilst Haystacks and Bruno complained quite rightly to MC Johnny Dale. For Daddy and Haystacks their paths would now diverge as Haystacks was making an ever increasing number of trips overseas and for Daddy there was a new threat looming just around the corner coming from North America.

The final contest of the week was between Butcher Bond against Pete Roberts. In what was a hard fought heavyweight tussle Bond got the first score with an upside down neck stretch which saw Roberts submit in the fourth round. Roberts was back on level terms in round six when he caught Bond by surprise with a folding press from the side for the count of three. Bond totally lost his cool in the seventh round and was disqualified. He delivered a reverse posting to Roberts and as he hung upside down in the corner Bond continued to kick him until finally referee Joe D'Orazio disqualified him.

The second half of the Aylesbury show completed the wrestling shown on World of Sport for 1978 on 30th December. The opener was a battle of the strongmen with John 'The Bear' Elijah tackling the ebony hercules Honey Boy Zimba. Perhaps as could be expected it turned into a rather slow affair with a propensity of strength holds dominating affairs. Elijah got the first fall in round three before Zimba equalised with a fall in the fifth round. Zimba got the winner in the final round pinning Elijah once more for a two falls to one victory.

The main event saw Brian Maxine make a rare defence of his British Middleweight Title and the challenger was none other than Mick McManus. McManus had lowered his sights from European levels to the domestic scene to try and get another title after being thwarted in his attempts to regain the European Middleweight Title from Mal Sanders. Maxine had defied all challenges for over seven years and was the second longest holder of the Lord Mountevan's belt after the inactive Mike Marino at mid/heavyweight. Once again Maxine retained his belt as a result of a two falls to one win coming in round eight but it was a tough battle with Maxine finishing the bout with blood coming from a cut over his right eye.

The last televised bout of the year saw Ringo Rigby taking on Johnny England. Rigby was a late replacement for Catweazle who had left Joint Promotions to wrestle on the independent circuit. Rigby got the first fall in the second round but he injured himself in round three when he slipped in the corner as a result of a wet canvas. Referee Max Ward deemed it to be an accident and so ruled it was a No Contest.

Around the halls -

Johnny Saint made another successful defence of his World Lightweight Title when Steve Grey once again was unable to step up to the highest echelons of the division. In the contest at Wolverhampton on the 5th Saint got a winning fall in the thirteenth round to seal a two falls to one victory. Mark Rocco

249

once again squared up to Marty Jones on the programme and it was Jones who notched up another win over his old rival. Rocco was counted out in the fifth round of another typically action packed match between the pair. Local lad Kashmir Singh stepped in at short notice for the show to take on Alan Dennison. Singh was unable to continue in the third round but sportingly Dennison refused to accept the win so a No Contest was called.

Steve Grey had another chance at Johnny Saint's title a week later at Croydon on the 12th. This time the match ended in a draw after fifteen classic rounds with Saint's fall in round ten cancelled out by Grey's in the twelfth round. A rather underwhelming rest of the bill with plenty of changes to the advertised line-up saw Caswell Martin make a comeback after his bouts abroad to face Big Bruno. Bruno was disqualified in the third round after losing his cool when Martin got the first fall. Johnny England beat Dean Brisco with a winning submission in the fourth round. Chris Adams beat Sid Cooper who was counted out in round three and the final bout of the evening had to be rushed to beat the venue's curfew with Johnny Czeslaw pinning Johnny Kwango in just over six minutes to win.

Steve Grey was in another title match that week on the 14th at Digbeth but this time he was defending his British Lightweight Title against John Naylor. It was another long night for Grey who once again showed supreme conditioning and fitness levels to wrestle a one fall each draw with Naylor. Grey got the first fall in round six before and equaliser in round eight from Naylor completed the scoring. At the end of the twelfth round the decision was a draw and Grey retained his title.

There was a strange bit of matchmaking on the bill with Mark Rocco booked against Billy Torontos in a definite clash of styles. Poor old Billy took a bit of a beating from Rocco in the five rounds the match lasted with Rocco getting a submission in that round to finish off Torontos. Chris Adams defeated Steve Logan who was disqualified in the fourth round whilst Ringo Rigby had an easy night of it with a two straight falls win in four rounds against Tim Fitzmaurice.

Wrestling started to ease down in the week before Christmas but Johnny Saint still had time to fit in another defence of his World Lightweight Title at Watford on the 19th. This time the challenger was Jim Breaks but it was Saint who retained with a winning fall coming in round ten. Mick McManus and Brian Maxine were developing quite a rivalry around this time and they had a special stipulation match on the show. It was the first fall wins with no rounds and a thirty minute time limit. McManus got the fall when he pinned Maxine in the eighth minute. When Maxine complained about the validity of the fall McManus pinned him again in thirty seconds of the restart. Pete Roberts chalked up a notable win when he defeated Mark Rocco by two falls to one in the fifth round. Caswell Martin who replaced Catweazle took advantage of a hefty weight advantage to beat Alan Dennison with the winner in the fifth round. Mal Sanders sent the fans home happy when he beat Johnny England in the evening's final contest.

The usual big crowds once again filled the halls in the holiday season and another packed crowd attended the show at Kilburn on 29th December. As per previous programmes there a raft of last minute replacements spoilt the show especially as one came in the main event. Mick McManus was billed to wrestle Bobby Barnes in a 'Battle of the bad boys' but Barnes didn't show and was replaced by Dino Skarlo. Skarlo was unable to continue at the end of round three but as McManus was deemed to have caused it by illegal moves the verdict was left open. Mohindar Singh was another no show so Rana Singh tagged with Caswell Martin against Big Bruno and Bronco Wells. Perhaps surprisingly it was the lighter team of Martin and Singh who ran out the winners with a winning fall in the seventeenth minute. Mal Sanders caused quite an upset when he defeated Mark Rocco by two falls to one in the fifth round. Pete Roberts beat Pat Roach who was disqualified in round four and finally Billy Torontos spoilt Sid Cooper's Christmas with a two straight falls win over him in five rounds.

The same night south of the River Thames there was another big Dale Martin show at Kingston-On-Thames with Big Daddy in the main event. Daddy with Jackie Turpin took on Steve Logan and Banger Walsh. Personally I didn't like seeing Logan in Daddy tags being on the end of the belly butts but being the true professional he was he just got on with the match. Daddy and Turpin won in the ninth minute when Walsh was knocked out by a Daddy double elbow drop. Steve Grey beat Johnny England by two falls to one in the sixth round. Chris Adams defeated Brian Maxine who was disqualified in the fifth round. Johnny Czeslaw beat Johnny Kwango with a fall in round five and finally the missing Mohindar Singh turned up here to lose to John Elijah.

The wrestling year came to an end on the 30th with two title matches on the programme at Hanley. Johnny Saint once more defended the World Lightweight Title against Steve Grey and Marty Jones defended the British Light/Heavyweight Title against Pete Roberts. Saint retained his belt once more and at this stage was a cut above any domestic challengers such as Grey. Grey got the first fall in round six before Saint equalised in the tenth round before Saint got the winner in twelfth. Jones had a much tougher battle to retain his title though and in the end only just kept hold of the belt. Jones as usual at Hanley was the villain of the piece and it was Roberts who got the first fall in the fifth round. The match came to an end in round seven when both wrestlers were counted out and Jones kept hold of his title by the skin of his teeth. Another match on the show to end with both wrestlers counted out was between Gil Singh and Ray Steele. With the score one fall each in round five it came to an end with the double countout. Pat Roach won a special challenge against Butcher Bond with no disqualification and the first fall wins. In an entertaining brawl Roach won when Bond was another wrestler to be counted out when he failed to beat the count of ten in the thirteenth minute.

So ended 1978 and as far as British wrestling was concerned for Joint Promotions it couldn't be any better. Since Max Crabtree had taken sole charge of the organisation it was in rude health. Big Daddy was drawing sell out crowds most nights backed up by good number of talented wrestlers such as Mark Rocco, Marty Jones, Tony St.Clair, Johnny Saint, Mal Sanders and Steve Grey all making breakthroughs to the top of the card as champions.

The independent scene was different as they didn't have the same publicity or public profile without a TV deal and it was hard at times to keep track with what was going on there. The ladies were still banned from wrestling in a lot of places notably London and unscrupulous promoters were still giving the independents a bad name with bait and switch advertising.

1979

January -

The first wrestling of the year shown on World of Sport on the 6th actually went straight back to 1978. The three bouts shown that week were recorded back in September at Woking and were part of the Jones v Rocco double title match programme. The opening match was at heavyweight between Wayne Bridges and Ray Steele. The only part of the match broadcast was the sixth and final round and two minutes in it was Bridges who got the winning fall. Earlier in the bout Steele had got the first fall in round three before Bridges levelled up in the fourth. In less than six months time these two would have a rematch on a much grander stage at Wembley Arena.

The main contest shown was another heavyweight contest this time between Tony St.Clair and Butcher Bond. The perils of showing a bill much later than it was filmed was illustrated when MC Bobby Palmer introduced St.Clair as the British Heavyweight Champion. In the real world of course he had lost his title to Giant Haystacks back in November. Not surprisingly the bout soon descended into a brawl with referee Peter Szakacs having a job keeping things in order. Bond attacked St.Clair as soon as the bell sounded for round two and weakened him with several postings with a few kicks for good measure. Straightaway Bond put St.Clair into a Boston Crab and got the first score via a submission. Bond got his first public warning from Szakacs early in round three as he continually attacked St.Clair whilst he was on the ropes. Bond then got his final warning from Szakacs in the same round for a punch to St.Clair's stomach as St.Clair was dishing out some substantial retaliation. Bond got a stern warning from Szakacs after he posted St.Clair after the bell sounded at the end of the round. St.Clair finally evened things up in the fourth round with a flying tackle from the top of the corner post flooring Bond. St.Clair covered him with a cross press and got the equaliser much to the crowd's delight. Bond was most upset and as the

254

bell sounded to start the fifth round referee Szakacs was distracted by something in Bond's corner. Bond took advantage and landed several punches to St.Clair's face before Szakacs paid attention to what was going on. An incensed St.Clair retaliated with punches of his own right in front of Szakacs and received a public warning. As Szakacs was informing the timekeeper of the sanction yet again he had his back to the action and St.Clair attempted a dropkick onto Bond. Bond ducked out of the way and the dropkick landed directly onto Szakacs' back instead. Rightly this led to the instant disqualification of St.Clair but as MC Bobby Palmer got into the ring to announce the decision he shamefully persuaded Szakacs that it was an accident and Bond's fault. The disqualification was overturned although there is nothing in the Lord Mountevan's rule book stating you must allow yourself to be kicked in the face instead of ducking. The match therefore was restarted much to Bond's disgust and within seconds St.Clair had pinned Bond with a cross press after a backdrop for the winning fall.

The final match that week saw funny man Catweazle taking on Steve Logan who had never shown a sense of humour in the ring. Logan had over a stone weight advantage and used it to great effect and finally finished off Catweazle in the fourth round. Logan delivered a forearm smash and Catweazle was unable to beat the count of ten.

One of the most infamous contests or rather incidents in British wrestling history was shown on World of Sport on the 13th. The three bouts on the programme were recorded at Hemel Hempstead earlier that week and featured the ITV debut of one John Quinn. Quinn had arrived in Britain after competing in the German tournaments in late 1978 but unless you had knowledge of these or of wrestling in North America it was doubtful the name John Quinn would have meant much. Quinn's opponent was veteran Manchester heavyweight Beau Jack Rowlands but it wasn't what happened in the match that caused such a fuss as what happened after it. Rowlands actually got the first fall in round two but he was counted out in the fifth round when Quinn landed an over the top forearm smash right on Rowlands jaw. The ferocity of the blow knocked out

Rowlands and would go on to be a familiar finish to Quinn's matches here. As MC John Harris announced the win Quinn grabbed his microphone and started speaking. At first it was quite concilliatory until he brought up the Second World War and how his Father was in Britain then and he had told Quinn that all the limeys were yellow. In 1979 most of the audience both in the hall and watching at home would have remembered the war and the ill-feeling between the British and Americans over certain things. This speech didn't just open up old wounds it ripped them apart. It was a sensational way to get yourself over and made Quinn detested by grapple fans and of course would make great business at the box office.

The other two matches shown that week were totally overshadowed but the opening contest saw Caswell Martin take on Mel Stuart. With the only the first fall needed to win it was Martin who got it in round three. Martin rolled up Stuart with a folding press from the side to end what was quite a ponderous contest.

The final match was between Steve Grey and Tim Fitzmaurice who had got the first fall in round two. Coverage started in round three with both Grey and Fitzmaurice showing some nice wrestling moves and counters in it. Grey got the equalising fall in the fourth round with a nice reversal of a double leg nelson from Fitzmaurice into a folding press. Grey won the match in round five when he made Fitzmaurice submit from a surfboard which was now becoming a regular move in Grey's repertoire.

Big Daddy once again was on parade with his 'TV All-stars' team in a tournament shown on World of Sport on the 20th and 27th January from Middlesbrough.

Daddy's team of six took on one captained by Mick McManus in six single's matches followed by a six man tag to finish with. Mark Rocco got McManus' team off to a flying start when he demolished Kid Chocolate. Chocolate did in fact get the first fall in round three when he pinned Rocco with a folding press after a headbutt had stunned him. Rocco wasn't behind for long though and in the fourth round he made Chocolate submit from single leg Boston after a nasty looking throw saw Chocolate's leg caught in the ropes. Rocco got a

256

second warning in round five for a similar move but it did the trick and another single leg Boston saw Chocolate submit once again to lose the match.

The second match saw Big Daddy level the match up with a win against King Kong Kirk. Daddy got the first fall in the second round with a mighty double elbow drop which saw nearly 50st. of body mass land on the canvas at the same time. The bell sounded for the third round and Kirk said he wanted to fight Daddy on the stage beside the ring and not inside the ropes. Referee Emil Poilve was having none of that kind of behaviour and made Kirk forfeit the bout to make it one-one in the tournament.

The next contest saw Mal Sanders for the 'All-stars' wrestle a one fall each draw with Mick McMichael. Sanders got the first fall in round four before McMichael equalised in the fifth.

Bert Royal took on Judd Harris in the fourth contest. Harris had recently returned from wrestling in Germany and hadn't wrestled for Joint Promotions for quite a while. Harris now based in Dortmund rejoiced in the name of Gunboat Harris as result of his naval service in the past. Harris had a hefty weight advantage of over 5st. and made it count in the third round when he made Royal submit from a Boston Crab after delivering several weakeners to Royal's back. Royal came back though in round four with an equalising fall which Harris took exception to. He then proceeded to attack Royal in his corner and as he had already received two public warnings he was disqualified by referee Poilve.

There was more controversy in the match between Mick McManus and Jackie Turpin. McManus won with a fall in the fifth round but afterwards Turpin challenged him to a boxer v wrestler contest as a result of the punches continually thrown by McManus.

The final single's match saw Bobby Ryan tackle Sid Cooper with the tournament score level at two-two. Ryan got the first fall in he third round when he reversed a flying tackle from Cooper into a reverse double knee hold in a beautifully executed move. In round four Cooper was thrown between the ropes by Ryan to the outside of the ring. Instead of returning immediately back to the ring he started arguing with the ringsiders and not paying attention to the count. Despite most of the audience counting along with the referee Cooper wasn't heeding them and was counted out.

The six man tag saw Daddy, Ryan and Turpin take on Rocco, Cooper and Harris. Daddy started when he took on all three of them at the same time with Cooper launched at Daddy by Rocco and Harris. Rocco got the first score in the fourth minute when a backbreaker on Turpin saw him submit. Daddy made the hot tag and got an equaliser a minute or so later with a big splash on Rocco followed by a cross press for the fall. The end came shortly after when Ryan backdropped Harris over the top rope and he failed to return to the ring in time so the tournament ended with a four-two win for Daddy's 'All-stars'.

Around the halls -

John Quinn made the lowest of low key starts to his tour of Britain when his first match in this country was as a substitute. He replaced Big Bruno in the main event against Wayne Bridges at Chelmsford on 2nd January. All Quinn's early matches were booked in the same way with some kind of disputed finish such as a count out or disqualification so a rematch could then be arranged with a stipulation such as 'All-in' rules. Quinn's first British match against Bridges ended with Quinn disqualified in the fifth round.

It was Pete Roberts turn to face John Quinn on the 8th at Tunbridge Wells, in the early weeks of Quinn's visit it was Bridges or Roberts who he mainly wrestled on a Dale Martin show. Roberts won this one when Quinn was counted out in round seven unaware in Britain there is a count of ten whilst outside the ring whilst he was used to a count of twenty. There was an intriguing co-main event on the show with Wayne Bridges taking on both Mick McManus and Brian Maxine. It didn't faze Bridges and he won by two straight falls in the twelfth minute.

John Quinn had another match with Pete Roberts on the 15th this time at Wembley with this time Quinn winning. Quinn knocked out Roberts in the sixth round when an over the top forearm smash left Roberts with no chance of beating the count.

Also on the bill was a match between Brian Maxine and Steve Grey. There had been a feud involving them as well as Mick McManus since the show there on 11th December and it only got worse in this match. Maxine thought he had made Grey submit in round four but it was disallowed. As Maxine argued with the referee Grey rolled him up for the first fall. An irate Maxine then attacked Grey and got himself disqualified.

The first show of the year at The Royal Albert Hall and the first of the now monthly programmes was on 17th January. For the fifth consecutive time Big Daddy was in the main event but with a host of other interesting matches on the bill it didn't matter. Big Daddy partnered Mick McMichael to take on King Kong Kirk and Gunboat Harris. It was an easy night for Daddy and McMichael with a two straight falls win in less than ten minutes. Mick McManus was scheduled to have his rematch with Mal Sanders for the European Middleweight Title but blew his chance before the first bell even sounded. McManus weighed in 6lbs. overweight at the pre-show weigh in and perhaps because of this he gave Sanders quite a beating in the now non-title bout. Sanders was forced to retire in the fourth round as he bled heavily from a head wound following a fall from the ring.

John Quinn made his Albert Hall debut against Wayne Bridges and Quinn received a heated reception from the crowd. Bridges won when Quinn was disqualified in the fifth round but both wrestlers claimed unfinished business and wanted to carry on with the bout. New British Heavyweight Champion Giant Haystacks took on Pat Roach in a non-title match. Roach won when Haystacks was disqualified in round two when he used a foreign object to split Roach's head open. As with Quinn and Bridges earlier both wrestlers again wanted to continue and it was announced that hopefully a tag match with the four involved would be organised for the next show there.

On a bumper seven bout programme the other three matches were somewhat forgotten amongst all the other action. Steve Grey beat the comebacking Ken Joyce by two straight falls in five rounds. Big Bruno beat Lee Bronson who was counted out in the third round whilst another heavyweight match saw Pete

259

Roberts beat Caswell Martin with the winning fall coming in the sixth round.

The first Croydon show of 1979 on the 23rd should have seen Giant Haystacks have another match against Pat Roach but Roach was absent. The replacement opponent was Len Hurst who had recently returned from the USA where had been wrestling regularly for the WWWF in recent times. Hurst had left Britain as a middleweight but now was around 14st or so in weight which was nowhere near enough to give Haystacks any problems. A splash from Haystacks on Hurst in the second round was enough for the referee to stop the match without even bothering to count. John Quinn was also on the show wrestling Pete Roberts and Quinn was disqualified in the fourth round.

On most of his January appearances John Quinn was placed somewhere down the bill as was the case at Brighton on the 24th when Big Daddy was the headline attraction that packed the crowd in once more. Quinn was in another brawl with Wayne Bridges on the night and they had already built up a connection that made their bouts excellent to watch. Bridges was the winner when Quinn was counted out after the pair of them had been fighting on the stage instead of inside the ring. Big Daddy led a team against one captained by Steve Logan in a team match which Daddy's team won by four-one. The highlight of it was the six man tag in which Daddy, Steve Grey and Mal Sanders beat Logan, Bruiser Muir and Sid Cooper with a winner in the twelfth minute.

The perils of the 'Winter of discontent' hit me the next evening when I was at Burgess Hill for the usual monthly show. The railway workers had gone on strike and I had a ten mile or so journey home, luckily I hitched a lift some of the way and walked the rest. It wasn't even that good a show with Big Bruno wrestling a six round draw with Johnny Wilson as the best match.

The Mick McManus, Brian Maxine and Steve Grey feud came to a head at Wembley on the 29th. After Grey's win against Maxine a fortnight previously a tag match was booked with Grey teaming up with none other than Steve Logan to take on Maxine who had chosen Mick McManus as his partner. This

260

was one of the few if ever times that McManus would face Logan in the ring. In the end Grey got the winning fall over Maxine with a little help from Logan. Logan and McManus never came into any contact much to the disappointment of the fans.

The 'Winter of discontent' had more victims on the 31st when grapple fans turning up to the The Pavilion in Bath for the fortnightly show there and saw the doors locked. A notice saying the show was cancelled due to the council workers having walked out was posted on the door for disappointed punters to see.

February -

The ITV cameras had been to Wolverhampton to record the three matches shown on World of Sport on the 3rd. John Quinn was the main attraction but first the opening bout saw the Yorkshire strongman Alan Dennison take on Wolverhampton's own Johnny England. England took exception to Dennison showing him up in front of his hometown crowd and quickly resorted to the rough stuff to quieten Dennison. The only fall needed to win came in round three and it was Dennison who got it. England was showboating as usual and trying to tempt Dennison to put him in a Full Nelson. As England broke the hold Dennison grabbed his legs and pinned him with a folding press. England went beserk and attacked Dennison who retaliated with a rather botched attempt to send England over the top rope. Curiously MC Brian Crabtree announced the verdict to be a disqualification win for Dennison rather than by the winning fall.

The match everyone wanted to see was John Quinn who was taking on a late notice change of opponent in Barry Douglas. Douglas had replaced the advertised Gil Singh. Before the bell rung to start the contest Quinn took the microphone from MC Crabtree and firstly thanked the crowd for their warm welcome which he appreciated. Quinn went onto state that he was not afraid of any wrestler in the world and he had heard of Pat Roach, Giant Haystacks but especially one wrestler in Britain. Quinn said it was somebody called Big Daddy but he hadn't

261

seen him yet and he wanted to wrestle Daddy under American rules. Quinn finished by saying what he had said on his first TV appearance was a really bad thing calling British people yellow. In fact he said it was inadequate and not only were British people yellow but they were stupid too. MC Brian Crabtree took the microphone back and told Quinn if he were bigger he would have a go at him himself and told him not to worry he would be meeting Big Daddy soon. Barry Douglas was spotting Quinn a 5st. weight advantage and that was far too much for him to give away in the match. Quinn got the first fall in round three after a high kick to Douglas' jaw followed by a forearm smash had weakened him. Quinn personally had broken several pinfall attempts on Douglas until he finally pinned him with a cross press. Quinn's feet were on the ropes during the count but referee Dave Reese didn't spot it but MC Crabtree had and pointed it out. Reese disallowed the fall and Quinn was furious. It didn't last much longer though as Quinn caught Douglas with the familiar forearm smash which knocked him out in just over a minute of round four. As Quinn was ranting at Crabtree who was trying to announce the result in came Pat Roach who was wrestling in the third match. Roach told Quinn that fifteen million viewers were at home watching this and he said normally he didn't get on with any of them but today he would stand with the British people against Quinn. It was an absolutely superb way to establish John Quinn as the number one hated villain in British wrestling.

Roach was then joined by his opponent Pete Roberts in the ring for his match. For once Roach wrestled within the rules with Roberts getting the first fall in round three. Roberts took Roach down coming off of the ropes and pinned him with a folding press from the side and he even got a congratularly hand shake from his opponent. Roach quickly levelled the bout in the fourth round with an equaliser. Roberts had barely got to his feet following a 'Brumagen bump' when Roach picked him up and slammed him to the mat and followed up with a cross press. The end came in round six when Roach sent Roberts flying over the top rope where he failed to beat the count after a heavy landing at ringside.

The other half of the show from Wolverhampton was shown on World of Sport the next weekend. The preliminary contest saw Steve Logan who was now entering the veteran stage of his career against Marty Jones who was continuing to go from strength to strength. Logan flew out of his corner at the sound of the first bell to attack Jones who hadn't left his corner and Kent Walton sounded astounded at the speed of Logan. Logan continued to roll back the years and give Jones all the trouble he could handle with moves both fair and foul. The first score came in round three and surprisingly it was Logan who got it with a submission. Logan had landed several punches behind referee Dave Reese's back before making Jones submit from a neck twist. Jones finally got back into the contest in round five when he got an equalising fall from a cross press following a body slam. Jones quickly wrapped up the bout in the sixth round with a winning fall from a similar move and he left for a North American tour in good spirits.

Giant Haystacks was on next when he took on Honey Boy Zimba who weighed less than half of Haystacks' now reported weight of 35st. Zimba was absolutely dwarfed by him and the only surprising thing was that the match lasted until round two. The end came when Haystacks reversed an attempted flying tackle and slammed Zimba to the floor. He then flattened Zimba with a shuddering splash and referee Dave Reese never bothered to complete the count as there was no chance of Zimba beating it.

It was tag team time to finish the week's show with the Martial Arts Fighter's team of Clive Myers and Chris Adams meeting Ed and Gary Wensor. The speed of Adams and Myers somewhat negated the weight advantage of the brothers and but it was the brothers who got the first score. Ed Wensor made Adams submit from a straight arm lift in the thirteenth minute after both brothers had weakened Adams' shoulder. Myers eventually made the hot tag and straightaway got the equaliser when he pinned Gary with a folding press following a victory roll. It didn't take Myers long to end the match with a winning fall in the twentieth minute. Myers delivered several kicks and chops before catching Gary Wensor coming off of the ropes and pinned him following a hip toss.

After a year or so of inaction the Board of Control finally decided to do something about the British Welterweight Title. It had been left vacant since Dynamite Kid was stripped of it following his decision to leave for North America. An eight man tournament was set up along similar lines to the recent one for the vacant heavy/middleweight title. The eight wrestlers nominated to compete in it were Jim Breaks, Steve Grey, Zoltan Boscik, Pat Patton, Ken Joyce, John Naylor, Johnny England and Jeff Kaye. The four first round heats were scheduled to be shown across two weekends of TV coverage on a show recorded at Reading.

The first two heats of the welterweight tournament were shown on World of Sport on the 17th with the first heat seeing Steve Grey take on Zoltan Boscik. Boscik tested referee Max Ward's patience in the third round and ended up getting a public warning. Grey responded in the best way possible by pinning Boscik with a double leg nelson following a sunset flip for the first fall. Boscik was now only wrestling part-time as he had taken over as landlord of the Imperial pub in Soho, London and maybe ring rust was effecting him ? Finally in round five after many attempts Boscik finally managed to lock Grey into his three-in-one speciality which saw Grey submit to level the contest. Although it looked that Boscik was using the middle rope to add additional pressure which of course Max Ward failed to spot. To make things worse he posted Grey before the bell rang for the sixth and Boscik got his final public warning from Ward for it. Boscik continued to attack Grey throughout the round as he sought out a winner but in the end it was Grey who won the bout. In the opening minute of round seven Grey pinned Boscik with a cross press after back dropping him to the mat. So Grey was the first wrestler to go through to the semi finals.

Before the second heat there was a heavyweight match between Pat Roach and Wayne Bridges shown and Roach had definitely forgotten his recent good behaviour in the ring. Bridges got the first fall in the second round before Roach equalised with a fall in round five. As the fall was announced by MC John Harris both Bridges and Roach got involved in a punch up and referee Max Ward disqualified the pair of them.

The final contest seen that week was the next heat of the welterweight tournament and it featured the favourite to win it, Jim Breaks. Breaks was matched with Pat Patton who was making his TV debut. As many suspected before the first bell rang Breaks' experience would be far too much for Patton. Breaks got the first score in round three when his 'Breaks' special' saw Patton submit. Breaks followed up with an arm lever in the fifth round to make Patton submit again and seal a two straight submissions win.

The other two heats in the welterweight tournament were shown the following week. The first of them featured two wrestlers both very much in the veteran stages of their careers in Ken Joyce and Jeff Kaye. This was very much a technical wrestling match between two fine exponents of the art. In what must have been an annoying thing for TV viewers both wrestlers wore identical blue trunks and black boots which made identification hard for those watching at home. It was Kaye who got the first fall in round three with a hip toss followed up by a cross press before Joyce levelled things up in the fifth with a folding press. Joyce joined Steve Grey and Jim Breaks in the semi finals with a winning fall in round six. Joyce reversed a folding press from Kaye into one of his own and secured it by a handstand giving Kaye no chance of kicking out.

As was the case last week the two tournament matches were split by a heavyweight contest and this week it saw Big Bruno take on his former pupil Johnny Wilson. Bruno relied on his strength and weight advantage in the first two rounds rather than any rough stuff for a change. Wilson shocked his former mentor when he got the first fall in the third round. He caught Bruno coming in and pinned him with a folding press from the side. Bruno upped the tempo in round four and quickly finished off Wilson although in an unfortunate way. Wilson tried a knee drop but on dropping Bruno's 20st. weight on to it something gave out. Wilson was unable to continue and Bruno made sure that MC John Harris knew he was accepting the win. The first aiders made their way to the ring to assist Wilson who had damaged a cartilage in his knee. Wilson had to be placed on a stretcher to be carried from the ring for further treatment.

The final tournament heat saw John Naylor face Johnny England. Predictably in the first round England was more concerned about showing off his very impressive physique as Kent Walton reeled off a list of body building titles he had won. Naylor though concentrated on his wrestling and to good effect as he pinned England with a folding press in round two. England was back on level terms in the fourth round after Naylor had caught his leg between the top two ropes. England pounced on him and immediately applied a single leg Boston which saw Naylor submit. It was Naylor though who completed the line-up for the semi finals when he got the winning fall in the seventh round. England was caught rushing in by Naylor who rolled him up for a folding press from the side.

Around the halls -

Big Daddy and John Quinn had their first in-ring encounter at Hanley on the 3rd as part of a tag match. Daddy teamed up with Bobby Ryan whilst Quinn partnered King Kong Kirk. Daddy got first blood over his soon to be bitter rival when both Quinn and Kirk walked away from the match in the ninth minute.

Controversy seemed to follow John Quinn everywhere he wrestled and his match with Wayne Bridges at Croydon on the 6th followed the same pattern. Bridges was in front from a fall in the second round and the match was now in round four with Quinn's conduct enraging the fans there. Someone from the crowd threw a coin towards the ring aiming for Quinn but it actually hit Bridges. Bridges was unable to continue so the bout was stopped and a No Contest verdict was recorded. It was rather a poor programme for the rest of the show there that night with Terry Rudge beating Romany Riley by two falls to one in round six the best of the other bouts.

As a result of their disputed match ending at Maidstone on 13th January both John Quinn and Wayne Bridges were booked for a return match at the same venue on the 10th. The stipulation for this bout would be that it would be a ladder match but outside matters forced it to be cancelled. Quinn's wife Linda was heavily pregnant at the time and instead of battling Bridges at Maidstone Quinn was with his wife as she had gone into labour on the way to giving birth to a son. Grapple fans in attendance at Maidstone had to be content with a rejigged bill which saw Bridges take on Ed Wensor in a ladder match in which Bridges won in less than four minutes.

The independent promoters were having a fair old time of it up in Scotland with fake advertising of shows or in the case of a show at Govan on the 13th a rotten gimmick. There was no name of the promoter on the poster but the main event of the show was advertised as featuring 'The Gestapo Twins' who claimed to be former members of the Hitler Youth. They were booked against the team of Andy Robbins and Jock Thompson. Also on the show was a ladies' match between Rusty Blair and Cherokee Princess but no results of the show ever came to light.

The fans who turned up at Bath on the next evening were again disappointed as the second consecutive show there was cancelled due to industrial action which seemed to spreading throughout the country.

As hoped for the bill for the February spectacular at The Royal Albert Hall on the 21st featured the tag match between Giant Haystacks and John Quinn taking on Pat Roach and Wayne Bridges. Bridges was out of action early on when a splash on him from Haystacks resulted in the first fall. Bridges was unable to play no further part in the match. Roach bravely carried on alone and managed to get an equalising fall but was soon overpowered. Haystacks and Quinn beat on Roach at will but as usual Haystacks went too far and was disqualified. This left Roach and Bridges somewhat fortunate winners and the feud far from over.

The main supporting match on the bill should have seen Mark Rocco defending his British Heavy/Middleweight Title against Bert Royal. Unfortunately Rocco was out of the country on an overseas tour so he was replaced by Zoltan Boscik. It was no substitute for the title match and again the promoters hid beneath the small print but fans were short changed once again. Royal beat Boscik by two straight falls in just three rounds in a quite forgettable match. Tony St.Clair warmed up for his rematch for the British Heavyweight Title when he defeated Butcher Bond by two falls to one in the sixth round. Len Hurst made a welcome reappearance at the Albert Hall when beat Ray Thunder who was counted out in round four. Jim Breaks once again demanded another title match when he beat Johnny Saint with submissions coming in round's five and six. Alan Dennison was victorious when his opponent Bobby Barnes was disqualified in the fourth round. The final contest of the evening saw crowd favourite Johnny Kwango beat Johnny England who once again spent more time showing off his muscles than wrestling. England was counted out in the fourth round.

The Belle Vue show on the 24th saw Manchester's grapple fans get their first look at John Quinn live. Quinn gave them an impressive showing when his opponent Ray Steele was knocked out in the fifth round with the over the top forearm smash disposing of another opponent. Big Daddy was also on the bill there in a tag match with one of his regular partners Bobby Ryan to face Gunboat Harris and a masked Red Devil. In a rather brief affair the Red Devil was knocked out in the fourth minute and a few seconds later Harris suffered the same fate. The Red Devil was unmasked as Brian Hunt. Jim Breaks was brought back down to earth after his Albert Hall win against Johnny Saint when he lost to Jackie Robinson. Robinson won by two falls to one with a winner coming in round six. Johnny England beat Pat Patton who was counted out in the fifth round whilst Ringo Rigby defeated Lucky Gordon who was also counted out, this time in round three.

March -

March's wrestling on World of Sport started on the 3rd and came from Oldham with Big Daddy in the top of the bill slot. But first up was a preliminary contest featuring 'Farmer's Boy' Pete Ross taking on the unpredictable Irishman Lucky Gordon. Coverage commenced at the start of round five with Gordon already in front from a submission on Ross in the third round. It wasn't long though till Ross equalised with a pinfall in the fifth and with no further score the bout ended in a draw.

Next up was the main event with Big Daddy and his partner Bobby Ryan taking on King Kong Kirk and Gunboat Harris. The ring looked minute with the three big heavyweights in it

268

and in the early stages Ryan clambered on top of the corner post to view proceedings. Unbelievably Daddy lifted up Kirk and slammed him to the mat but didn't follow up with a splash and Kirk immediately tagged in Harris. Harris was then floored by numerous belly butts before he left the ring accompanied by Kirk. They complained to MC Brian Crabtree that it was unfair that Daddy had refused to tag Ryan into the contest. Naturally Daddy fell into the trap and Ryan came into the ring where he managed to throw Harris who was more than 8st heavier around the ring. It didn't last long and Harris picked up Ryan so high he was about ten feet off of the ground and slammed him into the canvas. Ryan's problems were only beginning as Kirk was tagged in and he delivered one of his flying elbow drops onto Ryan. Another elbow drop saw Ryan in a sorry state and Kirk lifted him up high into a neck lift and Ryan submitted in just under six minutes. After another submission attempt from Kirk was foiled, Harris was tagged in before Ryan finally tagged Daddy in. Naturally referee Emil Poilve didn't spot the tag so Ryan had to continue before a legal tag was finally made. Daddy slung Harris about the ring before clubbing him down to the mat where he covered him for the equalising fall following the customary splash. Kirk continued instead of Harris and Daddy caught him coming from a posting and it was some sight seeing Kirk come over Daddy's shoulder for the double elbow drop. Kirk managed to beat the count but scrambled to the outside of the ring where he made his way back to the dressing room accompanied by Harris. The official verdict was that he had been counted out by Poilve in the eleventh minute. It was announced that the winners of the match would be taking on Mick McManus and Steve Logan in a tag to be held at Leamington Spa and shown sometime in April. There was a postscript to the match where Bobby Ryan informed Max Crabtree that he no longer wished to do tag matches alongside Big Daddy in the future. Ryan had a full time job with a brewery in the midlands and taking on guys like Kirk and Harris who were more than twice his weight was too much of an injury risk.

The last contest that week was something of a battle of the bad boys with Brian Maxine taking on the heavier Ray Thunder who outweighed his opponent by over 3st. Thunder got a public warning from referee Kashmir Singh in the third round for refusing to allow Maxine to get to his feet. Singh was equally adept as a wrestler and would go onto make several appearances on TV in the 1980's with his boots and trunks on. Thunder got the first fall in the fourth with a kind of powerslam flooring Maxine which Thunder followed up with a cross press for the count of three. Maxine was quickly back on level terms in round five when he pinned Thunder with a reverse double knee hold after a bodyslam. Thunder charged into Maxine and sent him flying through the ropes as he celebrated and referee Singh rightfully disqualified Thunder for it.

John Quinn was back on World of Sport the next weekend as part of the second half of the show recorded at Oldham. Quinn faced a last minute switch of opponent again as the originally booked Gil Singh failed to appear for a second time and was replaced by Len Hurst. Hurst was making a first appearance on TV for six years. Hurst who was used to the American all-in style after his years stateside but was unable to make much impression in the match. Quinn thought he had taken the lead in round two when a single leg Boston saw Hurst submit but he had used the rope for assistance so it was disallowed. It didn't matter that much as once again Quinn knocked an opponent out with a forearm smash. Hurst was left seeing stars in round four after becoming the latest recipient of it. As Hurst was assisted from the ring none other than Big Daddy showed up as his feud with Quinn continued to boil up. Daddy had to be held back by the likes of John Naylor, Barry Douglas, Lucky Gordon and Pete Ross as matters threatened to get out of hand.

There was drama in the match between Pat Roach and Tony St.Clair with it abandoned in round six. Referee Kashmir Singh was hurt as Roach and St.Clair tumbled out of the ring and sadly the bout had to end. Roach had got the first fall in the third round before St.Clair equalised in the fourth and with the match boiling up to its conclusion it was brought to an unfortunate ending.

The other match was a poorly booked bout with Mark Rocco taking on Johnny Kwango. It was like asking an OAP in a mobility scooter to try and keep up with Lewis Hamilton in a race. Luckily someone as talented as Rocco was able to drag the match into the third round before ending it as a result of Kwango submitting to a single leg Boston.

The welterweight tournament's first semi final was shown on World of Sport on the 17th as part of three bouts recorded at Rotherham. The opener was a rematch between Mick McManus and Jackie Turpin although it wasn't the boxer v wrestler match that Turpin had demanded. It was fought under traditional free-style wrestling rules although the rulebook was ignored for most of the bout. Turpin got the first fall in round three but McManus came back to win. An injured leg caused Turpin to submit from a single leg Boston in round five and McManus quickly got the winner from the same hold in the sixth round.

The main match saw British Heavyweight Champion Giant Haystacks who now apparantly weighed in excess of 35st. take on Ray Steele. Steele gave a good account of himself in the first two rounds and even went so far as getting the first fall in the second round. Steele rattled the big man with some forearm smashes before a flying headbutt felled Haystacks. Steele quickly covered him with a cross press for the count of three from referee Ken Lazenby. Steele carried on with the attack at the start of the third round but as he rushed in Haystacks caught him with a blow to his head. Rather than finish him off with a splash Haystacks squashed him with a Samoan drop instead. As Steele rose unsteadily to his feet Haystacks posted him into a corner and followed up by splashing him there. Referee Lazenby called a halt to the contest and awarded the win to Haystacks by TKO.

Jim Breaks was the first wrestler through to the final of the welterweight tournament as a result of his win against John Naylor. Breaks had his work cut out throughout the bout and it was only in the eighth and final round that he was able to get the win. Breaks got the first fall in round four but it was quickly equalised by Naylor in the fifth round. Naylor's brave attempt was finally thwarted with a minute or so left in the contest when he submitted to a 'Breaks' special'.

Wrestling was missing from World of Sport on the 24th with boxing shown at 4pm instead. Larry Holmes' latest title defence of his WBC World Heavyweight Title against Ossie Ocasio from Las Vegas which had happened early Saturday morning was broadcast instead of grappling.

Wrestling was back on 31st March with it being the day of the Grand National there was a bonus for grapple fans with an extra bout screened at 3.30pm. The match was between Pat Roach and Marty Jones from a bill recorded at Blackburn back in December. Roach outweighed Jones by at least 5st. and put that advantage to good use with plenty of rulebreaking too. Jones did manage to get a fall in the third round but the end came in round five. Roach hoisted Jones high above his head and the 'Brumagen bump' came next. Referee Dave Reese stopped the count at six as it was obvious Jones was hurt and needed medical attention.

After the half-time football scores the main wrestling show started at 4pm as usual and was the second half of the show recorded at Rotherham and featured the second semi final of the welterweight tournament.

The opener was an interesting match with Johnny Saint facing Sid Cooper and it was a shame viewers had only a brief look at the bout. Coverage was joined towards the end of round four with Saint ahead from a fall in the second round and Cooper having received a final public warning. These were two superb professional wrestlers in action and the best part came in the early stages of the fifth round. Saint did his roll up into the ball trick with which Cooper wouldn't engage and instead Cooper told the crowd how he wouldn't be fooled. Cooper then rolled up into a ball of his own which naturally went wrong and ended with Saint breaking it up. Saint swiftly followed up with a winning fall coming from a folding press secured by a bridge for a two straight falls win.

The second semi final of the welterweight tournament was on next with Steve Grey wrestling Ken Joyce for the right to meet Jim Breaks in the final which would be part of the coverage on FA Cup Final World of Sport on 12th May. It was pretty obvious before the match began that it would be Grey who would be in the final and that was how it ended. It was a superb wrestling match with both of them masters of the holds and counterholds style. Surprisingly it was the veteran Joyce who opened the scoring in round four with a fantastic move with Grey's attempt at a folding press reversed by Joyce into a reverse folding press for the count of three. Grey levelled the match in the sixth round when he caught Joyce unaware. Joyce had taken his eyes off Grey who had rolled himself into a ball. Suddenly Grey sprung into action and took Joyce down before pinning him with a reverse double knee hold which left Joyce kicking himself for the loss of concentration. Grey quickly followed up with the winner in the seventh round when he reversed a double leg nelson into a folding press with a bridge to secure a two falls to one win. Afterwards Ken Joyce took the microphone from MC Mark Green to congratulate Grey and to say that he hoped Grey beats Breaks in the final.

It wouldn't be a Relwyskow & Green promotion for TV without at least one curiously booked bout and it was the last one with Mal Sanders taking on Butcher Bond who outweighed Sanders by a good 5st. To compensate for the weight discrepancy Sanders was given a fall start. The coverage started at the start of round two and it seemed the contest was all over in that round. Sanders attempted a flying tackle on Bond who was leaning on the ropes and both wrestlers toppled out of the ring over the top rope. Bond was seemingly back before the count finished whilst Sanders was outside of the ring and Kent Walton thought that was the end of the match with Bond winning. Walton remarked that he was pleased Bond had won as he was due a bit of good fortune as both his parents had passed away in the past nine months. Unfortunately it wasn't to be as Bond was spotted by referee Ken Lazenby pulling Sanders by the trunks as he attempted to climb back in. Therefore the contest restarted and Bond was furious and he started to give Sanders a hammering. Bond carried on with the weakeners in round three and it paid off when he forced Sanders to submit from a backbreaker. In the end Bond overdid the rough stuff and he was disqualified by referee Lazenby after he deliberately sent Sanders over the top rope. Different county councils or authorities banned some moves and in South Yorkshire a deliberate throw of your opponent over the top rope brought an instant disqualification.

Around the halls -

London's grapple fans were well catered for at the start of March with the start of shows at the Woolwich Odeon on the 2nd. A five bout programme was headed by Tony St.Clair taking on Mark Rocco in a typically fast paced and hectic meeting. St.Clair equalised a fall from Rocco with one of his own in the fifth and with that Rocco decided he didn't want to carry on so walked back to the dressing room. Two heavyweight contests saw firstly Len Hurst take on Ray Thunder and beat him by two falls to one in round six whilst Pete Roberts defeated Butcher Bond who was counted out in the sixth round. Johnny Czeslaw who was beginning to miss a few bouts through ill health beat Billy Torontos with a winner in round five. Steve Grey ensured the fans went home happy with opponent Bobby Barnes disqualified in round three of the evening's final contest.

The next night was the latest show at the Kilburn Gaumont with Big Daddy and Giant Haystacks opposing each other in the evening's main event tag. Daddy and partner Jackie Turpin beat Haystacks and his partner by Steve Logan with a winning fall coming in the thirteenth minute. A rather suprising result saw Johnny Kwango beat Brian Maxine by two straight falls in four rounds. Lee Bronson beat John Elijah by two falls to one in round six of a heavyweight encounter. The rest of the evening's programme featured the Martial Arts Fighters team of Clive Myers and Chris Adams taking on Butcher Bond and Banger Walsh in a variety of matches. Myers pinned Bond in round two and Walsh made Adams submit in round two in single's bouts. Myers and Adams beat Bond and Walsh in a tag with the winner coming in the eleventh minute. Finally Myers beat Bond in an arm wrestling match to complete the series.

For me Wednesday 7th March was something of a hectic afternoon and evening with firstly it being my fifteenth birthday. Then there was wrestling at my local hall The Dome in Brighton in the evening and finally I found out that Big Daddy was going to be the guest on ITV's This is Your Life programme that night. With video recorders being a thing of the future in those days the only way to catch a look at the

274

programme was to go along to a nearby TV rental's shop and watch it on one of the tv's in the window before getting back to The Dome for the first match. Host of the show Eamonn Andrews was dressed as a hooded monster to gatecrash a photocall alongside Kendo Nagasaki, Gorgeous George and Giant Haystacks who were all dressed in their ring gear. Andrews took off his hood to approach Big Daddy and utter the immortal words 'This is your life'. Apart from Nagasaki, George and Haystacks other wrestlers there included Mal Sanders, Bobby Barnes, Roy St.Clair, Tony St.Clair, Bert Royal, Vic Faulkner, Jim Breaks, Steve Grey, Pete Roberts, Mike Marino, Alan Dennison, Butcher Bond, Wayne Bridges, Johnny Kwango, Tally Ho Kaye, King Kong Kirk , Big Bruno and Brian Maxine.

Max Crabtree was there alongside brother Brian as well as Daddy's wife Eunice and their children. Mick McManus appeared later on in the show to reminisce about the days when Daddy was billed as the Battling Guardsman. Not only did being featured on the show illustrate how big a personality Big Daddy was at this time but it provided brilliant publicity for wrestling in general.

As for the wrestling at Brighton that night it was a good show and an excellent rematch between John Quinn and Wayne Bridges the highlight. Fought under All-in rules with a lot of action out of the ring it finished in the seventeenth minute with Quinn disqualified. The other main bout on the programme was a tag with Giant Haystacks and Big Bruno taking on Honey Boy Zimba and Johnny Kwango. It bordered on the sadistic at times with Kwango in particular taking quite a beating before Haystacks finished him off with a splash. Zimba wasn't allowed to fight on alone so the contest was stopped and an easy win awarded to the big guys after eight minutes.

An even bigger mismatch in a tag happened at Belle Vue on the 10th with this time Giant Haystacks and Big Bruno taking on Clive Myers and Chris Adams. The combined weight of Myers and Adams wouldn't even be half that of Haystacks and it showed in the bout. Apart from sporadic comebacks of chops and a few kicks it was Haystacks and Bruno giving a beat down to their opponents throughout. Surprisingly the match

275

lasted until the twelth minute before it was halted to stop further punishment for Myers and Adams. Pat Roach used his weight advantage to see off Colin Joynson who was unable to continue after a 'Brumagen bump' in the fifth round. Bert Royal gained a win over Mark Rocco who was disqualified in round four. The other two matches saw Alan Dennison overcome a substantial weight disadvantage to beat Bronco Wells with a winning fall in round five whilst John Naylor defeated Mike Jordan by two falls to one in the sixth round.

There was something of a farcical match at Hanley on the 17th when a bout between Alan Dennison and Kid Chocolate was refereed by Johnny England. Despite both wrestlers obeying the rules throughout and wrestling in their usual sporting manner England was dishing out public warnings for any imagined offence. The match ended in a No Contest in the fifth round when a submission from Dennison left Chocolate unable to continue.

Once again John Quinn was one of the featured attractions at the latest Royal Albert Hall show on 21st March. This time Quinn would be wrestling Pat Roach who he had plenty of beef with at the previous show there on opposing sides in a tag. Roach ended up the winner but in a controversial way when Quinn walked out of the match in the fourth round when the referee was injured. A rematch from the January show saw Mick McManus once again take on Mal Sanders with the match ending in a one score each draw at the end of the scheduled six rounds. Neither wrestler wanted a draw so referee Max Ward allowed an extra round to find a winner. McManus quickly got the winner forcing Sanders to submit but for refusing to break the hold in time he was disqualified by Ward. Tony St.Clair warmed up for his forthcoming rematch with Giant Haystacks for the British Heavyweight Title by beating Pete Roberts in a superb contest. St.Clair won with a winning fall in round five and it was announced the title match would be on the April Albert Hall show. Caswell Martin pinned Colin Joynson in the tenth minute of another heavyweight contest.

The rest of the evening comprised of a first for the Albert Hall in that of a tag knockout tournament. The four teams competing for the prize were Big Daddy and Steve Grey, The

Wensor Brothers, The Martial Arts Fighters and Bruiser Muir and Banger Walsh. The first semi final saw Daddy and Grey beat The Wensors and the second saw Muir and Walsh defeat Clive Myers and Chris Adams. Despite a furious start to the final by Muir and Walsh in the end it was Daddy and Grey who won with once again Walsh knocked out by a double elbow drop from Daddy.

Big Daddy and John Quinn would have another in-ring encounter on the 24th at Belle Vue in what should have been a blockbuster tag. Unfortunately Quinn's original opponent King Kong Kirk was replaced on the night by Ron Allcard which made him the weak link in the match. After tagging with a variety of lighter wrestlers Daddy had gone back to one of his original partners in Tony St.Clair to take no chances against Quinn. Without Kirk in the match Quinn was unable to dominate and the only public warning in the contest came for Daddy before the the bout had even started. In the end Daddy and St.Clair were easy winners with a winning fall coming in the eleventh minute but it was becoming obvious that the fans wanted to see Daddy take on Quinn in a singles match. The rest of the card wasn't up to the usual Belle Vue quality with nothing much to commend it. Mike Bennett made a welcome return to Best Wryton Promotions and wrestled an interesting one score each draw with Alan Woods. Johnny Saint easily defeated Blackjack Mulligan by two straight falls in four rounds. Pete Ross beat Don Michaels by two falls to one in the sixth round and Jackie Turpin beat Banger Walsh who was disqualified in the third round.

April -

The wrestling shown on World of Sport on the 7th was the second half of the Hemel Hempstead bill which featured the TV debut of John Quinn from back in January. It wasn't the best ever fifty minutes of wrestling broadcast with no discernible main event. Billy Torontos took on Blackjack Mulligan in the first bout with Torontos up to his usual antics. There was only a couple of minutes of the match shown as coverage was joined at the start of round two and it ended in that round. Mulligan had already received two public warnings from referee Peter Szakacs for roughing up Torontos when Mulligan trapped his opponent's arms in the ropes. Torontos quickly escaped and as Mulligan rushed towards Torontos he threw him over the top rope. Mulligan had no chance of returning to the ring in time and Torontos was the winner by a countout.

The second contest featured a traditional wrestling match between two Lancashire based grapplers with John Naylor meeting Mike Jordan. Naylor got the first fall in the third round when he grabbed Jordan's legs and pinned him by a folding press secured by a bridge. Jordan was quickly back on level terms with an equaliser coming in the fourth round. Naylor's attempt at a folding press was quickly reversed by Jordan for a folding press of his own. Naylor went on to clinch the win with a winning fall coming in round six from a folding press after Jordan had attempted a victory roll.

The final match that week was a heavyweight contest between Lee Bronson and Johnny Czeslaw. Czeslaw got the first fall in round four with a folding press before Bronson equalised in the fifth round. Bronson reversed a posting attempt and pinned Czeslaw via a double leg nelson which was the end of the scoring and the contest ended in a draw.

Leamington Spa was the venue for the wrestling shown on World of Sport on the 14th with Big Daddy in the main event. The opener was a typically hard-fought heavyweight contest with Pete Roberts taking on Colin Joynson. Roberts got the first fall in round four before an equaliser from Joynson came in the first minute of round five. Roberts went onto win with the winning fall coming in round seven.

The main event was the tag which had been mentioned at the TV show from Oldham with Big Daddy and Bobby Ryan taking on Mick McManus and Steve Logan. Ryan's reluctance to do tags with Daddy gave an opening to Dave 'Boy' Smith to parther Daddy instead. Smith had now taken up wrestling full-time after finishing his studies. It was quite a poor contest with neither McManus or Logan having the weight to do anything with Daddy. Instead they double teamed Smith and the first score came in the third minute with McManus forcing Smith to submit from a Boston crab. Once Daddy made the tag the

278

match came to a swift conclusion with a slam and splash on McManus for the equaliser in the sixth minute. That was quickly followed by a similar move on Logan for the winning fall in the seventh minute. The fans there and I dare say the vast majority watching it at home loved it which at the end of the day is the most important thing.

The show finished with a rather dull heavyweight match with Antigua's Caswell Martin taking on 'Jamaica Kid' Len Hurst. Hurst got the first fall in the opening minute of round three before Martin equalised in round five. The bout ended in the seventh round after Hurst accidentally fell from the ring and couldn't continue. Martin refused to accept the win so a No Contest was the verdict.

Grapple fans had an Easter bonus with the Bank Holiday World of Sport on Easter Monday 16th April having wrestling from Croydon on at 4pm. The show featured a Battle Royale with three single's matches followed by the traditional over the top rope finale. The first match saw Chris Adams defeat Lucky Gordon with a winning fall coming in round five. Next up Bobby Barnes took on the much smaller Steve Grey and it was Barnes who won courtesy of a fall in the sixth round. The final single's bout ended with both wrestlers counted out in the the fifth round. Both Kid Chocolate and Johnny England took a tumble from the ring and neither could make it back inside of the ropes before referee Peter Szakacs had counted ten. The over the top rope match was surprisingly won by Steve Grey who was the lightest wrestler competing in it. The last three left were Grey, Bobby Barnes and Johnny England and it was Grey who threw the others out to win in a shade under six minutes of frenetic action.

It was back to a regular Saturday World of Sport on the 21st with the second half of the Leamington Spa show screened. The opener was another of those traditional British style heavyweight matches with John Elijah's fall in round five equalising Romany Riley's fall in the fourth round. The bout ended in a draw at the end of the scheduled six rounds.

The main event was another rematch between Mark Rocco and Bert Royal but again it was a non-title fight. The coverage began at the start of round two with Royal riling up Rocco with

279

slaps to his face before a couple of punches back soon stopped it. Referee Dave Reese gave Rocco a public warning after all manner of transgressions before both wrestlers started to fight outside of the ring. Rocco had torn off the corner post covering but Royal took advantage by slamming Rocco's head into the uncovered turnbuckle. It was Rocco though who got the first score in the third round when he pinned Royal with a reverse double knee hold after a piledriver had laid him out. Kent Walton remarked during the interval between rounds that he thought the piledriver should be made illegal and that is something many agreed with. Royal finally levelled up the match in round five when he pinned Rocco with a cross press after he had floored Rocco with a flying tackle from the corner post. Rocco though simply upped the tempo of the bout in the sixth round and forced a submission from Royal with a reverse shoulder lever. Referee Reese had other ideas and decided to disqualify him for the illegal move that had weakened Royal's shoulder leading to the submission hold. As MC Brian Crabtree anounced the decision Brian Maxine entered the ring to challenge Rocco. Maxine told Rocco he wouldn't take bloody liberties with him and that he liked to fight. Rocco told Maxine he was lucky that it wouldn't be his arm he jumped on but his neck and he would break it. The action ended with both Crabtree and Reese trying to keep them apart as they tried to brawl.

The final contest of the week saw local lad Banger Walsh take on Ringo Rigby with Walsh accompanied by a manager. The bout was over a twenty minute time limit and no rounds. Rigby won when Walsh was outside of the ring arguing with the crowd and was counted out in the twelfth minute.

The World of Sport cameras were on Merseyside on the 28th for a scheduled four bout show recorded at the Kirkby Suite. The first match was a clash of middleweight champions with British No.1 Brian Maxine taking on European title-holder Mal Sanders. After Maxine's confrontation with Mark Rocco seen the previous Saturday on World of Sport viewers would be interested to see if Maxine behaved himself this time. Sanders got the first fall in the second round before an equaliser for Maxine came in round three from a single leg Boston submission. The match ended in the fourth round when Sanders missed an attempted dropkick and hurt his neck. Referee Emil Poilve stopped the contest and awarded the win to Maxine but surprisingly he refused to accept the decision and it was revised to a No Contest.

The rest of the show comprised of a heavyweight knockout tournament featuring Giant Haystacks, John Quinn, Tony St.Clair and Pete Roberts. The first semi final was between Quinn and St.Clair which turned out to be a very good contest. St.Clair gave Quinn his most competitive televised match since his arrival. Quinn was forced to use the ropes to stop St.Clair's momentum in the early stages. Quinn then started with the punches behind referee Emil Poilve's back which got the crowd furious. St.Clair retaliated with punches of his own which Poilve allowed before a near fall as St.Clair took Quinn down into a double arm hold. In round three Poilve finally had enough and dished out a public warning to Quinn for attacking St.Clair whilst he was down. The first fall came in round four and it went to Quinn who pinned St.Clair with a cross press helped by a handful of St.Clair's trunks. Quinn had floored St.Clair with the over the top forearm smash and there was no chance of St.Clair kicking out of the fall. St.Clair was reluctant to start the fifth round as he nursed an injured shoulder which wasn't helped by Quinn kicking it. Finally St.Clair got his revenge in round five when he floored Quinn after a posting and followed up with a leg drop before St.Clair pinned the his opponent for the equaliser. Despite their best efforts neither could get a winning fall in the final round. Therefore there had to be a toss of a coin to decide the winner and who would progress to the final and whilst MC Brian Crabtree announced it Quinn and St.Clair preferred to continue to fight. It was St.Clair who called but called it incorrectly so it was Quinn who went into the final to face the winner of Giant Haystacks v Pete Roberts.

It was Haystacks who won the second semi final when he knocked out Roberts in round two. Despite Haystacks being hated by those in attendance and probably most of those watching at home everyone couldn't wait to see him take on Quinn and no doubt he would be the fan's favourite in the match. It wasn't meant to be though as when both wrestlers were being announced by Crabtree they had some sort of discussion which ended with a handshake. They then left the ring together and it was announced that they wouldn't wrestle each other and would share the winner's purse money. A very disappointing ending to the week's show.

Around the halls -

April saw the Big Daddy and John Quinn feud continue to build up with the announcement that they would wrestle on the FA Cup Final edition of World of Sport in a tag match. Also on the show to be recorded at Guildford would be the final of the welterweight tournament between Jim Breaks and Steve Grey to find the new British champion at that weight.

John Quinn got bragging rights over Big Daddy on the 2nd at Bradford when he notched up a win over the 'Mam's and Dad's favourite' in a tag match. Quinn had teamed up with his new best friend Giant Haystacks to take on Daddy who was partnering the much lighter Mick McMichael. Obviously McMichael was the weak link and he was targetted by both Haystacks and Quinn throughout the match and in the end McMichael submitted in the tenth minute to lose the match for him and Daddy.

Big Daddy got some revenge on the 7th at Maidstone when he tagged with Steve Grey against John Quinn and Sid Cooper. There was so much demand for tickets that the start of the show was delayed as the fans queued at the box office. Daddy and Grey won by two falls to one with a winning fall coming in the thirteenth minute in front of a delighted capacity crowd.

The tag team of Giant Haystacks and John Quinn were now appearing on a regular basis and their only problem was them keep getting disqualified as happened at Wolverhampton on the 10th. Pat Roach had teamed up with Tony St.Clair to take on Haystacks and Quinn and with Roach and St.Clair a fall in front their opponents were disqualified in the eleventh minute.

Haystacks and Quinn took on Big Daddy again in a tag match at Leicester the next night with this time Daddy teaming with Tony St.Clair rather than one of his usual lighter partners.

It worked as Daddy and St.Clair won the contest but only with Haystacks and Quinn getting disqualified once more. The same match and the same result happened at Southampton on the 13th with another packed crowd turning out to see them wrestle.

Giant Haystacks and John Quinn parted ways on the 14th with both competing in knockout tournaments at different venues. Haystacks was at Belle Vue and Quinn was at Kilburn. Haystacks was competing alongside Tony St.Clair, Caswell Martin and Lee Bronson who replaced the advertised Bruiser Muir. The first semi final saw St.Clair get the winning fall in the first round to beat Haystacks. The second semi final between Martin and Bronson had reached the end of the first round when it was announced that St.Clair had been injured and would be unable to participate in the ladder match finale. Therefore the match between Martin and Bronson was declared to be the final and was restarted as a ladder match in which Martin got the money in five minutes. The rest of the bill wasn't that brilliant but a host of wrestlers from the south made it interesting. Steve Grey beat Johnny Saint by two falls to one in round five. Len Hurst defeated Barry Douglas who was disqualifed in round five. Johnny Kwango beat Jeff Kaye with a winning fall in round five and Mick McMichael won when Johnny England walked out in round five and was counted out.

John Quinn's opponents in the knockout tournament at Kilburn were Wayne Bridges, Big Bruno and Ray Steele. Quinn beat Steele in the first semi final when he was knocked out by Quinn's forearm smash in round three. Bridges joined him in the final when he pinned Bruno in round three to win the second semi final. Bridges won the final when Quinn who was out of control from the very start was disqualified in round two. A rather uninspiring supporting programme saw Alan Dennison beat Blackjack Mulligan by two straight falls in four rounds. Johnny Czeslaw defeated Bronco Wells with a winning fall in round five. Irish strongman Jim Fitzmaurice was the crowd favourite against Gary Wensor and he repaid their support winning in round five. Another winning fall came in the fifth round for Romany Riley against Johnny Wilson.

If two heavyweight tournaments weren't enough on one night there was also one at Hanley with a ladder match final too. Pat Roach beat Colin Joynson in the first semi final with a 'Brumagen bump' in round three finishing off Joynson. Pete Roberts joined Roach in the final when he defeated Butcher Bond who was counted out in the fifth round. Roach won the ladder match when he was first to climb up the ladder in the fourth minute.

Perhaps the most bizarre tournament advertised for the 14th was one at Paisley up in Scotland. It bought back memories of the days of independent promoters advertising anyone they wanted to. Then on the night it would be announced that they couldn't wrestle due to injuries and wrestlers that they had never heard of would replace them. The bill at Paisley saw a top of the bill featuring Big Daddy taking on Klondyke Bill. That was backed up by Andy Robbins wrestling Bruno the Bear, no word on whether Bruno was human or an actual bear. Jackie Pallo was billed against the fearsome Dago Sotello and a ladies match would see Mitzi Mueller face Lady Jane. There is no record of this show actually happening or whether fans who bought tickets in advance got a refund.

The show at Croydon on the 17th saw John Quinn team up with Mark Rocco for the main event tag match there. Rocco had been announced as Quinn's partner for the tag against Big Daddy to be seen on Cup Final day and they were getting in some practice together here. They took on Tony St.Clair and Wayne Bridges at the Fairfields Halls and it was obvious they needed to do some more team work as they lost inside of fifteen minutes. Quinn was disqualified in the eleventh minute and Rocco deciding he didn't want to carry on alone followed him back to the dressing room a couple of minutes later. A car load of wrestlers from Yorkshire made the journey to Surrey to appear on the bill with Mick McMichael beating Jim Breaks by two falls to one in round six whilst Alan Dennison's match with Gary Wensor ended in a No Contest. Wensor was injured in the sixth round and Dennison wouldn't accept the win in such circumstances. Butcher Bond beat Clive Myers who was unable to continue in round four whilst Len Hurst continued his fine run of form since returning to Britain beating Ray Thunder by the only fall needed in the twelfth minute.

There was a hectic week for Max Crabtree and those in the office running things during the week commencing Monday 23rd April. On the Monday night there was the TV taping at Kirkby followed by a trek south for another TV taping at Guildford on the Tuesday. The Guildford show would see the show for the FA Cup Final World of Sport recorded before everyone headed a few miles east to the Royal Albert Hall on the Wednesday night.

Tony St.Clair got his long awaited opportunity to regain the British Heavyweight Title he had lost to Giant Haystacks back in November on the 25th. The match was the main event on the April show at the Royal Albert Hall with a World Lightweight Title defence by Johnny Saint also on the bill. St.Clair was successful in his attempt to become champion again but once more his opponent Haystacks was the agent of his own demise. Unlike the match in November where Haystacks stuck to the rules this time he adopted a far wilder approach during the match. Haystacks got the first fall in round three but had already received two public warnings from referee Joe D'Orazio for rather indulging in too much rough stuff. St.Clair got an equalising fall in the fifth round and as he celebrated Haystacks attacked St.Clair in his corner. As D'Orazio tried to separate them Haystacks shoved him away with a hand to the referee's face. D'Orazio immediately called for the bell and Haystacks had been disqualified. Tony St.Clair was the new British Heavyweight Champion and once more wearing the Lord Mountevan's belt around his waist.

In the other title match challenger Jim Breaks once again failed in his bout with World Lightweight Champion Johnny Saint. In a rather bad tempered encounter even the normally mild mannered Saint received a public warning as Breaks' antics provoked him beyond breaking point at times. Saint's opening fall in the sixth round was equalised by Breaks in round eight when a 'Breaks' special' saw the champion submit. The winner came in the tenth round when Saint pinned Breaks for yet another successful title defence. Ringo Rigby made an Albert Hall debut in a tough assignment against Bobby Barnes.

Despite showing up well for the first five rounds Barnes' experience eventually told as did the rule breaking. A weakened Rigby was forced to submit in round five and retired from the match to hand Barnes the win. An excellent lightweight match between Jackie Robinson and Mike Jordan enthralled those in attendance with their array of wrestling skills. Robinson even had time to do a spot of cossack dancing before beating Jordan with a winning fall in round six.

The rest of the programme saw a team match with Clive Myers, Len Hurst and Honey Boy Zimba taking on a rather uncomprising trio of Steve Logan, Sid Cooper and Ray Thunder. Myers beat Cooper pinning him in round two. Zimba defeated Thunder who was counted out in the second round. Logan's rather enthusiastic approach to his match with Hurst saw him disqualified in the first round. The concluding six man tag saw Myers, Zimba and Hurst record a straight falls win over Logan, Cooper and Thunder.

April ended with a title v title match at Rotherham on the 30th with Johnny Saint putting his World Lightweight Title up and Jim Breaks' European Lightweight Title would be on the line too. There was a perfect ending for the promoters when the match ended in the ninth round with both wrestlers disqualified. Therefore both Saint and Breaks retained their own titles and a rematch could be booked. On the same show there was the return of Jon and Pete LaPaque, the Leicester brothers who were now known as 'The Rockers' and wore matching leather jackets to the ring. They took on old rivals The Royals at Rotherham and despite breaking every rule in the book were unable to beat Bert and Vic who won by two falls to one in twenty minutes of great action.

May -

There was another busy month of wrestling on TV in May with the two Bank Holidays having coverage as well as the traditional Saturday shows on World of Sport.

The month kicked off with three bouts from Guildford shown on the 5th which was the first time the TV cameras had been at the Civic Hall. The hall was packed to capacity as the show also featured the bouts shown on FA Cup Final day. I was lucky enough to have been there and it was a good job I'd booked a ticket in advance as it was a complete sell out before the night. It was also a nice little earner for the council and Dale Martin as ticket prices were increased to £2 everywhere from the usual £1.50 and £1.25.

The show on the 5th featured three heavyweight bouts with the opening match seeing Count Bartelli's final match on TV for Joint Promotions. The Count was very much a veteran come 1979 and had been wrestling for at least 30 years but having switched to the independent scene he went onto wrestle till 1986. Bartelli's opponent was Butcher Bond and the television coverage started at the start of round four. Bond had already got a public warning from referee Max Ward in the second round for kicking Bartelli whilst he was on the mat. Bartelli took the lead in the third round after taking a bit of a pasting from Bond in the first two rounds. Bartelli seemed curiously out of sorts complaining about a problem with his eye. That all changed when Bartelli caught Bond and pinned him with a folding press from the side and the Count looked a lot happier. Bond continued the rough stuff on Bartelli in round four but referee Ward refused to issue another public warning. Ward preferred to give several stern private warnings by way of jabbing his finger in Bond's face as he made his point. Bond's aggression finally paid off in the fifth round when he got an equalising fall. Bond picked up an onrushing Bartelli and switched into a powerslam before pinning him with a reverse double knee hold. The end came in the final round and the win went to Bond who had twice sent Bartelli flying over the top rope and on the second occasion he took a heavy landing onto Kent Walton's ringside table. When Bartelli returned inside the ropes Bond pounced and forced Bartelli to submit from a reverse neck lift. It was quite sad to see the Count go out on a losing note especially after taking such a beating during the bout.

The second contest saw Pat Roach very much revert to type against his opponent Wayne Bridges and their tag team of a couple of months ago was very much forgotten. Whilst frowned on by the purists having two big heavyweights throw everything at each other is what the fans love to see as was the

287

case here. Tempers became frayed in the very first minute of the first round with Roach already incurring the wrath of referee Max Ward for not breaking the hold when told to do so. Roach got his first public warning in the second round for kicking Bridges three times whilst he was on the mat but Kent Walton thought it was rather a soft way to get yourself a warning. Roach began to rough up Bridges during the second and third rounds with bodychecks continually sending Bridges onto the mat. It paid off in the third round when Roach slammed a weakened Bridges to the mat and pinned him with a cross press to take the first fall. Bridges fought back in the fourth round flooring Roach with a couple of his flying headbutts which landed perfectly. A posting from Bridges followed and Roach was taken down courtesy of a kneedrop. Bridges was then able to pin him for the equaliser with a cross press. Things started to get out of hand in the fifth round with both wrestlers using punches and in the end Max Ward gave Roach his final public warning for not breaking a hold which was across Bridges' throat. The sixth round saw a fast start from Bridges who posted Roach who then retaliated by landing a punch right on Bridges jaw which knocked him clean out. Ward immediately disqualified Roach who complained to all and sundry before stomping his way back to the dressing room.

The final match saw another heavyweight in the last stages of a great career with Johnny Czeslaw taking on Ray Thunder. Thunder was never one to worry about such details as the Lord Mountevan's rules and got an early public warning from referee Max Ward in round two. Ward took exception to Thunder continually kneeing Czeslaw whilst he was down and eventually issued Thunder his first warning. Kent Walton remarked during that round that Czeslaw seemed subdued and as future events told he was suffering from a brain tumour that ended his career later in 1979 which later on tragically left him blind. In round four Czeslaw finally managed to put some offence together and delivered one of his famous chops which sent Thunder flying over the top rope. Despite Thunder's best attempts he couldn't get back into the ring before referee Ward had counted ten. This would turn turn out to be Johnny Czeslaw's last match on World of Sport.

The May Day Bank Holiday on the 7th saw an extra helping of televised wrestling on World of Sport with three bouts taped at Croydon shown. The opening match was between Mick McManus and Billy Torontos and had been seen many times around the various halls on the circuit. McManus won when Torontos was unable to continue in round five but it wasn't a match to engage with.

The main event saw new British Heavyweight Champion Tony St.Clair face the former No.1 Giant Haystacks but the contest had in fact been recorded at the beginning of April when Haystacks still held the belt. The strange thing this was the first and only time that Haystacks and St.Clair would have a single's match shown on World of Sport. After a fast start by St.Clair in round one it ended with Haystack's clubbing forearm blows slowing St.Clair up and the weight difference told. St.Clair delighted the fans though when he managed to floor Haystacks and pin him for the first fall. Haystacks took grave exception to this and slammed St.Clair's head into the outside of the corner post. St.Clair suffered a badly cut forehead and referee Peter Szakacs had no hesitation in disqualifying Haystacks. Szakacs also reported Haystacks to the Board of Control for further sanction.

The final match was a dour heavyweight match with Pete Roberts taking on Ray Steele. Roberts equalised Steele's fall in round four with a fall in the fifth as the match ended in a draw.

The 1979 FA Cup Final was on 12th May and wrestling featured on the Cup Final World of Sport in two time slots. The first match shown at 12.35pm was the final of the welterweight tournament between Steve Grey and Jim Breaks. This would turn out to be the first of three beautifully crafted matches between the two to decide the winner and the new British Welterweight Champion. The coverage on TV commenced at the start of round seven of a twelve round bout with no score and surprisingly no public warnings for Breaks either. As the round started Breaks continued with arm weakeners which he had commenced in the sixth and everyone knew where this would be heading. Breaks did get a submission shortly into the seventh but not from the 'Breaks' special' as usual but a nasty looking armbar from which Grey submitted immediately.

Naturally Breaks started the eighth round trying to get a second submission to seal a two-nil win and used a punch to try and soften Grey up. Grey lost his cool and punched and slapped Breaks in return as things got a little out of hand before Breaks once more went back to the arm weakeners. Fortunes reversed in round ten when Grey finally got the upper hand in the match when he softened up Breaks with several kicks to his leg. Grey grabbled Breaks' legs then got hold of his arms and a surfboard was on and Breaks submitted instantly. So there were two rounds to go and Grey went straightaway into another attempt at a surfboard with Breaks straining every sinew in trying to resist it. It came down to the final round with the score still one each, Breaks started by trying a 'Breaks' special' before once more Grey tried to get him into the surfboard to no avail. The bell sounded to end the match with no winner and Kent Walton assured us that there would be a rematch and it would be seen on TV.

The match millions tuned into see was at 2.10pm and finally Big Daddy would get his hands on John Quinn live on TV. Daddy and his partner Ringo Rigby were taking on Quinn and Mark Rocco. Rocco started off against Rigby with Rocco quickly taking control before Quinn was tagged in. Daddy tried to enter the ring but was quickly sent packing by referee Max Ward which gave Quinn the chance to beat up Rigby with a ample helping of rough stuff. Rocco then entered the fray via the top rope to continue the beating on Rigby whilst Daddy was left standing impotent outside of the ring holding his tag rope. Rocco then delivered a vicious looking piledriver on Rigby but made the cardinal mistake of taking his eye off his opponent and a weakened Rigby managed to crawl to his corner to tag in Daddy. The crowd erupted as Daddy came into the ring and he finally came into contact with Quinn. After the usual belly butts and body checks Daddy knocked Quinn to the mat and following a big splash pinned him for the first fall. Rocco restarted against Daddy instead of Quinn but all that meant was Rocco was rag-dolled around the ring before Daddy flattened him with another big splash. Rather than pinning Rocco Daddy walked away and tagged in Rigby which was a big mistake. Quinn came back into the match against Rigby and delivered some hefty kicks before a posting left Rigby in his opponent's corner. Whilst the legal men Rigby and Rocco tried to continue the match Quinn had snuck over to Daddy's corner to try and attack him with referee Ward having no control over the bout whatsoever. The beating on Rigby continued and eventually Quinn got the equaliser when he forced Rigby to submit from a backbreaker in the ninth minute. Rigby and Quinn restarted the match with Rocco taking the corner post pads off as Quinn delivered a splash on Rigby that had Kent Walton giving out an 'Ay, ay, ay'. Finally Rigby made the tag and the crowd went wild as Daddy re-entered the match against Rocco and immediately posted him onto the corner post with the pad removed. Daddy sent Rocco into the ropes before sending him what must have been 10ft. into the air with a huge back drop. On landing Daddy delivered another big splash and pinned Rocco for the winning fall despite Quinn trying to break it up. As MC John Harris announced the verdict the crowd mobbed the ring to celebrate. Kent Walton then said what everybody wanted to see was Daddy and Quinn meet in a solo wrestling bout on TV which surely must happen soon. Walton was correct and arrangements had already been made for the big fight which was going to be held at Wembley Arena on Wednesday June 27th. This would be the biggest wrestling show held in Britain for many a year.

Things were back to normal on World of Sport on the 19th with the second half of the show recorded at Kirkby shown. First match shown was Pat Patton taking on Johnny England who would go onto be regular opponents over the next three years and I think every hall would have seen the match once if not numerous times. Patton got the first fall in round three with England once again being his own worst enemy. England had press-slammed Patton over the top ropes but Patton had landed on his feet. Patton quickly nipped back into the ring and whilst England was posing Patton took him down with a flying crucifix to pin him for the first fall. England used his considerable strength to weaken Patton's back and once more sending him flying over the top rope. There was no soft landing this time for Patton and when he finally clambered back inside the ropes England was waiting and applied a Boston Crab.

Patton submitted right away and with his back injured Patton had to retire so giving England the victory.

The second match saw Alan Dennison go against Mike Bennett in a 'Yorkshire derby'. Dennison got the first fall in round four before Bennett equalised in the fifth round. It was Dennison who got the winning fall in the final round to secure local bragging rights.

The main event match was a curious tag with the Martial Arts Fighters Clive Myers and Chris Adams taking on Bruiser Muir and Johnny Kwango. Kwango was a replacement for Bronco Wells and it would be hard to think of a worse possible choice. Kwango was totally out of place in the match and subsequently it was a poor match. Muir got the first score in the ninth minute forcing Adams to submit from a neck hold with Kwango refusing to congratulate his partner. Myers got an equalising fall in the twelfth minute with an impressive splash off of the top of the corner post onto Muir led to a cross press for the count of three. It was slightly botched as Myers' momentum saw him bounce off Muir for the first attempt at the pin before repeating it for a successful second time. The match came to an end in fourteenth minute when Kwango headbutted his own partner Muir who then left the ring and went back to the dressing room. Shortly after Myers pinned Kwango for the deciding fall and to end a match that wasn't a good watch.

Wrestling was missing from World of Sport on the 26th with the England v Scotland football match shown instead. Grapple fans who read the Daily Mirror's TV pages that morning would have seen a large advert telling readers that next week in the Mirror would be 'The painful truth about professional wrestling', 'Getting to grips with the grapplers' as the Mirror's Murray Davies brings you the inside story of the grunt and groan game.

There was wrestling seen on TV on the Bank Holiday Monday though on the 28th with two bouts from Wembley shown on World of Sport. Three matches were actually advertised to be shown but time constraints saw the contest between Steve Logan and Len Hurst canned. The match everyone wanted to see was the rematch between Steve Grey and Jim Breaks to decide the new British Welterweight

Champion. Once again though at the end of the twelfth round it was a draw. Grey thought he had got the first fall in round five but it was ruled out by referee Peter Szakacs as Grey had his feet under the ropes. It wasn't till round nine that a legitimate score happened and it was Breaks with one of his 'Breaks' specials' that opened the scoring. Despite Grey's best attempts at a surfboard failing and several fall attempts falling short the contest entered the twelfth and final round with Breaks still leading from his submission in the ninth round. Finally though with a minute or so gone of the round Grey was finally able to pin Breaks for the count of three and with which the match ended in a draw. For those who already knew the proposed bill for the Wembley Arena show a third match between Grey and Breaks was on it so this drawn match didn't come as a surprise.

The other match shown saw Johnny Saint take on Mick McMichael in one of those bouts that seemed to see both wrestlers enjoying themselves. Saint got the first fall in the second round which was equalised by a fall in the fourth for McMichael. Saint got the deciding fall for the win in the fifth round of an enjoyable wrestling match.

Around the halls -

There was a surprise at Croydon on the 1st when Giant Haystacks picked up a win over Big Daddy in a six man tag. Haystacks with partners Big Bruno and Bronco Wells beat Daddy and his partners Pete Roberts and Young McAllister (who was Peter Wilson under an assumed name) by two straight falls. Earlier on in the evening Daddy had pinned Haystacks in the first round to win a solo match. Roberts had beaten Bruno and McAllister had defeated Wells before the losers took their revenge in the tag. There were three other matches on the bill with Terry Rudge and Colin Joynson wrestling an entertaining and hard fought one fall each draw. Brian Maxine's match with Len Hurst ended in a No Contest when Hurst was injured in round four. Also ending in the fourth round was Bobby Barnes' bout with Steve Grey with Barnes being disqualified in that round.

293

Big Daddy was also in action on the 5th at Belle Vue when he captained his 'TV All-stars' team against a team captained by Big Bruno. The six solo matches saw Chris Adams beat Bruno who was disqualified in round four. Banger Walsh defeated Pat Patton who was unable to continue in the fifth round. Big Daddy squashed Bronco Wells in the first round. Johnny England beat Young David who was injured in round six. Mike Jordan defeated Tommy Warboys who was making a rare appearance away from Yorkshire with a winning fall in the fifth round. The final solo bout saw Kid Chocolate face Lucky Gordon with Gordon's over enthusiastic approach seeing him incur the referee's wrath. In the end the match was stopped in round four but instead of being disqualified Gordon was forced to take part in the concluding six man tag. Gordon and his partners Johnny England and Banger Walsh were defeated by Big Daddy, Chris Adams and Young David in six minutes.

A sign of the popularity of wrestling at the time saw Belle Vue putting on shows on a weekly basis on some weeks instead of the usual fortnightly. Grapple fans were back at the Manchester venue on the 12th with local hero Tony St.Clair taking on John Quinn in the main event. As expected the atmosphere was at fever pitch in the hall during the match with no quarter given by either wrestler. Quinn quickly received public warnings in round's two and three as he overdid the rough tactics before getting an opening fall in the fourth round. St.Clair wasn't behind for long as he equalised in round five and as he celebrated in his corner he was attacked by Quinn who was then disqualified for doing so. Ray Steele took on Tommy Warboys who was making a quick reappearance at Belle Vue after being on the previous week's show. Warboys was a late replacement for Pat Roach and was beaten by Steele by two straight falls in four rounds.

Mark Rocco had another all action match when he took on John Naylor and Naylor gave him all the trouble he could handle. The lighter Naylor matched Rocco all the way and even got two public warnings to go with the two given to Rocco. In the end Rocco came out on top when he forced Naylor to submit in round six but it was a win he earnt the hard way. Colin Joynson beat John Elijah with a winning fall coming in round six whilst another heavyweight contest saw Honey Boy Zimba defeat Ray Thunder who was disqualified in the fourth round.

Mark Rocco had another tough match three days later at Croydon on the 15th when he took on the much heavier Wayne Bridges. The match ended in the fourth round with Bridges injured but because it was caused by Rocco's illegal moves the result was a No Contest. Pat Roach was again missing and was replaced by Clive Myers against Butcher Bond. Bond took exception to being on the end of Myers' chops and kicks and in round five walked out of the ring and forfeited the contest. Young David made a rare appearance for Dale Martin on the show when he tackled Tally Ho Kaye. David was the winner when Kaye was disqualified in the fourth round. Johnny Saint defeated John Naylor by two falls to one in round six of a superb lightweight match whilst Mal Sanders was unable to overcome the weight advantage Steve Logan had in their bout and was counted out in round four.

Mark Rocco made a successful defence of his British Heavy/Middleweight Title at Belle Vue on the 26th when his challenger Alan Dennison was disqualified. Dennison was in front from a submission in round six when he totally lost the plot in the seventh round and attacked Rocco. It reminded ringsiders of matches in the past when Dennison would become uncontrollable and it happened here when Dennison was provoked by Rocco's non-stop foul moves. There was no justification for it and the referee had to disqualify Dennison with Rocco retaining the title as a result. Brian Maxine had an easy night when he beat Blackjack Mulligan who was counted out in the third round. Another grappler to have an easy night was Johnny Saint who surprisingly defeated Jim Breaks by two straight falls in three rounds. Marty Jones had a tough time overcoming Butcher Bond in the main supporting bout but finally pinned Bond for the winner in the sixth round. Clive Myers defeated Mal Sanders by two falls to one in round five to complete the show.

The final spectacular of the season at The Royal Albert Hall on 30th May was somewhat overshadowed by the announcement of the Big Daddy's match with John Quinn at

Wembley Arena on June 27th and its top quality supporting programme. Daddy and Quinn would meet in a last man standing match with the added stipulation that the loser would leave the country. Backing this up would be the third and final match to decide the new British Welterweight Champion between Steve Grey and Jim Breaks and there must be a winner this time. Mal Sanders would defend the European Middleweight Title against highly rated Spanish challenger Chato Pastor. Tony St.Clair would face Japanese star Tokyo Joe and amongst other attractions the Martial Arts Fighters would be in tag action on the seven bout card.

It wasn't a bad night's action at the Albert Hall on the 30th but the highlight for me was being able to grab a poster advertising the Wembley Arena show that had been stuck to the ring beforehand. Big Daddy and John Quinn were both in action on the night but in separate matches. Daddy and Steve Grey took on Mick McManus and Mark Rocco in the main event tag with Rocco once again being the most important component of the match. Apart from Rocco once again taking some really impressive bumps for Daddy it was routine stuff with Daddy and Grey winning in the twelfth minute. Meanwhile John Quinn made shortwork of his opponent Lee Bronson who was knocked out in round three by Quinn's forearm smash.

Pete Roberts defeated Marty Jones by two falls to one in the fifth round with Jones at times showing signs of bad temper. They would meet again at Wembley Arena with the Dale Martin Trophy at stake. Brian Maxine beat Butcher Bond who was disqualified in round five whilst Vic Faulkner made something of a rare Albert Hall appearance beating Alan Dennison courtesy of a winning fall coming in the sixth round. To complete the evening Caswell Martin and Terry Rudge wrestled a one fall each draw over twenty minutes duration. It was now full steam ahead to Wembley and the publicity team went into overdrive.

That was the good publicity but to balance it there was the bad publicity of the Daily Mirror running a series of articles bashing wrestling or rather bashing Joint Promotions. The front page of the Mirror on the 28th had a headline 'OUCH Murray Davies gets to grips with the grapplers'. More interesting to me was the headline next to that saying 'Dear Marje' was back as Britain's best loved agony aunt.

The whole centre pages were given to an article headed 'KING CON' but one of the wrestlers doing the hit job wasn't surprising as it was Jackie Pallo. Pallo had been bitter towards Joint Promotions since he left in 1974 and couldn't wait to get a dig in towards the Crabtrees. Pallo would have been better off concentrating on his own promotion as his lack of business acumen was seeing it lose money hand over fist. Pallo would put on a show at a venue where there would be 200/300 punters at the most paying to get in but would have up to twelve wrestlers or sometimes more on the show with their wages to pay. The other wrestler involved in the article was a lot more surprising as it was Kendo Nagasaki and he was featured in the first article.

Nagasaki was wrestling the journalist Davies for the article and supposedly showing him the tricks of the trade. Davies went on to tell how fights were fixed and wrestlers got their orders in the dressing room beforehand. He also said televised bouts were even more carefully planned and they were told 'Make it spectacular, plenty of movement, plenty of aerial work'.

The other part of the article mentioned the hold all wrestlers respected which was the 'Office hold'. It mentioned how Joint Promotions controlled the wrestling seen on TV and how Mick McManus was the liason man between the promoters and London Weekend Television. Jackie Pallo went onto say he hadn't been seen on TV for six years and had formed his own promotion. Pallo then said he was trying to break the office hold to get a better deal for wrestlers. Max Crabtree , managing director, of Joint Promotions was not available for an interview.

Billy Abbey chairman of Joint Promotions told the Mirror 'We have absolutely no comment to make'. Abbey also said 'It's up to you to get your facts straight. If you do not we will take action for libel'.

At the bottom of both pages was the banner headline 'Tomorrow - the man who did the dirty on Mick McManus'.

The second of the articles in Tuesday's Daily Mirror had another two page spread with the main article telling of the infamous televised bout between Mick McManus and Peter Preston. This was the contest between them recorded at Lime Grove Baths and shown on TV in January 1967. Preston had got the first fall as planned in the second round but then went off-script with Preston refusing to allow McManus to win by knockout in round four. The article stated that Preston had been told by a rival Northern promoter to become the first man to beat McManus on TV and you'll be looked after. With the match going wrong referee Don Branch warned Preston to stick to the plan and his career would be over if he didn't. It also said that Preston had a dilemma as he was told not to hurt McManus as he was wrestling in the North the next week and the promoters wanted him there. In the end a desperate McManus got himself disqualified by punching Preston and trying to yank his trunks off so Preston was indeed the winner. McManus was asked for a comment and said 'I've nothing to say. The fight was a long time ago and I can't remember it. A lot of water has passed under the bridge since then'.

Kent Walton was quoted saying professional wrestling was not fixed and that it was absolute rubbish saying it. Walton admitted there was a certain amount of hokum which he preferred to call showmanship as it made a better spectacle for viewers.

The final part of the piece was a glossary of terms with readers informed what a shoot was, what blade job meant and the meaning of cheap heat amongst other things.

This sort of article came along every so often but it didn't mean anything or have any great effect on wrestling. What Jackie Pallo didn't understand was that if you tell newspaper readers that wrestling is fixed , it is fake etc. that they will take it to mean all wrestling is. Readers wouldn't think it's only Joint Promotions' wrestling which is fake and Pallo's shows weren't they would think all of it is so he ended up disrespecting his own shows as well.

June -

Unfortunately for grapple fans there were blank screens for three weeks as the World of Sport time slot was given over to other sports.

On the 2nd there was boxing from South Africa shown instead with John Tate taking on Kallie Knoetze in a heavyweight match. Mind you there was time allotted earlier in the show for coverage of the World Frisbee Championships which could have been used for some wrestling.

There was a schoolboy's football match between England and West Germany shown on the 9th and the following Saturday it was tennis and the Stella Artois Championship on instead of wrestling.

It was a great shame as the build up to the Wembley Arena show suffered slighlty with the lack of TV coverage and the ability to hype it up even more.

Wrestling finally returned to World of Sport on the 23rd with the final chance to publicise the extravaganza on the 27th. The first match featured Mal Sander's challenger at Wembley Chato Pastor who was matched against Gary Wensor on the show recorded at Southend. The first impression of Pastor was he looked quite elderly but he seemed very good technically against the heavier Wensor. Pastor got the first fall in round three with a nice move that ended in a double leg nelson pinning Wensor for the count of three. Wensor came straight back in the fourth round and got an equalising fall after a body slam with a reverse double knee hold. Pastor got the winning fall in the sixth round after taking Wensor down into a double knee hold. It felt very low key with no crowd reaction and not a good way to sell a major championship match.

The main event saw John Quinn take on Lee Bronson who he had easily beaten at the Albert Hall a few weeks before. Quinn received his usual warm welcome from the fans as he was introduced by MC John Harris and Quinn then grabbed the microphone from him. Most of what Quinn said was drowned out by the jeers of the fans but he was upset at the welcome he had received by the good people of Southend and hoped one day they would visit the USA where he could return the favour.

He also hoped a tidal wave would come in one day and drown the bloody lot of them. Quinn used his weight and power advantages through the first two rounds and everytime Bronson tried to rally Quinn halted him through tactics that saw him get two public warnings from referee Max Ward. The end came in the third round when Quinn's over the top forearm smash caught Bronson flush and knocked him out. Afterwards Quinn tore up a big picture of Big Daddy as he went on a tirade of what he was going to do to Daddy at Wembley Arena.

The final match should have featured two of the advertised wrestlers booked on the big show tag match wrestle in a solo bout. Sadly Clive Myers had given notice and left Joint Promotions at the end of May so not only was he missing from this one but also from the Wembley tag too. Myers was replaced by former partner Chris Adams to take on Mark Rocco instead. Adams' career had plateaued in recent months after the explosive start he had had in the second half of 1978 despite him improving with every bout. The match was joined in progress at the start of the third round with Rocco already receiving a public warning from referee Max Ward in round two. It was Rocco who got the first fall in round four after plenty of rough stuff had weakened Adams. Rocco hoisted Adams aloft and brought him down with a piledriver which was followed up by a reverse double knee hold which Adams had no hope of kicking out of. Adams did respond though in the fifth before which Kent Walton gave out full details of the Wembley Arena show the following Wednesday and gave out the dates when it would be screened on World of Sport. As Walton listed the matches Adams retaliated with several chops and kicks and Rocco got out of the ring before Adams threw him back inside the ropes. Adams quickly got to the top of the cornerpost and landed a flying tackle on Rocco and followed up with a cross press for the equaliser. With one round left Rocco wasn't to be denied the win and as Adams charged to him across the ring he backdropped Adams into the front row of fans sitting at ringside. Adams landed right onto an elderly lady's lap and he had absolutely no chance of getting back into the ring before he was counted out.

Wrestling once more was missing from World of Sport on the 30th as the Lada Classic golf tournament was shown instead.

Around the halls -

Everytime I was in London from the start of June you couldn't fail to spot a large poster advertising the Wembley Arena show, there were even posters on buses and at London Underground stations. Nobody could claim not to know the Big Daddy v John Quinn fight was at Wembley Arena on 27th June. Unfortunately there were two forced changes to the proposed bill with firstly Clive Myers being replaced in the tag by Pat Patton to form a new version of the Martial Arts Fighters with Chris Adams. Secondly the Japanese heavyweight billed as Tokyo Joe failed to arrive in Britain as scheduled for a short tour before his match at Wembley against Tony St.Clair. There was no explanation for Joe's non arrival who was also known as Kurenai Hayato amongst other names in the USA and he would be replaced by Len Hurst at Wembley.

Most of the action in the early part of June was pretty low-key with the emphasis on everything to do with Wembley Arena. Whilst Big Daddy was allegedly doing special training which seemed to be knocking out the usual cannon fodder, John Quinn was doing his best to rile up just about everyone as the countdown to the big fight continued.

Quinn was at Bradford on the 13th for a rare Wednesday night show there when he took on Tony St.Clair. St.Clair was a good match for Quinn and in the end St.Clair won a bad tempered bout when Quinn was disqualified in the fifth round. Spanish challenger Chato Pastor took on Vic Faulkner and again looked anything but special when held to a one fall each draw at the end of the sixth round. Marty Jones impressed with a two falls to one win against Colin Joynson as he made his preparations for his match with Pete Roberts at Wembley. The final two matches had to be switched around with the absence of both Tokyo Joe and Clive Myers. Young David who was now a full time pro after finishing his studies had the unenviable task of wrestling Mark Rocco and suffered a four

301

round beating before being counted out. Rocco did a double duty as he then took on Alan Dennison and when Dennison lost his cool in round four Rocco didn't fancy continuing and walked out.

Once again Young David was brought into replace Clive Myers on the 16th at Hanley to face Mark Rocco. It didn't work out well for the youngster and Rocco gave him an absolute hammering in the first round. Tony St.Clair who was at the venue without an opponent as he was scheduled to wrestle Tokyo Joe then entered the ring during the interval and said he would take over and wrestle Rocco instead. St.Clair was a much more suitable opponent for Rocco and in the end St.Clair was the winner with Rocco counted out in round five after walking out. Chato Pastor took on Mick McMichael and beat him by two falls to one in the fifth round. Mal Sanders for once shut Jim Breaks' mouth when he defeated him with a winning fall in round six. With all the changes to the bill there was added attraction to the show and it was well worth seeing with John Quinn taking on Pat Roach with no rounds or a time limit. Quinn was the winner when he pinned Roach in the twelfth minute. Finally Young David had a chance to show what he could do against a far more suitable opponent in the last bout. David took on the masked UFO who was Brian Hunt under the mask and David won when the UFO was disqualified in the third round.

Big Daddy and John Quinn faced each other on the 23rd at Belle Vue as a teaser for the Wembley show. Daddy teamed with Tony St.Clair whilst Quinn tagged with his regular partner now in Giant Haystacks. The match was fought under 'Calgary' rules and Daddy with St.Clair had the ideal Wembley warm up when they got the winning fall in the twelfth minute. Chato Pastor once again looked unimpressive in a one fall each draw with Bert Royal over six rounds. Johnny England overpowered Kid Chocolate and finished him off with a submission in round five. Colin Joynson defeated Ray Steele by two falls to one in the sixth round whilst the evening's final match finished prematurely. Jackie Robinson and Mike Jordan were both counted out in round three to bring the match to an early ending.

The night before the Wembley show on the 26th saw differing fortunes for Big Daddy and John Quinn. Daddy was given a rare night off so he could rest up and prepare for the next night whilst Quinn was given a booking at Weymouth. Weymouth was one of the worst places to get to from the London area with a lack of decent roads and a long time sat in the van travelling for Quinn. There was a show at Croydon on the 26th with the main event between Giant Haystacks and Pat Roach ending with both disqualified in the fourth round. Chris Adams and Pat Patton had a tune-up for the next night's match when they defeated Jim and Tim Fitzmaurice with a winning fall in the tenth minute. Chato Pastor had a hard fought win over Zoltan Boscik by two falls to one in the fifth round. Brian Maxine pinned Romany Riley to win in round six whilst Ringo Rigby beat Johnny England by two straight falls in the sixth round.

The Wembley Arena Extravaganza of 1979

Wednesday 27th June arrived and with it the biggest British wrestling show since the days of Haringey Arena in the 1950's. It must have been heartbreaking to be a wrestler at that time and when they got their bookings for the month to see that they were not at Wembley but elsewhere. There were three other Joint Promotions' shows that night with The Royals, Sid Cooper, Bobby Barnes and others at Leicester. Brian Maxine, Tally Ho Kaye and Young David were some of those appearing at Great Yarmouth. At Hastings Big Bruno, Bronco Wells and regular Big Daddy fall guy Banger Walsh were there with no need for them in a Daddy match that night.

On arrival at Wembley Park tube station in the afternoon there was a real big event feel to the place as fans turned up. Having met friends we then walked around to the stage door area where there was some sort of rumour that John Quinn wasn't happy and was thinking of pulling out. Unless there was the swerve of all swerves it was obvious Big Daddy was winning as he had a full month of appearances booked for July whilst Quinn was leaving the country whatever the match stipulations said. It was said John Quinn was fearing a double-cross and wouldn't wrestle unless he was paid for the night in full and in cash beforehand. In a way you couldn't blame him as if he lost his value would plummet and he was leaving anyway. There was only one thing Max Crabtree could do and that was to pay Quinn as there were ten thousand fans arriving and if they heard that the biggest British wrestling match in years was off they would riot. Once the matter was sorted then it was full steam ahead. The event was deemed to be a sell out but back in 1979 booking in advance was hard work with fans either having to telephone the venue to reserve a ticket and then sending a cheque or postal order to pay for it , going to the venue's box office in person beforehand which was hard if you lived outside of London or turn up on the night and buy a ticket at the box office then. Ticket prices were £10 for what was described as special ringside, then £8, £6, £4 and £2. £10 then is now worth around £46 which makes it seem very reasonable cost wise considering the importance of the show. For comparison a top price ticket at Belle Vue at this time was £1.50 and at the Royal Albert Hall it was £5.

The first bout of the evening was for the Dale Martin Trophy and to be wrestled for by Marty Jones and Pete Roberts. It was a nice solid start to the evening with Jones once again letting his temper get the better of him. Jones got the first fall in round two when Roberts mistimed a monkey climb and Jones pinned him with a folding press. Roberts was quickly back on level terms when he got an equalising fall in the third round. Jones continued to test referee Peter Szakacs' patience and was given a final public warning for kicking Roberts during the interval between round's five and six. Roberts went on to get the winning fall in the sixth round when he rolled up Jones for a folding press from the side.

Having not been that impressed by the matches I had seen Chato Pastor in before Wembley I wasn't expecting too much when he challenged Mal Sanders for the European Middleweight Title. I was therefore pleasantly surprised by the good showing he put up in the bout and he made Sanders work throughout the match. It was Pastor who got the first fall in the fifth round when the Spaniard totally outfoxed Sanders who had rushed into the corner post. Pastor took him down and pinned him with a double leg nelson in a nice reversal. The crowd were beginning to warm to the bout which had been a bit of a slow burner as Pastor was now well on top as the contest progressed through the sixth round. The contest entered round eight of twelve with Pastor still well on top but it would soon change. Sanders finally managed to get in some offence and he sent Pastor flying headfirst into the cornerpost. As the Spaniard rebounded out he was caught with a backdrop which took him down and he was covered by Sanders with a cross press for the equaliser. Sanders was now firmly on top and having finally worked out how to counter Pastor's awkward style he went on to win the match in the ninth round. Pastor attempted a flying headbutt but was caught by Sanders who took him down and covered him with a folding press secured by a bridge. Sanders had retained the European Middleweight Title and Pastor was first to congratulate him. As Pastor placed the title belt around Sanders' waist the editor of the Wrestling Scene magazine Russell Plummer presented Sanders with a nice, big bouquet of flowers.

When it was announced that Tokyo Joe had been replaced by Len Hurst to wrestle Tony St.Clair I and many others felt disappointed with the choice of substitute. But on the night both wrestlers had their working boots on and it turned out to be a good match. Surprisingly it was Hurst who got the first fall in round two when he reversed an attempted double leg nelson from St.Clair into a folding press with a bridge to secure the pinfall. Something which was strange was that MC John Harris wasn't around to announce the fall and it was left to timekeeper John Curry from his ringside table to do the honours instead. Kent Walton remarked it must have been a surprise as the MC wasn't around when needed. St.Clair wasn't behind for long in the match and got an equalising fall in the third round. St.Clair produced a superbly timed moved that ended in an over the top shoulder press that pinned Hurst for the count of three. Kent Walton made a pointed remark that John Harris was back to announce this fall ! I believe it wasn't Harris' fault as there had been problems with the PA system and he was using two microphones taped together so he had disappeared to try and deal with the fault. St.Clair went on to get the winning fall in round five with a cross press after an over the top slam had floored Hurst. Whilst St.Clair won it was Hurst who had pushed him all the way and made it such a competitive match.

Next up was the main event, the contest grapple fans all over the country wanted to see and the atmosphere inside Wembley Arena was white hot. The first wrestler to enter the hall was John Quinn who was now having Manfred Mann's song 'The Mighty Quinn' played as his entrance music but it was pretty much drowned out by the boos of the crowd there. Quinn was accompanied by Giant Haystacks and they had to fight there way through loads of fans on their way to the ring. One idiot tried to attack Quinn at ringside and he was shoved to the ground and received a couple of powerful kicks from Quinn for good measure. It was then time for Big Daddy to enter the hall and 'We shall not be moved' began to play on the PA. Daddy was accompanied by brother Brian Crabtree as well as a Pearly King and Queen and he was mobbed by his fans on the way to the ring. It really did have such a big time, big fight atmosphere and I doubt anything like it had been seen before and was definitely never seen since on a British wrestling show. As MC John Harris waited patiently to do the introductions Haystacks grabbed his microphone and shouted towards Daddy 'No more Big Daddy' as security tried to restore order outside of the ring. It was an amazing sight to see before finally Harris could announce the contest stipulations and then introduce both wrestlers. Referee Peter Szakacs had the tough job of keeping order in the match and ensuring a fair fight. At last the ring was cleared and it was just Daddy and Quinn waiting for the first bell to sound. As the fight got underway Quinn tried a couple of bodychecks on Daddy which had no effect before Daddy tried one which Quinn blocked. Daddy then sent Quinn into the ropes who rebounded off them and hit Daddy on the side of his head with a forearm smash. The move that had had devastating effects on other heavyweights was shrugged off by Daddy and so were three forearm smashes delivered from close up by Quinn. Quinn then attempted another forearm smash as Daddy was propped up on the ropes and the forearm smashes seem to stun him for a moment. Another forearm smash was then delivered but not to Daddy but to Brian Crabtree who was standing on the ring apron. Crabtree was knocked flying onto the floor and he had to receive medical attention. Daddy was now back at the top of his game and picked up Quinn and slammed him into the mat before doing it again and then a third time. Quinn was looking shaken as Daddy then posted him to one corner and then posted him to the opposite corner. As Quinn rebounded from the corner Daddy delivered a devastating double elbow drop and referee Szakacs counted to ten over the unconcious North American in just 1 minute 41 seconds of the contest. Kent Walton was excited, the ten thousand fans were excited and luckily even Brian Crabtree had recovered to join in the celebrations. The ring was surrounded by hundreds of joyful fans and the medical staff had to fight their way through them to be able to attend to the stricken Quinn. There was a plan on the night for the 42st. Incredible Bulk Fatty Thomas to come to the ring to challenge Daddy but luckily due to the chaos at ringside the idea was abandoned. Whilst the match lasted less than two minutes I don't think anyone there that night was disappointed and it was the perfect end to Quinn's British tour and he deserved a huge accolade for the job he did in the six months he was in this country.

After a well deserved interval it was on with the show and a heavyweight match between Wayne Bridges and Ray Steele. As with Len Hurst earlier the normally dour Steele brought his working boots with him and gave Bridges a competitive match. Bridges opened the scoring in round three with a cross press after a bodyslam had floored Steele. Steele came back with an equalising fall in the fifth round with a suplex leading to pinfall on Bridges. It was Bridges though who continued his climb up the heavyweight rankings with a winning fall in the sixth round. After a collision had stunned both wrestlers it was Bridges who was quickest to react and he pinned Steele with a reverse double arm shoulder press.

The penultimate match on the show was the third and final attempt to decide the winner of the tournament to crown the new British Welterweight Champion. After two drawn contests between Jim Breaks and Steve Grey they would now face each other again with this time a winner must be found. The match stipulations would be a thirty minute time limit with no rounds,

307

the first fall or submission etc would win and if at the end of thirty minutes it was a draw then the referee would decide who the winner was. The match ebbed and flowed through the opening stages with Breaks trying plenty of arm weakeners before attempting a 'Breaks' special' whilst Grey was trying to get Breaks to submit from a surfboard. Grey nearly got the fall as a distracted Breaks was having a temper tantrum and Grey rolled him up for a count of two and a half by referee Peter Szakacs as the match continued scoreless. The match entered the final five minutes with both wrestlers looking increasingly desperate to get the winner but it seemed referee Szakacs would be deciding the winner. In the end there was a decisive winner and it happened with three minutes remaining in the bout. Grey had weakened Breaks' shoulder with a couple of wrenches and he went to bounce off of the ropes to carry on the attack. As Grey hit the ropes he mistimed it and instead fell between the top two ropes and landed heavily on the ringside table that had the TV equipment on. Peter Szakacs went straight over to check on Grey and called for the bell to end the match as there was no way that Grey could continue. Even the normally vocal Breaks seemed subdued until John Harris announced that he was the winner and therefore the new British Welterweight Champion. Breaks was presented with the belt and Russell Plummer was back with another bouquet of flowers to give to the new champion.

The final match of the night was the tag and fans had already started to drift away as it was past 1030pm and with the vast majority of those in attendance using public transport the need was there not to miss their last bus or train home. Chris Adams was now teaming with new partner Pat Patton in the revised version of the Martial Arts Fighters and their opponents were Mark Rocco and Steve Logan. As time was getting on the match was quite brief with Rocco and Adams starting off the action. It was Adams who got the first fall in the third round with a folding press on Logan after Adams had weakened him with a kick to the head. Rocco and Logan soon started to rough up Patton who was the weak link. Once Rocco gave Patton two piledrivers he was lifted up in a reverse neck lift and Patton submitted for the equaliser for Rocco and Logan. The match ended in the eighth minute with the winning fall coming for Rocco who delivered another of his dangerous piledrivers on Patton before pinning him with a reverse double knee hold but the bout felt rushed.

All in all the night delivered what it promised , the Daddy v Quinn match and the atmosphere was memorable with it setting standards for the future that could never be repeated. The two other shows presented at Wembley Arena paled in comparison with this night. As per the stipulation of their match John Quinn departed from Britain and the British wrestling scene was a lot duller without him. As for Big Daddy he went to new heights of popularity both inside and outside of the ring which would continue for the next decade or so.

July -

The first part of the Wembley Arena show was screened on World of Sport on the 7th. Surprisingly the second half of the show was seen first with Wayne Bridges v Ray Steele, Jim Breaks v Steve Grey and the tag broadcast.

The big one between Big Daddy and John Quinn was seen on World of Sport on the 14th. There was a nice article previewing it in that morning's Daily Mirror and telling those not in the know that it was a dramatic encounter. The other matches shown that week were Mal Sanders' title defence against Chato Pastor and Tony St.Clair's match with Len Hurst. Viewers would have to wait a few months to see the Marty Jones v Pete Roberts contest.

The wrestling on World of Sport on the 21st was a rather dull offering from Southend which was the second half of the show seen a month before. The opener was a heavyweight contest between Ed Wensor and Terry Rudge. The match was joined in progress in round four and shortly after Wensor pinned Rudge for the opening fall. Rudge quickly hit back with the equalising fall in the the fifth round. Both wrestlers were going all out for the win in the final round when they both fell through the ropes to the floor outside. Neither wrestler was able to return before referee Max Ward's count of ten so the decison was double knockout.

The main match of the afternoon was another heavyweight contest with John Elijah taking on Pat Roach who was a replacement for Johnny Czeslaw. Roach with a 4st. weight advantage over Elijah coasted through the match and even when Elijah got the first fall in the second round Roach didn't lose his temper. Roach immediately equalised in the third round before winning the match in round five. As soon as Roach lifted his opponent up above his head it was obvious a 'Brumagen bump' was on its way and it duly was. Elijah took a heavy landing from it and referee Ward stopped the contest and awarded the win to Roach.

Finally Brian Maxine faced Mel Stuart and it was Maxine who came out on top. Maxine got the first fall in round two and by the fourth round Stuart had decided he had enough and walked out of the contest to be counted out.

There was the first hint of the trouble that was coming at ITV and the forthcoming industrial dispute on the 28th. The advertised programme for World of Sport from Croydon was replaced by three bouts recorded at Gloucester. The first match saw British Heavyweight Champion Tony St.Clair take on long time friend and rival Colin Joynson. The match was only a few seconds old when Kent Walton told viewers that Joynson's nickname was the pocket tank. St.Clair went in front in round two with a cross press after an arm drag had took Joynson down to the mat and St.Clair was lightning quick in pinning him. Joynson nearly got the equaliser at the end of the third round with a Boston crab submission on St.Clair but the bell sounded and as Kent Walton noted Joynson released the hold immediately. St.Clair was slow to come out for the fourth round with the Boston crab having weakened his back, referee Jason Singh had to check St.Clair wanted to continue before allowing the bout to restart. Naturally Joynson targetted St.Clair's back and after a couple of postings and bodyslams he got an equalising fall with another bodyslam leading to a reverse double kneehold for the pin. St.Clair came out on top in the fifth round when he reversed a posting and sent Joynson high into the air with a backdrop. Once Joynson was back on his feet St.Clair suplexed him to the mat and covered him with a cross press for the winning fall. It was a great British heavyweight wrestling match and the crowd showed its appreciation at the end for both wrestlers. As St.Clair went to leave the ring there was a disturbance and the camera panned to the huge figure of Giant Haystacks standing at ringside. Haystacks had arrived early for his match with Wayne Bridges which was on next. MC Brian Crabtree explained to those in attendance and viewers at home that Haystacks wasn't happy with the way he lost the British Heavyweight Title to St.Clair back in April. Referee Dave Reese joined Jason Singh in trying to keep the pair of them apart as St.Clair wanted to get it on there and then with Haystacks. Unfortunately outside circumstances with the ongoing TV strike later in the year stopped there being a rematch between them.

With Giant Haystacks already in the ring his opponent Wayne Bridges joined him for the second match on the programme. Dave Reese would have his work cut out keeping order in the bout as they were already fighting before the first bell rung. Bridges played right into Haystacks' hands in the first round as he tried strength holds which would never work and if they looked likely to succeed the big man just reached for a rope break. Haystacks got his first public warning at the end of the first round for landing a forceful blow to Bridges' head when the bell had clearly sounded. Haystacks should have got a second warning right at the start of round two for punching Bridges in the stomach but Reese somehow missed seeing it. Bridges retaliated with a couple of forearm smashes before he attempted a flying tackle but Haystacks retained his balance and kept on his feet. He then slammed Bridges to the mat so hard it felt like Bridges would go through it and Haystacks then landed a big splash on him. There was not a chance that Bridges would or could kick out of the pinfall and Haystacks got the first fall. Bridges somehow got to his feet to continue the contest in round three and Haystacks trapped him in his corner and continually punched Bridges in his stomach. Finally referee Reese spotted one and gave Haystacks a final warning but Bridges with a surge of adrenalin came back into the bout. Bridges hit Haystacks with a couple of flying headbutts followed by a barrage of punches which finally floored him. Bridges covered him for the equalising fall although Haystacks

311

looked to be in the ropes but it counted and the bout was all square. The match ended in the first few seconds of round four , as soon as the bell rung Haystacks charged over and flattened Bridges who had yet to leave his corner. Haystacks followed up by posting Bridges into the opposite corner where for some reason referee Reese had his back turned to the action attending to the corner pad. Bridges hit him with all the force that being hurled by a 35st. man could do and Reese decided to disqualify Haystacks. For once I felt Haystacks was hard done by, the bell had rung so Bridges should have been ready. Reese should never had his back to the action and he should have been watching what unfurled. Hopefully Dave Reese was reprimanded afterwards by the Board of Control for his lack of professionalism.

The final match that week saw two Birmingham based grapplers, Lucky Gordon and Ringo Rigby face each other. It was Rigby who won courtesy of a fall in round three followed by one in round five for a two straight falls win.

Around the halls -

The start of July felt a little underwhelming after all of the excitement and the hype of the Wembley Arena show but it was soon business as usual with the coastal resorts opening up again. Big Daddy was once more at the forefront of things and the fans were filling every hall he appeared at. Without Quinn to focuse on Daddy once more turned his attention to Giant Haystacks and they met in the top of the bill tag at Picketts Lock on the 6th. Daddy and Steve Grey defeated Haystacks and Mark Rocco with a winning fall in the tenth minute. The most interesting match on the show saw Marty Jones tackle Chris Adams but it ended in a No Contest. Adams was injured and couldn't continue in round six but Jones sportingly wouldn't take the decision. Johnny Kwango beat Steve Logan who was disqualified in round five for refusing to break the hold once Kwango had submitted. Young David was finding life tough in the full time pro ranks and went down to another defeat here. Johnny England's strength was too much for the youngster who lost by submission in round six. Billy Torontos in his usual show closing slot sent the fans home happy once again when he defeated Sid Cooper by two falls to one in the fifth round.

The new British Welterweight Champion Jim Breaks was billed to make his first defence at Belle Vue on the 7th against none other than Johnny Saint who was fancying a crack at the higher weight division. In the end the match didn't take place as billed and was a straight forward non title match which was won by Saint by a winning submission in the fourth round. The whole night featured quick finishes and felt very rushed. Pat Roach beat Pete Roberts who was knocked out in round five following a 'Brumagen bump'. Roach would now get the opportunity for another title challenge against Tony St.Clair on the next Belle Vue show. Johnny Kwango defeated Sid Cooper by two straight falls in round four. Marty Jones beat Ray Thunder who was counted out in round three and Brian Maxine lasted just a round longer than Thunder against Mark Rocco when he was counted out in the fourth round. All in all the fans would have been disappointed that a good looking proposed programme ended in such a hurried manner.

Daddy and Haystacks made their way fifty miles or so the North West on the 8th to appear at Blackpool Tower on another of the Sunday spectaculars there. Daddy teamed with Jackie Turpin whilst Haystacks once more turned to Banger Walsh. Walsh was knocked out in the tenth minute by the double elbow drop as Daddy and Turpin won another match together. Tony St.Clair met Colin Joynson and had yet another great heavyweight match which was won by St.Clair by two falls to one in the seventh round. Ringo Rigby beat Lucky Gordon with a winning fall in round five whilst Chris Adams had an entertaining opening match with Tally Ho Kaye which Adams won in round six.

Tony St.Clair's defence of his British Heavyweight Title against perennial challenger Pat Roach topped the bill at Belle Vue on the 21st. The match went the full twelve rounds distance and by way of the only fall scored in round eight it was St.Clair who retained the belt and it was fair to say in title defences he had the measure of Roach. An international heavyweight contest between Honey Boy Zimba and Barry Douglas ended in a win for Zimba when Douglas was counted out in the fifth round. Chris Adams beat Steve Logan who was disqualified in round four. The rest of the programme comprised of a knockout tournament with Vic Faulkner pinning Johnny England in the third round to win the first semi final. Tally Ho Kaye defeated Young David who submitted in round three in the other semi final. Faulkner beat Kaye in the final with the winning fall coming in the second round.

Tony St.Clair made another successful defence of his British Heavyweight Title at Cardiff on the 27th. This time the challenger was Marty Jones who stepped up to the full heavyweight ranks to try his luck but it ended in failure. From the start Jones' temper was letting him down and those who thought they would be seeing a decent wrestling match were wrong. Jones actually went in front with a submission in round seven but shortly after receiving his final public warning in the ninth round he was counted out. Alan Dennison's match with Jim Breaks on the bill was halted in round four when it descended into chaos and was abandoned. Young David notched up a rare win when his opponent Tally Ho Kaye was disqualified in the sixth round. Colin Joynson beat Len Hurst by a submission in round six and John Naylor was another winner when his opponent Kid Chocolate submitted in the eleventh minute.

August -

The first and only edition of World of Sport shown in August was on the 4th and featured the second half of the Gloucester show and the first appearance of Big Daddy since his Wembley Arena triumph. The opening bout saw Alan Dennison take on Jackie Turpin and the match was joined in progress with Dennison already a fall in front. Two minutes had gone in the fifth round when Turpin pinned Dennison for an equaliser but Dennison got the deciding fall in round six for the winner.

The second match that week was between Mick McManus and Bert Royal with Royal taking the lead in round two with the first fall. McManus thought he had pinned Royal for the equaliser in the fifth round but he had pulled Royal's trunks to

314

help and referee Dave Reese disqualified it. Tempers then boiled over as Royal lost his cool and attacked McManus who retaliated. Reese decided he had seen enough and disqualified the pair of them.

Big Daddy received a heroes welcome as he made his way to the ring for the main event tag alongside partner Steve Grey. Their opponents Banger Walsh and Butcher Bond waited whilst they fought their way through the masses of fans congratulating Daddy on his win over Quinn. Eventually the match started and after the usual double teaming on Grey Bond made him submit in the eighth minute with a backbreaker. Once Grey had made the hot tag Daddy cleaned house and equalised in the twelth minute when he slammed Bond to the mat and covered him after a big splash. A minute later the match was over when Walsh was once again knocked spark out after being on the receiving end of a double elbow drop. That wasn't the end of the action though as once Bond and Walsh had departed from the ring a new threat to Daddy's dominance entered the ring. He was wearing a mask and was accompanied by former welterweight 'Kangaroo Kid' Ken Else. This character looked to weigh in excess of 30st. and was introduced as The Masked Blimp. Else on his behalf demanded that Daddy took on his man in a belly butts contest. Just a few weeks after the brilliance of the Quinn bout it had descended into this rubbish but Kent Walton assured us we would see the match on TV. Walton then bade us his usual farewell 'Have a good week, till next week' and it was back to the studio for Dickie Davies and the full time football results. Little did we know that the next time we would hear from Kent Walton would be on 27th October.

On the 9th the ITV technicians went on strike and the whole of the ITV network was blacked out by the 10th. They had been offered a 9% pay rise but with inflation at 13.4% had demanded 25% and this had been denied so they pulled the plug. Unbelievably both sides dug their heels in and refused to negotiate and it wasn't till October 22nd that another offer was made. The offer was increased to 17.5% and the strike was over. ITV came back on air on Wednesday 24th October and wrestling returned on World of Sport on the 27th.

The TV schedules were still there at the start of the strike as nobody thought when ITV went off air it wouldn't be for more than a day or two.

Wrestling would have been missing anyway on the 11th as World of Sport was meant to be showing golf from St.Merrion instead.

The wrestling on World of Sport on the 18th would have been from Wembley Town Hall and featured the following three matches. Tally Ho Kaye v Ron Marino. Johnny Saint v Pete LaPaque and Mark Rocco v John Naylor. The show would have been recorded on the 13th but the taping was cancelled and a revised programme that night was held instead.

By the 25th the newspapers had given up printing the ITV schedules and viewers were left with only BBC1 and BBC2 to watch now. The wrestling which was meant to be shown that day on World of Sport was from Catford and the attraction would have been Big Daddy taking on the Blimp who was now renamed the 40st. Masked Mr X in the belly butts contest. The other two matches that week would have been two from the following bouts with the other three shown on the following week. Jim Breaks v Kid Chocolate. Johnny Kwango v Ray Thunder. Chris Adams v Sid Cooper. Ken Joyce v Ring Gladiator and Pat Roach v Len Hurst.

The extra helping of wrestling shown on the Bank Holiday Monday World of Sport on 27th August would have been the second half of the show from Wembley. The first half of the bill had been seen on Whitsun Bank Holiday in May. It was a team match with the trio of Pete Roberts, Clive Myers and Chris Adams taking on Sid Cooper, Bobby Barnes and Butcher Bond. The solo matches saw Adams beat Cooper who was counted out in round five. Myers beat Barnes by two falls to one in the fifth round and Roberts beat Bond who refused to wrestle in the second round. Roberts, Myers and Adams completed a four-nil whitewash in the six man tag with a two falls to one win over Cooper, Barnes and Walsh in the eleventh minute.

316

Around the halls -

August was pretty quiet for news in the ring with mainly the seaside venues holding the majority of shows. Big Daddy was the number one attraction and he headed to Belle Vue on the 4th to top the bill there. Big Daddy partnered Bert Royal and Jackie Turpin to take on a trio of Bobby Blimp, Blackjack Mulligan and Banger Walsh. The first solo bout saw Royal defeat Mulligan by two straight falls in the fourth round. Turpin took on Blimp who turned out to be Slim Gillan and the match was abandoned in round two thanks to the interference of Walsh and Mulligan. Daddy came to the ring and took on both Walsh and Mulligan at the same time and beat the pair of them in the second round. Finally Daddy, Royal and Turpin beat Walsh, Mulligan and Gillan in the concluding six man tag by two straight falls in five minutes.

Old rivals Mark Rocco and Marty Jones faced each other in a chain match which was won by Jones. Ringo Rigby beat Lucky Gordon by two falls to one in the sixth round and finally there was some wrestling when Alan Dennison and Mick McMichael got a fall apiece in a six round draw.

Jones and Rocco fought again at Torquay on the 9th with this time the stipulation being that it was fought under 'All-in' rules. Jones won with a winning fall in the fifth round in a chaotic contest. Mike Jordan beat Young David by two falls to one in a complete contrast to the Rocco v Jones contest. The bout was full of excellent wrestling and the crowd showed their appreciation to both grapplers at the end. The other two matches on the 'English Riviera' saw Brian Maxine beat Honey Boy Zimba who couldn't continue in the fifth round and Ringo Rigby won a bad tempered match against Ray Thunder courtesy of a winning fall in round six.

There was a daft stipulation match at Hanley on the 11th with Alan Dennison taking on Banger Walsh in a shirt ripping contest. Dennison ripped two shirts to Walsh's one to win it. Far more interesting was the return of Gwyn Davies to the ring, Davies had been inactive for a year or so and he now made a full time return. Davies took on the giant Blackpool lifeguard Rex Strong and beat him by two straight falls in the sixth round.

317

Marty Jones defeated Jackie Turpin in a wrestler v boxer match with Turpin unable to continue in round three. Vic Faulkner beat Pete LaPaque with a winning fall in the sixth round and John Naylor beat Pat Patton who was counted out in round five to complete the show.

The first show to be recorded for World of Sport to be cancelled because of the ITV strike was at Wembley on the 13th. The programme was changed on the night and reverted back to the usual five bouts. The main event between Mick McManus and Young David went ahead as booked and McManus was the winner with a submission in round five. Wayne Bridges beat Barry Douglas who was counted out in the fifth round. Mark Rocco defeated John Naylor who was unable to continue for round six after a submission in the fifth. Johnny Saint beat Ron Marino by two falls to one in round five and Honey Boy Zimba defeated Pete LaPaque in the fifth round.

There was drama the same night at Bridlington during the match between Marty Jones and Colin Joynson. In the sixth round the ring boards broke and both wrestlers fell under the ring. The match had to be stopped and the verdict was left open.

The next TV recording to be cancelled was the one proposed for Catford on the 20th which should have hosted the belly butt challenge match between Big Daddy and the masked 40st. Mr X. Without the cameras present the bout was changed to a traditional tag with Daddy and Dean Brisco taking on Mr X and Sid Cooper. After eight minutes of farce Mr X was counted out for a two straight falls win for Daddy and Brisco. The six planned contests was reduced to five with the Jim Breaks v Kid Chocolate match taken off of the show. The other matches on the show saw Pat Roach beat Len Hurst by submission in round six. Chris Adams' match with Ray Thunder ended in the second round with Thunder suffering an accidental injury. Billy Torontos beat Tony White by two falls to one in round five and Ken Joyce defeated the Ring Gladiator who was disqualified in the sixth round.

The Masked 40st. Mr X was back in 'action' at Wembley on the 27th when he was booked to wrestle Heavyweight No.1 Tony St.Clair in a solo match. Fortunately it was changed on the night to a tag with the Johnny England v Pat Patton match on the card added to the mix. St.Clair and Patton beat Mr X and England by two straight falls in the tenth minute. Ron Marino beat Johnny Kidd with a winning fall coming in round six. Tony Costas beat Pete LaPaque by two falls to one in the eighth round. Bruiser Muir failed to show for his match with Terry Rudge so Johnny England did a double duty and lost to Rudge when he was disqualified in the fifth round.

The big news outside of the ring was the arrival of two top international heavyweights from the USA for the new season which was about to start. First up was The Sheik who was billed as the Heavyweight Champion of the Arabic World from Baghdad. The Sheik was Adnan Al-Kaissy who had wrestled in Britain a decade or so ago as the Native American Billy White Wolf. The other arrival was a sensational scoop by Max Crabtree as he secured the services of the World Heavyweight Champion 'The Iron (or Golden) Greek' Spiros Arion. Like The Sheik Arion had wrestled here previously when also known as Arion Manousakis. Unfortunately the rather nice looking belt that Arion carried with him and the title had no linear legitimacy and had been made up by Crabtree.

As well as the two international arrivals a couple of old faces returned from the independent circuit with the 'Golden Boy' Steve Veidor being one of them. Veidor was still insanely popular with the young and not so young ladies at ringside and remained one of the best 'baby-faces' in the game. The other one returning was not quite so popular as it was the Welsh strongman Johnny Yearsley who was still very capable of a good scrap and a welcome addition.

September -

With no sign in sight of any resolution to the ITV strike and screens remained blank.

There were three remaining bouts from Catford to be shown which may have been on the 1st. There may have been no wrestling shown on the 1st or on the 8th as the next scheduled taping for World of Sport wasn't until September 12th. The show on the 12th was to have been recorded at Oldham and would have been an absolute cracker with the introductions of

Spiros Arion and The Sheik to grapple fans watching at home. Arion was booked against Pete Roberts and The Sheik should have faced Mal Sanders. Apart from that Tony St.Clair would have taken on the challenge of Giant Haystacks after their disagreement seen on TV in July. Mark Rocco would go into the lions den to fight Marty Jones in front of Jones' hometown fans. The final two proposed matches were Brian Maxine v Vic Faulkner and John Naylor v Young David and a tremendous pity we were deprived of seeing the show.

That was the end of scheduling TV tapings as there was simply no point in the present situation.

Around the halls -

The Sheik was the first to arrive in Britain and was top of the bill at Belle Vue on the 1st when he took on Johnny Wilson. The Sheik's speciality was the sleeper hold and there was a question over its validity under Lord Mountevan's rules. The Sheik put Wilson to sleep in the fourth round and whilst the Board of Control debated whether to allow the move the result stood at Belle Vue. Gwyn Davies made a winning comeback to Belle Vue when he beat Big Bruno who was disqualified in the fifth round of the match. Vic Faulkner undressed Tally Ho Kaye in the third round to win a street fight. Johnny Saint beat Mike Jordan in an excellent lightweight match by two falls to one in the sixth round and Pat Patton beat Banger Walsh by disqualification.

Big Daddy was at Hanley on the same night where another new threat called Anaconda lined up in the opposite corner. Anaconda turned out to be another Daddy punchbag who was in excess of twenty stones with little wrestling ability. Daddy and his partner Steve Grey beat Anaconda and Butcher Bond with a winning fall in the seventeenth minute. The match was the conclusion of a feud between Bond and Grey at the Staffordshire venue.

Johnny Yearsley was back for Dale Martin at Catford on the 3rd as part of a tremendous tag featuring twenty minutes of non-stop action. Tony St.Clair and Wayne Bridges beat

Yearsley and Mark Rocco when both Rocco and Yearsley walked out in the twenty first minute.

I had my first glimpse of Spiros Arion at Worthing on the 11th on only his second date here. Arion battered opponent Romany Riley from the first bell and the crowd were outraged by some of his tactics. In the end Arion got the first submission in round four from an abdominal stretch type hold and Riley was so hurt he couldn't continue. Afterwards Arion gave a speech reminiscent of those delivered by John Quinn. The problem with Arion unlike Quinn was that Arion didn't seem to have a filter or realise when he was going too far and needed to calm down. Therefore a lot of Arion's matches resulted in crowd disturbances as irate ringsiders tried to attack him.

Both Spiros Arion and The Sheik were at Oldham on the 12th for what should have been the taping for their TV debuts. Arion faced his original opponent Pete Roberts and again the abdominal stretch submission saw Roberts submit and not be able to continue. The Sheik took on a replacement in Mick McMichael and he put McMichael to sleep in round three with the result allowed to stand. Tony St.Clair defeated Giant Haystacks who once more was disqualified this time in round four. Steve Logan wrestled an entertaining one fall each draw with Vic Faulkner over six rounds and Marty Jones beat Mark Rocco with the winning fall coming in round five. The advertised John Naylor v Young David match was cut from the show.

The perils of half of the wrestlers on a bill travelling in the same car was illustrated on the 14th at Cardiff. The car bringing Giant Haystacks, Tony St.Clair, Marty Jones and Honey Boy Zimba to the show failed to arrive and there was no time to bring replacements to South Wales. It was reported to the crowd that an accident on the motorway had caused severe traffic chaos. It was not reported why the wrestlers on opposing teams in the tag were in the same car. Haystacks and Jones were meant to team together against St.Clair and Pete Roberts in the main event tag and it took some creativity from the officials present to book a show at the last minute. The first match was the only one as advertised with Jim Fitzmaurice pinning Tony White in the fifteenth minute to win. Brian

Maxine beat Steve Logan by two falls to one in round six. Pete Roberts defeated Johnny England who walked out in the third round. Catweazle was another welcome return to Joint Promotions for the new season and he celebrated with a win against Billy Torontos in round six. Finally there was a tag match with Maxine and Roberts beating Logan and England by two straight falls in the fifteenth minute.

Spiros Arion made his first Belle Vue appearance the next evening when he tackled Colin Joynson. Once again an opponent had no answer to the power of Arion and Joynson was another wrestler who couldn't continue after submitting to the abdominal stretch hold. The Sheik made a quick return after beating Johnny Wilson last time out and this time faced a tougher test against Marty Jones. The Sheik was disqualified in round five and defied Jones' calls to carry on for another round. Beau Jack beat Rex Strong by the one fall needed in the tenth minute. Ray Thunder gave a beating to Pete Ross who couldn't continue in the fourth round and John Naylor wrestled a one fall each draw with Jackie Robinson.

The Sheik made a rare trip south to wrestle for Dale Martin on the 18th at Croydon. The Sheik preferred to be based and wrestle near Leeds where he had spent a lot of time on his previous British visits. The Sheik's match with Chris Adams was halted in the fourth round when his sleeper hold had put Adams out for the count. This time the referee refused to make a decision due to the continuing arguments over the validity of the move. Spiros Arion destroyed Len Hurst and the match was stopped with Hurst unable to continue after a submission from the abdominal stretch in round four. Tony St.Clair had an easy match on the show beating Ed Wensor by two straight falls in the fourth round. Tony Costas who travelled with Spiros Arion helping with translation and language problems beat Ken Joyce by two falls to one in round six. Zoltan Boscik defeated Tony White who submitted twice to Boscik's three-in-one speciality hold.

The Royal Albert Hall's first show of the season was on 26th September with a triple main event that ensured another packed crowd. Spiros Arion was involved in a wild contest against Tony St.Clair in one of the main events. St.Clair was seeking a win to press his claim for a world title match but Arion had other ideas. Arion was out of control from the first bell and gave St.Clair a beating that was only halted when St.Clair somehow managed to pin him in round two for the first fall. The brawl continued in the third round and St.Clair had his head split open as they fought outside the ring. Once St.Clair returned to the ring the match was stopped and the win awarded to Arion.

Bert Royal stepped up to heavyweight to take on The Sheik and The Sheik's ultra aggressive style didn't endear him to the crowd. Royal was put to sleep in round four by The Sheik but this time he was disqualified for not breaking the hold when called on to by the referee.

The third of the main events saw the return to the Albert Hall of Steve Veidor after the best part of a three year's absence. Veidor seemed to have lost some of his dash and opponent Giant Haystacks looked set to win as Veidor struggled to overcome the massive weight difference. Once more Haystacks' temper let him down and he was disqualified in the fourth round which meant it was Veidor who would meet The Sheik on the October Albert Hall show.

The fourth heavyweight bout on the card saw Pete Roberts defeat Colin Joynson with a winning fall in the sixth round. The rest of the show comprised of a knockout tournament which was hurt by the absence of Jim Breaks. The first semi final saw Steve Grey beat Breaks' replacement Gary Wensor by a submission in round three. Tally Ho Kaye joined Grey in the final when he too won in the third round when his opponent Kid Chocolate was forced to submit. Grey won a brief final by two straight falls in the second round in a match lasting less than two minutes.

One unwelcome change for me came in towards the end of the month with a new design for the posters as well as the programmes used for Dale Martin shows. The previous posters used to advertise Dale Martin shows to me were iconic, they were easy to spot, easy to see what it advertised, where the show was and when the show was. The new design was more fussy with the stars around the edge and wasn't so clear to read. The new style was also used by Best Wryton which made them lose some of their originality. Russell Plummer, the man behind the Wrestling Scene magazine got the contract to produce event programmes and took the business away from long time printers Baileys.

October -

October came and still no resolution to the ITV strike and no sign of it ending yet. There was another failed attempt to tape a TV show on the 1st but luckily most of the bill would be moved to Guildford later in the month and be broadcast as the first proper show back on World of Sport.

Eventually the strike was settled and ITV recommenced broadcasting on the 24th. It was too late to save a show at Leeds on the same night that was meant to be taped for World of Sport. The proposed bill at Leeds was intended to be another attempt to show Big Daddy taking on the opponent who had now been renamed as The 42st. Incredible Bulk in a tag match. The match was rescheduled to be held at Catford later on in the year. Several of the matches that should have been recorded were booked on future TV shows instead.

Finally on 27th October World of Sport was back and wrestling returned to the 4.00pm slot. The problem was that ITV didn't have any matches ready as the tapings had all been cancelled so the comeback show featured highlights from the Wembley Arena show instead. Big Daddy v John Quinn was given another airing and the only match not broadcast at the time Marty Jones v Pete Roberts was shown too.

Around the halls -

The Sheik should have faced Wayne Bridges at Croydon on the 2nd but he had returned to the USA. The explanation given was that he wouldn't wrestle here due to his sleeper hold being banned by the Board of Control. He eventually returned at the end of the month. Bridges took on a replacement in the hapless Anaconda who Bridges defeated by two straight falls in two rounds. Luckily there were a couple of decent matches on the show with Steve Grey's surfboard submission once more taking

324

care of Jim Breaks in the fifth round for Grey to win. Steve Veidor wrestled a bruising contest with Johnny Yearsley which ended in the seventh round with Yearsley disqualified. Catweazle took on another replacement opponent in Romany Riley which ended in a No Contest in round six when Catweazle was injured. Finally young Johnny Kidd who was now appearing regularly pinned Karl Heinz in the tenth minute to win their match.

Big Daddy was at Belle Vue on the 13th when he captained his 'TV All-star's' team against one led by Giant Haystacks. On the night Haystacks' team was weakened by the absence of Mark Rocco and not so much by the absence of The Bulk. Lucky Gordon was called up to replace both of them in a rather cheap move. The solo bouts saw Mal Sanders beat Gordon who was disqualified in round six. Bert Royal defeated John Elijah by two falls to one in the sixth round. Ringo Rigby's match with Blackjack Mulligan was stopped in the fifth round and no decision was given. Big Daddy took on Giant Haystacks and beat him when Haystacks was counted out in the first round. Finally a tag saw Kid Chocolate team up with Daddy to defeat Mulligan and Gordon by two straight falls in just two minutes. All in all not a Belle Vue show to be fondly remembered.

Both wrestlers in the main event booked at Cleethorpes on the 14th were missing so The Sheik v Marty Jones was replaced by an impromptu tag match. King Ben partnered Roy Scott to defeat Pete LaPaque and Steve Peacock by two falls to in a shade over twenty minutes. The flamboyant blond haired Peacock had wrestled on the independent circuit for many a year and had now crossed over to Joint Promotions. Also on the show that night was Johnny Kidd who took on Bob Nickerson and beat him by two falls to one in round six. Nickerson also sometimes billed as Ron rather than Bob was another Ken Joyce trainee from the East Midlands. A short while later Nickerson was changed to Barratt and Bob to Blondie and Blondie Barratt became a regular name on the circuit. Not only did Barratt have a long time rivalry with Kidd which stretched over decades but he made his name as Kendo Nagasaki's tag partner in the latter days of wrestling on ITV.

The October show at The Royal Albert Hall on the 24th featured a sad occasion when Steve Logan bid farewell to the game he had graced with his presence for so long. Logan who had been wrestling for the best part of thirty years had been hampered by injuries in recent times and decided now was the time to bow out. From his debut Logan had always been the 'South London tough guy' and had never courted popularity with the fans but they always respected him. His tag team with Mick McManus was the stuff of legends and their matches with the likes of The Royals packed halls up and down the country. Logan's wrestling style was always the same, plenty of rough stuff, devastating forearm jabs to the opponent's body and not worrying too much about adhering to the rules. Outside the ring he was an incredibly nice guy, when I was seconding or working with the ring crew he always spoke and if you ran an errand for him to the shop he would always be grateful. The great thing about him was due to hair dye he never changed in appearance and his jet black hair was the same on the day he retired from the day he made his debut. After his retirement he moved to his wife Hazel's hometown of Morecambe where he lived till he died aged eighty in 2003. Unfortunately Logan's match at the Albert Hall ended in a defeat when Logan and partner Mick McManus were beaten by another revamped version of the Martial Arts Fighters with it now being comprised of Chris Adams and Ringo Rigby.

The main event that night featured Spiros Arion taking on the one man who had given him plenty of problems in matches on the circuit, Wayne Bridges. Bridges seemed to be the one British heavyweight who had the power and skill to cause Arion problems and Bridges did so at the Albert Hall. The packed crowd were behind Bridges to a man during the contest and even when Arion went in front in round three from the abdominal stretch submission their support didn't waiver. Bridges shrugged off the pain to rally strongly in the fourth round and pinned Arion for the equaliser. Sensationally Bridges got a winning fall in round five and out of nowhere he had become the leading British contender for Arion's World Heavyweight Title.

With The Sheik still having a temper tantrum over his sleeper hold being barred he was missing from the show and replaced by John Elijah for the match with Steve Veidor. Elijah gave his usual honest performance but it wasn't the match the crowd wanted to see and in the end Veidor got the winner in round six of a dull contest. Big Bruno derailed the progress Len Hurst had made in recent months with Bruno's height and power advantages too much for the Jamaican to overcome. Hurst was counted out in round five to end his recent impressive record. Johnny Wilson took on fellow Hampshire wrestler and Albert Hall debutant Barry Jones and won by two straight falls in the fifth round. This was by far the worst contest of the night and the Albert Hall bars did a roaring trade during it. Catweazle sent the fans home happy in the final match of the night when Bobby Barnes was disqualified in the third round of their contest.

The show at Belle Vue on the 27th was again hit by wrestlers not showing and this seemed to be a common theme throughout October. The main event tag should have seen Marty Jones and Johnny Saint taking on The Sheik and Steve Logan but with both of them missing they were replaced by Mel Stuart and Steve Peacock. That was a downgrade by many degrees and no way were they adequate substitutes for a main event. In the end Jones and Saint won by two straight falls in thirteen minutes in an uncompetitive match.

Steve Grey had a heated contest with Jim Breaks on the show with Grey winning by submission in the fifth round. Alan Dennison beat the Masked UFO who walked out in round five as Dennison tried to unmask him. Newcomer Dave Finch beat Tally Ho Kaye who was disqualified in the fifth round and Chris Adams defeated Banger Walsh on what was a sub-par show.

The big news at the end of October was the return home of Dynamite Kid who had finally come back to Britain after his successes in North America. Dynamite Kid's first match back was at Derby on the 29th when his opponent was another arrival back in the country as The Sheik had decided to return. The Sheik never got the opportunity to use the sleeperhold as Dynamite defeated him by two falls to one.

327

November -

Finally normal service was resumed on World of Sport on the 3rd saw three new bouts from Guildford shown. The opening contest saw Mick McManus face Catweazle for the umpteenth time in front of the cameras. It was Catweazle who got the first fall which came in round two from an old trick of his. McManus had hit him with a knee lift and it seemed left Catweazle out for the count. As referee Max Ward counted nine with no sign of Catweazle rising McManus turned his back on him and suddenly Catweazle sprung to life and pinned McManus with a side folding press. McManus got the equalising fall in the fourth round with a typical move of his. He hit Catweazle in the stomach with a forearm jab then grabbed his legs for a folding press and levelled the bout. McManus won in the fifth round when he neatly sidestepped a move from Catweazle who then fell between the ropes to the floor outside. He clambered back into the ring as the count reached nine and McManus went in for the kill. After several more leg weakeners he forced Catweazle to submit from a single leg Boston Crab.

The main event saw Spiros Arion make his first TV appearance of his tour taking on Romany Riley. After MC John Harris had introduced him Arion grabbed the microphone but unfortunately what he was trying to say was drowned out by the boos and jeers of the fans. Kent Walton told viewers that Arion had recently won the National Wrestling Association of America world championship title and that was the belt that he wore to the ring. I'm not sure if Walton was confused with the National Wrestling Alliance back in the USA but their champion in November 1979 was Harley Race who had recently won it from Giant Baba in Japan. Walton also told those watching that Arion had already been here for six weeks and was beating everybody put in front of him. Riley tried a bit of wrestling with Arion in the first round but Arion continually went to the ropes to break the hold. Referee Max Ward gave Arion his first public warning in the first round as he forgotten that he was meant to obeying the Mountevan's rules. Ward was having a hard job controlling Arion who yet again in a match was out of control and as the bell sounded to end the round he kicked Riley out of the ring. Arion started the second round as he ended the first by sending Riley flying out of the ring and smashing his head into the iron corner post as he tried to return. As with previous contests the crowd were incensed and trying to attack Arion as he continued to batter Riley. Riley tried to get back into the match and dropkicked Arion who went over the top rope to land at ringside. Arion stopped the Riley revival by kicking him in his groin area which Ward somehow failed to spot. Arion got a final warning from Ward at the end of round two as he again kicked Riley out of the ring after the bell had rung. Ward had lost all control of the bout as the third round started but it didn't matter as Arion had grabbed Riley and forced him to submit from the abdominal stretch which had finished off most of his opponents. Riley's second threw the towel in as the bell sounded for round four and he was another wrestler who was unable to continue after being a victim of the hold.

The final bout that week was a heavyweight contest which saw a TV comeback for Steve Veidor who was booked to wrestle John Elijah. It was Elijah who got the first fall after a bodyslam had floored Veidor and he pinned him with a reverse double kneehold. Veidor quickly equalised when he caught Elijah with an over the top double arm shoulder press for the count of three. Veidor got the winning fall in the final round of what was a very one paced contest when he rolled Elijah up from the side for a folding press.

The second half of the Guildford show was shown on World of Sport the following week and saw The Sheik make his first TV appearance under that guise. First up was a catchweight match seeing Ringo Rigby take on Tally Ho Kaye. It didn't take long for Kaye to use illegal tactics to subdue Rigby and he got a public warning for it in round two. Kaye thought he had got the first score with a submission in the third round from a Boston crab after Rigby had been hurt falling from the ring. Referee Max Ward had other ideas though and disallowed it as Kaye was on the ropes. Kaye started round four going all out for a legitimate score but it was Rigby who got it instead. Rigby reversed a backbreaker into a double leg nelson for the first fall and he quickly followed that up with a winner in round five. Rigby flung Kaye into the ropes and caught him when he bounced off with a hip toss and keeping hold of Kaye pinned him with a cross press for a two straight falls win.

The next match was a heavyweight contest between Pat Roach and Ray Steele in a bout that was seen far too many times in front of the cameras. Before the match could start Max Ward had to insist the ring canvas was dried as it was soaking wet from the previous match after Ringo Rigby had emptied the contents of his water bottle over the head of Tally Ho Kaye. Once the bout started it was just a repetition of previous bouts they had had and would go onto have. Roach was just about obeying the rules and relying on his 4st. weight advantage to deal with Steele through power moves instead. It was Roach who got the first fall in the third round with a cross press after a knee drop had put Steele down on the mat. Steele though came back with an equalising fall in the fourth round with an impressive move. Steele picked up Roach and slammed him to the canvas and covered him with a cross press which must have taken some strength to do. But it was to no avail as in round five Roach was the winner when the 'Brumagen bump' finished off another opponent with Steele being counted out.

The final match of the week was the most interesting with The Sheik meeting Len Hurst. As MC John Harris announced him The Sheik grabbed the microphone and went on to berate the crowd in Arabic. He then proceeded to attack Hurst and slam his head into the corner post and this was before the first bell had even rang. Referee Max Ward gave him a public warning before the match had even started ! Finally the bell sounded to start round one and Hurst was looking for revenge and returned the favour by slamming The Sheik into the cornerpost. Kent Walton told viewers that The Sheik's sleeper hold had yet to be ruled whether it was legal or not which was a factor later in the bout. Hurst gave The Sheik plenty of problems in the first two rounds and eventually pinned him for the first fall in round two. But first referee Ward gave The Sheik his final public warning for a low blow. Hurst delivered a couple of dropkicks to his opponent and followed up with a bodyslam before pinning The Sheik with a cross press to open the scoring. The bout came to a controversial end in the third round when The Sheik caught Hurst off the ropes with the sleeper hold and put him out for the count. The Sheik released the hold whilst Max Ward stood over the stricken Hurst and even John Harris came into the ring as they pondered what to do. Harris announced that Ward had stopped the contest and the verdict would remain open until the Board of Control had made a ruling on its validity. An elderly nurse came into the ring to attend to Hurst before The Sheik was ordered by Ward to bring Hurst back to full conciousness. Unfortunately The Sheik missed far too many of his booked matches to make much of an impact on his tour but when he did appear he certainly attracted plenty of heat from the crowd.

The World of Sport cameras were at Leicester for the show seen on the 17th and the highlight would be Big Daddy in the main event. First though was a replacement match with Gary Wensor taking on TV debutant Dave Draper. In that week's TV Times it was advertised to be a heavyweight match between Wayne Bridges and Lee Bronson but that was scrapped. Draper made a winning debut with a two falls to one win over Wensor. Draper never appeared on TV again and disappeared from the ring not so long afterwards.

Big Daddy teamed up in the tag to face Giant Haystacks and Mark Rocco in a match which had the crowd at fever pitch. First into the ring was Haystacks and Rocco before Daddy and Sanders appeared with Daddy's song 'We shall not be moved' accompanying them. Daddy had a job getting to the ring as the crowd mobbed him with security needed to clear the way. Once MC Brian Crabtree who was wearing an all-in-one rather tight catsuit and a frilly shirt underneath had done the introductions the match commenced with Rocco starting against Sanders for some fast paced moves and excellent action. Rocco took charge thanks to an assist from his partner Haystacks who was outside on his tag rope but hit Sanders on his head after he was posted. Referee Dave Reese gave Haystacks a public warning for it to match one given earlier to Rocco. Sanders managed to tag in Daddy who sent Rocco flying all over the ring who was again taking some incredible bumps before Haystacks was tagged in but he was very reluctant to get into the ring. Daddy sent

Haystacks flying with some hefty belly butts before a forearm smash sent Haystacks out of the ring and Rocco back in. Daddy sent Rocco flying high with a backdrop and on landing he splashed Rocco and covered him for the first fall. The second session started with Daddy hurling Rocco into the ropes before he tagged Sanders back into the action which was a mistake. Rocco kicked the onrushing Sanders in the head and followed up by a kick down below. Sanders was picked up by Rocco who delivered a piledriver and tagged in Haystacks to finish him off. Haystacks slammed Sanders and landed on him with a splash that seemed to have killed him. Kent Walton commented 'Mama mia' as poor Sanders lay there having conceded the equalising fall. Just to make things worse Sanders was then kicked in the head by Rocco. Brian Crabtree announced the fall but was also told by referee Reese that he had disqualified Rocco for the kick. That should have been the end of the contest with one fall and one disqualification counting as the other score for the win by two to one. For some reason it didn't count and with Sanders unable to continue it was left with Daddy and Haystacks to continue without partners. After two belly butts and two forearm smashes from Daddy it was all over. Haystacks left the ring and joined Rocco and they walked back to the dressing room.

The final match of the week saw Chris Adams with a fall and Butcher Bond with a submission wrestle a draw over six rounds. Once again Kent Walton repeated his idea that in the case of drawn bouts that public warnings should count and therefore Adams would have won with Bond receiving two warnings in the match.

It was back to Leicester for World of Sport the next weekend for the second part of the show recorded there and one of the most controversial matches of the time if not all time shown. Firstly though there was a middleweight contest to start between Brian Maxine and Bobby Barnes. Maxine was trying to convince everyone he had turned over a new leaf and was not a rulebreaker or even a rule bender anymore. Barnes was certainly not turning over any new leaves and acting as he always did by cheating and using foul tactics whenever he could. The match entered the sixth and final round with both wrestlers having got one fall each. Barnes was hit by Maxine behind referee Dave Reese's back and didn't get up. Referee Reese was not sure if Barnes had been punched by Maxine and with Barnes refusing to continue he abandoned the contest.

The second match saw Dynamite Kid back on World of Sport for the first time in about eighteen months and he would be facing Marty Jones. Dynamite looked vastly different from what we remembered with him now sporting a skinhead haircut and a lot more developed physique which saw him a couple of stones heavier than before he left. The first couple of rounds were pretty quiet with both wrestlers testing each other out. The action livened up in the third round with plenty of stiff looking moves and it was Jones who got the first fall in round four. Jones caught Dynamite coming off of the ropes and rolled him up into reverse folding press. As the fifth round started Kent Walton told viewers that he had been speaking to his good friend in the USA, the promoter Vince McMahon (this would have been Vince McMahon Senior). McMahon had told Walton that Dynamite would be headlining at Madison Square Garden shortly when he would be taking on Nelson Royal. As the match continued Dynamite weakened Jones with a diving headbutt as Jones lay on the mat and after Dynamite was foiled in an attempted small package he got the equaliser. Dynamite hit Jones with a knee lift and then picked him up and dropped him to the canvas with a ferocious looking piledriver. There was no chance of Jones kicking out of the cross press follow up and it was now one fall each. That left one round for either wrestler to get a winning fall in a match that Walton described as one of the best he had seen in the weight division. Jones had the first attempt at a winner with a pile driver and then a massive suplex failed too. Dynamite then sent Jones flying with a backdrop before he picked him up to suplex him. Unfortunately he was too near the ropes, he lost his balance and both him and Jones went out of the ring over the top rope and landed in a heap at ringside. Both wrestlers were surrounded by the fans and seconds trying to assist them but neither could beat referee Dave Reese's count of ten and it was announced that it was a draw.

The main event saw Spiros Arion in action again with this time he took on Colin Joynson. At the time the ITV authorities were very strict in what was deemed to be acceptable to be shown at 4.00pm and wanted it to be a sport hence Kent Walton's introduction every time of welcoming viewers to an afternoon of freestyle wrestling. This was one of the most violent matches shown on World of Sport and it was such a surprise it was shown. A month or so later in January 1980 one of Mark Rocco's matches was deemed unsuitable to be broadcast because of the violence and of course 'American Dream' Chris Colt's televised debut was banned. Once again Arion was out of control even before the bell rung making another speech which was made inaudible by boos. Joynson wasn't impressed when Arion said he would finish him off inside two rounds. Kent Walton now told us that Arion was the National Wrestling Alliance heavyweight champion of the world which wasn't true but I doubt many viewers had knowledge of the NWA and its title. Arion was straight on the attack with kicks to Joynson and punches as referee Dave Reese tried to control him. Arion got his first public warning in the first round as he overpowered Joynson and threw him out over the top rope. As Joynson tried to return inside the ring he had blood pouring out of his nose from Arion's punches. Kent Walton then let viewers know that John Quinn had applied to return to Britain in January to tag with Arion. That didn't happen, Quinn did return but Arion had left the country beforehand. As the round continued Arion then removed the cornerpost pad and slammed Joynson head first into the uncovered steel with the crowd starting to get very angry. The ringside security were having a hard job stopping fans getting to the ring as Arion once more slammed Joynson's head into the cornerpost. Dave Reese had absolutely no control as Arion continued to kick Joynson in the head as he sat in the corner with blood streaming from his nose. Finally Reese had no other option but to call for the bell and disqualify Arion in the first round. Some fans were now trying to climb into the ring and they were sent flying by Arion before Joynson totally lost his cool and attacked Arion. Missiles were being thrown into the ring as Arion and Joynson brawled in the middle of it. It was absolute mayhem both in the ring and outside of it with nobody able to control things. As if things couldn't get any more chaotic enter Big Daddy who made his way into the ring. Daddy then sent Arion flying out of the ring with a forearm smash as Kent Walton mentioned of the pair of them meeting in another Wembley Arena main event. Whilst there was no wrestling, it was ten minutes or so of superb entertainment.

Around the halls -

Tony St.Clair finally got a win over Spiros Arion and in front of his hometown fans too at Belle Vue on the 10th. St.Clair joined Wayne Bridges at the head of the queue for a world title match courtesy of a two falls to a submission win. Arion had got the first score in round two with his abdominal stretch making St.Clair submit. Luckily unlike many St.Clair could continue and equalised with a fall in round three before following up with a winner in the fourth. Pat Roach defeated Colin Joynson in the main support with Joynson counted out after receiving a 'Brumagen bump' in the fifth round.

Brian Maxine continued his new tactic of wrestling within the rules and showed sportsmanship too against Vic Faulkner. Faulkner was injured in round five and couldn't continue but Maxine refused to accept the win and a No Contest was called. In the two other bouts on the bill Tony Costas beat local lad Eddie Riley with a winning fall in the fifth round and Billy Torontos defeated Johnny England who was disqualified.

The same night at Gloucester saw the formation of a new tag team and one which was the heaviest in Europe. Weighing in excess of 80st. Giant Haystacks teamed up with The Bulk to take on Pete Roberts and Lee Bronson. Haystacks and Bulk squashed their opponents and won with a submission in the eighth minute. On the same bill Chris Adams notched up a rare win over Mark Rocco with a winning fall in the sixth round.

Steve Grey got a rematch with Jim Breaks for the British Welterweight Title at Croydon on the 13th. Breaks managed to hang onto the title as a result of a tremendous twelve rounds draw. Breaks had got the first score in the seventh round with a

335

'Breaks' special' seeing Grey submit before an equalising fall for Grey came in the ninth.

Pat Roach beat Pete Roberts who was unable to continue in the fourth round on the bill that night. John Elijah defeated King Ben with a winning fall in the fifth round. Billy Torontos beat Zoltan Boscik who was disqualified in the fourth round and Alan Dennison beat Tally Ho Kaye who refused to wrestle in round four.

Dynamite Kid cut short his British visit after a win against Mel Stuart at Wolverhampton on the 20th and returned back to North America which meant he was unable to appear at the November show at the Royal Albert Hall.

The aforementioned show at the Albert Hall took place the following night and was weakened by the absence of the Dynamite Kid. He should have been part of Big Daddy's squad in a team match and would have been one of the few occasions in British wrestling when he would have been on the same show as future British Bulldog's partner Davey 'Boy' Smith aka Young David. David was booked to take on Johnny Saint and David showed plenty in the bout that earnt Saint's respect. In the end though Saint was far too clever and experienced for David and pinned him in round five for the winner. There was a four man heavyweight knockout tournament on the show with Pat Roach, Gwyn Davies, Ray Steele and Butcher Bond competing for the prize. The first semi final saw Davies beat a temperamental Bond who downed tools in the fourth round and refused to continue. Roach defeated Steele in the other semi final when Steele was counted out in the fifth round following a 'Brumagen bump'. The final promised to be a cracker but didn't turn out that way. It ended with Davies disqualified in the fourth round and Roach winning the tournament as a result.

The rest of the programme saw Big Daddy captaining a team of Mal Sanders, Steve Grey and Dean Brisco who replaced Dynamite Kid to take on one led by Mark Rocco who was assisted by The Bulk, Sid Cooper and Banger Walsh. The Bulk who was still wearing a mask faced Daddy in a solo match and it lasted seconds as Bulk left the ring after refusing to wrestle. The other solo matches saw Rocco beat Sanders. Grey beat Cooper in straight falls and Brisco making an Albert Hall debut defeated Walsh who was disqualified. Daddy only needed Sanders with him to beat Rocco, Cooper and Bulk in the tag finale with the winner coming in five minutes. The big news to come out of the show was the announcement that Spiros Arion would defend the World Heavyweight Title at the Albert Hall on 19th December, the next show there.

The most bizarre tag team of the year award went to that of Spiros Arion and The Bulk who teamed up on the 23rd at Picketts Lock. They took on the father and son duo of Wayne Bridges and Dean Brisco who won when their opponents were disqualified in the eleventh minute.

There was a Jackie Pallo show on the same night at Rochester. As it seemed with all Pallo's bills this was a five match programme and with some big names on it so there would be a hefty wage bill to pay at the end of the night. On the night Billy Whitecloud's fall in round two was equalised by one for John Kowalski in the fifth round as they wrestled a draw. Adrian Street defeated Bob Kirkwood with the winning submission coming in round five. Clive Myers beat Danny Lynch who not surprisingly was disqualified in the fourth round. Al Miquet defeated Jim West by two straight falls in round four and Blackfoot Sioux beat Lena Blair who was disqualified in the fifth round.

There were a lot of angry fans at Belle Vue the following evening when the main event match of Mark Rocco v Dynamite Kid was called off from the ring. Dynamite had already returned to North America and also missed his match at the Albert Hall the previous Wednesday but the fans at Belle Vue didn't know that. What made it worse was the vast majority of those in attendance would have seen Dynamite's fabulous match that afternoon against Marty Jones on World of Sport so would have been looking forward to seeing Dynamite take on Rocco. As if things couldn't get any worse the substitute was Roy Scott from Leicester, a grappler very few in the crowd would have heard of. It certainly made a mockery of the statement in the programme which stated 'the promoters will engage the best possible substitute when necessary'. It was like going into a restaurant and ordering a prime rib of beef and the waiter bringing a cheap beefburger to the table and telling you

337

they were out of steak and that was the best possible alternative. Just to make it worse we will charge you the same for the beefburger as you would have paid for a steak.

Joint Promotions' shows had been blighted by absences throughout the Autumn/Winter season in 1979 with numerous changes to advertised bills. Mark Rocco had missed several week's of shows in October, The Sheik had missed over half of his bookings plus wrestlers like Johnny Czeslaw and Steve Logan had retired due to ill health and injury but were still being advertised. Promoters have hidden behind the card subject to change since the year dot and even do so to this very day and it is a wonder it has never been challenged by consumer law.

Anyway back to Belle Vue and as expected Mark Rocco gave Roy Scott a beating before he was counted out after a couple of rounds. Luckily The Sheik turned up after missing his last scheduled match there otherwise there would have been a riot but his match was once again mired in controversy. The Sheik put opponent Marty Jones in the sleeper hold and when he was told it was not legal he left the ring and was disqualified. The rest of the show saw Bert Royal beat Blackjack Mulligan by two straight falls. John Naylor gave a wrestling lesson to Young David before beating him by two falls to one. Finally two Belle Vue debutants met with Dave Draper beating Steve Peacock by two falls to one.

November ended with Mal Sanders finally making another defence of the European Middleweight Title, his first since beating Chato Pastor at Wembley Arena. His opponent on the 30th was former champion Mick McManus and surprisingly it was not on TV but at Chatham. Sanders retained the title with quickfire falls in round's seven and eight which followed a submission for McManus in the fifth round.

December -

The final month of the decade kicked off on World of Sport on the 1st with a bumper four bout bill from Catford. Not only was there a four man heavyweight knockout tournament but also a match between Mick McManus and Steve Grey shown.

338

The first of the tournament semi finals which were both fought over a twenty minute time limit with only one fall etc. to decide was between Gwyn Davies and Rex Strong. Davies progressed through to the final when he pinned Strong in the eighth minute. Big Bruno won the other semi final when his opponent the much lighter Terry Rudge was counted out in the eleventh minute.

Before the final the McManus v Grey match was shown with each wrestler forcing the other to submit it ended in a draw at the end of the sixth round.

The final was fought over the traditional rounds system and the winner was Gwyn Davies. Davies was already in front from a fall in the third round when he was punched by Bruno in full view of the referee in round four who was then disqualified. Davies was making his first TV appearance in a long time and therefore was the winner. It marked a successful beginning to a comeback which lasted about six months before injuries forced Davies into a permanent retirement.

The rest of the show from Catford was never shown at the time as it featured one of the worst matches of all time filmed for TV. Big Daddy and The Bulk finally 'fought' in front of the cameras. This wasn't the 'Belly butts challenge' but a regular tag with Daddy partnering Jackie Turpin against Bulk and Blackjack Mulligan. The match did surface several years later as part of the wrestling shown on the Men & Motors satellite TV channel and it hadn't improved with age.

The wrestling on World of Sport on the 8th came from Aylesbury with the usual three bouts on the show to enjoy. The opener that week saw Kid Chocolate take on Johnny England with all the action coming in the second half of the contest. England as usual spent the first round showing off his magnificent physique which always had Kent Walton drooling over. England opened the scoring in round four when he one handedly lifted Chocolate by the chin who instantly submitted. Chocolate came fighting back in the fifth round and he got an equaliser when he rolled up England from the back whilst he was busy posing for the crowd. It was England though who got the winning submission in the final round with an upside down chin lock which saw Chocolate submit for the second time. But much to England's fury instead of MC John Harris announcing he was the winner Harris announced that referee Max Ward had disqualified him. Ward had taken exception to England dropping Chocolate throat first onto the top rope as a weakener before the submission hold was applied.

The second match that week saw a special challenge match between Young David and Jim Breaks with a stipulation being that if David gets a fall then Breaks will give him £100. There was a further stipulation added with Breaks giving David a fall start so when the first bell rang David was already a fall ahead in the match. Breaks didn't take long to start the rough stuff and begin to weaken David's arm. Max Ward gave Breaks a first public warning in round two for kicking David's arm whilst he was on the mat. It was worth it though as the arm weakeners paid off in the third round when finally David was forced to submit from a 'Breaks' special'. Unbelievably to much excitement from Kent Walton and the crowd David managed to get the one fall he needed in round four to not only win the match but to win Breaks' £100 too. Breaks tried to blindside David but he caught Breaks rushing in and flipped him over into a folding press which David secured with a bridge.

The final contest that week saw a change to the advertised match with Pat Roach replacing The Sheik to take on Johnny Wilson. The Sheik had once again departed these shores which was a great shame as it would have been nice to see Wilson put to sleep in a bout when it was usually Wilson who sent the fans to sleep in many of his matches ! At least Roach was on one of his going days and after a slow opening round it became interesting. Roach was attended to in his corner by his trainer Dave Dynamite who interestingly was wearing an 'I hate Pat Roach' t-shirt. Whatever Dynamite told Roach in the interval it upset him as he started the rough stuff in the second round with some mighty power moves. But suddenly Wilson reversed a hip toss pinfall attempt by Roach into a flying tackle and he pinned Roach with a cross press for the first fall. Roach was not happy and shunned Wilson's attempted handshake. Straightaway into round three Roach was testing referee Max Ward's patience with illegal moves. Roach got a first public warning in the third round for pulling Wilson up by his hair as Roach now lost his cool. Ward was continually wagging his finger in Roach's face and giving private warnings 'I'm tellin' ya' but Roach was not for listening. Wilson now lost his cool and delivered several punches to Roach who was on his knees but referee Ward allowed them without a warning. Roach finally got a final public warning at the end of the fourth round for not breaking the hold when the bell rung and also for continually showing dissent towards the referee. It didn't matter as Roach went up a gear at the start of round five and within seconds he had lifted Wilson up above his head and the 'Brumagen bump' was next. He dropped Wilson to the mat where he was counted out by Ward and Roach was an unpopular winner.

The second half of the Aylesbury show was shown on World of Sport the next Saturday with Spiros Arion once more in the spotlight. The opening bout was a catchweight contest between Alan Dennison and John Naylor. Naylor got the first fall in the third round before Dennison equalised with a fall in the fifth. At the end of the sixth and final round it was still level and a draw was the result.

Spiros Arion was next and his opponent was Lee Bronson who wasn't expected to give him many problems. Arion's eyes were on his title defence the following Wednesday at the Royal Albert Hall against Wayne Bridges and he made short work of Bronson. As per Arion's other matches there weren't many freestyle wrestling holds as he once more ignored the Lord Mountevan's rule book. Arion got a public warning in the first round and a final one in the second as he overwhelmed Bronson but the match was soon over. Once Arion forced Bronson to submit from the abdominal stretch in round two it was obvious Bronson couldn't continue and the referee stopped the contest in favour of Arion.

The final match saw Sid Cooper take on Leicester's newcomer Ron Marino and it was Cooper who was far too experienced for Marino. Cooper got the winning submission in round five to seal a two one win.

The Christmas World of Sport on the 22nd featured three bouts from a show recorded at Blackburn. The first match saw a quick reappearance in front of the cameras for Johnny England when this time he took on 'Farmer's Boy' Pete Ross. Ross got the first fall in round three with a folding press as England once again played to the audience rather than concentrate on his match. England was the winner though when Ross was counted out in round four following a piledriver.

The second contest was completely different with a textbook wrestling classic between Johnny Saint and Steve Grey. Surprisingly it was Grey who got the winning fall in round seven when he pinned Saint with a reverse folding press.

The final match that week descended into the farce category with Big Daddy in a rare solo match taking on the masked Mr X. He replaced the originally booked Anaconda. It wasn't the Mr X renamed as The Bulk who had challenged Daddy earlier in the year but Chelmsford heavyweight Arthur Bice making a TV debut. Daddy gave Mr X nothing in the match just throwing him about and flooring him with bodychecks and belly butts. Daddy finished him off in round two with an awkward looking double elbow drop with Mr X failing to beat the count. The Bulk did appear though as after the match MC Brian Crabtree brought him to the ring as Max Crabtree tried to resurrect the belly butts challenge. The Bulk aka Fatty Thomas needed the help of the seconds and Mr X just to shove him into the ring where MC Crabtree introduced him as 'The Incredible Bulk'. Just for good measure Daddy then umasked Mr X. It was all so embarrassing as the show ended with Kent Walton wishing viewers a Merry Christmas.

The second half of the Blackburn show was seen on World of Sport following weekend. What was booked to be an intriguing main event between Giant Haystacks and The Sheik failed to materialise. Instead Haystacks took on Ray Steele which followed a rather dull opening bout. Pete Roberts wrestled a one fall each draw with Caswell Martin. Martin was another substitute on yet another show with many matches changed at short notice.

Haystacks towered over Steele as referee Emil Poilve issued his instructions to both wrestlers. Haystacks had already flattened Steele in a match shown on TV back in March and there was no chance of Steele doing any better this time. Steele did though manage to get the first fall in round two though when he pinned Haystacks with a cross-press after managing to floor the big man with a flying headbutt. Inevitably it didn't end well for Steele as he tried to floor Haystacks again in the early stages of the third round. Haystacks caught Steele's attempted flying tackle and nonchalently threw him to the canvas before landing a huge splash on him. This was the end for Giant Haystacks as a regular in British rings as Kent Walton announced that he was off to New York to wrestle in the New Year and as time went on through the 1980's he would wrestle more and more often overseas.

The final match of a rotten year for wrestling fans who enjoyed their sport on World of Sport was at least a dandy. After his victory over Jim Breaks at Aylesbury seen on World of Sport on the 8th Young David had demanded and received a match against Breaks with the British Welterweight Title at stake. David had matured over the last few months with regular matches and had become a firm favourite with the fans as well as becoming an excellent young talent. The early stages followed the usual Breaks playbook with plenty of arm weakeners on David as Breaks looked to apply his usual arm submission. Following the retirement of David's trainer Ted Betley he was accompanied by Alan Dennison who was in David's corner to give advice to the youngster. It was David who got the first fall with a folding press in round four with Breaks complaining as usual about its legality. Breaks got the equaliser in round six with a 'Breaks' special' forcing David to submit but he had been weakened by several punches which referee Emil Poilve failed to spot. The start of round seven saw Breaks rush over to attack David but as he threw David to the ropes the middle one came loose and David nearly fell out of the ring. The ring crew were attending to the ropes as the bout continued with Breaks dishing out some punishment which saw David bleeding heavily from his nose. Referee Poilve then gave Breaks a final public warning for a punch to David's nose which didn't help his nose bleed at all. Alan Dennison was seething in David's corner at Breaks' tactics and in round eight he jumped onto the ring apron to encourage David as Breaks once more tried a 'Breaks' special'. Breaks stopped the move and went over to Dennison to argue with him and incredibly Breaks turned his back on David. David grabbed Breaks from behind and rolled him up into a folding press for the count of three and there was a new British Welterweight Champion. Breaks was absolutely furious and there was mayhem both in and outside of the ring with the crowd celebrating. Emil Poilve put the belt around the seventeen year old champion whilst Breaks continued his protests about Dennison distracting him.

Jim Breaks immediately protested to the Board of Control that it was illegal for Alan Dennison to be on the ring apron and they agreed with Breaks. The result was then declared null and void. Breaks therefore was still the British Welterweight Champion and Young David had to be content with a rematch in the New Year.

Around the halls -

The final show of the year at Belle Vue was on the 8th and it was a complicated programme. Firstly there was a tag team knockout tournament and there was also an open weight knockout tournament too. In the open weight tournament the heats saw Young David beat Stud Baines who was disqualified in the fifth round. Ron Marino pinned Tommy Lorne for the winning fall in round six and Alan Dennison beat Pete LaPaque who walked out in the fourth round. Marino was unable to continue which left a teacher v pupil final with Alan Dennison and Young David facing each other. Dennison won the tournament with a two falls to one win in the fourth round over David.

The tag tournament semi finals saw The Masked Anaconda and Sid Cooper beat the strange pairing of Rex Strong and Mal Sanders with a winning submission in the ninth minute. Big Daddy and Jackie Turpin beat The Python and Mel Stuart by two falls to one in the fifth minute in the other. The Python had been taking part in Daddy tags in the last few months and was a rather ungainly, tall wrestler who departed the scene shortly after. Daddy and Turpin beat Anaconda and Cooper in the final so the crowd went home happy whilst the circus got ready to take over the venue until February.

The last show of the year at Croydon was on the 11th and saw Big Daddy captaining his 'All-stars' in a team match plus

Spiros Arion took on Pat Roach. The Roach v Arion match was an entertaining fight that didn't feature much wrestling. It was won by Roach when Arion was disqualified in the third round with Roach ahead courtesy of a fall in round two.

The team match's solo bouts saw Jackie Turpin knockout Sid Cooper in the sixth round. Catweazle beat the Gay One by two straight falls in the fourth round. Big Daddy defeated Banger Walsh in the first round with a double elbow drop rendering Walsh unconcious and Chris Adams beat Johnny England with a winning fall in round five. It was difficult to keep up with the tag finale at times but Daddy, Adams and Turpin won by two straight falls against all four of the other team who all seemed to be in the ring at the same time.

Spiros Arion finally met an opponent he wasn't able to bully let alone get in an abdominal stretch when he faced the might of Giant Haystacks at Cardiff on the 14th. Haystacks went ahead in the second round with a submission before Arion gave up in the third and left the ring. For once Haystacks heard the cheers of the fans as he was awarded the win via a countout decision.

The main supporting match at Sophia Gardens that night saw Marty Jones once again try his luck in the heavyweight division this time against Pat Roach. Roach was simply too big, too powerful and too strong for Jones who adopted an anything goes attitude to try and negate Roach's weight advantage. The end came for Jones in the sixth round when Roach pinned him via a crosspress following a bodyslam which appropriately for the festive season knocked the stuffing out of Jones.

The final Royal Albert Hall show of the seventies took place on 19th December and featured the long anticipated defence of his World Heavyweight Title by Spiros Arion. Arion would be defending the belt against Wayne Bridges who had already defeated him at the Albert Hall back in October. It was a drama filled evening but it was nearly called off at the last minute after Arion had decided that he wanted paying more than the agreed fee. Joint Promotions' chief Max Crabtree was not at the venue but was overseeing a TV taping at Blackburn. Crabtree had to take a call from Johnny Dale who was overseeing things at the Albert Hall for Dale Martin telling him what was happening down in London. Eventually all was sorted to everyone's satisfaction and the main event went ahead as booked. In the ring the title match was a tremendous tussle with the capacity crowd at fever pitch supporting their home town hero Bridges. Arion was mindful that he could lose the title by disqualification under British rules and toned down his usual rule breaking tactics. It turned into a hard hitting, action packed contest. Arion received a public warning in round four before he took the lead in the fifth round with his abdominal stretch making Bridges submit. Bridges came back strongly into the match in the seventh round and pinned Arion for the equaliser in that round. The roof came off the Albert Hall when Bridges turned the tables on Arion and forced him to submit from his own speciality, the abdominal stretch hold in the ninth round. Arion sportingly acknowledged the new champion after the contest and shook his hand as well as congratulating him over MC John Harris' microphone.

Spiros Arion was scheduled to remain in Britain and had a mandatory title rematch to take but he left the country immediately afterwards without fulfilling his booked obligations. As for Wayne Bridges he was now on top of the pile and immediately the target for any heavyweight who had aspirations on the world title.

The main event rather overshadowed the rest of the programme and it felt rushed through at times. Chris Adams pinned Tally Ho Kaye in the sixth round to win a lively opening contest. Brian Maxine beat Mark Rocco who was disqualified in the second round of a match where neither wrestler adhered to the rule book. Marty Jones was booked to wrestle Steve Veidor in what would have been an interesting bout but Veidor was unavailable on the evening and replaced by Johnny Wilson. Jones beat Wilson by two falls to one in the sixth round of an uneventful contest. There was tag action with The Royals who took on The Rockers who now consisted of original member Pete LaPaque and Tommy Lorne who had replaced Pete's brother Jon. The Royals won easily by two straight falls and finally Tony Costas defeated Albert Hall debutant Steve Peacock with a winning fall in the fourth round.

Post Christmas I saw my final show of the year on the 28th at Maidenhead which marked the welcome return to Joint

346

Promotions of Jon Cortez. Cortez who had been wrestling on the independent circuit for the best part of the previous three years jumped straight into title contention when he defeated Mal Sanders who was unable to continue in the seventh round.

Jon Cortez was also in action at Maidstone the next night which also marked the professional debut of Keith Haward, the former amateur champion. Haward had a tremendous pedigree in the unpaid ranks and had represented England at the 1978 Commonwealth Games where he won a bronze medal as well as competing at the 1976 Olympics. For some reason Haward was billed on the poster advertising the show as Pete Haywood where he was booked to wrestle Sid Cooper. Of course Cooper was the perfect opponent for a debut and Haward made a winning start with the deciding fall coming in round five. Cortez was part of a knockout tournament alongside Steve Peacock, Rajendra Singh and Kendo Nagasaki Mk.II. Cortez and Peacock were the finalists in a ladder match which was won by Cortez in seven minutes.

New World Heavyweight Champion Wayne Bridges took on the Masked Buffalo who was the masked Mr X who had recently wrestled Big Daddy on World of Sport. Bridges had an easy win with the Buffalo counted out in the third round. Completing an excellent night's wrestling was Young David beating fellow northerner John Naylor. The match originally ended in a one fall each draw at the end of the six scheduled rounds but David got a winning fall in a sudden death extra round.

At Yate down in the West Country on the same evening Big Bruno Elrington wrestled his final match of a distinguished career. Elrington was a formidable opponent in the ring and had won the famed Royal Albert Trophy as well as holding the Southern Area Heavyweight Title at times. Not only was Bruno a great wrestler he had also opened a gym in Portsmouth where he trained many wrestlers who went onto have successful careers in the ring.

Bruno was the fourth of four top stars who retired in the year joining Steve Logan and Johnny Czeslaw whose careers were ended by injury and illness respectively. Also forced to retire was Johnny Yearsley who had recently been diagnosed with cancer. Sadly Yearsley was to die in the February of 1980 after suffering a heart attack.

Thus the curtain came down on an eventful year's wrestling with the highs of the Wembley Arena show and the lows of the ITV blackout for over two months. British wrestling headed into the new decade in rude health with packed halls and strong viewing figures each Saturday afternoon for the wrestling shown on World of Sport.

The 1980's is covered in my first book The Saturday Afternoon War.

Acknowledgements

I'd like to thank Dave Icke for his help with the details of the World of Sport coverage and the use of his detailed records. Steve's Mitchell and Ogilvie for some of the posters used for illustrations in the book and also Bob Bartholomew and Steve Barker for their encouragement and inspiration in getting the project started.

Tony Earnshaw

tonyearnshaw64@gmail.com

POSTER PARADE

The following chapter contains a selection of posters from various shows held between 1975 and 1979.

Some of the posters contain language and references that are out-dated and may cause offence.

353

354

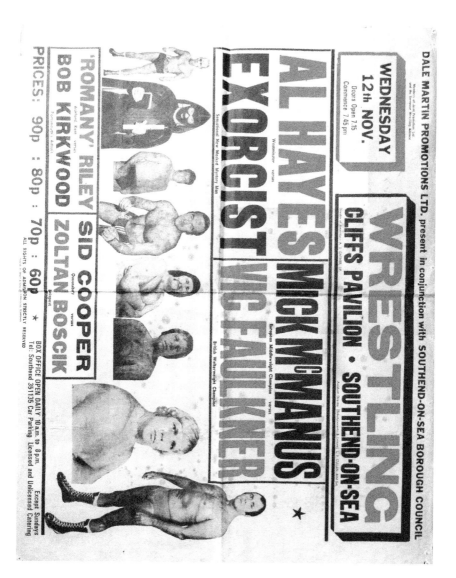

DALE MARTIN PROMOTIONS LTD. present in conjunction with SOUTHEND-ON-SEA BOROUGH COUNCIL.

WRESTLING
CLIFFS PAVILION · SOUTHEND-ON-SEA

WEDNESDAY
12th NOV.
Doors Open 7.15
Commence 7.45 pm

AL HAYES
Westminster
versus
EXORCIST
Sensational New Masked Mystery Men

MICK McMANUS
European Middleweight Champion
versus
McFAULKNER
British Welterweight Champion

'ROMANY' RILEY
Ashford, Kent
versus
SID COOPER
Queensbury

BOB KIRKWOOD
Farmingham
versus
ZOLTAN BOSCIK
Budapest

PRICES: 90p : 80p : 70p : 60p

BOX OFFICE OPEN DAILY 10 a.m. to 8 p.m.
Tel: Southend 351135 Car Parking Licensed and Unlicensed Catering

ALL RIGHTS OF ADMISSION STRICTLY RESERVED

Except Sundays

355

THURSDAY
11th SEPT.
at 7.30 p.m.

WRESTLING

KING GEORGE'S HALL
BLACKBURN

SUPER HEAVYWEIGHT KNOCK-OUT CLASH

Champion MIKE MARINO
WORLD TITLE AND BELT HOLDER — ONE OF WRESTLING'S ALL TIME GREATS

KENDO NAGASAKI
AND HIS PERSONAL MANAGER—GORGEOUS GEORGE — THE MERCHANTS OF VIOLENCE

BIG DADDIE
25 STONE BLOND GIANT — RECORDED 54 INCH CHEST — A MIGUN!

MAN MOUNTAIN MORAN
6 FT. 7 INS. 25 STONE. FORMER PRO FIST FIGHTER. A TOUGH GUY

BRILLIANT VIC FAULKNER
YOUNGEST OF THE FABULOUS ROYAL BROTHERS   Versus

TIGER WOODS
THE LANCASHIRE TORNADO

COUNT BARTELLI
A LEGEND OF VICTORIES TO HIS CREDIT   Versus

MARK ROCCO
A FIGHTER FROM THE FIRST BELL

★ TELEVISION SPECTACULAR (KENT WALTON AT RINGSIDE) ★

SPECIAL GUEST REFEREE
JACK PYE
(Yes, the one and only)

STRONGMAN ALAN
DENNISON
THE STRENGTH OF 2 MEN, AT TIMES POSSESSED OF THE DEVIL   versus

GOLDEN AGE
JOHN NAYLOR — 1975 T.V. TROPHY WINNER

PRICES: 75p : 65p : 50p
Advance Bookings at the Public Hall (Tel. 58424) or at the door on night of Promotion
PRINTED BY BAILEY & SONS LTD, SOMERCOTES, DERBYSHIRE

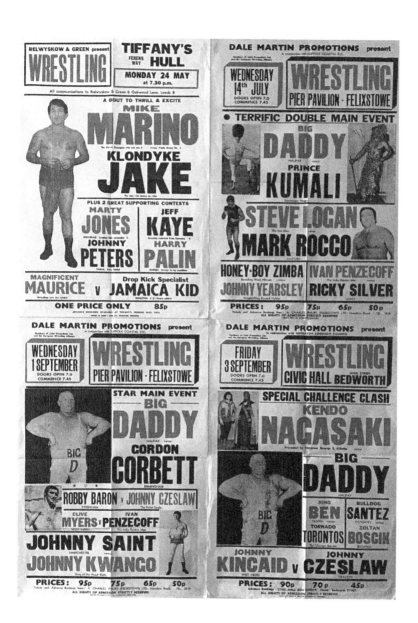

RELWYSKOW & GREEN present

WRESTLING

TIFFANY'S
FERENS WAY **HULL**

MONDAY 24 MAY
at 7.30 p.m.

All communications to Relwyskow & Green 6 Oakwood Lane, Leeds 8

A BOUT TO THRILL & EXCITE
MIKE
MARINO

KLONDYKE
JAKE

PLUS 2 GREAT SUPPORTING CONTESTS

MARTY
JONES
JOHNNY
PETERS

JEFF
KAYE
HARRY
PALIN

MAGNIFICENT
MAURICE v
Drop Kick Specialist
JAMAICA KID

ONE PRICE ONLY — 85p

DALE MARTIN PROMOTIONS present

WEDNESDAY 14th JULY
DOORS OPEN 7.0
COMMENCE 7.45

WRESTLING
PIER PAVILION · FELIXSTOWE

● TERRIFIC DOUBLE MAIN EVENT
BIG
DADDY
PRINCE
KUMALI

STEVE LOGAN
MARK ROCCO

HONEY·BOY ZIMBA | IVAN PENZECOFF
JOHNNY YEARSLEY | RICKY SILVER

PRICES: 95p   75p   65p   50p

DALE MARTIN PROMOTIONS present

WEDNESDAY 1 SEPTEMBER
DOORS OPEN 7.0
COMMENCE 7.45

WRESTLING
PIER PAVILION · FELIXSTOWE

STAR MAIN EVENT
BIG
DADDY
GORDON
CORBETT

ROBBY BARON v **JOHNNY CZESLAW**

CLIVE
MYERS v **PENZECOFF**
IVAN

JOHNNY SAINT
JOHNNY KWANGO

PRICES: 95p   75p   65p   50p

DALE MARTIN PROMOTIONS present

FRIDAY 3 SEPTEMBER
DOORS OPEN 7.0
COMMENCE 7.45

WRESTLING
CIVIC HALL BEDWORTH

SPECIAL CHALLENGE CLASH
KENDO
NAGASAKI

BIG
DADDY

KING
BEN
TORNADO
TORONTOS

BULLDOG
SANTEZ
ZOLTAN
BOSCIK

JOHNNY
KINCAID v
JOHNNY
CZESLAW

PRICES: 90p   70p   45p

KING'S HALL
BELLE VUE

BEST/WRYTON PROMOTIONS LTD. your T.V. Promoters present

WRESTLING

SATURDAY 3rd JULY commence 7.30 pm

★ **THE BEST OF TODAYS TOP T.V. STARS** (Exclusive) ★

THE GIANT IS ON THE WARPATH – LOOK OUT KENDO !!

6' 11", 31st. GIANT

HAYSTACKS
WILD ANGUS

KENDO

NAGASAKI
v
REX STRONG

SATURDAY NIGHT OUT – THRILLS, SPILLS

JIM BREAKS v **MICK McMICHAEL**

ROLLERBALL ROCCO v **MARTY JONES**

THE MATCH THAT THRILLED MILLIONS OF TELEVISION VIEWERS

DYNAMITE KID v **KENNY HOGAN**

British Heavyweight Championship   60 mins.

Champion **GWYN DAVIES**

Challenger **ROY ST. CLAIR**

Special Ringside **£1·50** : Reserved **£1 & 75p** : **50p** Unreserved

ALL RIGHTS OF ADMISSION STRICTLY RESERVED

KING'S HALL
BELLE VUE

BEST/WRYTON PROMOTIONS LTD. your T.V. Promoters present

WRESTLING

SATURDAY 14th AUGUST commence 7.30 pm

THE THRILL AND SPECTACLE OF BIG TIME WRESTLING

THIS IS MATCHMAKING AT ITS BEST

World Champion
MIKE MARINO

British Champion
GWYN DAVIES

NO HOLDS BARRED- NO ESCAPE SAYS THE BIG FELLOW

KENDO
NAGASAKI
v
6' 11", 31 STONE GIANT
HAYSTACKS

SPECIAL RETURN – THE YOUNG BULLS OF THE ARENA CLASH

Rollerball ROCCO v **MARTY JONES**

FOR THOSE WHO LIKE SCIENTIFIC WRESTLING

BERT ROYAL
GOLDEN ACE
JOHN NAYLOR

NOT A MATCH FOR THE SQUEAMISH

HANS STREIGER
COUNT BARTELLI

THE DYNAMITE KID
MIKE (FLASH) JORDAN

Special Ringside **£1·50** : Reserved **£1 & 75p** : **50p** Unreserved

ALL RIGHTS OF ADMISSION STRICTLY RESERVED

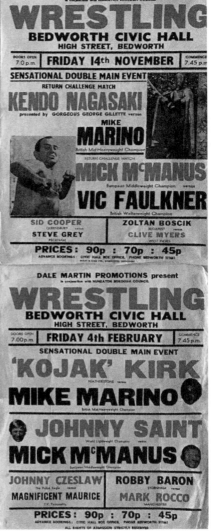

FAIRFIELD • CROYDON

General Manager: Mr. H. V. TEARLE
DALE MARTIN PROMOTIONS LTD. present

Wrestling Spectacular

TUESDAY 22nd MARCH Commencing 8.0 p.m.

ALL ACTION TAG TEAM CLASH

MICK McMANUS & STEVE LOGAN
European Middleweight Champion — Iron man of the South

VERSUS

JOHNNY KWANGO & CLIVE MYERS
King of the head butts — West Indies

WINNERS OF THE TAG CONTEST HELD HERE ON 8th MARCH

'IRON DUKE' IAN MUIR	TONY ST. CLAIR
Lanarkshire, Scotland v.	Redruth, Cornwall v.
PRINCE KUMALI	DAVID 'THE LION' BOND
Statuesque Negro Giant	Deptford
COLIN JOYNSON	CLAYTON THOMSON
Cheetham, Manchester v.	Glasgow v.
ROBBY BARON	MEL STUART
Sydenham	Gravesend

Prices: £1.25 £1.00 75p 50p
(including V.A.T.)
Tickets and advance Bookings from THE FAIRFIELD HALLS BOOKING OFFICE. Telephone 01-688 9291
All rights of admission strictly reserved

FAIRFIELD • CROYDON

General Manager: Mr. H. V. TEARLE
DALE MARTIN PROMOTIONS LTD. present

Wrestling Spectacular

TUESDAY 31st MAY Commencing 8.0 p.m.

• SUPER TAG MATCH •

LEE BRONSON partnered by **TONY ST. CLAIR**
Bolton — Redruth, Cornwall

MARK ROCCO Salford's speedy young star partnered by **JOHN HENRY YEARSLEY**
Weightlifting record holder

BIG DADDY	MICK SHANNON
Blond Giant from Halifax v.	Northfleet v.
REX STRONG	CARL HEINZ
Former Blackpool Lifeguard	Kent
ED WENSOR	Sid COOPER
Northampton v.	Queensbury, Yorks. v.
John ELIJAH	STEVE GREY
Walthamstow	Peckham

Prices: £1.25 £1.00 75p 50p
(including V.A.T.)
Tickets and advance Bookings from THE FAIRFIELD HALLS BOOKING OFFICE. Telephone 01-688 9291
All rights of admission strictly reserved

DALE MARTIN PROMOTIONS LTD. PRESENT IN CONJUNCTION WITH IPSWICH BOROUGH COUNCIL

WRESTLING

CORN EXCHANGE Grand Hall IPSWICH

Doors Open 7 p.m. **WEDNESDAY 1st JUNE** Commence 7.45 p.m.

ED. WENSOR Northamptonshire v.
TONY ST. CLAIR Redruth, Cornwall

GARY WENSOR Northampton v.
JOHN HURLEY Catford

Wrestling at its very Best

'ROMANY' RILEY Ashford, Kent v.
MEL STUART Gravesend

BOBBY BARNES Lewisham's blond arrogant star v.
Count BARTELLI Crewe, One of the all time greats

Prices: 90p : 70p : 60p : 50p
Advance Bookings from Corn Exchange Box Office. Telephone Ipswich 55265
ALL RIGHTS OF ADMISSION STRICTLY RESERVED

DALE MARTIN PROMOTIONS LTD. in conjunction with THREE RIVERS DISTRICT COUNCIL present

WRESTLING

WATERSMEET High St., Rickmansworth

Doors Open 7 p.m. **Thursday, 1st September** Commence 7.45 p.m.

SENSATIONAL TAG TEAM CONTEST

ZOLTAN BOSCIK Budapest, Hungary partnered by **CRY BABY COOPER** Queensbury, Yorks

STEVE GREY Peckham partnered by **MICK SHANNON** Northfleet

BOBBY BARNES	Lewisham v.
ROBBY BARON	Sydenham
WAYNE BRIDGES	Gillingham v.
BOB KIRKWOOD	Portsmouth
BILL TORONTOS	Chicago Express v.
MEL STUART	Gravesend

Prices: £1.20 : £1.00 : 80p : 60p
(including V.A.T.)
ADVANCE BOOKINGS PHONE RICKMANSWORTH 77541

361

362

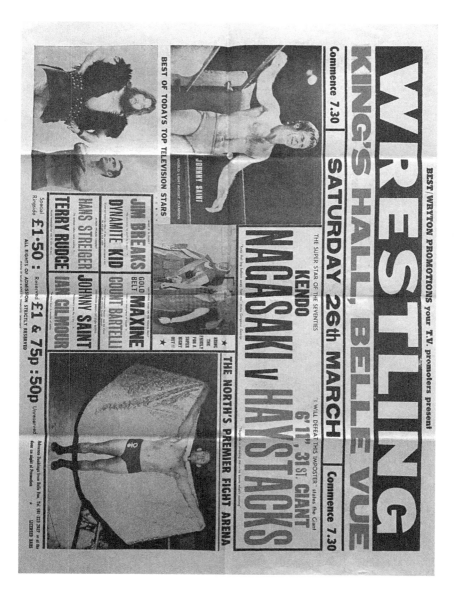

BEST/WRYTON PROMOTIONS your T.V. promoters present

WRESTLING
KING'S HALL, BELLE VUE

Commence 7.30 | SATURDAY 26th MARCH | Commence 7.30

BEST OF TODAYS TOP TELEVISION STARS

JOHNNY SAINT

WORLD LIGHT WEIGHT CHAMPION

THE SUPER STAR OF THE SEVENTIES

KENDO

NAGASAKI v HAYSTACKS

'I WILL DEFEAT THIS IMPOSTER' states the Giant

6'11", 31st. GIANT

THE NORTH'S PREMIER FIGHT ARENA

JIM BREAKS	GOLD BELT MAXINE
DYNAMITE KID	COUNT BARTELLI
HANS STREIGER	JOHNNY SAINT
TERRY RUDGE	IAN GILMOUR

Special
Ringside £1·50 : Reserved £1 & 75p : 50p Unreserved

ALL RIGHTS OF ADMISSION STRICTLY RESERVED

363

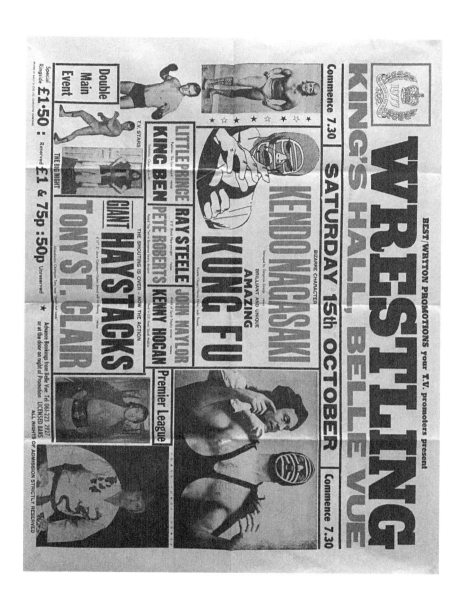

BEST/WRYTON PROMOTIONS your T.V. promoters present!

WRESTLING
KING'S HALL, BELLE VUE

Commence 7.30 — **SATURDAY 15th OCTOBER** — Commence 7.30

BIZARRE CHARACTER

KENDO NAGASAKI

BRILLIANT AND UNIQUE

AMAZING KUNG FU

Managed by Gorgeous George

Kamate Chops / Throws Man / Judo Throws

LITTLE PRINCE · **RAY STEELE** · **JOHN NAYLOR**

KING BEN · **PETE ROBERTS** · **KENNY HOGAN**

T.V. STARS

THE SHOUTING IS OVER — NOW THE ACTION

Premier League

GIANT HAYSTACKS

TONY ST. CLAIR

THE BIG NIGHT

Double Main Event

Special Ringside **£1·50** : Reserved **£1 & 75p** : **50p** Unreserved

Advance Bookings from Belle Vue. Tel. 061-223 2927
or at the door on night of Promotion LICENSED BARS
ALL RIGHTS OF ADMISSION STRICTLY RESERVED

365

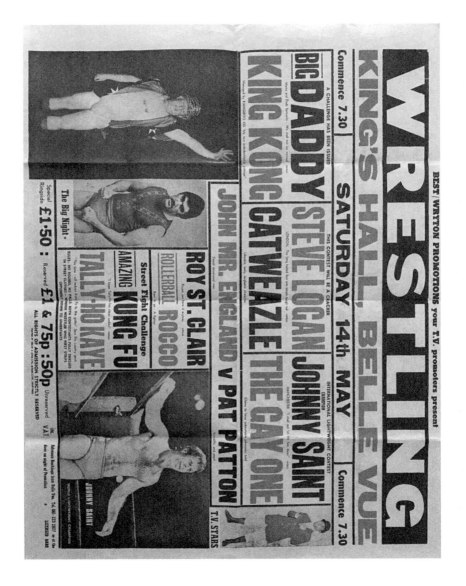

BEST/WRYTON PROMOTIONS your T.V. promoters present!

WRESTLING
KING'S HALL, BELLE VUE

SATURDAY 14th MAY

Commence 7.30   Commence 7.30

A CHALLENGE HAS BEEN ISSUED

BIG DADDY v STEVE LOGAN
THIS CONTEST WILL BE A CRACKER
LONDON.

KING KONG CATWEAZLE v JOHNNY SAINT
INTERNATIONAL LIGHTWEIGHT CONTEST
CHAMPION
MANCHESTER

THE GAY ONE

JOHN MR. ENGLAND v PAT PATTON

ROY ST. CLAIR v ROLLERBALL ROCCO
Street Fight Challenge

AMAZING KUNG FU v TALLY HO KAYE

T.V. STARS

JOHNNY SAINT
WORLD LIGHTWEIGHT CHAMPION

The Big Night

Special £1·50 Ringside

Reserved £1 & 75p : 50p Unreserved

ALL RIGHTS OF ADMISSION STRICTLY RESERVED

V.A.T.

BEST/WRYTON PROMOTIONS your T.V. promoters present

WRESTLING

VICTORIA HALL, HANLEY

SATURDAY 19th NOVEMBER

Commence 7.45 | Commence 7.45

TAG TEAM — BEST NEWS OF THE YEAR

DYNAMITE KID
v
THE OUTLAW ROACH

BOBBY RYAN
BARON
v
BARON DONAVAN ROBERTS

BIG PAT

JUDO PETE

SPECTACULAR ★ SATURDAY NIGHT OUT ★ THE IN CROWD

ROY ST. CLAIR
RAY THUNDER

BULLDOG JOYNSON
BRONCO BRUCE
HART

ACTION

ADMISSION: 80p : 75p : 65p : 60p

Inclusive of V.A.T. ★ It costs no more to book your seat in advance

★ T.V. STARS ★

WRESTLING at its Best

BEST/WRYTON PROMOTIONS your T.V. promoters present

WRESTLING
KING'S HALL, BELLE VUE

CHRISTMAS SPECTACULAR | SATURDAY 10th DECEMBER

Commence 7.30 | Commence 7.30

KING OF THE ACTION SPORTS

★ YOUR WRESTLING NIGHT OUT ★

12 Super-Size Heavyweights ★ Trophy Night ★ BIG NIGHT OF THE YEAR

★ ELEVEN CONTESTS TO KING OF THE RING ★

MAN AND LAD'S FAVOURITE

KENDO NAGASAKI

SENSATIONAL BIZARRE CHARACTER

STEVE LOGAN

Lou's famed London feeler

BARON DONOVAN

BLACKPOOL LIFEGUARD

REX STRONG

HILLBILLY HELL-ON

PLAYER OF HEART

MOUNTAIN

TONY ST. CLAIR

1977 British Heavyweight Champion

GWYN DAVIES

BIG DADDY

BACK FROM GERMANY

GIANT HAYSTACKS

COUNT BARTELLI

LUCKY GORDON MORAN

★ BELLE VUE — WISHES ALL A SWINGING CHRISTMAS ★

T.V. STARS

DALE MARTIN PROMOTIONS present
IN CONJUNCTION WITH WORTHING CORPORATION

WRESTLING
THE PAVILION, WORTHING

DOORS OPEN 7.0 p.m.	**TUESDAY 27th DECEMBER**	COMMENCE 7.45 p.m.

 **Christmas Spectacular**

SUPER TAG MATCH BY PUBLIC DEMAND

£100 aside   £100 aside

MIKE MARINO
British Mid-Heavyweight Champion **AND**

WAYNE BRIDGES
Champion of Kent

versus

THE CARIBBEAN SUNSHINE BOYS
Johnny Kincaid & Butcher Bond

STEVE **KELLY** BEXLEY HEATH versus	**CRY-BABY** COOPER QUEENSBURY versus	CLIVE **MYERS** Welterweight Champion of the West Indies versus
ZOLTAN **BOSCIK** BUDAPEST	MAL **SANDERS** MORDEN	STEVE **GREY** PECKHAM

PRICES : 90p   70p   60p   50p

All seats numbered and reserved obtainable from the Pavilion   Telephone : 202221
ALL RIGHTS OF ADMISSION STRICTLY RESERVED

Printed by BAILEY & SONS LTD., SOMERCOTES, DERBYSHIRE

369

BEST/WRYTON PROMOTIONS LTD your T.V. Promoters present

WRESTLING
CIVIC HALL · WOLVERHAMPTON

COMMENCE 7.45 p.m. | **TUESDAY 20th DECEMBER** | COMMENCE 7.45 p.m.

1977 CHRISTMAS SPECTACULAR
WORLD OF SPORT LIVE T.V. COVERAGE
Favourite Commentator KENT WALTON at the ringside

Sensational Ceremony of the UNMASKING of

KENDO NAGASAKI

Performed by Manager GORGEOUS GEORGE · Official Witness
MICK McMANUS
MILLIONS OF VIEWERS - WHO IS THE FACE BEHIND THE MASK ?

★ ☆ 6 TREMENDOUS CONTESTS - 2 REFEREES - TERRIFIC ☆ ★

AMAZING KUNG FU

IRON MAN
STEVE LOGAN

BIG   Champion TONY
DADDY & ST. CLAIR
"We shall not be moved"
versus
GIANT   BARON
HAYSTACKS & DONOVAN

BERT
ROYAL v ROCCO

ROLLER BALL

CATWEAZLE
TALLY-HO KAYE

DYNAMITE KID v KID CHOCOLATE | Golden Ace JOHN NAYLOR v JACKIE TURPIN

PRICES : £1.00 90p 85p 75p INCLUDING VAT

BOOK YOUR SEAT NOW

WRESTLING

ELMBRIDGE LEISURE CENTRE
SUNBURY LANE : WALTON-ON-THAMES

| DOORS OPEN 7.00 p.m. | **FRIDAY, 27th JANUARY** | COMMENCE 7.45 p.m. |

SUPER TAG MATCH!

THE ROYAL BROTHERS
BERT ROYAL partnered by
VIC FAULKNER
Bolton

v

STEVE LOGAN
Brixton's Iron Man
— partnered by —
CRY BABY COOPER
Queensbury, Yorks.

LEON FORTUNA v MAL SANDERS
The popular Friendly Islander   Morden

JOHNNY SAINT
Lightweight Champion of the World   V.

JIM MARTELL
Egham, Surrey

DAVID (THE LION) BOND
Deptford   V.
PHIL (SPRINGBOK) ROWE
Recently returned from South Africa

Prices: £1.25   :   £1.00   :   75p

Advance Bookings : Elmbridge Leisure Centre, Walton-on-Thames   Telephone 45679
Postal Bookings accepted with S.A.E.
ALL RIGHTS OF ADMISSION STRICTLY RESERVED

THE HEXAGON
READING
DALE MARTIN PROMOTIONS LTD. proudly present

WRESTLING

| Doors Open 7.00 p.m. | **FRIDAY, 10th March** | Commence 7.30 p.m. |

SUPER TAG CLASH!

The Fabulous ROYAL BROS.
BERT ROYAL &
VIC FAULKNER
Bolton

v

RAY THUNDER
As hard as the Canadian Rockies
—— partnered by ——
MARK ROCCO
British Heavy/Middleweight Champion

T.V. SPECTACULAR

JOHNNY KWANGO
King of the head butts   V.
STEVE LOGAN
Brixton's forearm smash tough guy

JOHNNY SAINT
World Lightweight Champion   V.
MICK McMICHAEL
Tough man star from Doncaster

BRUISER MUIR
Lanarkshire, Scotland   V.
JOHN WILSON
Fareham's handsome heavyweight

DYNAMITE KID
British Welterweight Champion   V.
CRY BABY COOPER
Queensbury, Yorkshire

BUTCHER BOND
Deptford   V.
WAYNE BRIDGES
Gillingham, Champion of Kent

Prices: £1.50   £1.25   £1.00   75p

Booking Hall Open 10 a.m. to 6 p.m., The Hexagon, P.O. Box 686, Civic Centre, Reading. Tel. Reading 56271.
ALL RIGHTS OF ADMISSION STRICTLY RESERVED

WRESTLING

WALTHAMSTOW ASSEMBLY HALL

| DOORS OPEN 7.00 p.m. | **WEDNESDAY, 17th MAY** | COMMENCE 7.45 p.m. |

SUPER MAIN EVENT TAG TEAM CONTEST

MICK McMANUS
The man you love to hate, partnered by
STEVE LOGAN
Iron man of the South

v

The Fabulous ROYALS
BERT ROYAL
and
VIC FAULKNER

CHRIS BAILEY versus SUPERSTAR SANDERS
London's slick of Dynamite   Golden Star of 1978

CLEVER ! THRILLING !!

THE VIKING
Giant of the North   V.
CASWELL MARTIN
Champion of the Wise Indies

THE MATCH YOU MUST NOT MISS

JOHNNY SAINT
World Lightweight Champion
— versus —
MARK ROLLERBALL ROCCO
Public enemy No. 1

Prices: £1.00   :   80p   :   60p

Advance Bookings : Recreation & Amenities Dept., Old Manors Buildings, High St., Walthamstow E17. Tel. 521 7111
ALL RIGHTS OF ADMISSION STRICTLY RESERVED

WRESTLING

PICKETTS LOCK CENTRE
PICKETTS LOCK LANE, EDMONTON

| Doors Open 7.0 p.m. | **FRIDAY, 26th MAY, 1978** | Commence 7.45 p.m. |

SUPER MAIN EVENT TAG TEAM CONTEST

The Fabulous ROYALS
BERT ROYAL
and
VIC FAULKNER

v

BAD BOY BOBBY BARNES
Bland, arrogant and mean, partnered by
THE GAY ONE
Is he or isn't he ?

CHRIS BAILEY v JOHNNY KWANGO
London's slick of Dynamite   King of the head butts

ACTION PACKED THRILLER

ALAN DENNISON
At times possessed of the devil   V.
CATWEAZLE
Hillarious, Loughtable, Lanky Lad

THE BATTLE YOU MUST ALL SEE

**WINNER OF 21st APRIL
4 MAN KNOCKOUT TOURNAMENT**
— versus —
TONY ST. CLAIR
British Heavyweight Champion

Prices: £1.25   :   £1.00   :   80p   :   60p   :   40p

ALL RIGHTS OF ADMISSION STRICTLY RESERVED

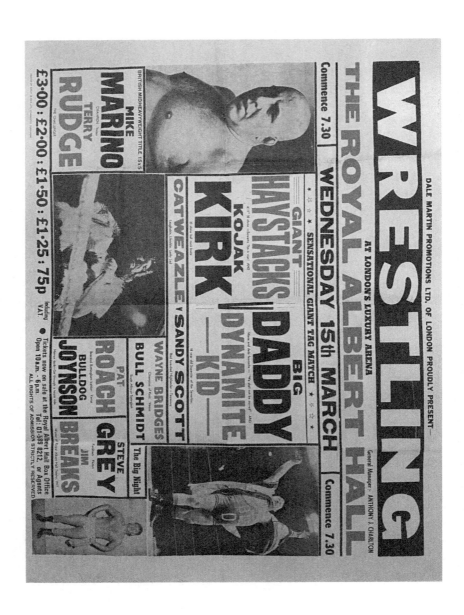

375

376

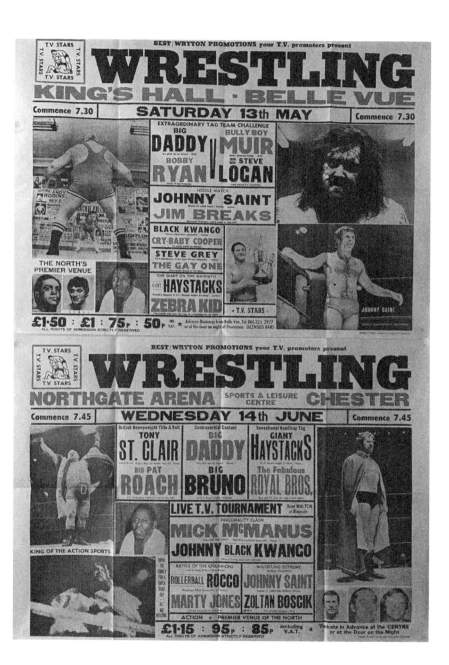

377

378

DALE MARTIN PROMOTIONS LTD. OF LONDON PROUDLY PRESENT—

WRESTLING

THE ROYAL ALBERT HALL

AT LONDON'S LUXURY ARENA

General Manager:- ANTHONY J. CHARLTON

WEDNESDAY 31st MAY

Commence 7.30

Commence 7.30

• WORLD LIGHTWEIGHT TITLE AND BELT •

JOHNNY SAINT

STEVE GREY

• RUBBER MATCH •
BERT
ROYAL
ROLLERBALL
ROCCO

VIC
FAULKNER
ALL ACTION BATTLE
RAY
THUNDER

• SUPER TRIPLE TAG MATCH – SIX IN THE RING •
BIG
DADDY McMANUS
MICK

AMAZING
KUNG FU
LEON
GIANT
HAYSTACKS
STEVE

FORTUNA
LOGAN

JIM BREAKS
TONY ST. CLAIR
"PAT ROACH"
ALAN DENNISON

★ GRAND SPECTACULAR '78 ★

£5.00 RINGSIDE : £3.00 : £2.50 : £2.00 : £1.25 •

Tickets now on sale at the Royal Albert Hall Box Office
Open 10 a.m. – 6 p.m.
Tel: 01-589 8212, or Agents

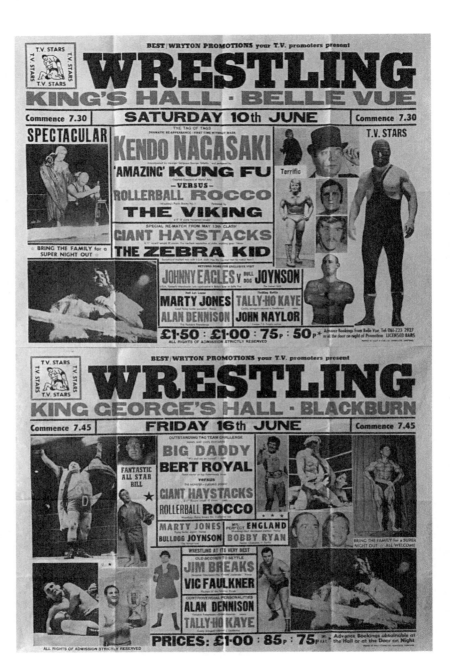

BEST/WRYTON PROMOTIONS your T.V. promoters present!

WRESTLING
KING'S HALL · BELLE VUE

Commence 7.30

SATURDAY 22nd JULY

Commence 7.30

T.V. STARS
T.V. STARS
T.V. STARS

BELLE VUE SPECTACULAR

EXCLUSIVE SCOOP - MATCH OF THE YEAR

BILL ROBINSON

BIG PAT ROACH

EXTRA-ORDINARY TAG TEAM CHALLENGE
EUROPE'S BIGGEST TWO versus ONE

GIANT HAYSTACKS
THE FABULOUS

ROYAL BROTHERS

BRING THE FAMILY
EVERYBODY WELCOME

WHIZZ KIDS

KID CHOCOLATE v FLASH JORDAN

A SPECIAL APPEARANCE OF

THIS IS IT! · RUBBER MATCH

BIG BRUNO JOHNNY SAINT

JOHN WILSON JIM BREAKS

DALE MARTIN PROMOTIONS present
in conjunction with NUNEATON BOROUGH COUNCIL

WRESTLING
BEDWORTH CIVIC HALL
HIGH STREET, BEDWORTH

Doors Open 7.0 p.m.	**WEDNESDAY 12th JULY**	Commence 7.30 p.m.

1978 SUMMER SPECTACULAR LIVE TELEVISED TOURNAMENT

First Appearance here Unmasked of the Sensational

KENDO NAGASAKI
Accompanied by Manager GORGEOUS GEORGE GILLETTE   Versus

JUDO PETE ROBERTS
just returned from a successful world tour

A Contest for the Bedworth Civic Hall Challenge Trophy

CRY-BABY JIM BREAKS
European Champion — Nasty submission   Versus

GOLDEN ACE JOHN NAYLOR
Former T.V. Trophy winner

Specially Appointed Referee for this Match   the One & Only
MICK McMANUS

Thrill a Minute Contest	Brains versus Brawn
Tally-Ho KAYE	**Mr. Perfect ENGLAND**
Cocky, arrogant — Almost a Gentleman Versus	Wrestling's best developed matman Mr. Midlands V.
BLACK BELT CHRIS ADAMS	**BOBBY RYAN**
4th Dan Former National Judo Champion	The Pride of the Potteries
Battle of the Giants	**International Clash**
Wayne BRIDGES	**TERRY RUDGE**
International star — Great warrior Versus	Mine Host — World travelled matman Versus
GWYN DAVIES	**TIGER SINGH**
6' 4" Handsome Welsh Champion	The Pride of India

BRING THE FAMILY EVERYBODY WELCOME

Favourite Commentator KENT WALTON at the Ringside

Prices for this Tournament   £1.10   90p   70p
ADVANCE BOOKINGS: CIVIC HALL BOX OFFICE. PHONE BEDWORTH 311661
PRINTED BY BAILEY & SONS LTD, SOMERCOTES, DERBYSHIRE

382

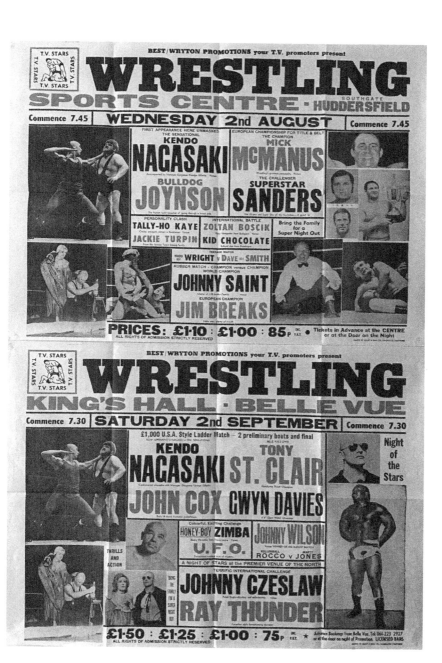

383

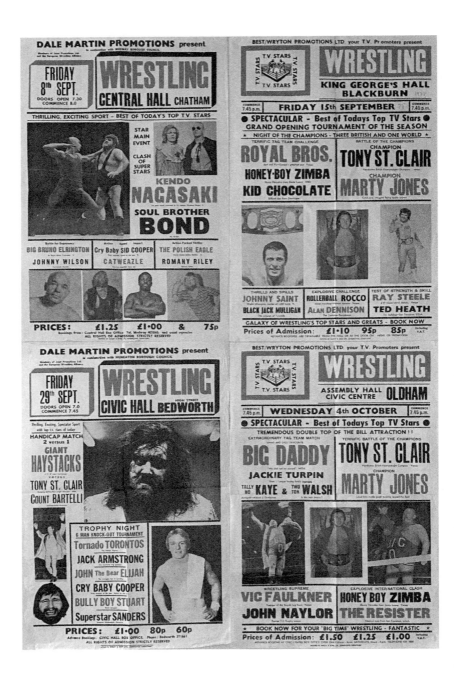

384

385

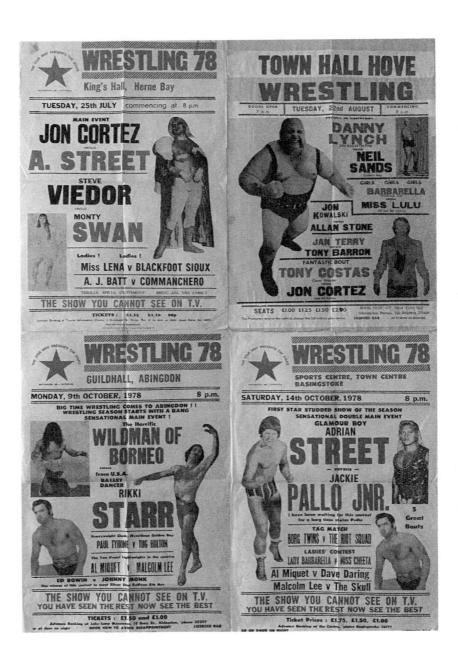

THE JOINT MITCHELL ORGANISATION presents
BRITAIN'S FIRST EVER

FESTIVAL OF WRESTLING

DIGBETH CIVIC HALL · BIRMINGHAM
SATURDAY 25th NOVEMBER

STARTS
2.30

MEET BIG DADDY

HAVE A CHAT - HAVE YOUR PHOTO TAKEN WITH BIG D - GET AUTOGRAPHS

HAYSTACKS HOLOCAUST

SWORN STATEMENT SENT BY GIANT HAYSTACKS — A DECLARATION OF WAR!

WRESTLING SPECTACULAR

STARTS 6.45 p.m. includes Triple Tag challenge and 'T.V. Stars Wrestling Magazine Trophy

BRIAN CRABTREE IS YOUR COMPERE

FANS FORUM
ARE REFEREES TOO SOFT?

ARM WRESTLING CHALLENGE
Battle of Skill and Strength

DISPLAYS   COMPETITIONS   PRIZES GALORE
BOOK NOW - A GREAT DAY OUT FOR ALL THE FAMILY

PRICES £1.25 [Adults] 75p [Children] 85p evening Only

Send P.O./Cheque to Joint Mitchell Organisation, 21 Wellington St. Edinburgh EH7 5EE Scotland
PRINTED BY BAILEY & SONS LTD. SOMERCOTES, DERBYS.

387

389

391

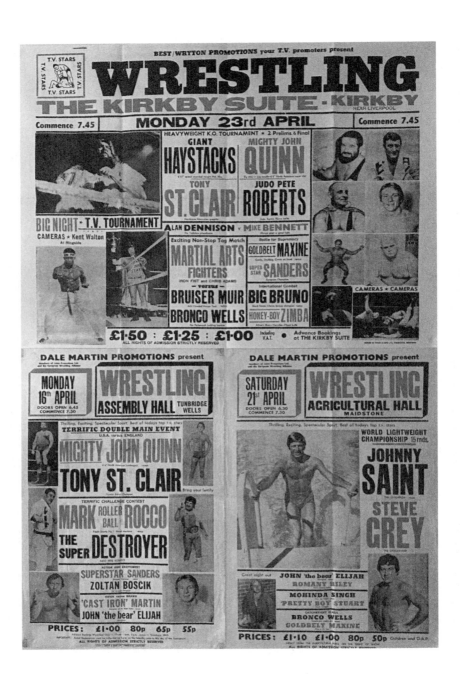

395

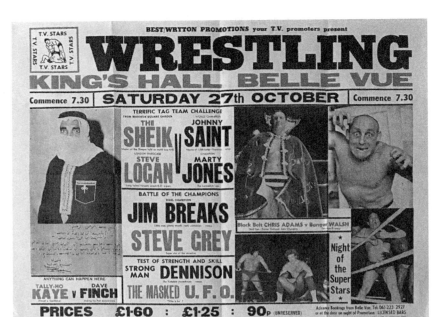

BEST/WRYTON PROMOTIONS your T.V. promoters present

WRESTLING
KING'S HALL BELLE VUE

Commence 7.30 | **SATURDAY 27th OCTOBER** | Commence 7.30

TERRIFIC TAG TEAM CHALLENGE
FROM MADISON SQUARE GARDEN

THE **SHEIK** v JOHNNY **SAINT**

STEVE **LOGAN** v MARTY **JONES**

BATTLE OF THE CHAMPIONS
DUAL CHAMPION

JIM BREAKS
STEVE GREY

TEST OF STRENGTH AND SKILL
STRONG MAN **DENNISON**

THE MASKED U.F.O.

Black Belt CHRIS ADAMS v Bangor WALSH

★ Night of the Super Stars

ANYTHING CAN HAPPEN HERE

TALLY-HO **KAYE** v DAVE **FINCH**

PRICES £1·60 : £1·25 : 90p (UNRESERVED)
ALL RIGHTS OF ADMISSION STRICTLY RESERVED

Advance Bookings from Belle Vue, Tel: 061-223 3927 or at the door on night of Promotion LICENSED BARS

DALE MARTIN PROMOTIONS LTD. present

WRESTLING

ASSEMBLY HALL : TUNBRIDGE WELLS
MONDAY, 29th OCTOBER at 7.30 p.m.

DON'T MISS THE "BIG TIME" WRESTLING ATMOSPHERE AND ACTION !

Extraordinary Challenge
No Holds Barred

STEVE **VIEDOR**

JOHNNY **YEARSLEY**

Sensational Battle of the Super Stars

ROLLERBALL **ROCCO**

THE SUPER DESTROYER

4 MAN KNOCK-OUT TOURNAMENT FOR SUPREMACY

Bad Boy BOBBY **BARNES**

GARY **WENSOR**

TICH **WHITE**

TONY **COSTAS**

Prices: £1.40 : £1.15 : 90p

KING OF THE ACTION SPORTS ★ THRILLS AND SPILLS ★ TERRIFIC

DALE MARTIN PROMOTIONS LTD. present

WRESTLING

PAVILION · BATH
WEDNESDAY, 31st OCTOBER at 7.45 p.m.

DON'T MISS THE "BIG TIME" WRESTLING ATMOSPHERE AND ACTION !

SENSATIONAL RE-MATCH
AMERICAN STYLE ALL-IN RULES

IRON **GREEK**
BATTLING **BRIDGES**

SUPERSTAR **SANDERS**

GARY **WENSOR**

ROLLERBALL **ROCCO**
THE SUPER DESTROYER

ROMANY **RILEY**

JOHN THE DEAR **ELIJAH**

Prices: £1.50 : £1.25 : £1.00

KING OF THE ACTION SPORTS ★ THRILLS AND SPILLS ★ TERRIFIC

BEST/WRYTON PROMOTIONS LTD. present

WRESTLING
KING'S HALL ★ BELLE VUE
SATURDAY 24th NOVEMBER commencing at 7.30 p.m.

BEST OF TODAY'S TOP T.V. STARS (Exclusive)

SPECIAL RETURN CHALLENGE MATCH
DIRECT FROM MADISON SQUARE GARDEN

THE SHEIK
MARTY JONES

THRILLS - EXCITEMENT - ACTION
NEAR MACHINE

ROLLER BALL ROCCO
DYNAMITE KID

SPECIAL SOAP PLUS BUCKET MATCH - If Mulligan loses, buckets of water, soap and scrubbing brushes will be in the ring and he will be scrubbed down

BERT ROYAL v BLACK JACK MULLIGAN

BRING THE FAMILY ★ ALL WELCOME

CLASH OF HEAVIES
RAY THUNDER
DAVE DRAPER

WRESTLING AT ITS BEST
GOLDEN ACE
JOHN NAYLOR
YOUNG DAVID

PRICES: £1·60 : £1·25 : 90p
ALL RIGHTS OF ADMISSION STRICTLY RESERVED

Advance Bookings from Belle Vue Tel 061-223 2927
or at the door on night of Promotion LICENSED BARS

BEST/WRYTON PROMOTIONS LTD. present

WRESTLING
VICTORIA HALL - HANLEY
SATURDAY 24th NOVEMBER at 7.30p.m.

BEST OF TODAY'S TOP T.V. STARS (Exclusive)

★ ACTION ★ SPEED ★ IMPACT ★ EXCITEMENT ★ ITS ALL HERE ★
FIVE TREMENDOUS OUTSTANDING CONTESTS - EIGHT MAN KING OF THE RING TOURNAMENT

TERRIFIC BATTLE OF THE GIANTS
THE
IRON GREEK v RAY STEELE

plus KING OF THE RING TOURNAMENT
8 RULES WRESTLERS MUST BE THROWN OVER THE TOP ROPE - LAST MAN STANDING IS THE WINNER

SUPER STAR **SANDERS**
'STUD' BAINES
KID CHOCOLATE
PAT PATTEN
THE ROCKER
JOHNNY ENGLAND
RON MARINO
TOMMY LORNE

Prices of Admission: £1.30 : £1.20 : £1.10
IT COSTS NO MORE TO BOOK YOUR SEAT IN ADVANCE
KING OF THE ACTION SPORTS ★ THRILLS AND SPILLS ★ TERRIFIC ★

BEST/WRYTON PROMOTIONS LTD. present

WRESTLING
QUEEN ELIZABETH HALL, Civic Centre, OLDHAM
WEDNESDAY, 21st NOVEMBER at 7.45 p.m.

BEST OF TODAY'S TOP T.V. STARS (Exclusive)

★ ACTION ★ SPEED ★ IMPACT ★ EXCITEMENT ★ ITS ALL HERE ★
HEAVYWEIGHT CHALLENGE

THE
IRON GREEK
MARTY JONES

STRENGTH versus SKILL
VIC
FAULKNER

STRONGMAN
DENNISON

Flash JORDAN v Eddie RILEY

Heavyweight Battle
BULLDOG JOYNSON
DAVE DRAPER

Thrills and Spills
THE MASKED
U.F.O.
KING
BEN

Admission: £1.50 : £1.25
KING OF THE ACTION SPORTS ★ THRILLS AND SPILLS ★ TERRIFIC ★

Printed in Great Britain
by Amazon